HEAVEN AND EARTH
IN EARLY HAN THOUGHT

SUNY Series in Chinese Philosophy and Culture
David L. Hall and Roger T. Ames, editors

HEAVEN AND EARTH IN EARLY HAN THOUGHT

∾

Chapters Three, Four, and Five of the *Huainanzi*

∾

John S. Major

With an Appendix by Christopher Cullen

STATE UNIVERSITY OF NEW YORK PRESS

The translation of *Huainanzi* Chapter 3 in this book is based in part on a draft translation by the late Dr. Herbert Chatley, obtained through the good offices of Dr. Joseph Needham and used with the kind permission of Dr. Chatley's daughter, Mrs. Theo Simmons.

Appendix A of this book, "A Chinese Eratosthenes of the Flat Earth," by Dr. Christopher Cullen, is reprinted by permission of the *Bulletin of the School of Oriental and African Studies* (London).

Pencil drawing of the funerary banner from Mawangdui Tomb #1 and of the Changsha Silk Painting by Sandra Smith-Garcès, copyright © 1991, 1992 by John S. Major. All rights reserved.

Published by
State University of New York Press, Albany

© 1993 State University of New York

For information, address the State University of New York Press,
90 State Street, Suite 700, Albany, NY 12207

Production by Cathleen Collins
Marketing by Nancy Farrell

Library of Congress Cataloging in Publication Data

Major, John S.
    Heaven and earth in early Han thought: chapters three, four, and
five of the Huainanzi / John S. Major ; with an appendix by
Christopher Cullen ·
        p.   cm. — (SUNY series in Chinese philosophy and culture)
    Includes bibliographical references and index.
    ISBN 0-7914-1585-6. — ISBN 0-7914-1586-4 (pbk.)
    1. Huai-nan tzu 2. Cosmology I. Huai-nan tzu. English.
Selections. 1993. II. Title. III. Series.
BL1900.H824E5 1993
523.1—dc20   92-27071
                                                                   CIP

10 9 8 7 6 5 4 3 2 1

For Valerie

Contents

Illustrations

Acknowledgments

This book has had a gestation period of more than twenty-five years, during which a great many people have given me encouragement, advice, and assistance. In attempting to express my thanks for all of this kindness, it seems appropriate to go back to the very beginning.

I first heard of the *Huainanzi* while I was an undergraduate at Haverford College, where the History Department permitted me to write my senior thesis (on Dong Zhongshu) under the direction of Professor Derk Bodde of the University of Pennsylvania. Dr. Bodde steered me onto a career path of research in early Han intellectual history. From then until now he has been unfailingly generous with his advice. Others who helped to set my feet upon the way during my undergraduate years were Professors Wallace MacCaffrey, Hugh Borton, Jonathan Mirsky, Harriet Mills, and Allyn Rickett. Above all, I am grateful for the intellectual and moral instruction of the late Professor Paul Desjardins, one of my dearest friends and an authentic sage in our own time.

This book had its concrete genesis in 1966, when I translated part of *Huainanzi* 4 (Sections VIII–XII, and later, Section XIX) for a graduate seminar in the history of Chinese science conducted by Professor Nathan Sivin, then at the Massachusetts Institute of Technology. Once again, I gained from that experience a wise mentor and a lifelong friend. When I decided to expand that work into a full translation of *Huainanzi* 4 for my doctoral dissertation at Harvard, I was fortunate enough to have as advisors three men who perhaps did not know that they were signing themselves up to be advisors for life: Professors Yü Ying-shih, Benjamin I. Schwartz, and John K. Fairbank. I feel greatly saddened that John Fairbank did not live to see this book in print.

During several periods of residence in Japan I was welcomed as a temporary research associate at the Research Institute for Humanistic Studies at Kyoto University. There, Professors Fujieda Akira and Yabuuchi Kiyoshi both gave me much valuable advice.

While in graduate school I received financial assistance from the Woodrow Wilson Foundation, the Harvard University Fellowships Committee, and Title VI of the

National Defense Education Fund; I am grateful to all of these organizations for their support.

I am deeply grateful, too, for the loving support given to me during my graduate years by my first wife, Dana.

I joined the faculty of Dartmouth College in 1971. During the next thirteen years, as I embarked on what sometimes seemed like the endless task of expanding my dissertation into a book, I enjoyed the friendship and encouragement of many colleagues there. I would single out especially Michael Ermarth, Gene R. Garthwaite, Robert Henricks, Hua-yuan Li Mowry, David Roberts, and Charles T. Wood. Mrs. Gail Patten, secretary of the Dartmouth College History Department, labored mightily and with unfailing good cheer typing and retyping drafts of various parts of this manuscript. The Dartmouth College Committee on Faculty Fellowships provided me with research support on various occasions. I also wish to thank the Social Science Research Council for a grant that enabled me to return to Kyoto in 1975.

During those years I sought and received advice and assistance from senior scholars at a number of institutions: Professor A. F. P. Hulsewé at the University of Leiden, the late Professor Schuyler Cammann at the University of Pennsylvania, Professor K. C. Chang at Harvard, the late Professor Edward Schafer of the University of California at Berkeley, Professor David Nivison at Stanford University, Dr. Li Xueqin of the Institute of History, Chinese Academy of Social Sciences, and Dr. Xi Zezong of the Institute for the History of the Natural Sciences, Beijing. All of them have my thanks. Most especially I am indebted to Dr. Joseph Needham, who early on took me under his wing, and who over the years has been unfailingly generous with his time and advice. Through Joseph Needham, I received invaluable help from someone I never met. In 1973 Dr. Needham gave me a copy of a rough draft translation of *Huainanzi* 3 prepared by the late Dr. Herbert Chatley (1885–1955), who, during a distinguished career as a civil engineer in China, also did much pioneering research in the history of Chinese science. Without the example of Dr. Chatley's work I would never have undertaken my own translation of the astronomical chapter of the *Huainanzi*; I therefore am grateful to Dr. Needham for sharing it with me, and to Dr. Chatley's daughter, Mrs. Theo Simmons, for granting me permission to use his draft translation as a starting point for my own.

In 1981–82 I was awarded a Visiting Fellowship at Clare Hall, Cambridge University; while there I benefited from both the friendship and the learned advice of Dr. Michael Loewe and Christopher Cullen. During that year I also had the great good fortune to meet the late Professor A. C. Graham, then at the School of Oriental and African Studies, London University. In later years, until his untimely death in 1991, Angus Graham was both a good friend and a stern (and therefore effective) critic who, by never tolerating sloppy thinking, inspired many improvements in this book.

Acknowledgments

The world of early Chinese intellectual history is a comparatively small one, and over the years I have received encouragement, advice, and criticism from practically everyone more or less of my own generation whose work has touched upon the *Huainanzi*. I should like to express my particular thanks to Sarah Allan, Roger Ames, Barry Blakeley, Francesca Bray, Suzanne Cahill, Elizabeth Childs-Johnson, Constance Cook, Riccardo Fracasso, Norman Girardot, Donald Harper, David Keightley, Charles Le Blanc, Sarah Queen, Jeffrey Riegel, Henry Rosemont, Jr., Hal Roth, Edward Shaughnessy, Kidder Smith, Wei-ming Tu, and Robin Yates. Elling Eide gave valuable advice on botanical and ornithological matters, as did Albert Dien on weapons and Christopher Cullen and David Pankenier on astronomy. I am very much indebted to Stephen Field for sharing with me portions of his as-yet-unpublished new translation of the *Chu ci* "Tian wen" (Heavenly Questions); his work has reinforced my own conviction that the "Tian wen" is of crucial importance for understanding the astronomical and topographical chapters of *Huainanzi*. Jay Sailey was especially generous with his time in reading drafts of these translations and suggesting solutions to thorny problems, and generous too in sharing with me an unpublished translation that he did many years ago of *Huainanzi* 16. Other friends—among them T. R. and Vicki Smith, Robert Oxnam, Tony Kane, Deborah Kaple, and Marc Aronson—who work in very different fields also helped me with their encouragement and moral support.

I am particularly grateful to Christopher Cullen for consenting to include his translation and study of the final section of *Huainanzi* 3 in this book as an appendix. I should like to note explicitly that he is the sole author of that appendix, and I make no claims to coauthorship of it; conversely, his responsiblity as author is limited to that appendix, and does not extend to any errors of translation or interpretation that may appear elsewhere in the book.

I also wish to thank my colleague Sandra Smith-Garcès of the Art Department of the Book-of-the-Month Club, who produced the splendid pencil drawings and computer-generated diagrams that grace these pages. I should also like to thank Cathleen Collins of SUNY Press for her inspired work on the design and production of this book, and David Goodrich for his extremely helpful and conscientious work in setting this book into type.

The usual disclaimer applies: If, after having received so much help from so many people, there are still things that I haven't gotten right, it is no one's fault but my own.

Because these pages, written in acknowledgment of so much friendship and aid received over so many years, amount almost to a brief intellectual autobiography, I should like to add a few additional perspectives to complete the story. This work was interrupted several times for extended periods, first to complete a book (with Joseph Needham, Lu Gwei-djen, and John Combridge) on Korean astronomical instruments and to work on shorter technical studies of issues relating to the cosmology of the *Huainanzi*, and later to complete several books on Asia for general audiences. The work was interrupted further when I left the academic world at the end of 1984. I wanted to pursue other career possibilities, first at the Asia Society, and currently in commercial publishing, while trying to keep active in research on early Chinese intellectual history—still my main avocation. In continuing to work on these chapters of the *Huainanzi*, it soon became clear to me that (as Allyn Rickett said about his own work on the *Guanzi*) the time had come to "finish it or forget it." Finishing it, however, had to be done without the customary benefits of an academic calendar and the leisure to pursue full-time research for extended periods. This is by way of expressing anticipatory gratitude to reviewers of this book, and to those who use it in their own research, for this reason: in the final stages of preparing this book for publication, I will undoubtedly have missed some recently published work—especially in Chinese and Japanese—that might have improved it, and I probably will also have made some errors that I might have been able to avoid under other circumstances. It will be the job of reviewers to point out such things, and of graduate students to pursue further research in avenues that I may have neglected. Anyone who does so will have my thanks.

Finally, to state the obvious, my greatest debt is to my family, for a lifetime of loving support. First to my parents, who, when faced with my decision to pursue a career in a field that must have struck them as arcane if not eccentric, never wavered in their belief that I was doing something valuable. Next to my brothers, and especially to Dr. David C. Major, whose enthusiasm for this project, and whose prodding when it threatened to become moribund, helped to keep me going; his meticulous reading of the penultimate draft of the entire book was enormously helpful. And most of all, thanks to my wife, Valerie Steele, for her unfailing love, encouragement, forebearance, and moral support.

Chapter 1

ༀ

PRELIMINARY CONSIDERATIONS

The two centuries or so spanning the late Warring States and the early Western Han periods were a time of astonishing intellectual fertility and creativity in China. Philosophers of every school were engaged in a great reexamination of the traditions that they had received from their ancestors, and the reformulation of those traditions—with the inclusion of many new insights and ideas—into a new synthesis. By the early Han, the "hundred schools" had been reduced to a handful.

The emerging philosophical synthesis of the early Han blended many strands of thought. From the Daoism of Laozi and Zhuangzi came the ideas of the primacy of the Dao and the existence of an ancient condition of primitive harmony before human schemes and contrivances brought disorder to the world. The astronomers, astrologers, and natural philosophers of the Naturalist School used their star maps and almanacs and observations of the natural world to develop an elaborate system of correlative and categorical reasoning, so that sense could be made, philosophically, of the organic, cyclical, self-created universe in which we live. At the same time, a school of statesmen sometimes known as the Technocrats blended the ideas of Laozi and others about sage government achieved through oneness with the Dao with Legalist ideas about how to organize an army and a bureaucracy and make them serve the purposes of the state. Added to the mixture were the theories of astrologers, especially those of the "Yin-yang Militarist School," who observed configurations of the celestial bodies to predict military success or failure. From these various strands of thought was produced a theory of statecraft according to which the enlightened ruler could align his own actions with those of the universe, and rule in accord with natural rhythms and harmonies. This synthesis was subscribed to by a growing number of thinkers, and came to be called the

1

Huang-Lao School—joining as it did the political, cosmological, and magical arts of Huangdi (the Yellow Thearch)[1] and the sage rulership of Laozi.

Among the key figures in this period of intellectual creativity were philosophers, astrologers, and magicians in the northeastern states of Qi and Yan and in the south-central state of Chu (which, by the late Warring States period, had shifted its center of gravity eastwards from its ancient heartland in the Han River Valley to the lower Yangtse and its hinterland, encompassing parts of the defunct states of Wu and Yue). These states, which represented regional variants of early Chinese civilization, had much in common not only in religion and intellectual life but also in material culture, perhaps in consequence of having been for a long time on the eastern periphery of the Chinese Zhongyuan cultural heartland, as well as being linked by maritime trade around the Shandong Peninsula. I refer to the shared cultural values of these states as the "coastal-riverine style" of early Chinese culture, and see that style as having contributed importantly to the development of Huang-Lao thought.[2] The fourth-century B.C.E. Jixia Academy of Qi, in which the notable Naturalist thinker Zou Yan was to play an important role several decades after its founding, was a center of cosmological speculation and other philosophical activity. A century or so after the lifetime of Zou Yan, an academy at Huainan (in the northeastern part of the former state of Chu) under the patronage of Liu An, king of Huainan, maintained and extended the Jixia tradition. The most famous product of this academy was the book now known as the *Huainanzi*.

The present work consists of a full translation of and commentary on three chapters of the *Huainanzi* that deal with cosmological issues: astronomy and astrology, topography, and the ritual/astrological calendar. Portions of these chapters have been translated and analyzed in the past by a number of scholars who have used them as examples of specific topics in early Chinese natural philosophy. They have not previously been studied in their entirety and as a unit; they deserve to be. Taken together, they present a remarkably clear and coherent account of a worldview that was shared by perhaps the majority of early Han intellectuals and that was to remain influential for centuries beyond the Han.

At the outset, it seems appropriate to give a brief account of the *Huainanzi*, its nominal author, and the textual tradition to which it belongs, and to discuss the conventions that I shall employ in this book. Readers well-versed in Han intellectual history may wish simply to skim the following sections of this chapter and proceed to the more detailed discussion of Han cosmology to be found in Chapter 2.

The *Huainanzi* has long been known as an important text of Chinese philosophy, although as a "miscellaneous" or "eclectic Daoist" work it never achieved the status accorded to the classics and other works in the Confucian tradition.[3] It is included in the Daoist Patrology (*Daozang*) and has been published in numerous noncanonical editions as well. It has been the subject of several commentaries and subcommentaries written over the course of many centuries. Both the work and its nominal author are known, in a general way at least, to most students of Chinese intellectual history.

Nevertheless, until a couple of decades ago the *Huainanzi* suffered from a certain neglect in comparison with other texts of the same general period. It seemed peripheral to the Confucian "high tradition" that occupied the attention of most scholars, and it tended to be mentioned only in passing in standard works on Chinese intellectual history.

Recently, however, many scholars have taken a fresh look at the *Huainanzi*. There has been, in fact, almost a boom in *Huainanzi* studies in the West, and to some extent in China and Japan as well. This renewed interest has occurred as part of a larger re-evaluation of the early Daoist tradition, and has benefited particularly from the general reassessment of early Han intellectual life prompted by the astonishing funerary library found in Tomb 3 at Mawangdui and by the discovery of long lost books in other tombs as well. Many scholars now see the *Huainanzi* as a seminal compendium: an attempt—largely successful in its own time—to define the dominant currents of thought in the early Han. Including, as it does, chapters on cosmology, politics, military affairs, and social philosophy (among other things), it was at the very least intended to address the principal concerns of rulers at the formative period of imperial Chinese history.

Recent books by Roger Ames[4] and Charles Le Blanc[5] have included excellent introductions to the *Huainanzi*, as well as discussions of its intellectual and textual background and of the remarkable growth of *Huainanzi* studies in the West. A new book by Hal Roth presents a detailed textual history of the *Huainanzi* and its commentaries.[6] It would be superfluous to repeat here information that is readily available in those works, or to provide more than a brief introduction to Liu An and the *Huainanzi*.

LIU AN AND THE *HUAINANZI*

Liu An (ca. 180–122 B.C.E.), king of Huainan, is known as the author of the work that bears his name, though nowadays we would be more likely to use the term general editor. He was a grandson of Liu Bang, known to history as Han Gaozu, founder of the Han Dynasty; Liu An's father was Liu Zhang, the first king of Huainan. Liu Zhang fell from imperial grace and died on the road to exile in 172 (some sources say 174) B.C.E. The ruler at the time, Zhang's half-brother Emperor Wen, regretted Zhang's death and enfeoffed his sons as an act of contrition. Thus Liu An, as the eldest son, succeeded to his father's title in 164, after some years of enfeoffment with the lesser title of marquis. During the reign of Emperor Wu, successor to Emperor Wen, Liu An seems increasingly to have harbored imperial ambitions; in particular, he was accused of *lèse-majesté* for having usurped certain imperial emblems. Ordered to present himself at the imperial court to face prosecution, he committed suicide in 122. According to a later legend, recorded in the Tang Daoist hagiographical collection called the *Shenxianzhuan*, at the moment of his death Liu An and the members of his household, including even his domestic animals, were transformed into immortals and rose bodily into the heavens in broad daylight.

In addition to whatever imperial ambitions he might have had, Liu An was an enthusiastic participant in the scholarly debates of his time; his interests ranged from administrative matters to cosmology, from natural philosophy to the occult. He attracted to his court a large number of men of learning and supported them with his patronage. One product of the scholarly atmosphere at the court of Huainan was the collection of essays now known as the *Huainanzi*. Liu An paid his respects at the court of Emperor Wu in 139 B.C.E., a year after the latter's enthronement. On that occasion, he presented a book to the emperor, which was duly added to the imperial library. It seems probable that that book was the first edition of the *Huainanzi*. Some scholars have argued that while portions of the work as it now exists date from the period between 164 and 139 B.C.E., work on the compendium continued until Liu An's death seventeen years later. Liu An's books and papers were confiscated by Emperor Wu's officials after his suicide, so any works written by Liu An or at his direction between the years 139 and 122 could easily have been incorporated into (or used to replace) the copy of the *Huainanzi* already in the imperial library. Elaborate arguments have been made on both sides of the issue of whether the *Huainanzi* is a work of 139 or 122 B.C.E.; the upshot of those arguments is that we really cannot know for sure.[7] The *Huainanzi* in its present form undoubtedly reflects the work of later redactors and editors as well. Overall, however, it seems that the *Huainanzi* is more likely to be a work of the middle, rather than near the end, of the second century B.C.E.; this general assessment is important for reasons that will be discussed below.

The early commentator Gao You, in his preface to the *Huainanzi* (ca. 212 C.E.), says that the book is the product of a formal symposium held in Liu An's court, and gives the names of eight of the participants.[8] It is impossible to say, however, whether or not the men named by Gao You are really the authors of any of the essays. Likewise, Liu An's exact role in compiling the book is unclear. It is possible that he is the author of some of the essays; Wallacker suggests that he may have posed topics or prepared outlines for his scholars to work on.[9] It is at least probable that he exercised some sort of editorial supervision and approved the essays in their final form. Even a casual reading of several chapters is enough to suggest that not all of the essays are by the same hand, although the book as a whole does manage to achieve a certain thematic coherence. The type of detailed stylistic study and statistical analysis of word use frequency that would enable us to assign the different chapters to authorship groups, as well as the phrase-by-phrase comparison of early Chinese texts (until recently a matter of arduous hand labor), will surely become much easier within the next few years with the development of new computer-based techniques. Pending the completion of such studies, one can only repeat the already well-known fact that the *Huainanzi* as a whole is the product of a group of scholars working under the supervision, and with the patronage, of Liu An.

THE PLACE OF THE *HUAINANZI* IN EARLY HAN INTELLECTUAL HISTORY

The Integrity of the Work

The uncertainty about the *Huainanzi*'s authorship, together with lingering doubts about its exact date, are not unusual problems; the same doubts can be raised about most early Chinese books. More important to the *Huainanzi*'s long-term historical reputation was the fact that it was catalogued as a "miscellaneous" (*za*) book in the Han imperial library. This designation reflects the fact that the *Huainanzi* did not conform ideologically to the Confucian syncretist doctrine established as the state orthodoxy of the Han by Emperor Wu's court intellectual and high official, Dong Zhongshu, around the turn of the first century B.C.E. Paradoxically, however, the *Huainanzi*'s status as a work that immediately predates the formulation of the Han Confucian synthesis is one of the things that now makes it seem of particular interest to students of early Han intellectual history.

Sources of the Huainanzi

Another reason for the *Huainanzi*'s relative obscurity during much of its history lies in its reputation as a work heavily dependent on other sources. Scholars have identified more than eight hundred direct quotations or close paraphrases of Zhou and very early Han works in the *Huainanzi*. Of those, by far the largest number are from four sources: *Zhuangzi* (269 references, in Le Blanc's tabulation[10]), *Lüshi chunqiu* (190 references), *Laozi* (99 references), and *Hanfeizi* (72 references). *Huainanzi* Chapter 1 is based heavily on *Laozi*, and Chapter 2 equally heavily on *Zhuangzi*; the importance of *Zhuangzi* and *Laozi* for the *Huainanzi*'s status as a Daoist work will be explored more fully below. The large number of quotations from *Hanfeizi* and *Lüshi chunqiu* have led some scholars, not unreasonably, to assign some chapters of the *Huainanzi* to the Legalist school.

Interestingly, in light of the very strong influence of *Zhuangzi*, *Laozi*, and *Hanfeizi* on the *Huainanzi* as a whole, their influence on the three cosmological chapters under consideration in this book is not very great. Conversely, while quotations from *Lüshi chunqiu* can be found throughout the *Huainanzi* (in twenty of its twenty-one chapters), they are of unusual importance in Chapters 3, 4, and 5. Much of Chapter 5, indeed, is quoted directly from the first sections of each of the first twelve chapters of *Lüshi chunqiu* (and thus also parallels the "Yueling" chapter of *Liji*, derived from the same source). The nature of *Huainanzi* 5's dependence on *Lüshi chunqiu* is explored in greater detail in the introduction to Chapter 5, below. Of equal significance, however, is the fact that *Lüshi chunqiu's* influence is apparent in *Huainanzi* 3 and 4 as well.

It would be quite wrong, nevertheless, to regard these three cosmological chapters of the *Huainanzi* as simply derivatives or restatements of *Lüshi chunqiu,* just as it would be wrong to regard the *Huainanzi* as a whole as an extended gloss on *Zhuangzi, Laozi,* and *Hanfeizi.* First, *Huainanzi* 3 and 4, and the final three sections of 5, show extensive links to other Warring States and early Han works as well. Second, it is as true for these three chapters as it is for the *Huainanzi* as a whole that the sources quoted are invariably selected, and often amplified or altered, in such a way as to show clear authorial intent. Like the *Lüshi chunqiu,* the *Guanzi,* and the *Shiji,* the *Huainanzi* forms part of the background of the Chinese encyclopedic tradition. These works, each of which may be seen as an attempted summa of contemporary knowledge from a particular politico-philosophical point of view, are not yet true encyclopedias, but they anticipate the tradition in which, especially from Tang times onward, enormous encyclopedic compendia were put together largely by quoting earlier sources. Both the *Huainanzi* as a whole and its individual chapters use sources to promote and expound a particular point of view, a kind of vade mecum of early Han syncretic thought.

Huainanzi 3, 4, and 5 show links to a wide range of sources (including those mentioned above) that share a distinctive philosophical outlook, which might be characterized as combining yin-yang/five phase cosmological theory, a schematic approach to cosmography, and mythic consciousness.

One of the most significant of these sources, especially for *Huainanzi* 4, is the *Shanhaijing,* or some group of hypothetical texts ancestral to it. But the *Huainanzi* does not draw uniformly from (or, one might say more cautiously, parallel) the *Shanhaijing,* at least as that work presently exists; rather, the passages quoted or paraphrased are mostly from *Shanhaijing* Chapters 6–9, entitled "Haiwai dong [nan, xi, bei] jing," the Lands Beyond the Eastern [Southern, Western, Northern] Seas. Indeed, *Huainanzi* 4 begins with lines closely similar to those that begin *Shanhaijing* 6, and the great majority of mountains, marshes, rivers, mythical personages, and strange foreign lands in *Huainanzi* 4 are also to be found—usually in amplified form—in those four chapters. It seems likely, for this and other reasons, that the *Shanhaijing* originally existed as several closely related but separate books, one of which may even in the early

Han have been known as the *Wuzang Shanjing*, with others corresponding (or being ancestral to) the *Haiwaijing* and the *Haineijing*. Those books were later put together by the noted editors Liu Xiang and Liu Xin during the late Western Han—and put together with scant regard for both repetitions and contradictions. Other materials ancestral to the present *Dahuangjing* (*Shanhaijing* 14–17) (along with another, shorter *Haineijing*, now *Shanhaijing* 18) would have been added to the collection in the post-Han period.[11] In any case, it would appear that Liu An's library included some version of all of these works.

Another important source for the *Huainanzi* is the poetic anthology *Chu ci*, particularly the "Tian wen" chapter; *Huainanzi* 3 and 4 both take the "Tian wen" as their points of departure, and share with it a distinctive mythic cosmology. The importance of the "Tian wen" for *Huainanzi* 3 and 4 has not been sufficiently appreciated; this point will be elaborated upon in the general introductions to Chapters 3 and 4 below, and in the relevant section-by-section commentaries that accompany the translations given in those chapters.

Other important sources for *Huainanzi* 3, 4, and 5 include the Mawangdui text entitled *Wuxingzhan*, which is quoted at length in *Huainanzi* 3; and the "Yugong" and "Hongfan" chapters of the *Shujing*. The latter were presumably important influences on the work of Zou Yan in the third century B.C.E. Because only a few scattered fragments of Zou Yan's own writings survive, it is impossible now to know how much his works influenced *Huainanzi* 3–5, but it is reasonable to suppose that such influence was substantial.

Huainanzi 5 bears what one might call a "family resemblance" to *Guanzi* III,8, a calendrical treatise entitled "You guan"; *Huainanzi* 3.XXII and XXIII are somewhat similar to a subsection of *Guanzi* XIV,41, entitled "Wuxing." In general, as Rickett notes, "No other text contains so many parallel passages to the *Guanzi* chapters contained in [the first volume of his translation of the *Guanzi*] as the *Huainanzi*."[12] The same statement would not be true in reverse form, but it nevertheless is clear that at least portions of the *Guanzi* were known at the court of Liu An, and in fact some of its chapters may have been edited there. It is certainly true that *Guanzi* and *Huainanzi* as a whole share many similarities, and I regard them both as exemplary texts of the Huang-Lao tradition.

The three chapters of the *Huainanzi* under consideration here also show some general affinities with *Zhuangzi* and *Laozi*, even though the amount of material directly quoted from those sources is fairly small. There also are thematic links to *Mu Tianzi zhuan*, *Heguanzi*, *Jinizi*, and *Huangdi neijing*, and probably also to other Mawangdui texts such as *Huangdi sijing*, though the question of the relationship between the Mawangdui corpus and the *Huainanzi* still requires much more work. The cosmological chapters of the *Huainanzi* also share some passages of text and some thematic characteristics with works that are probably in whole or in part later than the *Huainanzi* itself, particularly *Da Dai liji, Liezi,* and *Kongzi jiayu.* In some instances those works probably borrowed from the *Huainanzi,* while in other cases the texts perhaps share material from now-lost earlier sources. And, of course, both Dong Zhongshu (or, if as some scholars have suggested, he was not the actual author of the cosmological chapters of the *Chunqiu fanlu,* then whoever did write those chapters) and the savants whose discussions in the White Tiger Hall were recorded by Ban Gu in the *Bohutong,* seem to have been closely familiar with the cosmological chapters of the *Huainanzi.*

Conspicuous by its absence is any reference in these chapters to the *Yijing* (*Book of Changes*) or its appendices. This is not terribly surprising; as Fung Yu-lan long ago noted,[13] the cosmological theories of the *Yijing* and the Yin-yang/Five Phases schools remained quite separate until the early Han. It was, in fact, one of the achievements of Dong Zhongshu to unite the two schools; thereafter treatises combining the two proliferated among the Han apocrypha. Still, the absence of *Yijing* materials in the cosmology of the *Huainanzi* is worth noting, particularly in connection with the development of the Huang-Lao School in the late Warring States and early Han. As stated earlier, I regard the Huang-Lao School as characteristic of the coastal-riverine (or Qi and Chu) cultural style in ancient China, while the *Yijing* is characteristic of the cultural style of the northern inland states.

The commonality of sources shared by *Huainanzi* 3, 4, and 5 is naturally reflected in their content. These three chapters form a clear subunit within the *Huainanzi* as a whole. The treatment of heaven and earth in Chapters 3 and 4 is reciprocal and complementary; as mentioned above, some sources for both chapters were used selectively by the authors of the *Huainanzi,* with those portions of the (originally unified) source material referring to the heavens being allocated to Chapter 3, and the portions referring to the earth being placed in Chapter 4. The astrological sections of Chapter 3 are derived from the same calendrical tradition as Chapter 5; many difficult passages in Chapter 3 are clarified by Chapter 5. These three chapters, taken together, form in effect a contemporary summary of the cosmological theories of the Huang-Lao School in the early Han.

The Huainanzi *and Huang-Lao Daoism*

The nature of the Huang-Lao school of Han philosophy has been much debated by Sinologists since the publication in 1979 of Wei-ming Tu's influential article on that subject.[14] Many, perhaps most, specialists have adopted the view that the *Huainanzi* is a Huang-Lao work, perhaps even a paradigm of the school; other scholars, notably

Roger Ames, have remained skeptical. The point is an important one, because everyone can agree that Huang-Lao was one of the most important—perhaps the most important—philosophical schools of the early Han, but until recently no one was sure of exactly what its tenets were.

Whatever Huang-Lao was, it was syncretic in nature. Some scholars (for example Guo Moruo[15]) argued that Huang-Lao already existed as an identifiable school (though not necessarily yet with that name) at the Jixia Academy in the state of Qi in the fourth century B.C.E. If that plausible view is accepted, the idea of the *Huainanzi* as a Huang-Lao work emerges in turn, for Liu An's academy at Huainan was undoubtedly an heir to the Jixia tradition. This is evident not only in organization and character of Liu An's academy, but specifically in the academicians' interests in issues of the sort found in *Laozi* and the earliest strata of *Zhuangzi*, in various forms of Legalism (both "rewards and punishments" and "administration") and in the Daoist-Legalist synthesis of the *Guanzi*, and in the yin-yang/five phase cosmology of Zou Yan (who was, of course, a Jixia scholar).

The discovery of the funerary library in Mawangdui Tomb 3 brought about a dramatic improvement in our understanding of Huang-Lao thought.[16] If one follows the now generally accepted view that the Mawangdui corpus is Huang-Lao in character, a picture emerges of Huang-Lao as being grounded in a combination of *Laozi* Daoism and Legalism of exactly the sort found in the Mawangdui text *Huangdi sijing*. In light of this, the strong influence of *Zhuangzi*, *Laozi*, and *Hanfeizi* on the *Huainanzi* takes on great significance. Recent advances in peeling back the layers of the received text of *Zhuangzi*, and in understanding the relationship between *Zhuangzi* and *Laozi*, have also further clarified the issue. Hal Roth has even proposed that the received text of the *Zhuangzi* was edited and put into final form at the court of Liu An himself, making it in effect a sister text to the *Huainanzi*.[17]

In all of this, the assumption has been that the term Huang-Lao associates Legalism (whether of the Hanfeizi "punishments and rewards" or of the Shen Buhai "technocratic" variety), or at least state centralism, with Huangdi, while its Daoist elements derive from Laozi. Something is missing from the picture, however, and I believe that the missing piece is supplied by a proper understanding of the cosmological chapters of the *Huainanzi*. In my view, Huangdi stands not only for a Legalist, or statist, approach to government, but also for the integration of cosmology into political theory. If the leading candidates for exemplars of Huang-Lao thought are the Mawangdui corpus, the *Guanzi* (or at least major portions thereof) and the *Huainanzi*, it becomes a matter of significance that Huangdi is represented in some of those texts (e.g., *Wuxingzhan*, *Huainanzi* 3–5) as a thearch whose astral projection is identified with the planet Saturn and whose ritual emblems refer as much to a cosmological as to a political center.

In his response to Roth's paper on the editorship of *Zhuangzi*, Angus Graham argued against identifying the Han syncretism of the *Huainanzi* with Huang-Lao thought:

> Throughout the literature of the third and second centuries B.C.E. the legends of Shennong and the Yellow Emperor develop in interaction as representatives of rival tendencies to political centralization and decentralization. . . . The name of the Yellow Emperor, the inventor of the state and of war, may well have been chosen to represent the legalist side of Huang-Lao; whether this was the case or not, we can hardly class a text as Huang-Lao if it shows a positive preference for Shennong. But the main political chapter of the *Huainanzi*, the *Zhushu*, mentions only Shennong, in agreement with Roger Ames's claims in his *Art of Rulership* for the anti-authoritarian tendency of this chapter.[18]

This view, if applied to the *Huainanzi* as a whole, needs to be modified in light of the very strong preference for Huangdi found in its cosmological chapters. But the Yellow Thearch appears there, of course, precisely in his cosmological rather than his authoritarian guise. If the *Huainanzi* is to be regarded as a Huang-Lao work, it must be in large part because of this second—but, I would argue emphatically, not secondary—attribute of Huangdi as an exemplar of the cosmological arts.

Further advances in Huang-Lao studies appear to be heading for a new, initially surprising but upon reflection very compelling, consensus: That Daoism, as it was understood in the early Han (for example, in Sima Tan's essay on the "Six Schools" in *Shiji*), was essentially identical to the Huang-Lao School.[19] The old distinction between the "philosophical Daoism" of the pre-Han period and the "religious Daoism" of the late Eastern Han and beyond thus breaks down. Daoism as a named, identifiable school was itself a principal product of pre-Han and early Han syncretism, and was ancestral to both the Confucian syncretism of Dong Zhongshu and the religious movement that took the name Daoism in the second century C.E. If this view is correct, it amply justifies the interest that scholars have recently shown in the *Huainanzi*, for it propels that text from being a relatively obscure "miscellaneous" work of "eclectic Daoism" to being a key document of early Han thought.

This view of the *Huainanzi* as a Huang-Lao (= early Han Daoist) work has led to a gradual change in my own view of the cosmological chapters under consideration here. In my early work on this material,[20] I was mainly interested in the origins of certain strands of early Chinese science. I tended to adopt a Needhamesque point of view, seeing in *Huainanzi* 4, the "Treatise on Topography," examples of relatively "pure" early Chinese science, untainted by considerations of ethics, morality, and the art of rulership. It does not detract from my tremendous admiration for Needham's work to say now, however, that I regard the investigation of scientific "might-have-beens," promising scientific trends in early Chinese thought that later were led into dead ends by the weight of Confucian orthodoxy, as being a distraction from the greater task of trying to understand as fully as possible what the Chinese actually did think about certain aspects of the natural world at particular times. Rather than seeing the cosmological chapters of the *Huainanzi* as being among the last instances of pure natural philosophy in China before the whole field was forced into the mold of Confucian ideology, I now regard them—and I feel sure that Liu An and his savants intended them to be seen—as part of what a Chinese ruler needed to know to govern his kingdom properly. One of the messages of Huang-Lao Daoism was precisely that the cosmos is a unity, and there is no distinction between the affairs of nature and the affairs of humans—and their ruler.

The eighth chapter of the *Huainanzi*, entitled "Benjing xun," the "Treatise on the Fundamental Norm," is an extended essay on that very point; the treatise eloquently expounds a philosophy of history embracing a view of the remote past as a time when the actions of rulers were in perfect accord with the natural processes of the cosmos itself.[21] As *Huainanzi* 8 puts it, "All of spacetime is the body of one man; all within the six coordinates is under the rule of one man." In that view, it is as important for a ruler to know how to use an astronomical instrument or to understand how metals grow over time in the bowels of the earth as it is for him to know how to select good ministers or to understand the astrological auspices for success in war. The inclusion of chapters on these matters in the *Huainanzi* reflects the profoundly Daoist message that only a ruler who knows how to make his every action conform to the timeless workings of heaven and earth can succeed in controlling the affairs of man. Chapters 3, 4 and 5 of the *Huainanzi*, in addition to their intrinsic interest, are of importance to the intellectual history of Han China by making clear that yin-yang/five phase cosmology was fundamental to, and wholly integrated with, Huang-Lao philosophy in its fully developed state in the early Han.

This view of Huang-Lao has recently been reinforced by Randall Peerenboom from the point of view of the theory of law.[22] Peerenboom finds the Huang-Lao world view far more orderly and determined—verging on something like "natural law"—than the conventional view of early Daoism would suggest. This interpretation resonates with the cosmology of *Huainanzi* 3–5 which, particularly with respect to astrology, depicts human actions as constrained by cosmological principles. In *Huainanzi* 3, portents read from the position of Jupiter in the sky (in conjunction with the seasons, the sexagenary cycle, and other phenomena) are deterministic and not subject to human control; they contain no hint of Daoist "spontaneity." Similarly, the "Seasonal Rules" of *Huainanzi* 5 follow automatically from the annual waxing and waning of yin and yang; they are accompanied by dire warnings of the consequences of ignoring them.

At this point it will be useful to summarize my reasons for taking the *Huainanzi* as a whole, and these three chapters of that work taken individually, as being part of the Huang-Lao tradition. I take the essential philosophical stance of Huang-Lao to be as follows:[23]

1. *Dao* is the highest and most primary expression of universal potentiality, order, and potency. "It is undifferentiated, indeterminate, and ineffable. Yet it is generative, autonomous, unchangeable, and complete."[24]

2. Dao is expressed in cosmic order, which embraces both the world of nature and the human world; the human order is a subset of the natural order. "Huang-Lao privileges the cosmic natural order: the natural order has normative priority."[25]

3. The human order presupposes the existence of royal government. But royal government must conform to natural order. For a king to act "contrary to nature" is both futile and wrong; the proper stance of the king is *wuwei*, "non-striving" or "taking no action contrary to nature."

4. "A defining characteristic of the true king is the acquisition of . . . penetrating insight."[26] The king must learn all that can be learned about the natural order, so as to make his actions conform to it.

5. The government of the true king is neither sentimental nor vacillating, and neither arbitrary nor domineering. Being in all respects in conformity with the patterns of the Dao as expressed in the natural order, it is balanced, moderate, and irresistibly strong.

Lest this summary seem like a catchall of late Warring States and early Han political philosophy, it is important to note what Huang-Lao (in this view) does not include: It eschews the human-centered ethical consciousness and "benevolence" of Confucianism, the mechanistic despotism of law-centered Legalism, the anarchism of Zhuangzi, the undifferentiated fellow feeling of Mozi, the sophistry of the School of Names, and much else besides. On the other hand, as adherents of a syncretic school, proponents of Huang-Lao felt free to mine any and all other schools of philosophy for ideas congenial to themselves.

An entire book could (and probably should) be written on the theme of "Huang-Lao and *Huainanzi.*" Yet even a fairly cursory look at the *Huainanzi* as a whole will show that it conforms quite closely to the principles of Huang-Lao as outlined above. The primacy of the Dao is established in the *Huainanzi*'s first chapter, "Tracing the Dao," and this theme is pursued not only in the cosmological chapters under consideration here but throughout the work. So also is the idea of the primacy of the natural order; that idea is the defining motif of *Huainanzi* 5, the "Treatise on the Seasonal Rules," which makes clear that the ruler's actions must follow those of the seasonal round, lest dire consequences ensue. The primacy of the natural order is also explicit in *Huainanzi*'s philosophy of history, particularly in Chapter 8, the "Treatise on the

Fundamental Norm," which contrasts a Dao-centered golden age of antiquity with the human-centered and decadent contemporary world.[27]

That the rule of the true king proceeds from the natural order and is pursued through non-striving is spelled out in the opening lines of *Huainanzi* 9, "The Art of Rulership": "The art of the ruler is to deal with things through nonaction and to disseminate wordless instructions. Limpid and still, he does not move; even when moved he is not agitated. . . . Things proceed from what is naturally so and nothing arises from him personally."[28]

The obligation of the ruler to acquire "penetrating insight" is seen in the inclusion in the *Huainanzi* of Chapter 4, the "Treatise on Topography," one of the least politically involved chapters in the entire book. This raises a tricky question: would the "Treatise on Topography," taken in isolation from the rest of the *Huainanzi*, be definable as a Huang-Lao work? Or, to take another example, could the Mawangdui text "Xiang ma" ("The Physiognomy of Horses") be regarded as a Huang-Lao text if seen in isolation from the Mawangdui corpus? The honest answer is "not necessarily." But in dealing with Huang-Lao materials, context is of paramount importance. Such texts as the "Treatise on Topography" or "The Physiognomy of Horses" may be regarded as Huang-Lao texts *if they are clearly associated with other Huang-Lao materials*. In fact, given the stance of Huang-Lao regarding the primacy of the natural order, any text that promised to increase a ruler's knowledge and understanding of the natural world would shelter comfortably beneath the Huang-Lao umbrella. A dominant idea of Huang-Lao, and one important reason why the Huang-Lao school emerged so fruitfully from the late Warring States–early Han era of philosophical enquiry, is that *knowledge of the natural world translates into political power*. The cosmological chapters of the *Huainanzi* were included in the book in support of this view.

Finally, the Huang-Lao view that the power of the ideal ruler is possessed of irresistible potency, flowing as it does from the Dao as expressed in the natural order, is seen quite strikingly in the *Huainanzi*. Consider the astrological predictions derived from manipulations of the *shi* cosmograph in Chapter 3, the "Treatise on the Patterns of Heaven." There one reads, for example (in Section 3.XXXIV below), "As to the chronogram suspended in the balance-beam of the Angular Arranger, if there is war, it certainly will be victorious; if there is an assault, it must succeed." If the ruler allied himself with such forces, his potency would be so great as to seem itself like a natural phenomenon. As "The Art of Rulership" puts it, "The most excellent ruler is one of whom his subjects know only that he exists."[29] Thus I see no conflict between Roger Ames's claim that the *Huainanzi*'s political philosophy is antiauthoritarian and the characterization of that philosophy as Huang-Lao. In my view, authoritarianism (such as that found in Shang Yang's Legalism) rests on the whim of an all-powerful ruler; in contrast, the potency of the ruler in the *Huainanzi*'s Huang-Lao philosophy derives not from his arbitrary wishes backed by military and legal force, but from his being grounded in the Dao as manifested in the cosmic order.

When viewed as elements of Huang-Lao thought, the cosmological chapters of the *Huainanzi* gain in both interest and importance. Perhaps the most remarkable feature of these chapters, in fact, is the comprehensiveness and coherence of the worldview that they depict. Cosmogony, cosmography, astronomy, calendrical astrology, and other features of cosmology form a seamless web, the principles of which a ruler would ignore only at his peril. The principles are not yet imbued with *ethical* norms defined in Confucian terms: that would come a few decades after the *Huainanzi* was written, with Dong Zhongshu and the Han Synthesis. To that extent, they can still be described as a system of natural philosophy or (in Needham's term) "Naturalism"; still, they depict a moral universe. It is clear that, to the extent that these chapters contain what can legitimately be called science, then science in the Huang-Lao School no longer existed as an independent realm of intellectual enquiry (if it ever did, in ancient China), but was thoroughly integrated with the realm of human affairs.

In describing these materials as comprehensive and well-integrated, I perhaps risk overstatement, for in the section commentaries in the chapters that follow I shall sometimes point out apparent contradictions, as well as the sorts of inconsistencies that flow from an encyclopedic or anthologistic (rather than a synthetic) approach on the part of Liu An and his authors. At the same time, one must recognize the limits of one's ability to penetrate into the mind of a Han cosmologist; what now appear to be contradictions in these chapters may, in some instances, be nothing more than a failure of understanding.

CONVENTIONS EMPLOYED IN THIS BOOK

Chinese Characters in the Text

In order to keep typesetting costs within reasonable bounds, Chinese characters appear in this book only in the Appendices, the "Technical and Textual Notes," the Bibliography, and the Index. The Index thus also functions as a glossary for the main text of the book. In a few cases where it has been necessary to avoid ambiguity caused by romanization I have differentiated between Chinese words by the use of superscript letters, as for example with the two feudal states named Wei; they are distinguished as Wei[a] and Wei[b]. In another instance of possible ambiguity, I hope it will be obvious when the text speaks of a heavenly body appearing in *yin* that the *yin* in question is one of the twelve Earthly Branches, not the *yin* of yin-yang. In addition, because the section-by-section translations are keyed by page and line numbers to the Liu Wendian edition of the *Huainanzi*, interested readers will readily be able to locate the Chinese characters for transliterated but untranslated terms.

Divisions of the Text

The chapters of the *Huainanzi* are not divided into sections in the original text. I have supplied section divisions in the translations below and designated them by roman numerals and section titles (e.g., Section XXVI: Seasonal Yin and Yang), to provide some indication of the overall structure of the chapter texts and for ease in inserting passages of commentary following each section. At the beginning and end of each section of translation I also supply chapter, page, and line references to the Chinese text (e.g., 3:19b:5). I use as the reference text for this translation the edition of Liu Wendian, *Huainan honglie jijie*. While scholars differ as to which text of the *Huainanzi* is the most authoritative one, Liu's edition seems to me to provide the best combination of ready availability, textual accuracy, and typographical clarity.[30] This edition is particularly convenient in studying the cosmological chapters of the *Huainanzi*, because it includes, at the end of its second volume, Qian Tang's very helpful "*Huainanzi* tianwenxun buzhu" (Supplementary Commentary to the "Treatise on the Patterns of Heaven" of the *Huainanzi*; ca. 1788).

This book has two separate sets of notes. References to scholarly literature are supplied in endnotes, denoted in the usual fashion with superscript numbers in the text. In a large-scale translation project for which hundreds of scholarly works have been consulted over a long period of time, there is literally no end to the number of reference notes that could be supplied in this fashion. At some point such notes become more distracting than helpful, so I have tried to keep the endnotes to a necessary minimum. The bibliography contains a full list of works consulted in the course of writing this book. The second set of notes herein are the "Technical and Textual Notes," which are keyed to the translations themselves. Within each section of the translation, I have numbered the lines in what seems to me to be a "natural" order, generally one sentence (but sometimes a few closely linked sentences) per line number. These numbers, of course, also do not appear in the original text. Their primary purpose here is to serve as an indexing device for the technical and textual notes that appear near the end of the book. Technical and textual notes—including such matters as textual emendations, variant readings, and detailed comparisons with other early texts—that will be of interest only to the relatively small number of people who might read these translations with the original *Huainanzi* text in hand are designated by chapter, section, and line numbers of the translated text. Thus, for example, "3.XIV.8" refers to *Huainanzi* 3, section XIV, line 8. (The same line in the Chinese text would be designated 3:10b:2, i.e., chapter 3, page 10b, line 2 in Liu Wendian's edition of the *Huainanzi*.)

Each of the three translated chapters is preceded by a general introduction, which gives a synopsis of the chapter and general remarks about it. Thereafter, translated sections of text are followed by commentaries designed to elucidate both the general character of the section and some of the particular points of interest that it raises. Many of the chapter sections raise problems of great complexity and broad scope, problems on which—given the enormous expansion of scholarly activity in early Chinese studies in recent decades—whole articles or even monographs have been written (or on which they could and I hope will be written). The commentaries, then, cannot hope to be comprehensive, and I have tried as much as possible to limit them to questions fairly narrowly bounded by the text itself. In some instances—Chapter 3, Section XXVIII, on mathematical harmonics, is a good example—a very extensive literature already exists on the general problems raised by the *Huainanzi* text; in such instances, I simply refer to that literature and then add such comments as are necessary to explain particular points of interest in the text. In other instances—for example the passages having to do with the cosmography associated with the Kunlun Mountains in Chapter 4—I myself have commented in depth on the main issues in articles collected in my forthcoming *Essays on the Huainanzi and Other Topics in Early Chinese Intellectual History*; in those cases as well, I have kept my comments here appropriately brief while drawing the reader's attention to my more detailed studies.

Nevertheless, in an important sense the section commentaries are the real heart of this book. Although the *Huainanzi* presents all of the expected problems of any early Chinese text—textual corruption, variant readings, occasionally difficult or obscure passages—it remains true, as Benjamin Wallacker once remarked to me, that with the *Huainanzi* the problem is not so much to know what the text *says*, as to understand what it *means*. I hope, to some extent, to have drawn from these chapters something approaching the truth of how Chinese intellectuals in one of the most fertile of all eras of Chinese thought understood the cosmos to be put together, and how it worked.

TERMS IN TRANSLATION

Units of Measurement

I have followed the common practice of translating the Chinese words *chi* and *cun* as "foot" and "inch" respectively. Readers should remember, however, that a *chi* (the dimension of which changed over time)[31] was, in Han times, less than the length of an English foot; from the evidence of a folding bronze shadow-scale and gnomon excavated at Yizheng County, Jiangsu, a Han foot was 24 cm, or about nine inches, long.[32] Thus when 3.XXXI.9 below says that "the height of an average man is eight feet," that translates to about 6 feet in modern terms—a bit tall, perhaps, for a Han Chinese, but not out of the question. It is also important to remember that a Chinese "inch" (*cun*) represents one-tenth, rather than one-twelfth, of a Chinese "foot." (By chance, the length of a Han "inch" is thus 0.075 of an English foot or about 0.9 of the length of an English inch.)

On the other hand, there is no satisfactory English word roughly equivalent to the Chinese *li* (used as the standard measure for long distances), and I therefore leave that word untranslated. The exact length of a li varied over time, but a length useful at least for purposes of forming a mental image would be about a third of a mile, or about 500 meters.

From ancient times, the Chinese divided circles—the celestial circle in particular—into 365¼ "degrees." Such divisions of a circle are indicated in this book by the use of a superscript "d" (standing for "degree," and also for the Chinese equivalent term *du*): for example, 280^d. In contrast, in passages of commentary when I refer to the 360 degrees of a circle in accordance with modern usage, I use the standard superscript "o": 280°.[33]

For more on weights and measures, see Chapter 3, Sections XXXI and XLII below.

Other Terms

Yin and *yang* have become, in effect, part of the vocabulary of the English language; I follow the usual practice of leaving them untranslated. By Han times these terms had, of course, taken on a range of meanings greatly expanded from their original senses of "the shady side of a hill" and "the sunny side of a hill," or "cool" and "warm."

Qi is a more difficult matter. Many scholars have attempted to find an appropriate English equivalent, such as "breath," "vapor," "pneuma," or "specific activity." My feeling is that none of these is satisfactory. Any English word employed to translate qi carries with it its own semantic baggage, which usually is inappropriate to the meaning of the Chinese term. Accordingly, following in the footsteps of Joseph Needham, I choose not to translate qi, which in any case is also gradually edging its way into the English language via the martial arts and acupuncture and other aspects of traditional Chinese medicine; rather, I employ it as a Chinese technical term and explain its nuances, where necessary, in the commentary. The only exceptions to this rule are a few instances in *Huainanzi* 3 where, in the context of meteorological phenomena, qi clearly does mean "vapor," and I translate it thus.

For similar reasons, I choose not to translate the word *Dao*, which, depending on the context, has in the *Huainanzi* its familiar range of meanings, such as "the Way" (of philosophical truth), "natural process," and "the ultimate nature of things." As Sarah Allan pointed out in a recent paper,[34] Dao does indeed mean "way," but the image that the term called to mind in early China was neither a highway nor a pathway, but a *waterway*. The essential meaning of Dao is thus the path of least resistance taken by water flowing downhill.

On the other hand, some other technical terms do seem to lend themselves to translation.

My reasons for translating *wuxing* as "five phases" have been explained in the pages of *Early China*.[35] The use of the term five phases (which I owe to Nathan Sivin) for *wuxing* has provoked much discussion; see for example the early response of Richard Kunst, and the subsequent opinions of A. C. Graham, Derk Bodde, and Chauncey Goodrich.[36] Not to belabor a much-debated issue, it does seem fair to point out that for these chapters of the *Huainanzi*, the translation "five phases" does seem exactly right; the term was borrowed from modern chemistry, and the transformations of qi described here are comparable to the phase changes of matter.

Similarly, my reasons for translating *xiu* as "lunar lodges" have been explained and debated in the pages of *Early China*.[37] Most subsequent writers have agreed that "lunar lodges" is preferable to the old translation, "lunar mansions."

Tian has connotations in Chinese very much like those of the English word "heaven" in its senses of "the overarching sky" and of "a non-anthropomorphic divinity" (though not in the sense of a paradise to which the soul ascends after death); accordingly that translation is employed here in all instances.

The Chinese word *xing* is a much more inclusive term than the usual English translation "star" would suggest; it can mean "star," "planet," or even "constellation." Unless context requires a more specific translation, I translate *xing* as the equivalently inclusive "asterism."

Shen, when used as a noun, will normally be translated as "god" or "divinity"; or, when used as an adjective, as "divine."[38] *Xian* is translated as "immortal." Departures from these usages are indicated in parentheses in the translation.

I translate *di* as "thearch"—a felicitous word first used, I believe, by Edward Schafer—when it refers to specific personage such as the Supreme Thearch (*shangdi*) or the Yellow Thearch (*huangdi*), or to idealized rulers ("emperors"). Thearch captures well the character of ancient Chinese thought wherein divinities might be (simultaneously and without internal contradiction) high gods, mythical/divine rulers, or deified royal ancestors: beings of enormous import, straddling the numinous and the mundane. When *di* is used in a general or collective sense, I translate it as "god" (e.g., in *zhongdi*, "the many gods"); I also translate *di* as god when the implication of divinity seems to me particularly clear, as in the "gods" of the five planets in 3.VI below.

Chinese color words are notoriously difficult to translate; one can at best approximate. *Qing*, which can embrace a spectrum from grey through blue to green, I usually translate as "bluegreen"; *cang*, the brilliant blue of the dome of the sky, I translate as "azure."[39] *Chi*, the emblematic color of the south in Han cosmology, I usually translate as "vermilion," but occasionally as "red" when it seems to be used as a more generic color term.

The word *chen* occurs frequently as a technical term in *Huainanzi* 3, meaning an arc equal to 1/12 of the celestial circle, each such arc conventionally denoted by the name of one of the twelve Earthly Branches. Following the suggestion of Edward Schafer,[40] I translate *chen* as "chronogram."

The word *shi* denotes a device that came into widespread use in the Former Han for modeling or predicting significant configurations of certain astronomical bodies. It plays a very significant role in the astrology of *Huainanzi* 3. Various translations for *shi* have been proposed: "diviner's board" (Needham), "cosmic board" (Harper), "cosmic model" (Cullen).[41] Cosmic model is accurate, but risks ambiguity because of its plain-English character—that is, it is hard to distinguish between "a cosmic model" in general, and *the* cosmic model, the *shi*. A more specific technical term is needed. I prefer to follow Stephen Field's lead[42] and translate *shi* as "cosmograph"; this term, which applies to the *shi* and nothing else, also accurately depicts the device's function, which was to give a representation of the state of the heavens at any given time.

Other Untranslated and Untranslatable Terms

I have tried as much as possible to translate place names and the names of non-Chinese tribes, as well as such terms as the names of the twenty-eight lunar lodges and the twelve pitch pipes, since most such names obviously were intended to be meaningful. The names of the notes of the Chinese pentatonic scale, however, are so familiar (at least to readers of early Chinese materials) that I have left them untranslated, though they too were semantically meaningful in their time and place; were not convention so firmly against it, it would be tempting to translate *gong* as "ruler," *shang* as "minister," *zhi* as "intendant," *yu* as "wings," and *jue* as "horn."

Other exceptions to the rule that all nouns should be translated are well-known Chinese place names (Mt. Tai, the Yangtse River), and place names that do not yield (to me, at least) a plausible meaning (and which might be, in some cases, Chinese attempts to transliterate foreign words, e.g., the Nalü People in 4.XVI.20). In addition, I have left untranslated a few names of magical or extraordinary plants, animals, and things, such as the Chengruo plant in 4.XVIII.32, as well as the (almost certainly originally non-Chinese) names of the twelve years of the Jovian Cycle, either because I have not been able to find a translation that would not be speculative or bizarre, or because an English term that might seem equivalent would nevertheless carry misleading connotations.

Days and Dates

Like all classical Chinese texts, the *Huainanzi* denotes both days and years by the binary characters of the *ganzhi* sexagenary cycle. Premodern Chinese readers would have had as part of their mental equipment the ability to assign any such binary designation to its proper place in the cycle without having to think about it. Most readers of English do not have that ability; accordingly, I have given *ganzhi* dates in their Chinese form and, where appropriate, have also given the equivalent ordinal numbers in square brackets, for example, "*gengzi* [#37]." For the reader's convenience, the full *ganzhi* cycle is listed in Appendix B.

Months in this text are, of course, lunar months (from new moon to new moon), and are designated by the names of the twelve *zhi*, or Earthly Branches. The Chinese, from earliest times, regarded the winter solstice as the beginning of the solar year; the first "astronomical" month began with the new moon that immediately preceded the winter solstice, and was designated *zi* in the Earthly Branch cycle. The Chinese civil year did not always, or even usually, begin with the first "astronomical" month, however.[43] Historically, the commonest scheme was for the civil year to follow the so-called Xia sequence of the *Xia xiaozheng* ("Lesser Annuary of the Xia," the oldest extant calendar in China, now invariably published as an appendix to the *Da Dai liji*); whether that sequence had anything to do with the actual Xia Dynasty is subject to debate. In the "Xia sequence," the year began with the third "astronomical" month (the month designated *yin* in the duodenary Earthly Branch cycle), which began on the second new moon after the winter solstice. The *Huainanzi* invariably adheres to the Xia sequence; accordingly, I translate the Chinese phrase meaning "the first month" as "the first civil month."

In fact, however, the civil calendar of the Han did not follow the Xia sequence until the Taichu calendar reform of 104 B.C.E. Prior to that, the Han adhered to the Qin calendar, which began the civil year with the twelfth "astronomical" month, that is, the month designated *hai*, the last month before the winter solstice. Thus my translation "civil month" must be understood as referring to the Xia sequence rather than to the imperial Han calendar at the time the *Huainanzi* was written. Initially I considered using the translation "first [Xia] month" instead of "first civil month," but decided against doing so in order to emphasize the point that Liu An's state of Huainan, at least on the evidence of the *Huainanzi*, followed a different civil calendar from that of the Han imperial state.

The disparity between the *Huainanzi* month count and the legal civil calendar of the Han at the time may stem from any of several causes, or a combination of them. First, the Xia calendar was widely used in pre-Han times; it was employed, for example, in the "Shiji" chapters of *Lüshi chunqiu*, from which other versions of the "Yueling," including that in *Huainanzi* 5, are derived, and before that in the "Lesser Annuary of Xia." Because the *Huainanzi* is heavily derived from such texts of Zhou date (including perhaps some now-lost texts, especially texts in circulation in the old pre-Han state of Chu, of which the Kingdom of Huainan was once a part), it may have seemed to the *Huainanzi*'s compilers too troublesome, or too contrary to tradition, to convert the month count of those texts to the current Han civil month count. Second, the *Huainanzi* is a prescriptive text, a handbook for rulers in the Huang-Lao Daoist tradition; it is possible that its compilers had an ideological commitment to an ideal Huang-Lao Daoist state in which the Xia sequence calendar would prevail. Third, the use of the Xia sequence might have been an overt political act on Liu An's part; certainly the publication of a text the calendrical portions of which defied the Han civil calendar seems to have contributed to the political difficulties that led to Liu An's demise in 122 B.C.E. I believe Liu An's use of the Xia sequence indicates that he thought the Xia sequence should have governed the civil calendar, and so I translate accordingly.

Diagrams

In premodern China, maps and diagrams (such as diagrams of the celestial circle) were consistently oriented with south at the top. This orientation tends to be confusing and counterintuitive for most modern readers. Accordingly, all diagrams in this book are displayed in Western orientation, with north at the top.

A GENERAL INTRODUCTION
TO EARLY HAN COSMOLOGY

The general characteristics of early Chinese cosmology are well known. In this chapter I shall undertake only to provide a brief account of the main points of early Han cosmology to serve as an introduction to the translations of *Huainanzi* 3–5 that follow. In doing this I also call attention to certain specific features of Huang-Lao philosophy as it is expounded in the *Huainanzi* and other closely related texts.

COSMOGONY

Huainanzi Chapters 1, 2, and 3 offer different, but not necessarily incompatible, accounts of the coming-into-being of the cosmos; these accounts are supplemented by additional cosmogonic passages found in other chapters of the text.[1] Together they paint a picture of a cosmos that begins in formlessness and chaos, goes through a process of differentiation governed by principles inherent in the system itself (that is, without the intervention of a Demiurge or *deus faber*), finally producing the world-as-it-appears. This, however, persists for an unspecified duration in a mythic state of timelessness before entering the realm of time and history. The distinction between the *Urzeit* and the age of historical time is of fundamental importance; as Girardot has written, "the mythological theme of creation and paradise lost literally reverberates throughout the whole [of the *Huainanzi*]."[2]

    Huainanzi Chapter 1 is an enquiry into the nature of the Dao itself, which is depicted as anterior to time, space, and distinctions of every kind. It pervades the universe; it can be rolled up into a tiny ball—it is both macrocosm and microcosm. It has neither dimension nor form. It gives being to every thing that is, yet cannot itself be said either to be or not to be. *Huainanzi* 1 provides a cosmogonic vision of only a very sketchy sort, derived from *Laozi* 42, which says:

> The Dao gave birth to the one;
> The one gave birth to the two;
> The two gave birth to the three;
> The three gave birth to the Ten Thousand Things.
> The Ten Thousand Things carry yin and embrace yang,
> And create harmony through the blending of qi.

In *Huainanzi* 1, yin and yang "partake of the Dao," and the world is differentiated into duality; duality gives rise to the "ten thousand things." Always behind the appearance of all phenomena lies the Dao, which "defines the four seasons and harmonizes the five phases."

As *Huainanzi* 1 is in the tradition of *Laozi*, so *Huainanzi* 2 is in the tradition of the *Zhuangzi*. Thus, in its opening two chapters, the *Huainanzi* grounds its Huang-Lao philosophy in Lao-Zhuang metaphysics. *Huainanzi* 2 opens by quoting a famous set of propositions from *Zhuangzi* 2 (which itself is related to *Laozi* 15):

1. There was a beginning.
2. There was a time that preceded the beginning.
3. There was a time before the time that preceded the beginning.
4. There was Being.
5. There was Non-Being.
6. There was a time before Non-Being began.
7. There was a time before the time that preceded the beginning of Non-Being.[3]

Huainanzi Chapter 2 continues by explaining each of these propositions, in ways that Zhuangzi himself might not have recognized. The effect is to transform them into a seven-stage cosmogony, described by Le Blanc as follows:

1. Empty Non-Being.
2. Empty and Opaque Space.
3. Empty and Luminous Space.
4. The Space-Time Complex.
5. Blending of Earthly Qi and Heavenly Qi.
6. The Life Impulse.
7. The Birth and Flourishing of the Ten Thousand Things.[4]

As Girardot points out,[5] the first four of these stages are in effect internal to the primordial chaos of the undifferentiated universe. At the end of stage four, the Dao has evolved from a void to a state of chaos poised for coming-into-being, but as yet without visible manifestations. In the fifth stage, the qi of earth and heaven (yin and yang) can be described as discrete entities; in the sixth stage, germs and roots, eggs and pupae, mark the appearance of potential life-forms. Nevertheless, the cosmos is still soft, enfolded upon itself, egg-like, and without form. Only with the final stage does the manifest world appear. A major theme of the remainder of *Huainanzi* 2 is the adverse effects that follow from the imposition upon the primordial simplicity of the emergent cosmos of human-created values, distinctions, and devices.

To recapitulate, *Huainanzi* 1 gives us an enquiry into the Dao, and states with little elaboration that one produced two, two produced three, and three produced multiplicity. *Huainanzi* 2 sees the creative process as inherent in the Dao, which, however indescribable it may be, has a quality of yolk-like fecundity that gives rise to the ten thousand things.

From this perspective, the opening sections of *Huainanzi* 3 (see 3.I–II below) can be seen as an amplification of the final stage of *Huainanzi* 2's cosmogony. They provide, in other words, more detail on the mechanisms whereby chaos, impelled by the inherent qualities of the Dao, gives rise to order. Here I shall simply give in skeletal form the argument of this cosmogony.[6]

1.   Heaven and Earth inchoate and unformed: The Great Inception.
2.   The Dao begins in the nebulous void.
3.   The nebulous void produces spacetime.
4.   Spacetime produces primordial qi.
5.   Qi divides; the light and pure forms Heaven, the heavy and turbid forms Earth.
6.   Heaven and Earth produce yin and yang.
7.   Yin and yang produce the four seasons.
8.   The four seasons produce the ten thousand things.
9.   Yin and yang qi produce the heavenly bodies.
10. The fight between Gong Gong and Zhuan Xu causes heaven to tilt to the northwest.
11. Yin and yang cause the heavenly bodies to shine, and produce meteorological phenomena.
12. All things respond to yin and yang according to their kind.

The first stage in this cosmogony can be seen as a brief recapitulation of *Huainanzi* 2, while the second stage reaffirms *Huainanzi* 1's emphasis on the primacy of the formless and unbounded Dao. From the nebulous void, the cosmos begins to become self-organized and produces spacetime: "The nebulous becomes process enduring through time simultaneously with becoming material extended in space."[7] This produces qi, still described as "primordial," which is to say, undifferentiated. But the qi is a mixture of light and heavy, which drift apart and become separated by a "shoreline"; the lighter qi ascends to become heaven, the heavy descends to become earth. Heaven and earth "produce," that is, can be seen as paradigms of, yin and yang. Yin and yang produce the four seasons, and much of *Huainanzi* 3 is concerned with examining the consequences of the waxing and waning, in constantly shifting ratios, of yin and yang throughout the year. The four seasons produce the ten thousand (= all) things. This statement specifies the method of the *Laozi* 42 (and *Huainanzi* 1) cosmogony. The Dao is one and undifferentiated; the one Dao produces the two of yin and yang; yin and yang qi expressed as spacetime make three; the interactions of yin and yang with spacetime produce everything.

The introduction at this point of the famous battle between Gong Gong and Zhuan Xu that causes the northwestern pillar of heaven to be knocked aslant, making heaven lean to the northwest and earth to the southeast, is of key importance. This event is a mythic explanation of the noncoincidence of the ecliptic (the apparent path of the sun—and, approximately, the moon and the planets—around the earth) and the celestial equator (the projection into space of the plane of the earth's rotation). *Huainanzi* 6:6b tells how the goddess Nü Gua repaired the damage wrought by Gong Gong and Zhuan Xu by patching the sky with five-colored gemstones and using the legs of a giant turtle to replace the damaged pillars.

In *Huainanzi* 4, both Mt. Kunlun and the Jian tree (beneath the midpoint of the sun's daily journey across the sky) are depicted as cosmic pillars used by gods and immortals to ascend to and descend from heaven. This notion incorporates the idea of the "myth of eternal return," wherein the function of religious cosmology is the reestablishment of the sacred conditions of the *Urzeit* that allowed free communication between mortals and the divine. The rupture of that communication is thus seen as the fundamental human dilemma. The tilting of the cosmic pillar by Gong Gong and Zhuan Xu is one version of the cosmic disaster in Chinese sources; another is found in the "Luxing" chapter of the *Shujing*. "The charge was given to Chong and Li to break the communication between earth and heaven so that there was no descending or ascending."[8]

In the cosmogony of *Huainanzi* 3, both spacetime (time here considered as "process-as-it-endures") and the four seasons exist prior to the cosmic disaster; nevertheless, that event marks the true beginning of time as it is calculated in human terms. The *Urzeit* of cosmogony comes to an end; henceforth the ruler must search for ways (through calendrical and portent astronomy, the calculation of solar and Jovian years, and all of the other astrological methods described in *Huainanzi* 3) to avert celestial harm and recover a state of oneness with universal process and cosmic order. History begins with man's attempt—through Yu the Great's engineering works (alluded to in *Huainanzi* 4.III)—to recreate the cosmos after the universal deluge that was a consequence of the tilting of heaven and earth.

In this new era of time-dependent phenomena, the heavenly bodies shine; wind, rain, thunder, lightning, and other meteorological phenomena appear through the interactions of yin and yang. Each of the ten thousand things has its own distinctive yin-yang characteristics; all interact in accordance with them.

An important, but seldom noted, feature of this cosmogony is that it clearly states that *everything is made of qi.* Qi is both process and substance, and comes into being as the concrete manifestation of spacetime; differentiating into the light and clear, the heavy and turbid, qi (now describable in terms of yin and yang) becomes the basic stuff of the visible universe. The notion of qi (both clear and turbid) as the fundamental material is usually thought of as one of the defining characteristics of Song Neo-Confucianism; it is remarkable to see the same principle asserted here, some twelve centuries before Zhu Xi.

Up to this stage, the cosmogony of *Huainanzi* 3 deals only with the fundamental dualism of yin and yang, and sees all phenomena as reflections of their interactions; there is no hint as yet of the five phases. Those are introduced in 3.VI, in the guise of the five planets, with their associated gods, directional symbolic beasts, and other five-phase correlates. Significantly, each of the planetary gods is depicted as holding a construction tool: the compass, square, marking cord, balance beam, and plumb bob. In *Huainanzi* 5.XV, these (plus the water level) are described as the "standards" by which cosmic processes are measured. Here they have, at a minimum, that meaning; there is perhaps also a hint that the celestial (planetary) gods are the architects of the subcelestial world as it comes into being in its multiplicity of forms. At the least, in this passage the five phases are given equal status with yin and yang as part of the cosmology of differentiation-between-categories and resonance-within-categories that was central to Huang-Lao thought.

The five phases also provide (in *Huainanzi* 4.XVIII–XIX) more detail about the processes through which the ten thousand things emerge from a state of relative undifferentiation. The first of these two chapter sections describes the speciation of animals and plants from first ancestors (in the case of animals, according to the five phase categories of scaly, armored, feathered, hairy, and hairless; textual corruption has obscured what probably were five phase categories in the case of plants). The second describes the formation of minerals from qi of five colors corresponding to the five phases. Moreover, *Huainanzi* 4.XI provides a somewhat rudimentary attempt to devise a taxonomic classification of animals on the basis of physical characteristics.

The universe that emerges from the cosmogony of *Huainanzi* 3 (as Randall Peerenboom has pointed out with regard to the Huang-Lao philosophy of law[9]) is to a remarkable degree structured and determined. The coming-into-being of the cosmos is *wuwei*, "non-purposive," and *ziran*, "thus-of-itself," but it is also orderly, predictable, and subject to what one might cautiously describe as "natural law" even in the absence of a divine lawgiver.[10] The principles that make the cosmos orderly and predictable are elaborated in the theories of categorical or correlative thinking and *ganying* resonance.

CORRELATIVE THINKING AND SYSTEMS OF RESONANCE

In Huang-Lao cosmology, the principal means by which the ruler was advised to make his actions conform to the natural rhythms and processes of the cosmos emerged from a thorough understanding of systems of correspondence, or what Graham has termed "correlative thinking."[11] In this mode of thought, all things in the world can be grouped into numerical categories (corresponding to the dualistic yin and yang, the five phases, the eight directions, and so on); things within a category resonate with each other more strongly, reliably, and predictably than do things that are not in the same category. As *Huainanzi* 3.II.17–18 puts it, "Things within the same class mutually move each other; root and branch respond to each other." Or again, *Huainanzi* 4.VIII.17: "All things are the same as their qi; all things respond to their own class." Resonance (*ganying*) between or among things within a class is conveyed through qi, conceived of as both the basic stuff of concrete phenomena and as an intangible vibrating medium pervading empty space.[12]

Correlative thinking is the best-known aspect of early Han cosmology, and it need not be reviewed at length here. Modern Sinology has produced an enormous body of literature on its various aspects, including yin-yang and *wuxing* and other correlative categories. Much of this scholarship has been summarized by Michael Loewe; the best analytical treatments are those of Ho Peng Yoke, Nathan Sivin, Derk Bodde, and A. C. Graham.[13] Graham's structuralist analysis gives deep insight into the nature of correlative thinking, and his survey of the historical development of the categories of yin-yang and the five phases may be taken as authoritative.

Yin and yang entered the Chinese vocabulary sometime during the early– to mid– Warring States period, with the original meanings "the shady and sunny sides of a hillside" and "cool and warm." Although the words were not yet terms of philosophy, their meanings had important implications for their later use as technical terms; both "shady and sunny" and "cool and warm" imply gradients on a scale, rather than polar opposites. In the *Zuozhuan* (Zhao 1/8), they are two of the "six qi," the others being wind, rain, darkness, and light. As employed by Zou Yan and the Naturalist School from the mid–third century B.C.E. onwards, yin and yang became paradigms of a complementary (nonantagonistic) dualism whereby phenomena could be analyzed in terms of shifting proportions of yin and yang; a predominantly yin phenomenon always contained at least a germ of yang and vice versa.

As we have already seen, in the cosmological chapters of the *Huainanzi* yin and yang are used especially to describe cyclical dualistic phenomena, chiefly the shifting proportions of sunlight and darkness throughout the solar year. The waxing and waning of the seasons is characterized as the "accretion" and "recision" (*de* and *xing*) of yin and yang. Yin and yang also denote other dualistic pairs, such as:

Heaven :: Earth
High   :: Low
Male   :: Female
Light :: Dark
Flying :: Walking

The second most important correlative category in *Huainanzi* is the *wuxing*, or five phases. The earliest appearance of the concept of a set of five categories dates back to the Shang, with the "four directions" (*sifang*) plus, implicitly, the center.[14] Various references to sets of five can be found in Zhou texts, but, as Graham has shown, before the third century B.C.E. the Chinese showed no particular preference for the characteristic Huang-Lao sets of two and five; note, for example, the "six qi" mentioned above. In the thought of Zou Yan and his followers, fives were normally specified as "five materials" (*wucai*), "five powers" (*wude*), and so on, rather than being subsumed under the *wuxing*, which was simply one category among several.

By the time the *Huainanzi* was written, however, the system of the *wuxing* was already philosophically mature. The *wuxing*—Wood, Fire, Earth, Metal, and Water— had become paradigmatic, subsuming all other sets of fives (five musical notes, five tastes, five planets, etc.). The translation "five phases" becomes fully applicable to the *wuxing* at this point, because the five are clearly phases of qi in the same sense that ice, water, and vapor are phases of H_2O. The directional, numerical, and other key correlates of the five phases were securely established. The five phases had become, in other words, a fully correlative system; all things within a single phase mutually interacted according to the principles of *ganying* resonance, while the five taken together operated in regular and predictable cycles of transformation.

The originally separate themes of yin-yang and the *wuxing* were combined within a single cosmological framework. The five phases themselves could be correlated with cycles of yin and yang, as for example in the various versions of the "Yueling" (including *Huainanzi* 5), where the yin-yang annual cycle includes subcycles correlated with the five phases. Moreover, anything correlated with one or another of the five phases could have a yin or a yang aspect (that is, be *predominately* yin or yang; everything is always to some degree both yin and yang), or be yin in some features but yang in others. For example, birds (feathered creatures) are correlated with phase fire; they are yang, in that they fly, but yin, in that they are oviparous. In modern terms, the set of living creatures has a subset, creatures correlated with phase fire; this subset is intersected by a set of yin attributes and a set of yang attributes. The small area where the sets are congruent yields the category "birds."

Mutual interaction within a class of things defined by yin, yang, and the five phases (and other correlative categories) is conveyed by qi. The word qi originally meant breath, steam, or vapor. By the early Warring States period it had come to mean, more broadly, an active influence of some kind, as from the atmosphere (in weather) or within the body (in causing fever or chills). Qi could also be applied to temperament or mood; likes and dislikes, anger and joy were conceived of as arising from qi. (In modern Chinese, to become angry is still "to give rise to qi.") Qi also meant, in the contexts of medicine and hygiene, a kind of animating force, as in Zhuangzi's methods of *yangqi*, "nourishing the vital energy," and similar yogic practices.

The idea of qi as a conveyor of resonant influence, on the *ganying* principle of "like responds to like," seems to have originated with Zou Yan and his followers in the Jixia Academy of the state of Qi in the third century B.C.E. In this conception qi is an active correlative principle. As Graham puts it, "once spring is correlated with the color green and the ruler's bounty, [qi] will be conceived as changing the weather to spring, making leaves green and moving the heart to bounty."[15] In the *Huainanzi*, as we have seen, qi functions in that sense as an intangible conveyor of influence, but it also was regarded as an immaterial substance ("primordial qi") that, in the self-organizing cosmogonic process, condensed into the material fabric of all things in heaven and earth. Things within a correlative category (whether a simple or a complex one) interact (even over long distances, and without any mechanical connection) on the "like responds to like" principle not only because they emit imperceptible "vibrations" through the medium of qi, but because they are made of the same kind of qi.

While yin-yang and the five phases are the most important correlative categories in *Huainanzi*, several others deserve mention as well. A category of nine appears frequently in the opening sections of *Huainanzi* 4 in the form of the 3 x 3 grid of the nine provinces (which, in *Huainanzi* 3, is reflected in the nine palaces of heaven). This category of ninefold phenomena gives rise to a subset of eight (the nine minus the center), as in the eight directions, the eight winds, the eight outlying regions beyond the center, and so on. This category of eight would seem to invite a further correlation with the eight trigrams of the *Yijing*, but in fact until the end of the second century B.C.E. the *Yijing* was the exclusive preoccupation of the Confucian school, and it plays no role in Huang-Lao cosmology as exemplified by the cosmological chapters of the *Huainanzi*. (Trigram correlates for the eight winds etc. in *Huainanzi* were supplied by the late Eastern Han commentator Gao You. One of the achievements of Dong Zhong-shu in forging, around 105 B.C.E., the grand synthesis that laid the foundation for imperial Confucian ideology had been to incorporate the trigrams and hexigrams into the categorical thinking of the Zou Yan school and its Huang-Lao heirs. This provided a vehicle for the introduction into natural philosophy of the whole range of Confucian ethical philosophy, which had developed its own correlative categories—not only the trigrams and hexigrams, but also, for example, the "five virtues," which fit easily into five-phase reasoning.)

Other important correlative categories in *Huainanzi* are ten and twelve, associated with the Heavenly Stems and Earthly Branches. The latter were particularly important in their guise as the twelve chronograms that marked out the months, by denoting the position of the sun throughout the year, and the twelve years of the Jovian Cycle, by denoting the position of counter-Jupiter, *taiyin* (see below). The Earthly Branches also were correlated with the twelve pitch pipes of the duodecatonic scale. Both stems and branches, and some combinations of the two, were used in *fenye*, "field allocations" (for which see below) to denote certain states and territories. They also were used to name twenty of the twenty-four "seasonal nodes" of the solar calendar. The stems and branches together made still another category, the sexagenary cycle applicable to days and years.

Correlative thinking and *ganying* resonance operate in the cosmology of the *Huainanzi* to organize the world into a highly regular and predictable system. In that system, change and transformation, evolution and decay are still "organic" (to use Needham's term). The world remains unitary in a fundamental sense; the Dao embraces and underlies all things, and reduces distinctions among them to epiphenomena. Through the Dao, everything in the cosmos can affect everything else; a disturbance in one part of the system reverberates throughout the whole. For early Chinese of all schools of thought, there was no necessary cleavage between the world of man and the world of nature, between organic and inorganic, between ethics and instinct; nor was there any notion of a mechanistic universe, divine clockwork operating by mathematical laws that could be observed and formulated by people acting outside of and apart from the machine. But correlative thinking brings order to the organism by showing that certain effects are regular and predictable. In *Huainanzi* 5 we find, for example, that if a ruler acts benevolently during the months of spring, the (phase wood) germinative qi thus engendered will encourage the growth of plants. If on the contrary during the spring months he inappropriately acts with stern severity, thus generating the metallic qi of autumn, then the springtime growth of plants will be hindered.

Correlative thinking was not devoid of absurdities, as for example when categories were filled in artificaly to preserve symmetry; the season of "midsummer" in *Huainanzi* 5 is a good example. Some correlations, such as the five phase correlations of the "five viscera," were only weakly (if at all) tied to real phenomena. Nevertheless, to its practitioners correlative thinking must have seemed like a remarkably powerful tool for making sense of the world. It allowed them to act upon the view that while events in the universe might seem "spontaneous," they are not random. That the universe is describable and predictable was a fundamental doctrine of Huang-Lao cosmology, which was intended (as *Huainanzi* 3–5 in their entirety show) to provide a ruler with a practical program for promoting the success of human endeavors by ensuring that they conformed to the basic principles and rhythms of the cosmos itself.

COSMOGRAPHY

The Round and the Square

The most basic principle of Huang-Lao cosmography is that "Heaven is round, Earth is square." This concept, which apparently has its first explicit statement in the *Zhoubi* (or *Zhoubei*) *xuanjing*, a classic mathematical work of the third or second century B.C.E. but which certainly has much deeper roots in ancient Chinese thought, admits a variety of interpretations. Many of these have been explored by Sarah Allan in "The Shape of the Cosmos,"[16] the principal argument of which is that the Chinese, at least as far back as the Shang Dynasty, conceived of the earth as being shaped like the character *ya*, with four squares radiating out in the cardinal directions, surrounding a central square. As Allan notes, a common (and very old) metaphor for heaven and earth was the shells of a turtle; heaven covers earth as the round carapace covers the "square" plastron.

I believe, however, that the fundamental meaning of "round heaven, square earth," at least in the minds of Huang-Lao cosmologists, was astronomical. The roundness of heaven was taken for granted as being obvious; the only controversy was over whether heaven was flat or bowl-shaped.[17] The belief that the earth is square was based on more subtle reasoning. The cosmic disaster wrought by Gong Gong and Zhuan Xu knocked the ecliptic aslant from the celestial equator. This produced the astronomical phenomena that define the four seasons. Around the circumference of the celestial equator (the ideal circle of the round heavens), there are two points where it is crossed by the ecliptic. These points, in the northeast and southwest, mark the spring and autumn equinoxes. There are two further points, in the southeast and northwest, where the ecliptic and the equator are at their maximum distance from each other. These mark the summer and winter solstices. Thus there are four seasonal nodes, separated along the celestial circle by arcs of 90°. Connecting these points forms a square, and that square is the earth—an idealized earth, bounded by celestial time as defined by the four seasons.

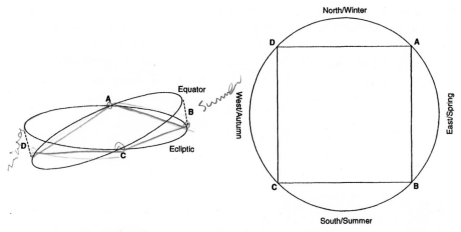

Figure 2.1. The equinoctial and solsticial nodes define the square earth.

For Han cosmologists, this conception of round heaven and square earth had the practical consequence that celestial measurements were normally expressed in degrees (*du*) and celestial motions in terms of leftward or rightward movement along the ecliptic and the equator; earthly measurements were expressed in terms of linear units and cardinal directions.

Several bits of evidence point to the conclusion that this astronomical basis of "round heaven, square earth" informed Huang-Lao cosmology as exemplified by the cosmological chapters of *Huainanzi*.

One domain of evidence is calendrical. As mentioned in Chapter 1 above, the *Huainanzi* uses two different systems for defining the solar year. The first is the "astronomical year," beginning with the month designated by the Earthly Branch *zi*; this month contains the winter solstice and is correlated with the direction north. It therefore occupies a point on the celestial circle corresponding to the midpoint of the northern edge of the square earth, formed by a line connecting the points at NW and NE on the celestial circle. The second calendrical system, the "Xia sequence" civil year (or astrological year), begins with the month designated by the third Earthly Branch, *yin*; this is the month immediately preceding the month in which the spring equinox occurs. It marks (astrologically, if not astronomically) the return of waxing yang and phase wood in the annual cycle. All twelvefold enumerations (months and their correlates) begin with *yin*; all eightfold enumerations (winds and other directional phenomena) begin with the direction northeast.

Another domain of evidence is what might be called schematic cosmography. When the twelve Earthly Branches are arrayed around the celestial circle as chronograms

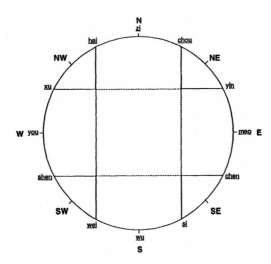

Figure 2.2. Twelve chronograms, eight directions, four hooks: a square within a circle.

to define the twelve months of the solar year (or the twelve years of the Jovian Cycle), each of the four "corner" points (NE, SE, SW, NW) is bracketed by a pair of chronograms. These pairs are called the "four hooks"; they correspond to (or are depicted as) the "V's" of a TLV mirror or a *liubo* game board. (For more on TLV mirrors and *liubo* boards, see below.) These V's define four points that can be connected to form a square within the celestial circle.

The image of the square earth within the round celestial circle was given concrete form in the so-called "mountain mirrors" (*shanzi jing*) of the late Warring States and early Han periods (see Fig. 2.3).[18] These mirrors customarily depict, within the circumference of the round mirror (conventionally understood as a heaven image), a central square (in the center of which is a boss, designed to hold the silken cord by which the mirror could be picked up, but also to represent the *axis mundi*); at some distance beyond the central square a larger square was indicated by four figures in the shape of skewed characters *shan*, representing the mountains at the ultimate edges of the earth. In some of these mirrors, the inner and outer squares have parallel sides. In others, the outer square (representing the outer limits of the earth, i.e., the celestial equator projected out into space) was set at an angle of 90° to the smaller central one (representing the *oikoumenè*). This perhaps indices some disagreement on the part of cosmologists, as seen in the instructions that they presumably gave to the artisans who cast these mirrors, over how to depict the orientation of the earth itself within the outer limits of the four directions. In mirrors where the sides of the squares are not parallel, the sides of

34

Figure 2.3. "Mountain Mirrors" of the Late Warring States Period (after Hunan Provincial Museum, "Hunan Changde Deshan Chumu fajue baogao," *Kaogu* 1963.9: 473.)

the inner square would run N–S and E–W, with the corners therefore at NW, NE, SE, and SW (i.e., at the solsticial and equinoctial nodes), while the corners of the outer square would point in the four cardinal directions. (Or perhaps vice versa, as the mirrors give no clear indication of absolute orientation.) Scattered among the squares (whether parallel or nonparallel) at equal intervals were eight (or sometimes eight outer and four inner) low bosses, indicating the cosmic pillars. These mirrors obviously were forerunners of the better-known TLV mirrors of the late Former Han and beyond, about which more will be said below in connection with the cosmograph.

Finally, it is important to note that the standard metaphor in the *gaitian* cosmological system (for which see below) for the relationship of heaven to earth was that heaven covers earth "like the canopy of a chariot." This clearly defines a square *within* a circle; as seen in numerous Han models and pictures of chariots, the umbrella-like canopy extends to the corners of the square chariot platform, not just to the midpoints of its sides (see Fig. 2.4)[19]. Wang Chong's famous complaint in the *Lunheng* that if heaven were round and earth square "the corners would not fit" could not apply to the canopy-and-chariot image. It would only become germaine when that image was displaced by another, namely the circle within a square of the cosmograph.

Divisions of the Circle and the Square

As we have seen, the circumference of the celestial circle was customarily divided by twelve points (the chronograms, used for celestial/calendrical measurements) and/or by eight points (the directions N, NE, E, SE, S, SW, W, and NW). The planes of the celestial circle and the earthly square were generally conceived of as being divided into five or nine segments.

Figure 2.4. A Han chariot, showing the characteristic round canopy above a square carriage body. Line drawing after a relief carving in stone from the Han tomb at Yinan, Shandong (from Zeng et al., *Yinan gu huaxiang shimu fajue baogao*, Plate 102).

The five "palaces" of heaven (see *Huainanzi* 3.XIII.1–6) consisted of a central circle surrounded by four radial truncated wedges in the four cardinal directions. The earthly counterpart of this scheme was the figure of a central square surrounded by four squares (or rectangles) in the four cardinal directions, in the shape of the character *ya* (see *Huainanzi* 5.XIII).

The "nine fields" of heaven (*Huainanzi* 3.V) similarly consisted of a central circular field surrounded by eight radial truncated wedges extending in the eight directions. Note that these outer eight fields were not formed by simply splitting the outer "four palaces" in two. Whether four palaces or eight fields, these truncated wedges were defined by arcs the midpoints of which correspond to the four, or eight, directions. Thus the northern "palace" extended for 45° to either side of true north; the northern "field" extended for 22.5° to either side of true north.

The earthly counterpart of the nine celestial fields was the 3 x 3 grid of nine squares filling a larger square. This figure, established by Zou Yan at the Jixia Academy in Qi in the third century B.C.E. and accepted by the Huang-Lao School as the sovereign image of the square earth, was applied to a very wide range of things, from the "well-field" system of Mencius to the *mingtang* "Hall of Light" to the "nine provinces" of Yu the Great as schematized by Zou Yan.[20]

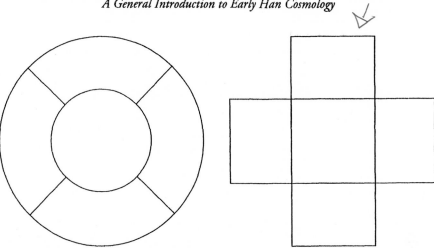

Figure 2.5. Fivefold Heaven and Fivefold Earth.

The dominant image in all of these schematic depictions of heaven and earth is that of axial centrality. The *axis mundi* was thought of as penetrating down to the Yellow Springs below the earth, and ascending through the Gate of Heaven into the sky. This image is found, for example, in *Huainanzi* 8:6a: "When Boyi bored the first well, the dragon mounted on a dark cloud, and divinely made its dwelling on Mt. Kunlun." The axis of heaven was usually taken to be the polestar, and the axis of earth a point lying directly beneath it, far to the north of China. The mythology associated with Huang-Lao cosmology offers, however, a bewildering variety of candidates for the *axis mundi*: Mt. Kunlun (or one of its peaks, Mt. Buzhou, the "Non-Circumscribing Mountain") in the northwest; Mt. Changhe, described as the Gate of Heaven but also as a mountain associated with the west wind; the Fusang tree of the east and the Ruo tree of the west, marking the beginning and end points of the sun's daily journey across the sky; and the Jian tree, marking the apogee of the sun in the south. There were also eight (or, in some accounts, four) pillars that separated heaven and earth. These presumably were arrayed around the periphery of the square earth or of the round heaven (though in either case, the geometry does not quite work for eight evenly spaced pillars); it was the northwestern one of these that Gong Gong and Zhuan Xu broke in their battle.[21] The important point here is that while axial imagery varies, the fundamental importance of centrality does not.[22]

A further feature of the 3 x 3 grid system of schematic cosmography was the *fenye* "field-allocation" theory of judicial astrology.[23] In its simplest form, associated with Zou Yan, this held that celestial events occurring in one of the nine fields of heaven would have concrete effects in the corresponding one of the nine provinces of earth.

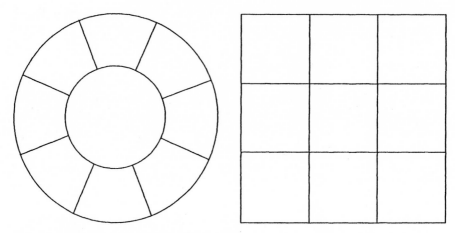

Figure 2.6. Ninefold Heaven and Ninefold Earth.

This concept is elaborated to a very considerable degree in *Huainanzi* 3, where such astrological "force-fields" are allocated according to the ten Heavenly Stems and twelve Earthly Branches, various significant stem-branch pairs, the twenty-eight lunar lodges, and so on. Later in the Han, the system would be extended still further to embrace the eight trigrams and sixty-four hexagrams of the *Book of Changes*.

The Gaitian System

In addition to laying out heaven and earth in various schematic configurations, cosmologists of the Huang-Lao School (and its competitors) had to explain the motions associated with the heavens—the diurnal movements of the sun and the fixed stars, and the more complex longer-term motions of the sun, moon, and visible planets. The most widely accepted theory to account for these phenomena, in the early Han, was the *gaitian* or "Canopy Heaven" system. The locus classicus for the *gaitian* system is the *Zhoubi xuanjing*, a work of the third century B.C.E. The *gaitian* system has been lucidly described by Nakayama[24] and is also discussed in detail below in Appendix A, by Christopher Cullen, with specific reference to *Huainanzi* 3. Accordingly, it will be appropriate here to mention only a few of the system's most salient points.

The *gaitian* system was an attempt to account for the perceived motions of the heavenly bodies in the absence of a concept of a spherical earth. The primary *gaitian* system assumed that earth and the sky were both flat, parallel planes. Variants of the system assumed that both were shallow arcs, or hemispheres, but parallel in either case. The heavenly bodies were assumed to rotate around the celestial north pole; the rising

38

and setting of the sun, moon, planets, and fixed stars were therefore taken to be not real phenomena, but optical illusions. The heavenly bodies were held to be visible in the sky, and hence to illuminate the earth, only within a restricted (and seasonally shifting) "circle of visibility" covering a portion of the earth's surface but not its entirety; thus they would seem to appear and disappear from time to time. The main goal of scientific investigation under the *gaitian* system was therefore to employ gnomons to measure the distance between the earth and the sky, the distance of an observer's location from a point located beneath the center of the sky, and the seasonal movement of the circle of visibility of the heavenly bodies.

The *gaitian* system would have been virtually by default the main cosmological model of the authors of the *Huainanzi*, but except in the case of the final section of *Huainanzi* 3 (generally assumed to be a later addition to the text) it does not play a conspicuous role in *Huainanzi* 3–5. Indeed one may question whether the *gaitian* system, strictly conceived, corresponded to the mental model of the authors of these treatises. That is, they might have employed the *gaitian* system for calculating purposes, while intuitively assuming that the real earth and sky in fact consisted, not of parallel flat planes, but a square flat earth covered by a circular, domed sky—the ancient tortoise shell-and-plastron analogy. This view is inherent, for example, in *Huainanzi* 3.XXV, which describes the path of the sun across the sky from east to west (and thence from west to east by subterranean channels) in terms redolent of archaic mythology.

The *gaitian* universe was given physical embodiment in the *shi* cosmograph, a device that plays a crucial role in the astronomy and (especially) the astrology of *Huainanzi* 3. However convenient that device was, however, for gauging the astrologically significant arrangements of the heavenly bodies at any given time, it may also, as we shall see, have played an unintended role in exposing the weaknesses of the *gaitian* system itself.

The Cosmograph

The cosmograph used the motion of an imaginary counterorbital asterism, called *taiyin* ("great yin") or, sometimes, *taisui* ("great year") to track (in mirror image) the actual motions of Jupiter, for reasons explained by David Hawkes:

> The Chinese were rather late in adopting an astronomical system of year numeration, preferring to designate the year, for whatever purpose, in terms of someone's reign. Texts dating from about the fourth century B.C. occasionally speak of the "Year Star" (i.e., Jupiter) being in such and such a constellation; but this system was felt to be an awkward one, because Jupiter moves in contramotion to the fixed stars, and so the twelve cyclical terms (*tzu, ch'ou, yin, mao* &c.), which were already used both in the naming of the days and in the clockwise designation of twelve

compass points, appeared—very confusingly—in reverse order if you applied them to the twelve years marked by the positions of Jupiter.

This difficulty was eventually overcome by inventing a "hypothetical correlate" of Jupiter which moved from *yin* to *mao* while Jupiter moved from *ch'ou* to *tzu*. The term "She T'i Ke" was used to designate the position of this imaginary planet in *yin* (approximately ENE), and eleven other very unChinese-looking terms were used to designate its positions in the other eleven years of the cycle. This new system is first found in use in a text dating from the third century B.C.[25]

The "invisible correlate" moved, however, not so much (conceptually) through the actual sky, but by being carried along on the moveable "heaven plate" of the cosmograph.

The cosmograph consisted of a round, rotatable "heaven plate" placed on a pivot atop a fixed, square "earth plate." The heaven plate typically was inscribed with a depiction of the Northern Dipper, the names of key asterisms, and the twenty-four seasonal nodes or "fortnightly periods." The latter were designated by the twelve Earthly Branches (which on the earth plate marked the cardinal directions, denoted as the "four hooks" and "four midpoints"—see below), along with eight of the ten Heavenly Stems and four named "corner points" to mark out twenty-four equally spaced points around the celestial circle. (The remaining two Heavenly Stems were correlated with the center, and so played no role in the function of the cosmograph.)

The TLV mirrors of a century or so after the compilation of the *Huainanzi* were in effect an elaboration of the "heaven plate" of the *shi*; as Cammann noted many years ago, TLV mirrors resembled a *bi* circular jade disc placed on top of a square *liubo* game board with TLV markings, those markings then being transferred to the round mirror itself.[26] The mirrors also depicted a square earth within the circular heaven, the eight cosmic pillars and, frequently, images of the four directional gods.[27]

The earth plate of the cosmograph was marked at the midpoint of each side, and at the corners, with eight broad lines (sometimes inscribed with the Eight Trigrams of the *Book of Changes*) indicating the directions, as well as with concentric bands indicating the Heavenly Stems, the Earthly Branches, and the twenty-eight lunar lodges. This explains the references to "midpoints" and "hooks" in *Huainanzi* 3.VII, and the rather puzzling (at first glance) statement there that "when *taiyin* is in any of the four hooks, Jupiter passes through two asterisms" but that "two times eight is sixteen" (one might expect "two times four is eight"): The "midpoints" (corresponding to the "L's" of a *liubo* board or TLV mirror) are marked by a single Earthly Branch at the four cardinal directions, while the "hooks" (corresponding to the "V's" of a *liubo* board or TLV mirror) at the corners each designate *two* directional points (approximately NNE and ENE, ESE and SSE, etc.), indicated by the names of two of the Earthly Branches flanking the

Figure 2.7. Drawing of the back of a Han TLV mirror (from *Gong nong kaogu jichu zhishi*, p. 163.)

corner lines themselves. These points, so marked and so named, were used in the operation of the cosmograph to trace the celestial movement of Jupiter by analogy with the indicated position of *taiyin* on the cosmograph itself. The handle of the Dipper—the "pointer" of the heaven plate dial—was said to "strike" a country or territory by indicating the presence of *taiyin* in the heavenly field (chronogram, lunar lodge, etc.) corresponding to that state or territory in *fenye* field-allocation astrology.

By regularizing celestial motions and making them observable under any conditions (regardless of daylight, clouds, or whatever), the cosmograph must have been a great boon to astrologers. It also gave a sort of physical embodiment to the *gaitian* universe, by depicting the world as a flat, square earth surmounted by a flat (or actually slightly domed) and parallel heaven. It was not, however, able to reproduce any of the sophisticated gnomon measurements that, in the *gaitian* system, were used to measure the height of the sky or the angle of the sun, nor could it indicate the supposed seasonally shifting "circle of visibility" of the heavenly bodies. Ultimately, therefore, the very simplicity of the cosmograph may have undermined the *gaitian* system (except for astrological purposes, and as it was understood in unsophisticated terms in the popular imagination). In any case, the *gaitian* system was discarded by the Latter Han in favor of the *huntian* system, in which earth was enclosed within a spherical heaven

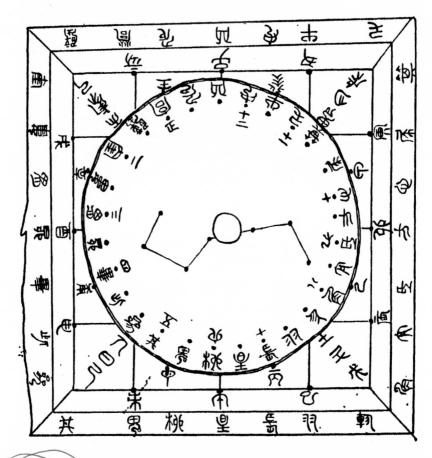

Figure 2.8. Shi cosmograph from the tomb of the second Marquis of Ju Yin, Anhui Province, ca. 165 B.C.E. (from Yan Dun jie, "Guanyu Xi Han chuqi de shipan he zhanpan," *Kaogu* 1978.5: 340).

as the yolk of an egg is enclosed by its shell.[28] As the cosmograph was the characteristic instrument of *gaitian* cosmology, so the armillary sphere would become the characteristic instrument of the *huntian* system.[29]

The cosmograph also created unintended confusion about the relationship of the round heaven to the square earth. As noted above, this concept originally visualized earth as an ideal plane the corners of which were at the equinoctial and solsticial nodes of the celestial equator: a square within a circle. Heaven covered earth as the canopy of a chariot covered the driver's compartment, with the corners neatly fitting under the canopy. For purely practical reasons, however, it would not have been possible to design the cosmograph to reflect this square-within-a-circle model; the earth plate had to be larger than the moving heaven plate in order for measurements to be read from one against the other. This uncoupled the "round heaven, square earth" concept from its astronomical underpinnings; as concretized in the cosmograph, and as Wang Chong would complain, the corners of the earth indeed did not fit under the canopy of heaven. However successful the cosmograph may have been as an astrological calculating device, it was clearly unsatisfactory as a physical model of the universe. If the *gaitian* system required the cosmos to be modeled as a small celestial disk atop a larger square earth, then something was wrong with the *gaitian* system. This problem did not apply to the cosmograph's cousin, the TLV mirror (because it had no moving parts, and thus did not involve considerations of scale), which continued to gain popularity as a magico-religious cosmos-in-miniature even as the *shi* cosmograph itself was yielding to Zhang Heng's armillary sphere.[30]

Both archaeological discoveries and careful textual analysis are beginning to make clear that the Chinese of the Warring States and Han periods made use of a number of astronomical instruments for observing (and for not needing to observe) the skies.[31] As other astronomical instruments emerge from archaeological excavations, or are identified as such in museum collections, further light will be shed on the cosmological theories of the Huang-Lao School as found in these chapters of the *Huainanzi*, as well as on competing schools of thought.[32]

TRADITION AND INNOVATION: MYTH AND RELIGION IN HUANG-LAO COSMOLOGY

As was noted at the beginning of this book, the philosophical synthesis that emerged from the vigorous intellectual life of the late Warring States and early Han periods obviously contained much that was new. Innovations were found not only in the realm of abstract ideas (such as correlative thinking) and improved theories of rulership, but also in new techniques of mathematical astronomy and new devices, such as the cosmograph and magically potent TLV mirrors. On the other hand, the Huang-Lao synthesis also built on ideas that were of considerable antiquity. The credibility of the Huang-Lao School in the early Han may have rested in part on the degree to which it was grounded in widely-shared assumptions that went back to the foundations of Chinese civilization.

A few examples will suffice here. One striking feature is the importance of the calendar, and of positional astrology, in Huang-Lao thought. Nivison and Pankenier have shown in separate studies[33] that the *Bamboo Annals* calendar is reliable back to the early second millennium B.C.E., that the lunar lodges probably date back to around the same time, and that the directional gods (vermilion bird, white tiger, etc.) are of similar antiquity. Sarah Allan has shown that the sun myths preserved in *Huainanzi* 3 date back at least to the Shang.[34] Li Xueqin recently introduced striking physical evidence for the antiquity of the conception that the heavens are round and divided into eight parts.[35] The formulation of *ganying* resonance through the medium of qi was probably an innovation of Zou Yan, but the idea of action at a distance, and particularly the idea that events in the subcelestial world can influence the heavens, underlies the theory of the Mandate of Heaven—an idea of the early Zhou, if not before. Taken together, these ideas would have made the calendrical astrology of *Huainanzi* 3 seem, in its own time, not simply credible, but nearly self-evident.

Another cluster of ideas has to do with symmetry and centrality. As we have seen, this is implicit in the Shang idea of the "four quarters" surrounding the central polity. This Shang notion of centrality finds concrete expression in the decor of many bronze vessels, most notably the celebrated Changsha square *ding* with all four sides decorated with human-like masks facing out in the four directions. In Cammann's view, these faces or masks represent unusually humanoid versions of the *taotie* monster mask, which he identifies as symbolic of a protective deity associated with the idea of centrality.[36] The idea of centrality is also found in the myth of the expulsion from the central realm of the San Miao "barbarians," a myth that dates back at least to the early Zhou. The concept of the periphery of the civilized world as being populated by monsters and terata persisted in Chinese mythology, and is found in *Huainanzi* 4.XV as well as throughout the *Shanhaijing*. The schematic cosmography of the Huang-Lao School has deep roots.[37]

The extent to which the philosophical synthesis that finds its near culmination in *Huainanzi* (the Confucianism of Dong Zhongshu may be said to mark the ultimate stage in Han syncretism) is rooted in antiquity may be seen in the extent to which that synthesis, for all its apparent rationalism, was intertwined with myth and religion. A central element in Huang-Lao cosmology is a Chinese version of the Grand Origin Myth. The Grand Origin Myth itself, as de Santillana and von Dechend have shown,[38] is a complex of ideas that pervade the civilizations of Eurasia and which in all likelihood, therefore, date back to neolithic times.[39]

We know almost nothing of Chinese mythology as it might have existed from the beginnings of Chinese civilization as an oral tradition, but it is clear from various fragments of evidence (both written and iconographic) that do exist that the Chinese Grand Origin myth is of considerable antiquity. Beginning in the early Zhou Dynasty, the Chinese began to compile written texts; by the late Warring States period and into the early Han Dynasty a large body of written works existed. Those works contain bits and pieces of ancient mythology, not as a continuous, coherent narrative, but rather as fragments, often out of context, often puzzling, of uncertain date and authorship.

Versions of many elements of this fragmented mythology can be found in several of the chapters of the *Huainanzi*, notably in the three under consideration here, and in *Huainanzi* 8 as well. The cosmology of the *Huainanzi* is intimately bound up with elements of religious or quasireligious belief; any description of that cosmology that deals only with the rational elements of "natural philosophy" and ignores the numinous would be seriously misleading.

Accordingly, it will be useful to recast the account given above of cosmogony and the origins of human history into a mythic narrative, drawing primarily on the three chapters of the *Huainanzi* under consideration here but filling in gaps, when necessary, from other chapters of the *Huainanzi* and other works in the Huang-Lao tradition. First, however, a few additional words of explanation are in order.

Myth has two essential characteristics. First, it exists in the form of a good story, one that will be told and retold from generation to generation in preliterate societies. Second, it admits of simultaneous multiple interpretations; it can be understood at the level of the obvious story being told, but also at various symbolic levels, some so sacred and taboo that they are among a culture's most closely guarded secrets, imparted in elaborate rituals of initiation or transmitted through closed lineages of shamans or other ritual specialists. Thus, for example, one can believe that the events of Genesis— or any other version of the Grand Origin Myth—happened exactly as they are written down in the sacred scriptures. Others see them as cultural memories of actual ancient events, mythicized over the centuries. It has been proposed, for example, that the myth of the Great Flood is a memory, preserved through hundreds of generations, of the worldwide inundation of coastal lands that occurred about 12,000 years ago when the glaciers of the Ice Age melted and raised the level of the sea by many meters.[40] Myth seems to lend itself particularly well to the phenomena of astronomy, the most ancient and sacred of the sciences—as for example in the myth of Gong Gong and Zhuan Xu, which, as we have seen, "explains" the tilting of the ecliptic relative to the celestial equator.

With these considerations in mind, let us look again at the mythic narrative implicit in the cosmological chapters of the *Huainanzi*.

The story begins in the *Urzeit*, the time before time began, the era of the first sages—Shen Nong, Fu Xi, the Yellow Thearch, and others—who are scarcely distinguishable from gods, who reigned for hundreds of years apiece and who bestowed the blessings of civilization upon the people. As that age drew to a close, under "Emperors" Yao and Shun, a mysterious people known as the San Miao committed the terrible sin of rebellion; they were then driven away from the central kingdom by Shun. Around the same time, two divinities, conceived of as giants, sought to gain celestial powers:

> Anciently, Gong Gong and Zhuan Xu fought, each seeking to become the thearch.
> Enraged, they crashed against the Non-Circumscribing Mountain; Heaven's pillars

45

broke, the cords of earth snapped. Heaven tilted in the northwest, and thus the sun, moon, stars and planets shifted in that direction. Earth became unfull in the southeast, and thus the watery floods and mounding soils subsided in that direction. (3.I.23–29)

As a consequence of this, a great deluge began, and a flood engulfed the whole earth. Shun chose a man named Gun to tame the flood; he tried to do so by stealing some magical earth from the gods to make dams. But the dams failed, and Gun was punished by being exposed on a mountainside, where he turned to stone. From his body, however, burst his son Yu, later to be known as Yu the Great. Yu, rather than opposing the waters, harnessed their natural tendencies. He observed the tracks left in the mud at the bottom of the floodwaters by the tails of passing dragons, and used them as markers to excavate channels; thus he returned the rivers to their natural beds and allowed the waters to drain away.

But in one version of the myth, Yu also availed himself of some magical earth:

> Yu also took expanding earth to fill in the great flood, making the great mountains. He excavated the wastelands of Kunlun to make level ground. In the center (of the world) is a manifold walled city of nine layers, with a height of 11,000 li, 114 double-paces, two feet, and six inches. (4.III.1–3)

When all of this was over, Yao and Shun had passed from the scene, and Yu became thearch. And not just thearch, but the first hereditary ruler in Chinese history; in legend, at least, the founder of the dynastic system of government that lasted into the twentieth century.

This myth is a very good story, but, as we saw earlier in this chapter, it also contains elements of a metaphor about the shape and character of the universe itself. The first sages were themselves gods, or god-like, and lived in contact with the gods. Their reigns lasted for hundreds of years. Under their rule, the people enjoyed the blessings of civilization and were totally free from strife. In their era, time had no meaning—time did not yet exist.

In the time of Yao and Shun, the sins of the San Miao led to their expulsion, and at the same time the ambitions of Gong Gong and Zhuan Xu led to the wrecking of one of the pillars of heaven. Heaven and earth tilted, so that the heavenly bodies flowed one way, the waters of the earth another. The old order was swept away in a world-engulfing flood. The square earth had to be drained, surveyed, marked out into its nine provinces, and set under the government of the flood tamer himself. With the tilting of the ecliptic relative to the celestial equator, time itself began—seasonal time, the endless round of years from winter solstice to winter solstice, the end of one year and the beginning of the next. The world became familiar, ruled by a human emperor

46

Adam + Eve

with a normal life span, and marked by the trouble and strife that is the lot of all mortals. For better or worse, we became masters of our own fate, but at a price—for the gods, those inhabitants of the celestial plane, withdrew from the plane of the earth, and were our constant companions no longer.

Yet it was thought that this rupture might be repaired, at least for some times and under some circumstances. Yu the Great was careful not only to drain the floods but to raise up the mountains, including Mt. Kunlun itself, the world pillar. We are told that

> Broad Palace, Revolving House, Hanging Garden, Cool Wind, and the Hedge Forest are within the Changhe Gate of the Kunlun Mountains. This is called the Carved-Out Garden. The pools of the Carved-Out Garden flow with yellow water. The water circulates three times and then returns to its source. It is called cinnabar water; if one drinks it, one will not die. . . . (4.III.14–18)

> If one climbs to a height double that of Mt. Kunlun, that mountain is called Cool Wind Mountain. If one climbs this mountain, one will not die. If one climbs to a height that is doubled again, that mountain is called Hanging Garden. If one ascends it, one will gain supernatural power, and be able to control the wind and the rain. If one climbs to a height that is doubled yet again, it reaches up to heaven itself. If one mounts to there, one will become a demigod. It is called the abode of the Supreme Thearch. (4.V.1–7)

Mt. Kunlun is, in effect, a stairway to heaven. Mounting the sacred pillar, one passes through the Changhe Gate, a circular door in the vault of the sky leading into the heavens beyond; there one encounters still higher peaks, with more and more marvellous powers, until one ascends to the abode of the celestial emperor himself.

In other words, ritually and under some circumstances, one can restore the conditions of the world before time, the world before cosmic disaster and engulfing flood severed the bonds between humans and the gods.

Nevertheless, in the cosmological chapters of the *Huainanzi*, the gods play a role that seems curiously divorced from religious faith. They appear to be embodiments of the principles of correlative thinking and calendrical astrology, an awe-inspiring part of, but not separate from, the cosmic unity grounded in the immanent and indivisible Dao. They occupy every niche of a pantheistic hierarchy from the Supreme Thearch (also called the Grand Monad) to high gods associated with the planets, the five directions, etc., to the assistants to those gods, to meteorological gods such as the Torch Dragon and local minor divinities like Shaman Xian, to "immortals" who ascend and descend the cosmic pillars, down to the not-divine but also other-than-human monsters of the lands far beyond the central realm. Many of these gods are scaly, draconic, or serpent-bodied, from the (to judge from the characters used to write their names) fishy Gun and the insect-like Yu to the dragon-like divinities of Thunder Marsh who drum on their bellies for the sheer pleasure of it. Strangely lacking in this pantheon are malevolent gods or deities of the underworld. All of these gods seem to be presented as being emblematic of the natural world—upholders of the cosmic order and symbols of its diverse processes, but not capable of acting upon it. There is no hint, in *Huainanzi* 3 and 4, of prayers to any of these divinities, or of the likelihood that they could intervene on behalf of humans to affect the nonhuman world in any way. *Huainanzi* 5, in contrast, is replete with mention of sacrifices to ancestors and to gods of the four directions; disaster—disruption of cosmic order—is held to ensue from neglecting these sacrifices. But the concrete benefit derived from such sacrifices is that the world will continue in its proper and harmonious course, not that the ruler might obtain a dispensation to depart from the inherent order of the cosmos.

The concept of the sacred in Huang-Lao thought thus seems to be subsumed into a broader concept of cosmic order. The stories, imagery, and dramatis personae of myth pervade the cosmology of the *Huainanzi*, but gods that once contended so fiercely that they knocked aside a cosmic pillar, or who struggled to control a world-engulfing flood, now are seen as simply part of a continuum that embraces all of the unitary cosmos, from heaven to earth, from the Supreme Thearch through lesser gods, from humans and animals to shellfish and worms. The role of the human ruler of the central polity mirrors that of the planetary gods who wield the construction implements that are the "standards" of cosmic order; both are charged with ensuring that nothing interferes with the harmony of the world. To the extent that an individual human religious goal appears at all in this cosmology, it does not involve worship and adoration, or even making bargains with the gods; rather it is to attain the quasidivine status of immortality.

Hints of the cult of immortality do appear in the cosmological chapters of the *Huainanzi*, as for example with the elixir of immortality drawn from the cinnabar springs of Kunlun mentioned above. Around the time the *Huainanzi* was written, the age-old question of religion—"what happens when we die"—was being asked anew, and some were beginning to add, "Is it possible not to die?" To ancient rituals of calling back the departed *hun*, or ethereal soul, of the deceased, were added positive attempts to forestall death, through breath control, yoga, and the earliest hints of metallurgical alchemy.

Cosmogony is explicitly linked to questions of immortality, or life after death, in the opening passages of *Huainanzi* 7:

> Anciently, in the time before there were Heaven and Earth, there were only formless simulacra. Obscure! Profound! Vast plain, mournful desolation, boiling turbulence, fathomless grotto! No one knew the gate (of Heaven). Two gods inchoately were born, giving structure [= "warp threads"] to Heaven and a plan to Earth. Vast! None knew its limits. Overflowing! None knew its resting-place.

48

From this (condition), they differentiated as yin and yang, separated as the eight ultimate endpoints [= cosmic pillars]; hard and pliant brought each other to completion, and the ten thousand things took form.

Turbulent qi became beasts, and subtle qi became humans. Thus the germinal and godlike belong to Heaven, the bony and corporeal belong to Earth. The germinal and godlike enter the gate (of Heaven), but the bony and corporeal return to their roots (in the Earth). (One asks,) "How then am I to be preserved?"

Thus the Sage patterns himself on Heaven and follows the flow of the essential nature of things; he does not adhere to the vulgar, nor entrap himself in the (merely) human. He takes Heaven as his father and Earth as his mother, yin and yang as his net and the four seasons as his fastenings. Heaven, in its tranquility, attains clarity; Earth, in its fixity, attains repose. Of the ten thousand creatures, those who lose these (fixed principles) die; those who pattern themselves on them live.

The tranquil and boundless is the dwelling-place of the godlike and enlightened; the empty and null is the dwelling-place of the Dao. This is why those who search in externals lose that which is within; those who stand guard over internalities lose that which is external. It is like roots and stems: The root leads into a thousand branches, and to ten thousand leaves—no one can follow them all. But that which is germinal and godlike is received from Heaven; that which has shape and substance is endowed by Earth. (7:1a:4–1b:8)

The prescription for immortality—or at least for finding some means for escaping the human predicament—here is reminiscent of Zhuangzi; the sage escapes the mundane by taking refuge in the Dao. But other contemporary evidence suggests that immortality was sought in more concrete ways as well, through the rituals of burial and through the escape of the soul into the realm of the gods. The notion that the *po*, or earthly soul, could continue to enjoy its funeral offerings after death so long as the body remained uncorrupted to house it, led to elaborate efforts at preparing corpses for burial—with spectacular success in the case of the Lady of Dai, the occupant of Mawangdui Tomb #1. The funerary banner draped over her coffin was probably intended to serve as a sort of cosmic road map for the journey of her *hun* ethereal soul—released from her body at the moment of death—to the afterlife. Beyond that, the idea was beginning to take hold that the departed *hun* soul might achieve an apotheosis after death. This too is evident in the Mawangdui banner: the Lady of Dai is pictured in the heavens with a serpentine tail, making her as one with such celestial deities as Fu Xi, Nü Gua, and the Torch Dragon.

Cosmology in Context

What might the Huang-Lao cosmology of the *Huainanzi* have meant to Liu An and his circle of savants at the court of Huainan? To answer this question, one must look at least briefly at the social and political circumstances of the early Han period.

Figure 2.9. The funerary banner from Mawangdui Tomb #1. Pencil drawing by Sandra Smith-Garcès.

Liu An was a grandson of Liu Bang, and thus a member of the third generation of the ruling family of the Han. He was one of many relatives or close supporters of the Han founder who held fiefs within the Han empire. It would have been natural for him, and others of his status, to view feudalism (in the Zhou Chinese manifestation of that concept) as the natural order of government; the brief statist experiment of the Qin Dynasty would have seemed like a temporary aberration. The ideal ruler that Liu An envisioned and sought to emulate, and for whom the *Huainanzi* might have been conceived as a sort of handbook of good government, would have resembled a Zhou king more than a later Chinese emperor. As the astrological predictions of *Huainanzi* 3 make clear, the old Zhou states—Wei, Chu, Lu, and the rest—were still thought of in the early Han as having a present reality, rather than as being mere historical memories.

At the same time, Liu An and his fellow feudatories found their world under siege. Liu An might well have been guilty of crimes against the imperial throne, but whatever they were, it is clear that Emperor Wu seized upon them to bring about the death of Liu An and the prompt incorporation of his fief into the imperial polity. A new political reality was beginning to take hold; Qin-style centralism was to prove to be no aberration, but rather the blueprint for a new style of government in China. Feudalism as a political system was dead, replaced by imperial bureaucratism.

The world was changing in other ways as well. Under Emperor Wu the borders of China expanded dramatically, bringing under Chinese rule many peoples who had been known only as half-wild "barbarians" to writers of such texts as the "Treatise on Topography." Legalism had been discredited by the harsh policies of Qin; Confucianism was enjoying a modest revival, but so far Confucian scholars found themselves valued mostly for their historical, archival, rhetorical, and clerical skills. Within the empire, commerce and industry flourished, bringing unheard-of wealth to nouveaux-riches commoners; the familiar distinctions of aristocratic rank were disappearing. Of course, these phenomena were not entirely new, and some of them merely continued trends that extended well back into the Zhou period itself. Nevertheless, a well-born Chinese of the early Han could legitimately have felt that his world was changing with baffling speed and in ways that defied comprehension.

These considerations are important for our understanding of the *Huainanzi*. In many ways the political program propounded in that work is conservative, even reactionary. It proposed solutions to the political problems of a world that no longer existed at the time when it was written. The Huang-Lao School was a product of the late Warring States period, even if it reached its full flowering in the early Han. Like other philosophical schools of the time, it asked the question, How is a ruler to prevail in a world of small kingdoms locked in a mutual, and deadly, struggle for survival? It rejected both the Legalist solution—arms and grain—and the Mencian one—benevolence and righteousness. As we have seen, the Huang-Lao prescription was rather for the ruler to align himself with the power of the Dao itself, to make his actions so conform to the patterns of the natural order as to be irresistible. Liu An was never to have a chance to put this program to a practical test.

Nevertheless, the Huang-Lao School taught much that was appealing to the rulers of the new age as well. If the ruler of a Zhou principality could fancy himself as occupying the fulcrum between heaven and earth, so too could an emperor of the Han Dynasty. The early Han was a time of intellectual ferment and discovery precisely because the new circumstances of the age demanded a new ideological synthesis—one that was soon to be provided, when Dong Zhongshu found the key to integrating Huang-Lao thought with Confucianism.[41]

The *Huainanzi* is of interest in part because of the lively picture it provides for us of the intellectual atmosphere at the court of an up-to-date Chinese ruler of the second century B.C.E. Liu An ensured for himself a good historical reputation, just as the kings of Qi had done a century earlier, by establishing himself as a patron of scholarship and the leading figure in a learned academy. On the evidence of the cosmological chapters of the *Huainanzi*, his court scholars would have included astronomers, calendrical specialists, astrologers versed in the manipulation of the cosmograph and in the interpretation of its positional readings, geographers, cartographers, and specialists in the natural sciences. The King of Huainan's meticulous attention to the phenomena of the natural world was to be emulated by Chinese emperors throughout the history of the empire.

With the establishment of a strong imperial capital and a rapid expansion of the frontiers, new ideas poured into the center from every part of the realm, including from such provincial centers of learning as the court of Huainan. This process was further encouraged by the expansion of bureaucratic government throughout the empire; officials returning to the capital from the provinces could and did bring with them new ideas, books, techniques, beliefs, and even customs and fashions.

Among many other signs of increasing cosmopolitanism at the imperial level, new forms of official worship were instituted in the Former Han, including sacrifices to the gods of the four directions and to Xiwangmu, the Queen Mother of the West. These innovations provide additional evidence of the acceptance at elite metropolitan levels of yin-yang/five phase philosophical and religious ideas, and of interest in the cult of immortality;[42] they hint at what was to become the formalized pantheon of Religious Daoism a few centuries hence.

The *Huainanzi* is of particular interest and importance for the intellectual history of Han China because it was written at a time that defined the turning point from an old order to a new one. However much the Huang-Lao cosmology found in the following chapters may have shared in the currents of new ideas and new techniques that swirled through the intellectual circles of the early Han, it also was grounded in beliefs and attitudes from the distant past. It was, in other words, in large part a reinterpretation of tradition; and it stood poised to usher in new trends in philosophy and religious belief in the centuries that followed.

Huainanzi Chapter 3: Tianwenxun

∽

THE TREATISE ON THE
PATTERNS OF HEAVEN

INTRODUCTION

The "Treatise on the Patterns of Heaven" provides a summary of astronomical and astrological knowledge in the early part of the Han period. It includes sections on cosmogony, cosmology, positional and calendrical astronomy, and astrology (including rules for the use of the *shi* cosmograph), and, prominently, on the interpretation of celestial portents and the assignment of their significance to territories corresponding to the pre-Qin feudal states.

The content of the chapter is inclusive rather than consistent in character, and contains information derived from a variety of Warring States and early Han systems and textual sources. Thus, for example, the length of the year is given variously in different sections of the treatise as 366, 365¼, and 360 days. The treatise includes material of an archaic and mythical flavor, such as an account of the stages of the sun[-crow's] daily journey across the sky, as well as astronomical data of considerable sophistication and accuracy, such as a calculation of the length of the Jovian Year as 4,340 days, only about 7.5 days more than the true figure.

In this translation the chapter has been divided into sections (which do not appear in the original text) for convenience in dealing with the material. These sections are also useful for discerning the overall organization of the treatise.

In this brief overall introduction to the "Treatise on the Patterns of Heaven" I provide a synopsis, section by section, of the treatise as a whole, followed by an outline of the major celestial periodicities given therein. I then go on to discuss briefly the question of the epoch (that is, the starting point for the celestial ephemerides), and the role of astrology in the treatise.

SYNOPSIS OF
"THE TREATISE ON THE PATTERNS OF HEAVEN"

COSMOGONY
Section I: The Origin of the Cosmos
  Evolution of the cosmos from primordial chaos; yang qi forms heaven, yin qi forms earth.
  The battle of Gong Gong and Zhuan Xu; tilting of heaven and earth.
Section II: Yin and Yang
  The nature of yang and yin qi.
  Yin-yang *ganying* resonances.
Section III: The Reciprocity of Heaven and Man

COSMOGRAPHY AND COSMOLOGY
Section IV: The Divisions of Heaven
  An introduction to the following sections.
Section V: The Nine Fields
  The nine fields of heaven with their associated lunar lodges.
Section VI: The Five Planets
  The planets with their associated gods and other five-phase correlates.
Section VII: The Motions of Jupiter
Section VIII: The Motions of Mars
Section IX: The Motions of Saturn
Section X: The Motions of Venus
Section XI: The Motions of Mercury
Section XII: The Eight "Wind Seasons"
  Eight seasons of 45 days, defined by the eight winds.
Section XIII: The Five Offices and Six Departments
  Correlation of named regions of the heavens with departments of bureaucratic government.
  Pairs of Earthly Branches forming six diagonals across the heavens.

SOLAR CYCLES
Section XIV: The Purple Palace
  Celestial circle defined as 365.25^d; tropical year defined as 365.25 days.
Section XV: The Callippic Cycle and the Grand Conclusion Cycle
  The Callippic Cycle of 76 years (= 4 x Metonic Cycle of 19 years), that is, the period in which whole numbers of years of 365¼ days and lunar months of 29 499/940 days recur at the same time of day.

THE COSMOGRAPH

Section XXVII: The Indications of the Handle of the Dipper
  Movements of the handle of the Dipper on the *shi* cosmograph, with associated pitch pipe
    notes and omens.

NUMEROLOGY AND MATHEMATICAL HARMONICS

Section XXVIII: Numerology and Harmonics
  Numerology of multiples of three.
Section XXIX: Harmonics of the Twelve Pitch Pipes
  Calculation of pitch pipe lengths.
Section XXX: The Notes and the Seasons
  Numerological correlation of pentatonic and duodecatonic notes with the calendar.
Section XXXI: The Numerology of Weights and Measures
  Numerological correlation of pentatonic and duodecatonic notes with weights and measures.

THE JOVIAN CYCLE

Section XXXII: The Twelve-Year Jovian Cycle
  Sexagenary day cycle correlations of the twelve-year Jovian Cycle.
  Omens of the twelve Earthly Branchs.
Section XXXIII: The Names of the Twelve Years of the Jovian
Cycle
  Names of non-Chinese origin of the twelve years of the Jovian Cycle.
  Lunar lodge positions of Jupiter and *taiyin* (hypothetical counter-Jupiter).

PORTENT CALCULATIONS

Section XXXIV: Astrological Meaning of the 60-Year Jupiter Cycle
  Sexagenary day cycle portent calculations according to the position of *taiyin*.
  Five-phase correlates of Stems and Branchs, in cyclical series.
  Miscellaneous prognostication rules.
Section XXXV: The Lunar Lodges
  Controlling lunar lodges for the twelve months.
  Angular extensions of the lunar lodges.
  Territorial apportionments of the lunar lodges.
  Territorial portents of Jupiter's position in the lunar lodges.
Section XXXVI: Seasonal Indications of *Taiyin*
  Actions appropriate to the seasons of the solar year govern the "seasons" of the Jovian Year
    indicated by *taiyin*.
Section XXXVII: Stem-Branch Correlations
  Territorial apportionments of the Heavenly Stems.
  Territorial apportionments of the Earthly Branchs.
  Stem and Branch correlations of the five phases.
Section XXXVIII: Relations of the Five Phases
  Production order of the five phases, and associated rules for conduct of affairs.

Section XXXIX: The Gods of the Northern Dipper
  Male and female gods of the Northern Dipper.
  Their annual motions correlated with yin-yang and *xingde* (recision-accretion).
Section XL: Omens of the Stems and Branches
  Miscellaneous Stem-Branch portents; Stem-Branch "concurrence pairs."
  Territorial apportionments of the Stem-Branch pairs (eight "concurrence pairs" and eight "lesser conjunctions").
  Miscellaneous portents.
Section XLI: Correspondences and Omens
  Portents of yin and yang.
  Macrocosm/microcosm.
Section XLII: Prognostications for the Jovian Cycle
  Rules for regulating food rations on the basis of prognostications for the twelve years of the Jovian Cycle.
  Chart of Stem-Branch directional correlations.
Section XLIII: Appended Treatise on Gnomonics
  Measurements of the universe by means of a ten-foot gnomon.
  This section appended to but probably not originally part of the "Treatise on the Patterns of Heaven."

PERIODICITIES IN THE "TREATISE ON THE PATTERNS OF HEAVEN"

Solar Years

1. The sexagenary-cycle year, defined as 366 days so that the winter solstice always falls on a day denoted *zi* or *wu*.
2. The soli-lunar calendar year:
    a. Length of the year = 365¼ days. Solstices defined as 182 5/8 days apart.
    b. Length of the lunar month = 29 499/940 days.
    c. Metonic Cycle of 19 years, with 7 intercalary months, so that the year and the month both recommence on the same day.
    d. Callippic Cycle of 76 years (4 Metonic Cycles) so that the year and the month both recommence on the same day at the same hour.
    e. Grand Conclusion Cycle of 1,520 years (20 Callippic Cycles) so that the year and the month both recommence at the same hour on a day denoted by the same sexagenary-cycle Stem-Branch pair.
3. The "lesser year" of 360 days, considered as:
    a. 24 solar nodes or "fortnightly periods" of 15 days;
    b. Twelve 30-day months, indicated by the handle of the Northern Dipper (or

its equivalent as represented on the cosmograph) pointing to one after another of the chronograms distributed around the celestial circle.

c. Eight 45-day "wind seasons."

d. Five 72-day "seasons" denoted by the five Heavenly Stems that take the Earthly Branch *zi* in the sexagenary cycle.

The Jovian Year

1. The Jovian Cycle of 12 years, governed by the period of Jupiter and its hypothetical counterorbital counterpart, *taiyin* (or *taisui*), and denominated by twelve year names evidently of non-Chinese origin.

Planetary Periods

1. Jupiter: 4,340 days, or 11.88 years, approximated as 12 years. (True period is 4332.5 days, or 11.86 years.)

2. Mars: 24 lunar months, or approximately 708 days. (True period is 693 days, or 1.88 years.)

3. Saturn: 28 years. Better figures were available at the time *Huainanzi* was written, however. The *Wuxingzhan*, from which the relevant passage in *Huainanzi* is quoted, gives 30 years; the *Taichuli*, or Grand Inception Calendar, of 104 B.C.E. gives 29.79 years. (True figure is 29.46 years.)

4. Venus: Visible in the east for 240 (a mistake for 224?) days, hidden for 120 days, visible in the west for 240 days, hidden for 35 days, then reappears in the east. (True figure is 224.70 days.)

5. Mercury: Visible for 20 days in each season (i.e., at about 91-day intervals), normally in the second, fifth, eighth, and eleventh months. (True figure is 87.97 days.)

THE QUESTION OF THE EPOCH

Calendrical cycles imply an epoch, that is, a point at which the cycles commence. The "Treatise on the Patterns of Heavens" defines an epoch in various ways, as the following passages suggest:

> The weft-cords of Heaven establish the epoch, which always begins with *yin*. Arising, (*taisui*) moves to the right (against the fixed stars) for one year and then shifts (to the next of the celestial chronograms). After twelve years it completes a great circuit and then begins again. (3.XIX.12–14)

> The beginning of the Jovian Cycle is established (on the day) *jiayin*. After one completion [i.e., 4,340 days], it (begins again), established (on the day) *jiaxu*. After two

completions it (begins again) established (on the day) *jiawu*. After three completions, it returns to its beginning in *jiayin*. The year's annual shift is one chronogram [i.e., an arc of 1/12 of the celestial circle]. (3.XXXII.1–5)

On the day *jiayin*, in the first year of the epoch, Saturn is in (the lunar lodge) Dipper. Each year Saturn moves through one lunar lodge. (3.IX.1–2)

From the above, and from similar passages elsewhere in the chapter, it is clear that an epoch (the starting point of a calendrical or concordance cycle of some kind) is taken to begin on a day denoted *jiayin* in the sexagenary cycle. The reasons for the importance of *yin* are twofold. Firstly, as was explained in Chapter 1 above, the *Huainanzi* follows the "Xia sequence" calendar, in which the civil year begins in the third astronomical month, that is, in the month designated *yin*; the winter solstice, the beginning of the astronomical year, occurs in the month designated *zi*. Secondly, and not by accident, the state of Chu is correlated with the Earthly Branch *yin*, and the *Huainanzi* is a work in the Chu tradition.

What is not clear is when the epoch (presumably a Grand Concordance Cycle) was held to have begun. Presumably it was in a year in which the first (i.e., *yin*) month began on a day designated *jiayin*, but in that case, which year? The sexagenary day cycle repeats on the same day of the year every eighty years, and it is not clear how far back into the past the epoch of the "Treatise on the Patterns of Heaven" was projected.[1]

ASTROLOGY

By far the greatest amount of material in the "Treatise on the Patterns of Heaven" is astrological in character, as one would expect; from the earliest times in China, as in other ancient civilizations, astronomy was of interest primarily for what information it was believed to yield about the conduct of human affairs (and especially political affairs). The astrological rules and portents in the treatise are extremely varied in character, having to do with such matters as seasonal observances, favorable and unfavorable conditions for the conduct of military campaigns, and predictions specific to different areas of China designated by the names of the pre-Qin feudal states. Several sections of the chapter show close affinities with *Huainanzi* 5, the "Treatise on the Seasonal Rules," indicating, most likely, descent from a common tradition of calendrical astrology. In all of these cases it is clear that the treatise is solidly in the tradition of Huang-Lao Daoism, amassing a great deal of material, varying in character from mathematical astronomy through numerology to portent astrology and mythology, in the service of a ruler who was expected to make use of all of the knowledge of the natural order that he could command in the conduct of his state's affairs.

જી

THE TREATISE ON THE PATTERNS OF HEAVEN

Section I: The Origin of the Cosmos

[3:1a:1]

1   When Heaven and Earth were yet unformed,
2   All was ascending and flying, diving and delving.
3   Thus it was called the Great Inception.
4   The Dao began in the Nebulous Void.
5   The Nebulous Void produced spacetime;
6   Spacetime produced the primordial qi.
7   A shoreline (divided) the primordial qi.
8   That which was pure and bright spread out to form Heaven;
9   The heavy and turbid congealed to form Earth.
10   It is easy for that which is pure and subtle to converge,
11   But difficult for the heavy and turbid to congeal.
12   Therefore Heaven was completed first, and Earth fixed afterwards.
13   The conjoined essences of Heaven and Earth produced yin and yang.
14   The supercessive essences of yin and yang caused the four seasons.
15   The scattered essences of the four seasons created all things.
16   The hot qi of accumulated yang produced fire;
17   The sun is the essence of fiery qi.
18   The cold qi of accumulated yin produced water;
19   The moon is the essence of watery qi.
20   The overflowing qi of the essences of the sun and the moon made the stars and planets.
21   To Heaven belong the sun, moon, stars, and planets;
22   To Earth belong waters and floods, dust and soil.
23   Anciently Gong Gong and Zhuan Xu fought, each seeking to become the Thearch.
24   Enraged, they crashed against Mt. Buzhou;
25   Heaven's pillars broke, the cords of Earth snapped.
26   Heaven tilted in the northwest, and thus
27   The sun and moon, stars and planets shifted in that direction.
28   Earth became unfull in the southeast, and thus
29   The watery floods and mounding soils subsided in that direction.

[3:2a:2]

Commentary to Section I

The treatise begins with this powerful and quite beautiful cosmogonic passage, describing the evolution of spacetime from the primordial chaos by means of the operations of a dualism inherent in the Dao itself. Quite remarkably, it treats qi—usually thought of (at least until the advent of Neo-Confucian metaphysics) as an entirely immaterial resonant medium—as the basic stuff of the physical universe. Spacetime as it emerged from this initial coming-into-being is then seen to have been disrupted and disordered through a cosmic accident, producing the "unbalanced" world of catastrophe and flood that confronts humans in the era of historical time.

Much of the cosmological significance of this section has already been discussed in Chapter 2 above.[2] It is not necessary, therefore, to repeat that analysis here.[3]

However, the language of this section, almost liturgical in its lofty formality, deserves further comment. Here I shall rely heavily on the recent work of Stephen Field, who has had the brilliant insight that the individual lines of the "Tian wen" chapter of *Chu ci* can each be split into declarative and interrogative halves, and that the declarative half of such a "bifurcated" translation itself forms a narrative of early Chinese cosmology, myth, and history.[4] When the opening section (verses 1–14) of "Tian wen" is treated in this way, it becomes immediately obvious that Section I (as well as parts of Sections IV–VI) of *Huainanzi* 3 are directly based on the "Tian wen" narrative:

> In the beginning of old,
> All is yet formless, no up or down.
> Dark and light are a blur,
> The only image is a whir.
> Bright gets brighter, dark gets darker,
> The yin mingles with the yang—
> Then was the round pattern manifold.
> What an achievement that was!
> Around turn the cords on the pivot of Heaven;
> Eight pillars are the buttresses;
> Spread out are the nine fields of Heaven
> With their numerous edges and angles.
> The Heavens mesh with the twelve;
> Sun and moon bond, and the asterisms line up.

Two points need to be emphasized here. First, the cosmogonic narrative in *Huainanzi* 3.I is unquestionably based on that of the "Tian wen" narrative. This is clear from such terms as *fengyi*—my "flying and ascending," Fields's "a blur"—and *yu* (*Huainanzi*) or *yuwei* ("Tian wen")—my "junctures" (3.IV.1 below), Fields's "edges and angles." Second, the narrative aspect of "Tian wen" lends itself naturally to the kind of amplification that we find here in *Huainanzi*, because the "Tian wen" does in fact ask questions that invite answers:

> The yin coupled with the yang [what was basic? what transformed?]

or

> Eight pillars are the buttresses [why the gap in the southeast?]

The last part of this section recounts the famous story of the fight between Gong Gong and Zhuan Xu that led to the tilting of heaven and earth—in cosmological terms, to the astronomical fact that the ecliptic (the sun's apparent path around the earth as seen against the fixed stars) does not coincide with the celestial equator (the earth's equator as projected onto the fixed stars). This accounts for the seasons of the solar year; the solstices mark the sun's furthest distance from the celestial equator, while the equinoxes mark the points at which the equator and the ecliptic cross. The fight between Gong Gong and Zhuan Xu, then, marks the transition from the *Urzeit*, the era of "timelessness" when there were no seasons to mark solar time, to the historical era of human rulers and the march of time.

This story also answers several of the "heaven questions" of "Tian wen":

> Kang Hui [= Gong Gong] was enraged; the land leaned southeast [why?].
> The nine provinces were askew; the river valleys were fouled [how?]
> The eastward flow never fills the sea [who knows why?]

Here, as in a surprising number of instances throughout the cosmological chapters of *Huainanzi*, we find Liu An's scholars undertaking to answer and flesh out the questions of "Tian wen."

This amplification can be seen, for example, not only in the onomotopoeic reduplication of *fengyi* as *fengfengyiyi*, but in its pairing with a parallel phrase, *tongtongshushu*, "diving and delving," making explicit that the Cosmic Pillar both ascends to the apex of heaven and bores through to the depths of the subterranean waters.[5]

The *Huainanzi* also introduces, as "Tian wen" does not, the technical term *yuzhou*, literally "eaves and roof-beams," but in cosmology, "spacetime" (or, in Graham's felicitous phrase, "cosmos-as-it-extends and cosmos-as-it-endures.").[6] Thus the overall effect of this and the next few sections at the beginning of *Huainanzi* 3 is to make more explicit—and, perhaps one can say, more fully realized—an understanding of cosmogony that was already deeply imbedded in Chinese mythology and natural philosophy a century or more before the *Huainanzi* was written.

Section II: Yin and Yang

[3:2a:2]
1 The Dao of Heaven is called the Circular;
2 The Dao of Earth is called the Square.
3 The square governs the obscure;
4 The circular governs the bright.
5 The bright emits qi, and for this reason

6   Fire is the external brilliance of the sun.

7   The obscure sucks in qi, and for this reason

8   Water is the internal luminosity of the moon.

9   Emitted qi endows, retained qi is transformed.

10   Thus yang endows and yin is transformed.

11   The unbalanced qi of Heaven, becoming perturbed, causes wind;

12   The harmonious qi of Earth, becoming calm, causes rain.

13   When yin and yang gather together their interaction produces thunder.

14   Aroused, they produce thunderclaps; disordered, they produce mist.

15   When the yang qi prevails, it scatters to make dew;

16   When the yin qi prevails, it freezes to make frost and snow.

17   Feathered creatures make up the class of flying things, and are subject to yang;

18   Creatures with scales and shells make up the class of creeping and hiding things, and are subject to yin.

19   The sun is the ruler of yang. Therefore,

20   In spring and summer animals shed their fur;

21   At the summer solstice stags' antlers drop off.

22   The moon is the fundament of yin. Therefore,

23   When the moon wanes, the brains of fish shrink;

24   When the moon dies, wasps and crabs shrivel up.

25   Fire flies upward, water flows downward; thus

26   The flight of birds is aloft, the movement of fishes is downward.

27   Things within the same class mutually move each other;

28   Root and twig mutually respond to each other. Therefore,

29   When the burning-mirror sees the sun,

30   It ignites tinder and produces fire.

31   When the square receptacle sees the moon,

32   It moistens and produces water.

33   When the tiger roars the valley winds rush;

34   When the dragon arises the bright clouds accumulate.

35   When *qilins* wrangle, the sun or moon is eclipsed;

36   When the leviathan dies, comets appear.

37   When the silkworm spins cocoons (shaped like) ear ornaments, the *shang* string (of a stringed instrument) snaps;

38   When meteors fall, the sea suddenly swells up.
     [3:3b:11]

Commentary to Section II

With this section the text shifts from cosmogony to cosmology: from how the cosmos came to be to how it acts in being. The section begins by stating the familiar equations heaven = circular = yang; earth = square = yin (on which see Chapter 2 above). It then proceeds to a discussion of *ganying* "resonance" or "responsive action within categories," one of the fundamental concepts of early Chinese cosmology.[7] Significantly, all of the resonant relationships mentioned here are expressed in terms of yin and yang alone; the five phases do not yet play a role. Many of the examples given here anticipate the fuller treatments that they receive in *Huainanzi* 4, the "Treatise on Topography." For instance, the tumultuous (and overtly sexual) interaction of yin and yang to produce thunder and lightning reappears in 4.XIX; the description here of the effects of yin and yang on animals anticipates the elaboration of that theme in 4.VIII and 4.IX as well as in many places throughout *Huainanzi* 5. Many of the statements made in this section—for example, that when the moon wanes the brains of fish shrivel up— apparently formed part of the conventional wisdom of the early Han, for they appear in numerous texts of the time. The statement that deer shed their antlers at the solstices recurs in 3.XVI.36 below, as well as in 5.V.32 and 5.XI.31. Gao You's commentary here explains that *mi* deer shed their antlers at the winter solstice, while *lu* deer shed them at the summer solstice.

Another such bit of conventional wisdom concerns the (yang) burning-mirror and the (yin) "square receptacle" (*fangju*), a square metal vessel that apparently was used by would-be immortals and other adepts to collect the nighttime dew (by condensation) that was thought to be the perfect nourishment for immortals (as in 4.IX.17, "Creatures that feed on qi are sage-like and enlightened, and have great longevity").

Of particular interest in this section are lines 33–37, which demonstrate that *ganying* resonance operates reciprocally in both directions between the animate and inanimate worlds (to use categories that would have struck an early Chinese intellectual as entirely too rigid). If the waning of the moon can shrivel a fish's brain, so also the roaring of a tiger can raise the wind. So too, by implication (here—the lesson is made explicit in the next section, as well as throughout *Huainanzi* 5 and in some later chapters of the *Huainanzi*) inappropriate actions on the part of a ruler can bring down upon his realm such catastrophes as drought, whirlwinds, and celestial portents.

The statement in line 37 that "when the silkworm spins cocoons (shaped like) ear ornaments, the *shang* string (of a stringed instrument) snaps" is an interesting example of *ganying* resonance. The statement seems quite mysterious, but a plausible clarification emerges when one analyzes it in terms of five phase theory: Ear ornaments are made of gold or some other precious metal. *Shang*, the second note of the pentatonic scale, is correlated with phase metal (see 4.XIV.17); the strings of musical instruments are made of silk. Thus when silkworms produce "metal" cocoons, the "metal" string of a musical instrument will snap (in response to this unnatural phenomenon).

In this section we encounter the first of many mentions in *Huainanzi* 3 and 4 of magical animals of mythic potency. The dragon, the *qilin* (often translated as "unicorn," but that word has too many implications inappropriate to the Chinese composite beast) and the leviathan (here *jing*, literally "whale," but clearly intended as a magical ocean-beast, akin to the *kun'geng* of 4.XVIII.18–19 below) are joined by the *feng* and *huang* "phoenixes," the *luan* "symurgh," and a number of other beasts familiar from a wide range of Warring States and Han texts. The tiger in line 33 above should probably also be added to this list, especially inasmuch as Han iconographic representations of tigers (as for example in the numerous depictions of the four directional animals) show it to be not only ferocious, but also—except for the head—hardly distinguishable from a dragon with its long, serpentine body. There is a very large literature on such mythical animals, among which the works of Jean-Pierre Diény and Edward Schafer are outstanding.[8] Here it will suffice to note that the appearance of such beasts in these chapters of the *Huainanzi* is a signal to look for embodiments of cosmological processes, the mythic landscapes of superterrestrial fairylands, or both.

Section III: The Reciprocity of Heaven and Man

[3:4a:2]

1   The natures of the rulers of men penetrate to Heaven on high.
2   Thus if there are punishments and cruelty, there will be whirlwinds;
3   If there are wrongful ordinances, there will be plagues of devouring insects.
4   If there are unjust executions, the land will redden with drought.
5   If (lawful) commands are not accepted, there will be great excess of rain.
6   The four seasons are the officers of Heaven.
7   The sun and moon are the agents of Heaven.
8   The stars and planets mark the appointed times of Heaven.
9   Rainbows and comets are the portents of Heaven.
[3:4a:7]

Commentary to Section III

Here the lessons of Section II are made explicit and brought specifically to the attention of the ruler who was the presumed "ideal reader" of the *Huainanzi*. Cosmology operates to create a moral universe, in which human actions resonated along the celestial axis to create—literally—good or bad vibrations both in the heavens and on earth. As the text says below (3.XXIV.10), "Heaven is round, Earth is square; the Dao is in the exact center." The ruler (the possessor of the Dao), in other words, sits at the fulcrum of what Nathan Sivin has called a "vibrating dipole," where the ruler mediates between the celestial and terrestrial realms.[9]

[handwritten annotation:] What about the center?

67

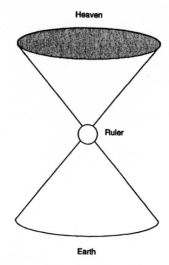

Heaven

Ruler

Earth

Figure 3.1. The ruler as the fulcrum of the "vibrating dipole" of heaven and earth.

Section IV: The Divisions of Heaven

[3:4a:8]

1 Heaven has nine fields and 9,999 junctures.
2 It is 150,000 li distant from the earth.
3 There are five planets, eight winds, and twenty-eight lunar lodges.
4 There are five offices and six departments.
5 These are called the Purple Palace, the Great Enclosure, the Chariot Pole, the Pool of Xian, the Four Guardians, and the Heavenly Slope.
[3:4b:6]

Commentary to Section IV

This short section serves as a general introduction to Sections V–XIII below. It begins by answering the questions of "Tian wen" 11–12:

> Spread out are the nine fields of Heaven [where do they reach to? Where do they touch?]
> With their numerous edges and angles [who knows how many?]

The boundaries of the fields of heaven are defined in the following section. Here we are told that its height (presumably at the apex) is 150,000 li; there is no indication of the diameter of the dome of heaven (which presumably is parallel to the earth, whether both are flat or slightly domed) from edge to edge, but in 4.II.4–7 below, we are told that the expanse of the earth from east to west and south to north is something over

233,500 li. (For more on the configuration of heaven and earth see Appendix A below.)

The 9,999 "junctures" joining the fields of heaven (traced perhaps, at least in imagination, from star to star across the vault of the sky) recall the numerous folds in the fused joints of the skull bones. The image of the dome of heaven as a skull is one of several instances of cosmos/man::macrocosm/microcosm in the *Huainanzi* (see Section XLI, lines 11–17 below, and also *Huainanzi* 7:2a–3a, quoted below in the commentary to Section XLI). The "junctures" also recall the sutures in the shell of a turtle; taken together, the shell and plastron of a turtle constituted a well-known image for the round, domed heaven above the square, flat earth.[10]

Section V: The Nine Fields

[3:5a:11]

1   What are the Nine Fields?
2   The central one is called Balanced Heaven.
3   Its asterisms are Horn, Neck, and Root.
4   The eastern one is called Azure Heaven.
5   Its asterisms are Room, Heart, and Tail.
6   The northeastern one is called Transforming Heaven.
7   Its asterisms are Winnowing-Basket, Dipper, and Ox-Leader.
8   The northern one is called Umbral Heaven.
9   Its asterisms are Serving-Maid, Emptiness, Rooftop, and Encampment.
10   The northwestern one is called Secluded Heaven.
11   Its asterisms are Eastern Wall, Stride, and Bond.
12   The western one is called Luminous Heaven.
13   Its asterisms are Stomach, Pliades, and Net.
14   The southwestern one is called Vermilion Heaven.
15   Its asterisms are Turtle-Beak, Triad, and Eastern Well.
16   The southern one is called Fiery Heaven.
17   Its asterisms are Spirit-Bearer, Willow, and Seven Stars.
18   The southeastern one is called Yang Heaven.
19   Its asterisms are Extension, Wings, and Chariot-Platform.
[3:5b:11]

Commentary to Section V

The nine fields of heaven are comparable to the nine continents of earth described in *Huainanzi* 4.I below.[11] They are an elaboration of a scheme called the "five palaces," correlated in 3.XIII below with five departments of government. The five palaces and nine fields were described by my collaborators and myself in a previous work[12] as follows:

> The Five Palaces. One of the simplest, and one of the oldest, divisions of the heavens was into five "palaces." These comprised the central circle of the north circumpolar stars (which never, for an observer in northern China, dip below the horizon), called the *ciweigong*, "Palace of Purple Tenuity"; and four truncated sectors extending from the circle bounding the north circumpolar stars to the south circumpolar circle of perpetual invisibility, these sectors being designated as the palaces of East, South, West, and North. The five palaces were correlated with the Five Phases (*wuxing*), the four cardinal directions (plus the center), the seasons, etc. The four non-central palaces were symbolized by four animal emblems: the Blue-Green Dragon of the East, the Vermilion Bird of the South, the White Tiger of the West, and the Dark Warrior of the North (a paired turtle and snake).
>
> The Nine Fields. This was similar in conception to the five palaces, except that the portion of the sky surrounding the north circumpolar stars was divided into eight, rather than four, truncated sectors. The nine fields corresponded to the "nine continents" into which the earth was schematically divided; the eight noncentral fields were correlated [N.B.—but not in *Huainanzi*] with the eight trigrams of the *Yijing* (Book of Changes).

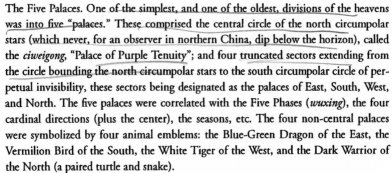

Note that the nine fields are enumerated here in counterclockwise order, in contrast to the clockwise order in which terrestrial directions are usually given (as for example in 4.I.8–16 below). This undoubtedly is in imitation of the counterclockwise (i.e., east to west) motion of the fixed stars across the visible sky.

Note also that each of the nine fields is given an allotment of three (four in the case of the northern field) of the twenty-eight lunar lodges. These lodges, however, are not *in* the fields to which they are assigned, because the lodges are not uniformly distributed throughout the sky (they all lie approximately along the ecliptic, the path of the sun across the sky). Instead, the assignments are made for astrological purposes, as is made clear in Section XXXV below.

Section VI: The Five Planets

[3:5b:11]

1 What are the Five Planets?
2 The East is Wood. Its god is Tai Hao.
3 His assistant is Gou Mang.
4 He grasps the compass and governs spring.
5 His spirit is the Year-star [Jupiter].
6 His animal is the bluegreen dragon.
7 His musical note is *jue*;

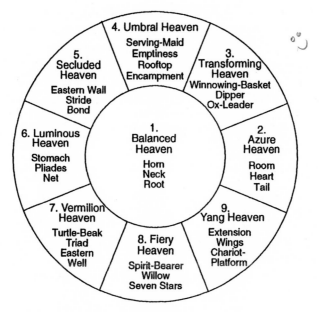

Figure 3.2. Diagram of the nine fields and their assigned lunar lodges.

8   His days are *jia* and *yi*.

9   The South is Fire. Its god is Yan Di.

10   His assistant is Zhu Ming.

11   He grasps the balance-beam and governs summer.

12   His spirit is Sparkling Deluder [Mars].

13   His animal is the vermilion bird.

14   His musical note is *zhi*;

15   His days are *bing* and *ding*.

16   The Center is Earth. Its god is the Yellow Thearch.

17   His assistant is Hou Tu [Sovereign of the soil].

18   He grasps the marking-cord and governs the four quarters.

19   His spirit is Quelling Star [Saturn].

20   His animal is the yellow dragon.

21   His musical note is *gong*;

22   His days are *wu* and *ji*.

23   The West is Metal. Its god is Shao Hao.

24   His assistant is Ru Shou.

25   He grasps the T-square and governs autumn.

26   His spirit is Great White [Venus].

27   His animal is the white tiger.

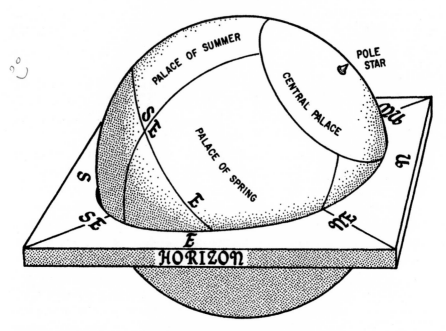

Figure 3.3. The Chinese celestial sphere, showing the five celestial palaces in relation to the celestial equator.

28   His musical note is *shang;*
29   His days are *geng* and *xin.*
30   The North is Water. Its god is Zhuan Xu.
32   His assistant is Xuan Ming.
33   He grasps the plumb-weight and governs winter.
34   His spirit is Chronograph Star [Mercury].
35   His animal is the Dark Warrior.
36   His musical note is *yu;*
37   His days are *ren* and *gui.*
      [3:6b:5]

Commentary to Section VI

This entire passage is quoted verbatim (allowing for textual variation and damage) from the Mawangdui text "Wuxingzhan" (Prognostications of the Five Planets), but interestingly, only portions of the latter text are quoted here.[13] In "Wuxingzhan," the introductory passage for each planet (the portion quoted in this section) is followed by highly detailed information about the movements of that planet. Here in "The Treatise on the Patterns of Heaven," these introductory sections have been grouped together—quite consciously, I believe, to emphasize their parallel structure and cosmological meaning—and additional sections on the movements of the five planets (similar to, but less detailed than, those in "Wuxingzhan") have been added below (Sections VI–X). It appears that the author of this treatise, in making use of his earlier source, altered it so as to convey a general cosmological message to his (presumably royal) reader, and to give the essentials of planetary motions and periodicities without asking him to get bogged down in the technical details of professional astronomy.

With the introduction of the five planets, the text introduces the five phases to complement the workings of yin and yang discussed in Sections II and III above. Each planet is correlated with a phase, a direction, a color, a season, a musical note, and two of the ten Heavenly Stems, all in accordance with standard five phase theory. It is of particular interest that each of the five planetary gods is depicted as holding a builder's tool, suggesting the role of the five phases (personalized as cosmic deities) in bringing the world of myriad phenomena into being from the primordial cosmogonic processes that produced the one, the two, and the three, and in sustaining that world through the course of time. The five planetary gods and their "assistants" appear again in 5.XIV as rulers of five regions of the earth—obviously terrestrial equivalents of the five palaces of heaven. Their five tools (in slightly different form), plus the water level, appear again in 5.XV as the "six regulators" (*liudu*), taken as emblems for and paradigms of cosmic order as reflected in the proper conduct of the ruler of an ideal state.[14]

The translations of the names of the planets used here are those of Edward Schafer, whose discussion of planetary symbolism in Tang times is of great interest.[15]

Section VII The Motions of Jupiter

[3:6b:5]

1   When *taiyin* is in any of the four midpoints, the planet Jupiter passes through three of the lunar lodges.

2   When *taiyin* is in any of the four hooks, the planet Jupiter passes through two of the lunar lodges.

3   Two times eight is sixteen, three times four is twelve. Therefore,

5   In twelve years (Jupiter) traverses (all) twenty-eight lunar lodges.

6   The (average) daily motion (of Jupiter) is (approximately) one-twelfth of a [Chinese] degree.

7   In one year, (Jupiter traverses) $30\frac{7}{16}^{d}$.

8   In twelve years, (Jupiter) completes a circuit (of the heavens).
    [3:7a:9]

Commentary to Section VII

The orbital period of Jupiter is approximated in this section, as was conventional in early China, as twelve years; the exact figure as computed from the angular velocity given here is 11.88 years or 4,340 days.

This is the first of several sections in *Huainanzi* 3 that refers to the use of the *shi* cosmograph.[16] As explained in Chapter 2 above, the cosmograph used the motion of an imaginary counterorbital asterism, *taiyin*, to track (in mirror image) the actual motions of Jupiter. The celestial position of Jupiter could, in theory, be deduced from the location of *taiyin* on the cosmograph; in fact, errors would creep in very rapidly because of the unrealistically standardized motions required by the way the device was constructed.

In this section, the names of invisible counter-Jupiter, *taiyin*, and Jupiter, *suixing* or "year star," are distinct and unambiguous. Problems arise in other sections below when the term *taisui*, "great year," is employed; it is not always clear whether that term refers to astronomical Jupiter, hypothetical counter-Jupiter, or to the twelve-year period of the "Jovian Year."

Section VIII: The Motions of Mars

[3:7a:8]

1   Mars normally enters the asterism Grand Enclosure in the tenth month.
2   [The corresponding state thereupon] comes under its control.
3   Then it emerges, passing through the lunar lodges in turn.
4   (Mars) governs states that lack the Way,
5   Causing disorder, robbery, sickness, mourning, famine, and warfare.
6   When its leavings and enterings (of lunar lodges) are irregular, there is disputation and change.
7   Its color is sometimes visible and sometimes unnoticeable.
[3:7b:1]

Commentary to Section VIII

This brief section on the motions of Mars is somewhat vague, but it provides enough information to suggest that the orbital period of Mars was approximated as twenty-four lunar months, or about 708 days. (The Grand Inception Calendar of 104 B.C.E. gave the quite accurate figure of 693 days or 1.88 years.) Presumably the statement "in the tenth month" above is a reference to the position of Mars in every second year (disregarding intercalary months). The Great Enclosure is one of the "six departments" mentioned in 3.IV.5 above and described in more detail in 3.XIII.7–15 below.

how did it become that way?

This section also makes clear that Mars, the "sparkling deluder," was an asterism of ill omen. In particular, later astrological works specify that the appearance of Mars in the Grand Enclosure boded ill for the ruler.[17]

Section IX: The Motions of Saturn

[3:7b:1]

1. On the day *jiayin* [#51], in the first year of the Epoch, Saturn is in (the lunar lodge) Dipper.
2. Each year Saturn moves through one lunar lodge.
3. If Saturn should be (in a particular lunar lodge) and is not there,
4. The state (corresponding to that lodge) will lose its land.
5. If Saturn ought not yet to be (in a particular lunar lodge) but (already) occupies it,
6. The state (corresponding to that lodge) will increase its land and the year will be ripe.
7. The (average) daily motion (of Saturn) is 1/28 of a [Chinese] degree.
8. Its annual motion is 13 5/112^d.
9. In twenty-eight years it completes a circuit (of the heavens).

[3:7b:5]

Commentary to Section IX

This section gives the ancient and traditional, but highly inaccurate, figure of twenty-eight years for the orbital period of Saturn; the seemingly precise figure of 13 5/112^d for the annual motion of Saturn given in line 8 is simply 365.25^d divided by twenty-eight. Despite its known (by early Han times) inaccuracy, the approximation of 28 years was probably considered essential in an astrological text so as to preserve the link between Saturn and the twenty-eight lunar lodges. (These may have originated as early as the beginning of the Xia period, around 2000 B.C.E., and certainly had assumed their fixed identity—both their names and their angular-extension values—by the mid-fifth century B.C.E.[18]) The "Wuxingzhan" gives the orbital period of Saturn as 30 years; the Grand Inception Calendar gives it as 29.79 years;[19] both of those texts are more concerned with calendrical accuracy than with astrological considerations.

Saturn, the planet of the Yellow Thearch, is here assigned a fundamental role in military astrology; each of the lunar lodges was allocated to a pre-Qin state or territory (see Section XXXV below), and the planet's failure to appear, or early appearance, in a particular lodge foretold disaster or victory, respectively, for the state concerned.

Section X: The Motions of Venus

[3:7b:5]

1. In the first month, on the day *jiayin*, in the first year of the Epoch, Venus rises at dawn in the east in (the lunar lodge) Encampment.
2. After 240 days it disappears.
3. It remains hidden for 120 days and then appears in the evening in the west.
4. After 240 days it disappears.
5. After 35 days it once again appears in the east.
6. It appears in *chen* or *xu* and disappears in *chou* or *wei*.
7. When (Venus) should appear but does not appear,
8. Or should not yet disappear but does disappear,
9. Throughout the world, armies will be withdrawn.
10. When (Venus) should disappear but does not disappear,
11. Or should not yet appear but does appear,
12. Throughout the world armies will set forth.

[3:8a:4]

Commentary to Section X

The "Wuxingzhan" has gives the period of initial visibility of Venus as 224 days rather than the 240 days given here; it is likely that the *Huainanzi* figure of 240 days perpetuates an early copyist's error. The true orbital period of Venus is 224.70 days, but because Venus (and Mercury) are within the earth's orbit around the sun, and thus never very far above or below the sun in its passage across the sky, early Chinese astronomers found it difficult to conceive of single orbital periods for those planets, but rather described them as "appearing and disappearing" for different periods of time. The "Wuxingzhan" also gives 16.96 days, rather than the 35 days of line 5 above, as the period between Venus's disappearance as an evening star and its reappearance as a morning star. It is not clear how this discrepancy can be accounted for; however, the *Huainanzi* figure of 35 days may accord better with the perceived interval under normal viewing conditions (because the planet is very difficult to see when it is too close to the sun), while the "Wuxingzhan" figure could have been derived by calculating from the synodic period of Venus (584 days, close to the implied figure in the "Wuxingzhan" for the synodic period, 224 + 224 + 120 + 17 = 585 days).

The astrological significance of Venus for the Chinese is made clear here; the glittering brightness of "Great White" had none of the gentle and romantic connotations that westerners saw, but was rather the flash of weapons of war. Venus, correlated with the phase metal, west, declining yang, and so on, was a dangerous planet, governing the advance or retreat of armies.

76

The Treatise on the Patterns of Heaven

Section XI: The Motions of Mercury

[3:8a:6]

1   (The movements of) Mercury correspond exactly to the four seasons.

2   Normally in the second month, at the spring equinox, it appears in (the lunar lodges) Stride and Bond.

3   In the fifth month, at the summer solstice, it appears in (the lunar lodges) Eastern Well and Spirit-Bearer.

4   In the eighth month, at the autumn equinox, it appears in (the lunar lodges) Horn and Neck.

5   In the eleventh month, at the winter solstice, it appears in (the lunar lodges) Dipper and Ox-Leader.

6   (Mercury) appears in (the chronograms) *chen* or *xu* and disappears in *chou* or *wei*.

7   It appears for twenty days and then disappears.

8   At dawn it attends (the sun) in the east,

9   In the evening it attends (the sun) in the west.

10   If in any season it does not appear, that season will be unfortunate;

11   If for four seasons it does not appear, throughout the world there will be famine.

[3:8a:11]

Commentary to Section XI

This section implies an orbital period for Mercury of about 91 days (i.e., it appears once in each season; the true value is 87.97 days), and notes that in each season it appears (i.e., is sufficiently far from the sun to be visible) for 20 days before disappearing again. Mercury—small and difficult to see—played a very small role in Chinese portent astrology, and its astrological meaning in this section is correspondingly vague. Mercury was correlated with the phase water and the direction north; the icy connotations of that correlation perhaps suggested the famine portents described here.

Section XII: The Eight "Wind Seasons"

[3:8b:1]

1   What is the span of days for each of the eight winds?

2   Forty-five days after the winter solstice the *tiao* wind reaches its limit.

3   Forty-five days after the *tiao* wind limit, the *mingshu* wind reaches its limit.

4   Forty-five days after the *mingshu* wind limit, the *qingming* wind reaches its limit.

5   Forty-five days after the *qing-ming* wind limit, the *jing* wind reaches its limit.

6   Forty-five days after the *jing* wind limit, the *liang* wind reaches its limit.

7   Forty-five days after the *liang* wind limit, the *Changhe* wind reaches its limit.

8   Forty-five days after the *Changhe* wind limit, the *Buzhou* wind reaches its limit.

9   Forty-five days after the *Buzhou* wind limit, the *guangmo* wind reaches its limit.

10   During the *tiao* wind season, issue unimportant dispatches, dismissing, delaying, or restraining.

11   During the *mingshu* wind season, rectify boundaries and repair the fields.

12   During the *qingming* wind season, issue presents of silk cloth and send embassies to the feudal lords.

13   During the *jing* wind season, confer honors upon men of position and reward the meritorious.

14   During the *liang* wind season, report on the fruitfulness of the land and sacrifice at the four suburbs.

15   During the *Changhe* wind season, receive magistrates and put aside amusements.

16   During the *Buzhou* wind season, repair palaces and dwellings, and improve dikes and walls.

17   During the *guangmo* wind season, close up gates and bridges and execute punishments.

    [3:9a:3]

Commentary to Section XII

The wind names given here have the following meanings and implications:[20]

Tiao = "branch, shoot; drawn-out" as in lengthening of days after the winter solstice.

Mingshu = "bright abundance."

Qingming = "clear bright"; this wind gave its name to the later Qingming Festival, held around the time of spring equinox.

Jing = "bright, brilliant"; the connotation apparently is of the sun reaching its maximum brightness at the summer solstice.

Liang = "cool"; this hardly matches the actual weather of north-central China immediately after the summer solstice, but its connotation is perhaps of shortening days as the year enters its yin cycle.

Changhe = the Gate of Heaven; in some other contexts equated to the north circumpolar stars, Changhe here is correlated with the west, the direction of sunset.[21]

Buzhou = The northwestern pillar/Gate of Heaven; see below.

Guangmo = "broad dimness"; i.e., the long evenings of the approaching winter solstice.

The name of the Buzhou wind comes from Mt. Buzhou (mentioned in 3.I.24 above, in connection with the myth of Gong Gong and Zhuan Xu), and is of considerable interest. The name of Mt. Buzhou is sometimes translated as "Unrotating Mountain," but *zhou* does not really mean "to rotate about an axis." Mt. Buzhou is, rather,

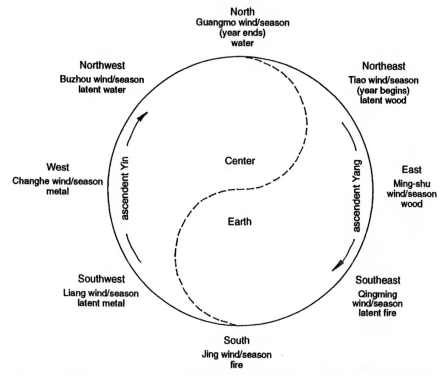

Figure 3.4. Diagram showing the correlations between the winds, directions, yin and yang, and the five phases: the regulators of seasonal behavior. The phase earth occupies the center, where yin and yang come together harmoniously. It plays no active role in this diagram and is not correlated with a wind or a season. Compare Fig. 4.2 on page 160.

the mountain which *does not describe a circle around something else.* The "something else" in question is the midpoint of the heavens, or in other words the celestial axis (equivalent to the polestar but here, for rather complicated cosmological reasons,[22] located in the northwest rather than in the north). Mt. Buzhou is, in short, both a mountain and an asterism, but unlike all other stars, which inscribe circles in the sky around the polar axis, it remains motionless in one place. For this reason the most accurate translation of Mt. Buzhou would be something like "Non-Circumscribing Mountain" or "Non-Circumambulating Mountain," though in view of the awkwardness of both of those constructions it may be best to avoid translating this name in most cases.

The actions called for in the eight wind seasons are regulated by the reciprocal waxing and waning of yin and yang; they reflect the prescriptions of *Huainanzi* 5, the "Treatise on the Seasonal Rules," which operate according to the same principles.

Section XIII: The Five Offices and Six Departments

[3:9a:7]
1 What are the Five Offices?
2 That of the east is Agriculture.
3 That of the south is the Military Command.
4 That of the west is Public Order.
5 That of the north is Public Works.
6 That of the center is Metropolitan Affairs.
7 What are the Six Departments?
8 They are *ziwu, chouwei, yinshen, maoyu, chenxu,* and *sihai.*
9 The Grand Enclosure is the hall of the Son of Heaven.
10 The Purple Palace is the dwelling-place of the Grand Monad.
11 Chariot Pole is the residence of the Imperial Concubine.
12 The Pool of Xian is a park of water and fishes.
13 The Heavenly Slope is the gate-tower of the assembled gods.
14 The Four Guardians are those who bestow rewards and punishments.
15 The Grand Enclosure governs the Vermilion Bird.
[3:10a:2]

Commentary to Section XIII

The Five Offices are the (astrological) civil/bureaucratic allotments of the Five Palaces of the heavens; see the commentary to Section V above. The Five Palaces correspond to a fivefold division of the earth (the center plus peripheral regions of the east, south, west, and north). The Five Offices here reflect, though not perfectly, the seasonal/directional correspondences of the changing proportions of yin and yang throughout the calendar year, as elaborated in Chapter 5, the "Treatise on the Seasonal Rules," below, and summarized in V.XIII.

Briefly stated, the east governs agriculture because spring (correlated with east) is correlated with the rebirth of waxing yang at the beginning of the year, with growing things, and with phase wood.

The south, correlated with phase fire, governs military affairs; in the "Treatise on the Seasonal Rules," in summer, when yang reaches its maximum, the ruler begins to make preparations for warfare. The south is also correlated with Mars, the "fire planet," the astrological portents of which usually relate to military affairs.

The west, correlated with phase metal, marks the beginning of the waxing of yin in the seasonal round; in autumn the ruler turns his attention to public order, carrying out punishments and issuing prohibitions. See also 4.VIII.30, which associates the west, and phase metal, with maiming and killing.

The north, correlated with winter, phase water, and maximum yin, is in general a time of quiescence, but in the first month of winter the ruler orders the repair of buildings, roads, and walls; hence the correlation here with the Ministry of Public Works. The correlation with phase water is perhaps strengthened because public works in China also frequently involved projects for water control.

The correlation of the center (and midsummer; balanced yin and yang; the metropolis of the ruler; the altar of the soil; and phase earth) with metropolitan affairs is obvious.

The Six Departments are defined in line 8 as six diametral chords across the celestial circle, drawn between six opposite pairs of Earthly Branches arranged around the horizon; these "departments" correspond to the "Six Co-ordinates" of 5.XIV, a section that elaborates on the astrology associated with the six diametral chords.

Here, in lines 9–15, the Six Departments are associated with the names of six asterisms, or more exactly six regions of the sky.[23]

The Purple Palace, described in 3.XIV immediately below, denotes the circle enclosing the north circumpolar stars; it, like Chariot Pole, is associated with the center. The "Treatise on Astronomy" of the *Jin shu* says, "The five stars of *beiji* ('North Pole Asterism') and the six stars of *gouzhen* ('Angular Arranger') all lie within the Purple Palace. . . . The North Pole Asterism ranks supreme among the stars in the north . . . its second star, known as *diwang* ('Sovereign King') governs the sun. It also forms the throne of the deity *Tai Yi* ('Grand Monad')."[24]

The Grand Enclosure is an asterism that is thought of as making a "wall" around the north celestial pole; here the name is used to denote the northern quadrant of the sky extending from the horizon to the Purple Palace. The *Jin shu* says, "*Taiwei* ('Grand Enclosure') . . . is the court of the Son of Heaven . . . (containing) the thrones of the Five Emperors."[25] Line 15 (which looks like a stray line of commentary that has crept into the text) associates the Grand Enclosure with the Vermilion Bird, and hence with the south and phase fire.

Chariot Pole is a cognomen for the Yellow Thearch (see the commentary to 4.XVIII below). The *Jin shu* says, "*Xian yuan* ('Chariot Pole') consists of seventeen stars to the north of (the lunar lodge) Seven Stars. Chariot Pole is the spirit of the Yellow Thearch and the body of the Yellow Dragon. The stars govern the court secretary (who attends to the needs) of the Empress and the Imperial Concubine."[26] The linkage with the Yellow Thearch and the imperial court make this a clear symbol of celestial centrality and phase earth.

Of the Pool of Xian (which can also be translated as "Broad Pool"), the *Jin shu* says, "Three stars called *xian chi* ('Broad Pool' [or 'Pool of Xian']) south of *tian huang* ('Heavenly Lake') represent the fish-pond."[27] In 3.XIX below, the Pool of Xian is associated with the Jovian Year, and is said to "govern the Great Season"; though the exact meaning of that phrase is unclear, the Pool of Xian is certainly used here as a term for the eastern quadrant of the sky. In 3.XXV.2, the sun "bathes in the Pool of Xian" before beginning its daily journey across the sky. Possible connections between the asterism called the Pool of Xian and the mythical personage known as Shaman Xian (and the mountains associated with him) are explored in the commentary to 4.XVIII below.

Neither the Four Guardians (*si shou*) nor the Heavenly Slope (*tian a*) are mentioned in the astronomical chapter of the *Jin shu*, and their identification as constellations is uncertain. Interestingly, the *Jin shu* does identify a specific constellation called the Six Departments, with no apparent reference, however, to the way that term is used here. The text says, "The six stars of *wen chang* ('Literary Brilliance') are in front of the head [i.e., the bowl] of *bei dou* ('Northern Dipper,' i.e., *Ursa major*), forming the Six Departments (*liu fu*) of the heavens. They govern the computations of the Dao of the heavens."[28]

It must be stressed, however, that the Six Departments (which are simply diametral chords across the celestial circle) do not represent the boundaries of any of these constellations or asterisms. Nor does there seem to be enough of a link between these diametral chords and specific asterisms to form the basis for any sort of positional astrology. The main intent and effect of this passage is, rather, to depict the heavens as a kind of celestial imperial metropolis, with palaces and gardens for the emperor and his empress and concubines, and buildings for the imperial functionaries.

Section XIV: The Purple Palace

[3:10a:2]

1   The Purple Palace controls the Dipper and turns to the left.
2   The sun moves 1^d each time it makes a revolution across the heavens.
3   At the winter solstice, the sun is in Lofty Wolf Mountain.
4   The sun shifts 1^d per day; therefore, after it has travelled $182\frac{5}{8}^d$,
5   At the summer solstice the sun is in Ox-head Mountain.
6   Then it turns back, and (after travelling through) $365\frac{1}{4}^d$, completes one year.
[3:10a:7]

Commentary to Section XIV

The Purple Palace, which as we have seen is a name for the north circumpolar stars, controls the Dipper, which is the most prominent constellation of the Purple Palace and which serves as the "pointer" of an annual "celestial clock." Here, the term Purple Palace is being used in a special sense; it is equivalent to—another name for—the heaven plate of the cosmograph. The instructions given here for shifting the heaven plate (which has a representation of the Dipper inscribed upon it) by 1^d per day indicates clearly that this section refers to the use of the cosmograph (or some closely related astronomical instrument).

Lofty Wolf Mountain and Ox-head Mountain, despite their names, apparently are asterisms, not geographical features.

Section XV: The Callippic Cycle and the Grand Conclusion Cycle

[3:10a:7]

1 At the beginning of the Heavenly Singularity Epoch,
2 The first (civil) month being established in *yin,*
3 The sun and moon together enter the fifth degree of (the lunar lodge) Encampment.
4 Seventy-six years after the beginning of the Heavenly Singularity Epoch,
5 The sun and moon again enter the fifth degree of Encampment, without any remainder-fraction.
6 This is called an Era.
7 Twenty Eras make 1,520 years, called a Grand Conclusion.
8 (At the end of that period), the sun, moon, and asterisms all re-commence in *jiayin.*
   [3:10b:2]

Commentary to Section XV

This section implicitly takes as its starting point the Metonic Cycle (see 3.XXI below) of 19 years (encompassing seven intercalary months), the shortest cycle in which the beginnings of the solar year and the lunar month both repeat on the same day. The Heavenly Singularity Epoch here is the Callippic Cycle, equal to four Metonic Cycles; in the Callippic Cycle, the beginnings of the solar year and the lunar month both repeat on the same day at the same hour. The Grand Conclusion Cycle equals twenty Callippic Cycles. Its period of 1520 years represents the least common multiple of seventy-six and eighty, the latter figure being the number of years of 365.25 days in which the 60-day cycle recurs. Thus in the Grand Conclusion Cycle the solar year and the lunar month both should begin again at the same hour on a day denoted by the same sexagenary stem-branch pair. (In fact this will not happen, because of errors that accumulate through the approximation of the length of the year as 365.25 days.) See "Periodicities in the 'Treatise on the Patterns of Heaven'" in the introduction to this chapter.

Section XVI: Solar Cycles and Their Omens

[3:10b:6]

1 The daily motion of the sun is 1^d.

2   Thus in a year there will be a surplus of ¼ᵈ.

3   Thus after four years there will be an accumulation of 1461 days, and harmony is restored.

4   After eighty years, (the days of the 60-day cycle) will be repeated (on the same days of the year).

5   Thus it is said that *ziwu* and *maoyu* are the two diametral chords;

6   *Chouyin, chensi, weishen,* and *xuhai* are the four hooks.

7   Northeast is the weft-string of Returning Accretion;

8   Southwest is the weft-string of Reverting Yang;

9   Southeast is the weft-string of Perpetual Ocean;

10   Northwest is the weft-string of Penetrating Cleft.

11   When the sun is at the winter solstice, the Dipper (points) north, exactly on the (north-south) diametral chord.

11   The yin qi is at its maximum, and the yang qi begins to grow.

12   Thus it is said that the winter solstice produces accretion.

13   When the sun is at the summer solstice, the Dipper (points) south, exactly on the (north-south) diametral chord.

14   The yang qi is at its maximum, and the yin qi begins to grow.

15   Thus it is said that the summer solstice produces recision.

16   When the yin qi is at its maximum, north is at its furthest extent (from the sun).

17   The Northern Limit penetrates down to the Yellow Springs.

18   Hence one must not cut into the earth or bore wells.

19   The myriad creatures are shut up in hibernation, and insects head for their burrows.

20   Thus it is said that accretion is in the Room.

21   When the yang qi is at its maximum, south is at its furthest extent (from the sun).

22   The Southern Limit penetrates upward to the Vermilion Heaven.

23   Hence one must not level hills or raise roof-beams.

24   The myriad creatures flourish and increase, and the five grains grow abundantly.

25   Thus it is said that accretion is in the Field.

26   When the sun is at the winter solstice, water follows it.

27   When the sun is at the summer solstice, fire follows it.

28   Thus in the fifth month fire is dominant and water is reduced to a trickle;

29   In the eleventh month water is dominant and yin is victorious.

30   Yang qi produces fire, yin qi produces water.

31   (In years when) water is dominant, the summer solstice will be damp.

32   (In years when) fire is dominant, the winter solstice will be parched.

33   When (the year) is parched, charcoal is light.

34   When (the year) is wet, charcoal is heavy.

35   When the sun is at the winter solstice, wells are full of water and basins overflow.

36   Goats shed their hair, deer's antlers fall away, and magpies nest.

37   An eight-foot gnomon casts a shadow thirteen feet long (at noon).

38   When the sun is at the summer solstice, the yellow floods enrich the fields and mineral essences emerge from the soil.

39   Cicadas begin to sing, and the half-summer herb grows;
40   Flying insects do not bite foals and calves, and birds of prey do not seize nestlings.
41   An eight-foot gnomon casts a shadow 1.5 feet long (at noon).
42   When the gnomon-shadow is long, yin qi is dominant;
43   When the gnomon-shadow is short, yang qi is dominant.
44   When the yin qi is dominant, there is water;
45   When the yang qi is dominant, there is drought.
     [3:12a:6]

Commentary to Section XVI

This section begins by defining the sun's daily movement, as indicated by the handle of the Dipper (whether in the night sky or as inscribed on the heaven plate of the cosmograph) as 1^d, and by noting that in four years this movement produces a "surplus" of one day. This is in effect a rule for defining the leap year; it is followed by an observation that the sexagenary day names repeat on the same day of the year in a cycle of eighty years. These lines amount to a set of simple rules for employing the cosmograph for calendrical purposes; this theme is picked up again in Section XXVII below.

The section next turns to a consideration of the six diametral lines that can be drawn across the celestial circle between pairs of Earthly Branches arranged at equal intervals around it. These have already appeared as the "six departments" in 3.IV and the "midpoints" and "hooks" of 3.VII above; they will reappear as the "six co-ordinates" in 5.XIV below. Here the two lines denoting north-south and east-west are called "diametral chords." Those denoting northeast-southwest and southeast-northwest are defined by four named points, called "weft-strings." Each of the latter is flanked by a pair of Earthly Branches, called "hooks." (See the illustration of a Han cosmograph in Fig. 2.8.)

The names of the four weft strings show that this section will deal in the tradition of calendrical astrology to which Sections XVII and XXII–XXIV below, and all of *Huainanzi* 5, belong: the waxing ("accretion") of yang and the waning of yin during the first six months of the year, and the waning of yang and the waxing of yin in the second six months. The direction northeast is correlated with the branch *yin* and the first month of the Xia sequence calendar; it marks the beginning of the civil year, and thus the beginning of yang's ascendency: Returning Accretion. Six months later, southwest is correlated with the beginning of the waxing of yin, and the waning of yang: Reverting Yang. Perpetual Ocean in the southeast is a perplexing term. In the southeast, yang is nearing its maximum, and perhaps there is an implication here that heaven is a sort of celestial ocean. The name for the northwest, Penetrating Cleft, is clearer; yin is about to reach its maximum, at which time, line 17 says, the Northern Limit will penetrate downwards to the Yellow Springs. These names perhaps also refer to the tilting of the ecliptic relative to the celestial equator as described in the myth of the fight between Gong Gong and Zhuan Xu. After the northwestern pillar was knocked aslant by their combat, all of the rivers ran to the southeast (perhaps making a "perpetual ocean" in that direction), while the damaged and tilted northwestern quadrant could perhaps be described as a "penetrating cleft."

The problem that this section confronts, and that can be seen in the astrology of all calendars that follow the Xia sequence, is this: The Xia sequence begins the year in the third astronomical month, associated with the northeast. Yang therefore should begin to wax in the first Xia month, and continue to dominate the year until the end of the sixth Xia month; thereafter yin takes command. But, as this section shows clearly, the Chinese also recognized that the astronomical (as opposed to the civil) year began with the winter solstice, in the eleventh Xia month. Thus in astrological terms, the civil calendar had yang beginning to control the year two months after it had already done so according to the astronomical calendar. In *Huainanzi* 5 and other versions of the "Yueling," this leads to a clear contradiction: the sixth civil month is called the third month of summer, and also is treated as an artificial "midsummer" season of maximum yang; but yang had already reached its maximum at the summer solstice in the fourth month, several weeks earlier.

In the "Yueling" (in all of its versions), the astronomical year is largely ignored in favor of the Xia sequence civil (i.e., astrological) year. In this section, primary attention is paid to the astronomical year, and to the position of the sun as observed in the heavens or replicated with the cosmograph. Gnomon measurements at the solstices are also carefully noted. Wetness and dryness are treated as normal, cyclical half-yearly yin-yang phenomena, but whole years of flood or drought are seen as abnormal. The wetness or dryness of the climate is observed scientifically by the effect of humidity on the weight of charcoal.

In other respects, however, the seasonal portents described here, based on observations of the natural world, are those of the "Yueling" tradition. Statements such as those found here about the seasonal behavior of animals, insects, and plants (for example the notion that deer shed their antlers at the solstices) are ubiquitous in *Huainanzi* 5, as are such seasonal prohibitions as forbidding cutting into the earth at the winter solstice or forbidding the erection of buildings at the summer solstice.

The seemingly puzzling statements that "accretion is in the Room" or "accretion is in the Field" are explained in the following section, "The Seven Habitations."

Section XVII: The Seven Habitations

[3:12a:6]

1 Yin and yang, recision and accretion, have seven habitations.

2   What are these seven habitations?

3   They are the Room, the Hall, the Court, the Gate, the Lane, the Road, and the Field.

4   In the eleventh month, accretion dwells in the Room for thirty days, fifteen days before the winter solstice and fifteen days after.

5   Thereafter it shifts its place every thirty days.

6   When accretion is in the Room, recision is in the Field.

7   When accretion is in the Hall, recision is in the Road.

8   When accretion is in the Court, recision is in the Lane.

9   When yin and yang are of equal power, then recision and accretion are together in the Gate.

10   In the eighth month and the second month, the qi of yin and yang is equal, and day and night are of equal length.

11   Thus it is said that recision and accretion are together in the Gate.

12   When accretion is in the south there is birth;

13   When recision is in the south there is death.

14   Thus at the meeting (in the Gate) at the second month,

15   The myriad creatures come to life.

16   At the meeting (in the Gate) in the eighth month,

17   The herbs and trees begin to die.

18   Between the two weft-strings is a span of $91\frac{5}{16}^{\mathrm{d}}$.

     [3:21b:2]

Commentary to Section XVII

This section in effect defines a solar-year calendar by means of seven equally spaced positions, called "habitations" (*she*) on the eastern horizon from winter solstice to summer solstice.[29] From northeast to southeast (one-quarter of the celestial circle, as defined in line 18), these are called the Field, the Road, the Lane, the Gate, the Court, the Hall, and the Room. At the winter solstice, the sun rises in the southeast; at that point, yang begins a period of six months of increasing influence, seen in the daily movement of sunrise further and further to the north. Thus in the first half of the year, yang moves from the Room outwards (i.e., northwards) gradually being fully displayed in the Field, when the sun rises in the northeast. At the same time, yin moves reciprocally in the opposite direction. At the summer solstice, the movements are reversed. Yin and yang meet in the Gate (due east) twice each year, at the equinoxes. This whole section thus describes by means of a vivid and very appealing image the annual reciprocal waxing and waning of yin and yang.

    The terms used to describe the waxing and waning of yin and yang are *xing* and *de*. Here (and in certain other cosmological texts), these are used as technical terms, and do not have their usual meanings of "punishments" and "rewards." Rather, *xing* means "recision" or "paring away"; *de* means "accretion."

Section XVIII: The Solar Nodes

[3:12b:3]

1   The sun's daily motion being 1^d, fifteen days makes one node (*jie*). Thus are produced twenty-four seasonal changes.

2   When the (handle of the) Dipper points to *zi* (at midnight), it is the Winter Solstice (node). Its sound is like (the pitch pipe) Yellow Bell.

3   After fifteen days, (the handle of the Dipper at midnight) points to *gui*. This is the Lesser Cold node. Its sound is like (the pitch pipe) Responsive Bell.

4   After fifteen more days, (the handle of the Dipper at midnight) points to *chou*. This is the Greater Cold node. Its sound is like (the pitch pipe) Tireless.

5   After fifteen more days, (the handle of the Dipper at midnight) points to the weft-cord of Returning Accretion, and there is a surplus of yin in the land. Thus it is said that the forty-sixth day from the winter solstice marks the Beginning of Spring (node), when the yang qi dispels the cold. Its sound is like (the pitch pipe) Southern Regulator.

6   After fifteen more days, (the handle of the Dipper at midnight) points to *yin*. This is the Rain node. Its sound is like (the pitch pipe) Tranquil Pattern.

7   After fifteen more days, (the handle of the Dipper at midnight) points to *jia*. This is the Awakening of Insects node. Its sound is like (the pitch pipe) Forest Bell.

8   After fifteen more days, (the handle of the Dipper at midnight) points to *mao*. Thus it is called the Spring Equinox (node). Thunder is abroad. Its sound is like (the pitch pipe) Luxuriant.

9   After fifteen more days, (the handle of the Dipper at midnight) points to *yi*. This is the node of the Clear-Bright wind-maximum. Its sound is like (the pitch pipe) Median Regulator.

10   After fifteen more days, (the handle of the Dipper at midnight) points to *chen*. This is the Grain Rain node. Its sound is like (the pitch pipe) Maiden Purity.

11   After fifteen more days (the handle of the Dipper at midnight) points to the weft-cord of Perpetual Ocean, and the portion (of the year allotted to) spring reaches its limit. Thus it is said that that the forty-sixth day (after the spring equinox) is the Beginning of Summer (node). The great winds end. Its sound is like (the pitch pipe) Pinched Bell.

12   After fifteen more days, (the handle of the Dipper at midnight) points to *si*. This is the Lesser Fullness node. Its sound is like (the pitch pipe) Great Budding.

13   After fifteen more days, (the handle of the Dipper at midnight) points to *bing*. This is the Grain in Ear node. Its sound is like (the pitch pipe) Great Regulator.

cycle

14 After fifteen more days, (the handle of the Dipper at midnight) points to *wu*. Yang qi reaches its maximum. Thus it is said that the forty-sixth day (after the beginning of summer) marks the Summer Solstice (node). Its sound is like (the pitch pipe) Yellow Bell.

15 After fifteen more days, (the handle of the Dipper at midnight) points to *ding*. This is the Lesser Heat node. Its sound is like (the pitch pipe) Great Regulator.

16 After fifteen more days (the handle of the Dipper at midnight) points to *wei*. This is the Great Heat node. Its (chromatic) note is Great Budding.

17 After fifteen more days (the handle of the Dipper at midnight) points to the weft-cord of Reverting Yang. Thus it is said that forty-six days after (the summer solstice) is the Beginning of Autumn (node). This is the node of the Cool Wind wind-maximum. Its sound is like (the pitch pipe) Pinched Bell.

18 After fifteen more days (the handle of the Dipper at midnight) points to *shen*. This is the End of Heat node. Its sound is like (the pitch pipe) Maiden Purity.

19 After fifteen more days (the handle of the Dipper at midnight) points to *geng*. This is the Descent of White Dew node. Its sound is like (the pitch pipe) Median Regulator.

20 After fifteen more days, (the handle of the Dipper at midnight) points to *you*, on the central marking-line. Thus it is called the Autumn Equinox (node). Thunder ceases, and swarming insects turn toward the north. Its sound is like (the pitch pipe) Luxuriant.

21 After fifteen more days, (the handle of the Dipper at midnight) points to *xin*. This is the Cold Dew node. Its sound is like (the pitch pipe) Forest Bell.

22 After fifteen more days, (the handle of the Dipper at midnight) points to *xu*. This is the Descent of Hoarfrost node. Its sound is like (the pitch pipe) Tranquil Pattern.

23 After fifteen more days, (the handle of the Dipper at midnight) points to the weft-cord of Penetrating Cleft. Thus the portion (of the year allotted to) autumn comes to its end. Thus it is said that the forty-sixth day (after the autumn equinox) is the Beginning of Winter (node). Herbs, trees, and flowers die. Its sound is like (the pitch pipe) Southern Regulator.

24 After fifteen more days, (the handle of the Dipper at midnight) points to *hai*. This is the Lesser Snow node. Its sound is like (the pitch pipe) Tireless.

25 After fifteen more days, (the handle of the Dipper at midnight) points to *ren*. This is the Great Snow node. Its sound is like (the pitch pipe) Responsive Bell.

26 After fifteen more days, (the handle of the Dipper at midnight again) points to *zi*.

27 Therefore it is said that yang is born in *zi*, yin is born in *wu*.

28 Yang is born in *zi*. Therefore in the eleventh month, the sun is at the winter solstice; magpies begin to nest, and human qi accumulates in the head.

29 Yin is born in *wu*. Therefore in the fifth month lesser punishments are carried out. Shepherds-purse and wheat stop growing and wither. The herbs and trees that sprouted in the winter must die.
    [3:14b:7]

Commentary to Section XVIII

The term "node" here translates the Chinese word *jie*, the original meaning of which referred to the nodes that mark the linear sections of a stem of bamboo but which later was applied more broadly to denote periodic phenomena of various kinds. The nodes are usually termed in English the "fortnightly periods," but that term's meaning of two 7-day weeks (a "fourteen-night") is both inaccurate and inappropriate when applied to the Chinese calendar; something more evocative of the original Chinese term is preferable.

The text here specifies twenty-four *jie*; later calendars divided these into twelve *jieqi* and twelve *zhongqi*. Nominally each node was a period of 15 days, making a 360-day year; again, in many later calendars, adjustments were made so that the periods fit smoothly into the full solar year. The twenty-four nodes, the names of which seem to imply a very old folk calendar, are quite familiar and have been described often in the literature on Chinese calendrical science.[30]

The list of seasonal nodes here is essentially that used throughout China up until modern times. The only difference is that this list begins in the first astronomical month, with the Winter Solstice node; most lists[31] follow the "Yueling" tradition in beginning the year with the first (Xia) civil month, and hence with the Beginning of Spring node. The *Huainanzi* list also differs from the lists in *Lüshi chunqiu* (and hence also "Yueling") in the order of the five nodes following Beginning of Spring, as follows:

Huainanzi 3	"Yueling"
(4) Beginning of Spring	(1) Beginning of Spring
(5) Rain	(2) Awakening of Insects
(6) Awakening of Insects	(3) Rain
(7) Spring Equinox	(4) Spring Equinox
(8) Clear-Bright	(5) Grain Rain
(9) Grain Rain	(6) Clear-Bright
(10) Beginning of Summer	(7) Beginning of Summer

Wang Yinzhi argues[32] that a later editor must have changed the order of the *Huainanzi* list, which should be emended to conform to that of *Lüshi chunqiu* and "Yueling." Xi Zezong points out,[33] however, that the *Huainanzi* list accords somewhat better with actual phenomena than the "Yueling" list, and thus came to be accepted in its place. Wang Yinzhi also notes that the chromatic note correlations in the *Huainanzi* list differ from those in *Lüshi chunqiu* and "Yueling," and uses this to argue that the *Huainanzi* list is wrong. It would seem, rather, that the author of *Huainanzi* 3 chose not to follow *Lüshi chunqiu* exactly, but decided instead to make a few deliberate changes. There is no particular reason to assume that *Huainanzi* must conform exactly to the earlier texts on which it is based.

Xi also points out another "contradiction" in this text, which is that whereas in 3.XII.4 above, the Clear-Bright node (*qingming*) occurs 135 days after the winter solstice, in this list of the seasonal nodes the Clear-Bright node runs from 106 to 120 days after the winter solstice. The list of wind names in 3.XII *is* derived from *Lüshi chunqiu*, and if the *Lüshi chunqiu* order of the seasonal nodes were followed (i.e., if Clear-Bright followed rather than preceded Grain Rain), Clear-Bright would run from 121 to 135 days after the solstice, and the lists of wind names and seasonal nodes would be in harmony. This is not a complete contradiction in any case, however, because the Clear-Bright "wind season" in 3.XII runs from 91 to 135 days after the winter solstice, reaching its maximun on the 135th day; thus the Clear-Bright seasonal node is contained within that wind season, both in the *Lüshi chunqiu* and in the *Huai-nanzi* lists.

The twenty-four seasonal nodes here are specified as running from winter solstice to winter solstice, which in fact would mean 365.25 days; but each seasonal node is defined as 15 days, for a total of 360 days. In later times this discrepancy was rectified by adding "adjustment days" at appropriate intervals—easily done with the aid of the cosmograph or some analogous instrument. No such procedure is specified here, however.

What this seems to show is that at the time *Huainanzi* 3 was written, there existed both an exact "astronomical year" of 365.25 days, and an "ordinary year" of 360 days used in folk or astrological calendars, and variously defined as 24 × 15 days, 12 × 30 days, 8 × 45 days, and 5 × 72 days. In the different sections of this chapter, the author of *Huainanzi* 3 simply presents them as different systems, each apparently adequate for the uses to which it was put, and not in need of reconciliation. This "ordinary year" is clearly agrarian in origin, which incidentally argues strongly against the oft-repeated assertion that astronomy arose as the first of the exact sciences "because an accurate calendar is a necessity in an agrarian society." Refinements of the ephemerides were necessary for mathematical astronomy and political astrology (because, among other things, the ruler demonstrated his oneness with the heavens by promulgating an accurate calendar), but not for agriculture. The people reckoned their own seasons.

The handle of the Dipper, in the sky or—especially—on the cosmograph, is depicted as moving clockwise through the twenty-four seasonal nodes arrayed around the celestial circle. (See Fig. 3.5) The twenty-four points are laid out as specified in 3.XVI.5–10 above. N–S and E–W are designated by four of the Earthly Branches, *ziwu* and *maoyu* respectively. Each of the four cardinal points is bracketed by a pair of Heavenly Stems: E by *jiayi*, S by *bingding*, W by *gengxin*, and N by *rengui*. (The fifth and sixth of the Heavenly Stems, *wuji*, is assigned to the center, and thus plays no role in marking out the points on the celestial circle.) The "corners" between the cardinal directions are the four "weft-strings" named in 3.XVI.7–10, that is, NE, Returning Accretion; SE, Perpetual Ocean; SW, Reverting Yang; NW, Penetrating Cleft. Each of these points is bracketed by the remaining four pairs of Earthly Branches, NE by *chouyin*, SE by *chensi*, SW by *weishen*, and NW by *xuhai*; these are the "four hooks" of 3.VII.2 and 3.XVI.6 above.

Each of the twenty-four nodes is assigned to one of the twelve pitch pipes; the notes cycle though the standard order of the duodecatonic scale (see 3.XXIX below) from Yellow Bell at the winter solstice to Yellow Bell (an octave higher) at the summer solstice, and then repeat in reverse order. For each seasonal node, it is said that "its sound is like (*bi*)" one of the pitch pipe notes. This is not simply a case of assigning pitch pipes to the twenty-four nodes as a system of correspondence; rather, as Bodde has shown,[34] the qi of the nodes themselves were believed to resonate to these tones. With the arrival of each seasonal node, in other words, the appropriate pitch pipe was supposed spontaneously to emit its note.

The correspondence between the seasonal nodes and the twelve pitch pipes may be seen in Figure 3.5.

Section XIX: The Twelve Chronograms and the Jovian Year

[3:14b:7]

1   The handle of the Dipper makes the Lesser Year.
2   The Pool of Xian makes the Greater Year.
3   In the first (civil) month (the Dipper) is established in *yin*.
4   The months move from the left through the twelve chronograms.
5   The second month is established in *mao*.
6   The moon moves from the right through the four quadrants (*zhong*). When it finishes, it begins again.
7   As for *taisui*: One who faces is it humiliated; one who turns away from it is strong; one who is on its left is in decline; one who is on its right attains glory.
8   When the Lesser Year is in the southeast, there is birth; when it is in the northwest, there is death.
9   This is what is meant by the saying: It must not be met, but it may be turned away from; it must not be to the left, but it may be to the right.
10   The Great Season is (governed by) the Pool of Xian.
11   The Lesser Season is that of the month-establishments.
12   The weft-cords of Heaven establish the epoch, which always begins with *yin*.
13   Arising, (*taisui* moves to the right for one year and then shifts.
14   After twelve years it completes a great circuit and then begins again.
15   In the first year of (the King of) Huainan, the Grand Monad was in (the cyclical year) *bingzi*.
16   The winter solstice was on (the cyclical day) *jiawu*; (the node) Beginning of Spring (began) on (the cyclical day) *bingzi*.
     [3:15b:6]

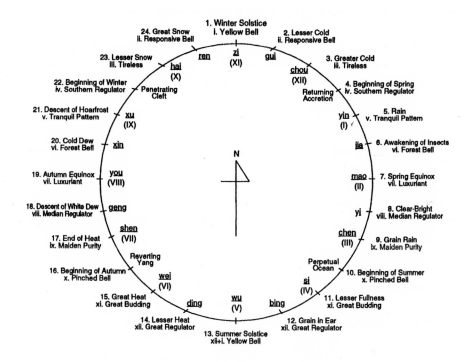

Figure 3.5. The twenty-four seasonal nodes, with associated pitch pipes.

Commentary to Section XIX

This section deals with the astrological implications of the lunar year and the Jovian Year in combination, with specific predictions for encounters between *taisui* (counter-Jupiter; see commentary to 3.VII above) and states correlated with the various Earthly Branches and Heavenly Stems arrayed around the earth plate of the cosmograph. While this much is clear, in its details this section contains much that is confusing, a situation made worse by a very considerable amount of textual corruption.[35]

It is apparent that all of the operations and astrological implications here depend on the cosmograph, rather than on actual observation. The year is established in *yin*, the third civil month, as in the Xia sequence calendar used throughout the cosmological chapters of *Huainanzi*. The statement in line 4 that "the months move from the left through the twelve chronograms" seems to imply the use of a ring or disk of some sort, inscribed with the twelve chronograms, and held overhead (actually or conceptually) while facing north, with *zi* alligned to the north pole. Lines 3 and 4 together thus refer not to the actual moon, but to the "Establishment" of the month, which moves through the twelve chronograms. If you imagine yourself looking at the pole holding the celestial ring overhead, as just described, with the signs arranged in a circle around it, then starting from *zi* on the bottom (north), the initial shift will be observed to move from left to right. This is not easy to visualize, however; references to 'left' and 'right' in texts of this kind tend to be hard to link with physical reality as we perceive it.

The Xian Pool is a well-known asterism, but the meaning of line 2, "The Pool of Xian makes the Greater Year" is unclear. We have already encountered this asterism as one of the "Six Departments" in 3.XIII.12 above. It seems to be on one level a "moving god" whose position in the cosmos can be as baleful as that of the better known *taisui*, or counter-Jupiter. It does seem clear that the Pool of Xian is more than just an asterism here, and it cannot be interpreted (though the text would seem to invite this) as the mark-point for the Jupiter (or counter-Jupiter) Cycle. The mark point for the Jovian Year is well attested as the initial Jupiter-station *xingji* "Stellar Sequence," which is not identifiable with, and in fact is not even close to, the asterism *xianchi*, "Pool of Xian." When the planet Jupiter is in its starting position at *xingji*, *taisui* starts from the cyclical sign *yin*. (All of this implies the idealized world of the cosmograph, rather than the heavens themselves. The regularized motion of *taisui* eventually loses synchronization with its real counterpart, so that station skipping has to occur from time to time if the linkage is to be preserved.)

Lines 7–9 refer to the cyclical signs of the "Lesser Year" (i.e., the soli-lunar year of the Xia sequence) in combination with the position of *taisui*, the regularized marker of the Jovian Year—all presumably as calculated (or demonstrated) by use of the cosmograph. The exact meaning of these lines is somewhat unclear, but their general import is that the cosmograph provides a means for calculating (by means of an idealized model of astral positions) times of good and bad fortune for the state.[36] The astrological principles here are similar to the those given below in 3.XXXIV.30: "In using *taiyin* (for prognostication), as a rule whatever is to its left, that is, ahead of it, suffers cutting-away; whatever is to its right, that is, behind it, obtains increase."

Section XX: Numerology and Harmonics

[3:15b:11]

1 Two yin and one yang make two qi.
2 Two yang and one yin make three qi.
3 Combining these qi makes the (pentatonic) notes.
4 Combining the yin makes yang.
5 Combining (this number with) the yang makes the pitch pipes.
6 Thus there are five notes and six pitch pipes.
7 The notes double to produce the number of the days.

8   The pitch pipes double to produce the earthly branches.

9   Thus there are ten days and twelve branches.

[3:16a:7]

Commentary to Section XX

This passage at first glance is very puzzling, and various commentators have argued that the numerology is wrong and that the first line should read "one yin and one yang make two qi." But this is really a perfect example of numerological reasoning, almost in the form of a riddle; it depends on an intermingling of number value and number symbolism. The logic is as follows:

1. Two is a yin (i.e., even) number, one is a yang (i.e., odd) number. This is equivalent to saying that one yin and one yang make two qi.

2. But two yang (dealing here with quantity, not number symbolism—because it is not permissable to say "yang is a two [even] number") and one yin make three qi.

3. Thus we have, in all, five qi, equivalent to the five pentatonic notes.

4. Now change the terms of reference: the two yin of line 1 are now taken in the sense of quantity (not "yin is a two [even] number" but "two yin"); these plus the one yin of line 2, make three—a yang number.

5. Adding this three to the three yang found in lines 1 and 2 make six, equivalent to the six pitch pipes. (The twelve tones of the duodecatonic scale can be produced by six pipes, each producing two notes.)

The rest of the passage is straightforward: Double five to get ten, making the ten days of the Chinese "week" (*xun*), which equate to the ten heavenly stems; double six to get twelve, making the twelve Earthly Branches.

Section XXI: The Metonic Cycle

[3:16a:7]

1   The moon's daily motion is 13 26/76^{d}.

2   A lunar month is 29 499/940 days. Twelve months make a year.

3   The (tropic) year is 10 827/940 days longer (than the lunar year).

4   Hence in nineteen years there are seven intercalary months.

[3:16a:11]

Commentary to Section XXI

The Metonic Cycle, as defined here, is the basis for the longer calendrical cycles already discussed in 3.XXV above.

In the following commentary, the fractions in the text have been converted to decimals for ease in calculation.

The "moon's daily motion" is the angular distance covered in its orbit around the earth. The figure given here, equivalent to 13.3421^d, cannot be arrived at by simply dividing the celestial circle, 365.25^d, by the length of the lunar month (given here as equivalent to 29.53085 days); a calculation of the angular distance traversed by the moon each day must also account for the moon's annual motion (see 3.XIX.6, above). 13.3421 times 29.53085 yields a total monthly orbital distance of 394.00355^d. That is to say, in a month the moon makes a full circuit of 365.25^d plus 28.75355^d. (In Section XIX, the angular distance of the moon's monthly "rightward" movement through the stars is implied as 30.4375^d.)

The length of the lunar month—the number of days from new moon to new moon—given here is quite accurate, 29.53085 days as compared to the true value of 29.53059 days. Twelve lunar months, using the figure given in the text, make a lunar year of 354.3702 days. The figure given for the excess number of days in the tropic year over the lunar year is derivative: the tropic year is taken as 365.25 days, which, minus the lunar year of 354.3702 days, yields 10.8798 "excess days." The true figure for the length of the tropic year as of 100 B.C.E. is approximately 365.24320 days.

All of this is based on the Metonic Cycle, the most simple reconciliation of the lunar and solar years, by which seven intercalary lunar months are inserted into each span of nineteen years. Using the figures given in the text, it works out almost exactly:

$$365.25 \times 19 = 6{,}939.75 \text{ days}$$
$$((12 \times 19) + 7) \times 29.53085 = 6{,}939.7499 \text{ days.}$$

In fact, it works out too exactly; it is immediately apparent that the length of the lunar month given here was simply derived from the Metonic Cycle. That is, nineteen years ($6{,}939.75$ days) was divided by 235 months, yielding a length for 1 month of 29.53085 days.

The true figures do not in fact match quite as well:

$$365.24320 \times 19 = 6{,}939.6208 \text{ days}$$
$$((12 \times 19) + 7) \times 29.53059 = 6{,}939.6886 \text{ days}$$

Thus after a few centuries, the Metonic Cycle becomes noticeably out of phase. The problem of reconciling the lunar year and the tropic year would plague Chinese astronomers (and astronomers in all other ancient cultures as well) for centuries to come.[37]

Section XXII: A Year of Five 72-Day Periods

[3:16a:11]

1   The days of the winter solstice take the branches *zi* and *wu*.

2   The days of the summer solstice take the branches *mao* and *you*.

3   Adding three days to the (branches of) the winter solstice yields the days of the summer solstice.

4   The whole year shifts by six days and begins again with *renwu*.

5   At the winter solstice, (the cyclical day) *jiazi* receives control.

6   (The phase) wood is used in all affairs, and the smoke of fires is bluegreen.

7   After seventy-two days, *bingzi* receives control.

8   (The phase) fire is used in all affairs, and the smoke of fires is vermilion.

9   After seventy-two days, *wuzi* receives control.

10   (The phase) earth is used in all affairs, and the smoke of fires is yellow.

11   After seventy-two days, *gengzi* receives control.

12   (The phase) metal is used in all affairs, and the smoke of fires is white.

13   After seventy-two days, *renzi* receives control.

14   (The phase) water is used in all affairs, and the smoke of fires is black.

15   After seventy-two (more) days, the year comes to an end, and *gengwu* takes control.

16   The year shifts by six days so that the number may extend (to the full count of 366).

17   After ten years, (the sequence) begins again with *jiazi*.

18   When *jiazi* is in control, act gently and graciously, and relax prohibitions. Open doors and covers, and penetrate barriers. It is prohibited to cut wood.

19   When *bingzi* is in control, promote the worthy and the good, and reward the meritorious. Enfeoff nobles and distribute wealth.

20   When *wuzi* is in control, nourish the old and the widowed, distribute food-alms, and bestow grace and favor.

21   When *gengzi* is in control, improve walls and enclosures, strengthen city walls and fortifications, scrutinize prohibitions [with a view toward strengthening them], refurbish the armor of the troops, admonish officials, and punish the lawless.

22   When *renzi* is in control, shut doors and gates, investigate strangers, execute punishments, kill the condemned, (command the people to) rest within their gates and under the beams of their roofs, and prohibit wandering abroad.

23   The qi of *jiazi* is dry and turbid.

24   The qi of *bingzi* is dry and hot/bright.

25   The qi of *wuzi* is damp and turbid.

26   The qi of *gengzi* is dry and cold.

27   The qi of *renzi* is clear and cold.

    [3:17a:6]

Commentary to Section XXII

Since half the year is about 183 days, that is, thrice sixty plus three, the solsticial days change by three places in the 60-day cycle. This, plus the statement that "the whole year shifts by six days" suggests a calendar year of 366 days, as in the "Yao dian" chapter of the *Shujing*.[38] The assumption in this passage is that the first year mentioned begins on the cyclical day *bingzi* (#13); the second year thus, as specified, begins with *renwu* (#19).

In the scheme of five 72-day "seasons" presented in this section, every day of the sexagenary cycle will appear at least once, and the 72-day period could, of course, begin on any day. The stipulation that *jiazi* (#1) "takes control" reflects an identification of the first day of the sexagenary cycle with the first season of the five-season cycle; in addition, the use of *jiazi* as an index number facilitates the calculation of subsequent "control days":

jiazi = #1
bingzi = #13, i.e., $1 + 72 - 60$.
wuzi = #25, i.e., $1 + 144 - 120$.
gengzi = #37, i.e., $1 + 216 - 180$.
renzi = #49, i.e., $1 + 288 - 240$.

Thus in the next year, the cycle shifts by six days, and begins with *gengwu*, #7, that is, $1 + 6 + 360 - 300 [- 60]$. With the 366-day year specified, the whole cycle repeats every ten years.

The five phase attributes of the five 72-day "seasons" are standard, as are the actions appropriate to each season. The specified phase is used as a standard for all activities during the season in question. The statement about the color of the smoke of fires during each season is somewhat puzzling; presumably this refers to the smoke of sacrificial or divinatory fires, but whether any chemical method of achieving such colors was actually used is questionable.

The tone of this section is similar to the calendrical section of Chapter 41 ("Wu-xing") of the *Guanzi*, but the details are rather different. In both cases, the activities enjoined are governed by five phase correlations. The author of *Huainanzi* 3 may have consciously paraphrased or emended *Guanzi* 41, or perhaps both texts are variants derived from a now-unknown common source.[39]

The specific rules for the conduct of government given for each of these five seasons in lines 18–22 are strikingly similar to those of *Huainanzi* 5, the "Treatise on the Seasonal Rules," which likewise has five seasons (the four natural seasons plus an artificial season of "midsummer" assigned to the sixth month of the year).

Section XXIII: Astrological Relations of the Five Seasons

[3:17a:6]

1   When (the day designated) *bingzi* opposes (the "season" governed by) *jiazi*, hibernating insects hatch forth prematurely, and there is (unseasonably) early thunder.

2   When *wuzi* opposes *jiazi*, the pregnant suffer calamities, eggs are infertile, and birds and insects suffer great injuries.

3   When *gengzi* opposes *jiazi*, there will be military operations.

4   When *renzi* opposes *jiazi*, there will be spring frosts.

5   When *wuzi* opposes *bingzi*, there will be claps of thunder.

6   When *gengzi* opposes *bingzi*, there will be bolts of lightning.

7   When *renzi* opposes *bingzi*, there will be hail.

8   When *jiazi* opposes *bingzi*, there will be earthquakes.

9   When *gengzi* opposes *wuzi*, the five grains will suffer calamaties.

10   When *renzi* opposes *wuzi*, there will be cold spells in summer, with rain and frost.

11   When *jiazi* opposes *wuzi*, silkworms will not mature.

12   When *bingzi* opposes *wuzi*, there will be great drought; aquatic grasses will entirely dry out.

13   When *renzi* opposes *gangzi*, fish will not grow.

14   When *jiazi* opposes *gengzi*, herbs and trees renew their growth.

15   When *bingzi* opposes *gengzi*, flowers bloom for a second time (out of season).

16   When *wuzi* opposes *gengzi*, the annual harvest may be preserved or may be lost.

17   When *jiazi* opposes *renzi*, (creatures) will not hibernate (as they should).

18   When *bingzi* opposes *renzi*, there will be meteors.

19   When *wuzi* opposes *renzi*, in winter insects depart from their places.

20   When *gengzi* opposes *renzi*, there will be thunder in winter.
     [3:17b:6]

Commentary to Section XXIII

This section provides rules for determining the astrological relations of two calendrical periods: the stem-branch sexagenary cycle and the five annual "seasons" of 72 days each. Obviously, within every such season, each sexagenary *ganzhi* day will occur at least once. In these lines, therefore, *gan* cannot simply mean "occurs in" (which would always happen); it must mean something like "opposes"—indicating some kind of unnatural or ominous situation. Here, *gan* perhaps refers to occasions when Jupiter (or, more likely, *taisui* counter-Jupiter as observed on the cosmograph) is located in a stem-branch pair "opposed" to the pair governing a given season.

These seasons of 72 days repeat in a cycle of ten 366-day years, as explained in the previous section. The seasons begin on a different day each year, and presumably the astrologer working with this set of rules would make the appropriate adjustments for day names for each year of the ten-year cycle.

The effects of a season's being "opposed" by the name day of another season are strikingly similar to the effects predicted in *Huainanzi* 5, the "Treatise on the Seasonal Rules," to occur if the ruler employs the ordinances of an inappropriate season at any

TABLE 3.1 EXPLANATION OF EFFECTS OF "OPPOSING DAYS"
IN A YEAR OF FIVE 72-DAY SEASONS.

Day ↔ Season	Phase ↔ Phase	Explanation
bingzi ↔ *jiazi*	fire ↔ wood	Excess yang; heat calamities.
wuzi ↔ *jiazi*	earth ↔ wood	Decay; calamities of gestation.
gengzi ↔ *jiazi*	metal ↔ wood	Cutting; injury and war.
renzi ↔ *jiazi*	water ↔ wood	Excess yin; cold calamities
wuzi ↔ *bingzi*	earth ↔ fire	Earth restrains fire; thunder.
gengzi ↔ *bingzi*	metal ↔ fire	Metal arouses fire; lightning.
renzi ↔ *bingzi*	water ↔ fire	Water opposes fire; hail.
jiazi ↔ *bingzi*	wood ↔ fire	Destruction; earthquakes.
gengzi ↔ *wuzi*	metal ↔ earth	Metal injures earth; crop destruction.
renzi ↔ *wuzi*	water ↔ earth	Excess water in earth; cold.
jiazi ↔ *wuzi*	wood ↔ earth	Yang influence underdeveloped; retarded maturation of crops
bingzi ↔ *wuzi*	fire ↔ earth	Excess yang; drought.
renzi ↔ *gengzi*	water ↔ metal	Excess yin; fish injured.
jiazi ↔ *gengzi*	wood ↔ metal	Excess yang; false growth of vegetation.
bingzi ↔ *gengzi*	fire ↔ metal	Excess yang; false flowering in autumn.
wuzi ↔ *gengzi*	earth ↔ metal	Retarded yin; plants do not ripen.
jiazi ↔ *renzi*	wood ↔ water	Excess yang; winter unseasonably warm.
bingzi ↔ *renzi*	fire ↔ water	Fiery apparitions in dark sky.
wuzi ↔ *renzi*	earth ↔ water	Excess yang; hibernating insects awaken.
gengzi ↔ *renzi*	metal ↔ water	"Sounds of warfare" in winter.

time. They are also similar to the effects predicted in 5.XIV.14–25, where if government "fails in its duties" in any given month, disasters of various kinds will occur six months later.

Whatever the meaning of "opposes" here, the astrological principles involved may be explained in terms of standard five-phase reasoning, as shown in Table 3.1.

Section XXIV: The Qi of Months and Seasons

[3:17b:6]

1 In the third and final month of spring, abundant thunder sounds forth, bringing in the rains.

2 In the third and final month of autumn, the qi of earth has not yet become (completely) quiescent, and one gathers in the killed [= harvested] things.

3 All crawling things become torpid and hide away, and country-dwellers shut their gates.

4 Bluegreen Woman comes out and brings down frost and snow.

5 Thus the qi of the twelve times of the year progress, until they reach an end (again)

in the second month of spring, when that which has been stored away is received
forth (again) and the cold is shut away.

6 Then Tranquil Woman drums and sings to regulate the harmony of Heaven and to
make grow the hundred kinds of cereals, the beasts and birds, and the herbs and trees.

7 In the first month of summer the crops ripen; the cries of pheasants and pigeons
become prolonged, causing the thearch to look forward to the annual harvest.

8 Thus if Heaven does not give forth yin, the myriad things cannot be born;

9 If Earth does not give forth yang, the myriad things cannot grow to maturity.

10 Heaven is round, Earth is square; the Dao is exactly in the middle.

11 The sun (produces) accretion, the moon (produces) paring away.

12 When the moon reverts (in its course), the myriad creatures die.

13 When the sun attains its apogee, the myriad creatures are born.

14 Separated from mountains, the qi of mountains is hidden away.

15 Separated from water, aquatic insects become dormant.

16 Separated from trees, leaves wither.

17 When the sun is not seen for five days, (the ruler) will lose his throne. Even a (ruler
who is a) sage cannot withstand this.
[3:18a:10]

Commentary to Section XXIV

As with the preceding two sections, Section XXIV derives from a tradition of calendrical astrology that also includes the various versions of the "Yueling," such as *Huainanzi* 5, the "Treatise on the Seasonal Rules." The yin-yang correlations here are standard, and the seasonal omens are similar to those in *Huainanzi* 5. Here the text also employs the terminology of *xingde*, as in 3.XVI and 3.XVII above.

The arrival of winter and spring are attributed here to Bluegreen Woman and Tranquil Woman, who presumably are seasonal goddesses, part of a pantheon of minor divinities that included "jade women" and other deifications of natural phenomena.[40] This section, like other texts in the "Yueling" tradition of calendrical astrology, has the flavor of folk wisdom as well as of systematic cosmology.

As was noted above in the commentary to 3.III, line 10 here is emblematic of the ruler's key position as the "possessor of the Dao." The implication of the lines immediately following is that the waxing and waning of yang and yin create the annual seasons, but the ruler must act in accordance with this natural cycle in order to bring order, prosperity, and tranquility to his realm.

Line 14, "Separated from mountains, the qi of mountains is hidden away," sounds *Laozi*-like; a thing cannot exist apart from that which supplies its essence. But lines 14–16 here have a function that is principally aphoristic. They lend weight to line 17, which is a portent warning addressed specifically to the ruler.

101

Section XXV: The Path of the Sun

[3:18a:10]

1 The sun rises up from the Bright Valley,
2 Bathes in the Pool of Xian,
3 And rests in the Fusang Tree.
4 This is called Dawn Light.
5 Ascending the Fusang Tree, it thereupon commences its journey.
6 This is called Emergent Brightness.
7 (When the sun) reaches the Bent Slope,
8 This is called Dawn Brilliance.
9 (When the sun) reaches the Steaming Spring,
10 This is called the Morning Meal.
11 (When the sun) reaches the Mulberry Field,
12 This is called the Late-morning Meal.
13 (When the sun) reaches the Balance-Beam of Yang,
14 This is called Within the Angle.
15 (When the sun) reaches Kun Wu,
16 This is called the Exact Center.
17 (When the sun) reaches the Bird-Roost,
18 This is called the Lesser Return.
19 (When the sun) reaches the Valley of Grief,
20 This is called the Dinner-Hour.
21 (When the sun) reaches Woman's Sequence,
22 This is called the Great Return.
23 (When the sun) reaches the Angle of the Abyss,
24 This is called the Raised Pestle.
25 (When the sun) reaches Carriage-Stone,
26 This is called the Descending Pestle.
27 (When the sun) reaches the Fountain of Grief, it halts; its female attendant rests her horses.
28 This is called the Suspended Chariot.
29 (When the sun) reaches the Abyss of Anxiety,
30 This is called Yellow Dusk.
31 (When the sun) reaches the Vale of Obscurity,
32 This is called Definite Dusk.
33 The sun enters the floodwaters of the Abyss of Anxiety;
34 Sunrise emerges from the drainage-stream of the Vale of Obscurity.
35 (The sun) travels over the nine continents, (passing through) seven resting-places, (covering a distance of) 507,309 li.
36 Yu (the Great) employed (the stages of the sun's journey) to make (the distinctions between) dawn, daylight, dusk, and night.
[3:19b:4]

Commentary to Section XXV

The sun myths of early China have been expertly analyzed by Sarah Allan in her article "Sons of Suns";[41] this section of *Huainanzi* 3 is replete with the sorts of mythic images discussed there.

As early as the Shang period, the Chinese thought of the sun as a glowing chariot guided across the sky by a female charioteer, Xihe. (Later, Xihe was split into two male quasi divinities, said to be the court astronomers of the "Emperor" Yao; in the "Yao dian" chapter of the *Shujing*, these are depicted as each having two younger brothers, also named Xi and He.) In an alternative vision, the sun was depicted as a crow or raven, usually three-legged, that flew across the sky from the Fusang tree in the east to the Ruo tree in the west. (See Fig. 2.9 above.) These images are to some extent conflated here; the sun climbs the Fusang tree before rising at dawn to begin its journey across the sky, implying the sun-crow, but otherwise the dominant image here is of the sun-chariot. (For example, in line 27, the sun's "female attendant"—specifically Xihe in later quoted variants of this line—rests her horses just before dusk.)

This section, mythic and archaic in tone, gives a clear impression of having been derived from a folk or oral tradition, quite certainly one that is more ancient than the relatively technical astronomical/astrological sections that dominate *Huainanzi* 3 as a whole. It is in part an elaboration of the famous passage in the "Yao dian" in which Yao commands the brothers Xi and He to attend to the four cardinal directions:

> [Yao] particularly ordered the younger brother Xi to reside among the Yu barbarians at the place called Yanggu [the Bright Valley] and to receive as a guest the rising sun, in order to regulate the labors of the east. . . .
>
> [Yao] particularly ordered the younger brother He to reside in the west at the place called Meigu [= Menggu, the Vale of Obscurity], and to bid farewell respectfully to the setting sun, in order to regulate the western accomplishment.[42]

The impression of this passage in *Huainanzi* 3 as a "story" is heightened by its careful mention of stopping places for meals and snacks. It is the sort of story that may have lain behind the later, and far more polished and literary, poetic accounts of spirit journeys across the sky, traversing enormous distances past mythical landmarks in a shamanistic quest for an elusive goddess—poems such as the "Li sao" and "Yuan you" of the *Chu ci*, and their many later imitations.

The connection to the *Chu ci* is by no means accidental, for this section of *Huainanzi* 3 specifically responds to "Tian wen" 15–16:

> Leaving from Hot-Water Valley, arriving in the Vale of Obscurity,
> On the journey from brightness to dark [a pass of how many li?]

Hot-Water Valley (*tanggu*) is cognate to the Bright Valley (*yanggu*) here; they are nothing more than two closely related alternate names for the same place. Hot-Water Valley can also be understood to mean the Valley of Tang (the Victorious), founder of the Shang Dynasty. In answering the question posed by "Tian wen" 16, this passage specifies that the journey is 507,309 li in length, and elaborates by listing all of the stages along the way. That the sun is said to "travel over the nine continents" also places this passage in the cosmographic tradition of Zou Yan that informs *Huainanzi* 4, the "Treatise on Topography."

The Ruo tree, on which the sun alights in the west at sunset, is not mentioned in this section, but its presence in the Vale of Obscurity may be inferred from other accounts of the myth of the sun's journey. Both the Fusang tree and the Ruo tree are mentioned in *Huainanzi* 4.V, along with another tree, the Jian tree, that marks the midpoint of the sun's path. Sunrise Valley and the Fusang tree are also mentioned in 4.XVI, along with Kun Wu: "The Hill of Kun Wu is in the South" (4.XVI.13). Kun Wu was the mythical ancestor of the state of Chu; here apparently his astral projection or celestial counterpart inhabits a point in the sky at the midpoint of the sun's daily journey; the Hill of Kun Wu and the Jian tree are thus two different names for the same celestial/mythographical place. In its daily journey across the sky, the sun is described as passing through fifteen stages, from the Pool of Xian to the Vale of Obscurity, including the "seven resting-places" mentioned in line 35. (Interestingly, the sun reaches the midpoint of its journey at stage seven, not stage eight as one would expect for the sake of symmetry.) Like the Pool of Xian—encountered above in 3.XIII.12 and 3.XIX.2—such places as "the Balance-Beam of Yang" and "Bird-Roost" are to be understood as asterisms of some kind, archaic constellations lying roughly along the ecliptic.

The statement in line 34 that "Sunrise emerges from the drainage-stream of the Vale of Obscurity" is of considerable interest, for it provides the means for the sun-crow, or Xihe and her chariot, to return from west to east, completing the sun's journey so as to allow it to set out anew on the following day. The Vale of Obscurity is drained by the Ruo River, which is also said in some sources to swirl around the Hollow Mulberry (a variant of the Fusang tree) in the east.[43] As Allan notes, this "can be explained by regarding [the Ruo River] not as an ordinary river, but as another name for the watery underworld also known as the 'Yellow Spring' (*Huang Quan*), which ran everywhere beneath the earth and which came to the surface at the feet of the Fu Sang and the Ruo Tree."[44] Wolfgang Bauer has noted the semantic relations within a family of Chinese words pronounced *tong* (e.g. the words for "cave" and "pipe"), and comments that "it was not the darkness of the cave that attracted attention [in the later Daoist tradition], but rather the light of day shimmering far away at its end, and which promised a new world."[45] Bauer's remarks refer specifically to the later Daoist concept of the cave or grotto as a fairyland or paradise, and moreover not simply an enclosed subterranean space but rather a passageway or tunnel. The image here in *Huainanzi* 3 of the sun's return to the east through such a tunnel recalls (or perhaps presages) the adept's passage through a cave/fairyland as a symbol of "returning to the Dao."

The comment in line 36 that Yu the Great employed the stages of the sun's journey to mark the distinctions between dawn, daylight, dusk, and night is of particular interest in connection with the Grand Origin Myth discussed in Chapter 2 above; the world-engulfing flood tamed by Yu is to be understood, in light of that myth, as a consequence of the battle between Gong Gong and Zhuan Xu that resulted also in the tilting of the ecliptic relative to the celestial equator. Yu's reign marked the transition from the timelessness of the precatastrophe world and the historical time of the human world. Yu "marked" the solstitial and equinoctial nodes passed by the sun in the course of its journey from the Fusang tree to the Ruo tree and back again, bringing time to the world in the form of both quarters of a day and quarters of a year.

Section XXVI: Seasonal Yin and Yang

[3:19b:5]

1   At the summer solstice, yin (begins to be) ascendant over yang.
2   For this reason, the myriad creatures come to an end and die.
3   At the winter solstice, yang (begins to be) ascendant over yin.
4   For this reason, the myriad creatures lift up their heads and come to life.
5   Daylight is the portion of yang, night is the portion of yin.
6   Thus when the yang qi dominates, days are long and nights are short.
7   When the yin qi dominates, days are short and nights are long.
    [3:19b:7] [3:20b:10]
8   Appearing in *mao* and *you* (at the equinoxes), yin and yang divide day and night equally.
9   Thus it is said that when the compass is born, the T-square dies, the level-beam is growing, the plumb-weight is hidden away, and the marking-cords dwell in the center as the foundation of the four seasons.
    [3:21a:3]

Commentary to Section XXVI

This brief section at first seems like hardly more than a summary of Section XVI above; it gives in abbreviated form an account of the yin and yang portions of the year and the day.

This passage gains some additional force, however, when lines 8 and 9 are transposed to here from their present position in the Chinese text (following Section XXVII below); they are clearly out of place there, and probably were originally part of this section. For the five phase connotations of the five construction implements in line 9 here, see Section VI above, as well as 5.XV below. In plainer language, this line says that when spring is born, summer is growing, autumn is (still) dead, and winter, having preceded spring, is now buried away. The phase earth plays no direct role in the seasonal round, but dwells in the center and regulates the other four. Compare the very similar language in 4.XIV, where, however, all five phases are in a state of dynamic change.

Section XXVII: The Indications of the Handle of the Dipper

[3:19b:7]

1 The Celestial Thearch stretches out over the four weft-cords of Heaven,
2 And employs the Dipper to revolve (through) them.
3 In a month it shifts by one chronogram, its location being successively displaced.
4 In the first (civil) month, it points to *yin*; in the twelfth month it points to *chou*.
5 It completes a circle in one year; finishing, it begins again.
6 When (the Dipper) points to *yin* [in the first civil month], the myriad creatures stir like earthworms underground. The pitch pipes take the note Great Budding. Great Budding means that there are buds but they have not yet emerged.
7 (In the second civil month, the Dipper) points to *mao*. *Mao* means "burgeoning," thus (living things) burgeon forth. The pitch pipes take the note Pinched Bell. Pinched Bell means that seeds first begin to swell.
8 (In the third civil month the Dipper) points to *chen*. *Chen* means "to stir up." The pitch pipes take the note Maiden Purity. Maiden Purity means that what is withered is done away with and the new comes forth.
9 (In the fourth civil month the Dipper) points to *si* ("fetus"). There being a fetus, there is sure to be birth in consequence. The pitch pipes take the note Median Regulator. Median Regulator means that the center grows large.
10 (In the fifth civil month the Dipper) points to *wu*. *Wu* means "to oppose." The pitch pipes take the note Luxuriant. Luxuriant means that all is tranquil and fitting.
11 (In the sixth civil month the Dipper) points to *wei*. *Wei* means "flavor." The pitch pipes take the note Forest Bell. Forest Bell means to extend forth and then stop.
12 (In the seventh civil month the Dipper) points to *shen*. *Shen* means "chanting." The pitch pipes take the note Tranquil Pattern. Tranquil Pattern means that the pattern is changed. The (force of) accretion is expunged (from the annual cycle).
13 (In the eighth civil month the Dipper) points to *you*. *You* means "satiety." The pitch pipes take the note Southern Regulator. Southern Regulator means that it is recognized that the satiety is great.
14 (In the ninth civil month the Dipper) points to *xu*. *Xu* means "destruction." The pitch pipes take the note Tireless. Tireless means that there is bringing in without satisfaction.

106

15   (In the tenth civil month the Dipper) points to *hai. Hai* means "hindrance." The pitch pipes take the note Responsive Bell. Responsive Bell means to respond to the bell.

16   (In the eleventh civil month the Dipper) points to *zi. Zi* means "black." The pitch pipes take the note Yellow Bell. Yellow Bell means that the bell is beginning to be yellow.

17   (In the twelfth civil month the Dipper) points to *chou. Chou* means "to tie." The pitch pipes take the note Great Regulator. Great Regulator means to go out one after the other.

[3:20b:10]

Commentary to Section XXVII

Which is?

Here the "Treatise on the Patterns of Heaven" returns to astrological observations carried out by means of the cosmograph. The (Celestial) Thearch of line 1 is *di*, the God of the Pivot, specifically the star Kochab (beta Ursa Minoris), which for the Chinese was the second star of the asterism Northern Culmen (*beiji*). Sima Qian, in *Shiji* 27, calls it "the fixed place of the Grand Monad" (*tai yi chang ju*). It is described in the astronomical chapter of the *Jin shu* as follows: "[The] second star [of Northern Culmen], known as *di wang* or *da di*. . . . governs the sun. [It] also forms the throne of (the deity) *tai yi* [Grand Monad]."[46] Although this star was several degrees away from the celestial north pole in Han times, it was the brightest star in the vicinity of the pole, and was conventionally taken to be the polestar. This explains the reference to its stretching out over the four weft cords of Heaven, which are, of course, great circles denoting north-south and east-west, as described in 3.XVI.5 above. The star *di* thus marks the pivot of the heaven plate of the cosmograph, around which the image of the Dipper inscribed on the plate rotates to serve as a pointer. The Dipper points, in this instance, to the zone of the earth plate that is divided twelve segments, equivalent to the chronograms (*chen*), each denoted by one Earthly Branch and thus coincident with the twelve months of the year.

This section is very obscure; the meanings of each monthly line are heavily dependent on puns, both phonetic and logomorphic. The language of the original passage seems somewhat tortured and difficult; many of these lines are translated only provisionally, on a "best guess" basis. Specific details on the puns are given in the Textual and Technical Notes below. In general, the puns refer both to the names of the twelve Earthly Branches, and to the names of the twelve pitch pipes. The use of puns here amounts to almost a kind of logomancy; the puns, in other words, would have been thought to have magical qualities, in a manner exactly equivalent to the numerological resonances found in several sections of this chapter.

Figure 3.6. The Dipper, which acts as a celestial pointer in its daily angular motion of 1^d, is conceived of in this stone relief carving from the Wu Liang Shrine as the chariot of a celestial deity. Cf. 3.XXVII.1: "The Celestial Thearch stretches out over the four weft-cords of heaven." (From Zheng Wenguang, *Zhongguo tianwenxue yuanliu*, p. 133.)

In each month, the pitch pipes (collectively, as a set of twelve) are said to take (lit. "receive," *shou*) one or another note. As in 3.XVIII above, this refers to the practice of "watching for the ethers"; the appropriate pitch pipe was supposed to sound spontaneously during the month with which it was correlated. It is interesting to note, however, that in 3.XVIII and in the present section the author of *Huainanzi* 3 is content to offer two different, and unreconcilable, versions of this magical resonance. In the earlier section, the pitch pipes responded to the twenty-four seasonal nodes by emitting tones first in the standard order of the duodecatonic scale, beginning with Yellow Bell (C) at the winter solstice and then in reverse order back to Yellow Bell again; here the month in which the winter solstice occurs is also correlated with Yellow Bell, but the notes go through only one cycle of the standard order (i.e., C-G-D-A-E-B-F#-C#-G#-D#-A#-F) beginning with Great Budding (D) in the third month.

Section XXVIII: Numerology and Harmonics

[3:21a:3]

1   Thus it is said, "The Dao begins with one."

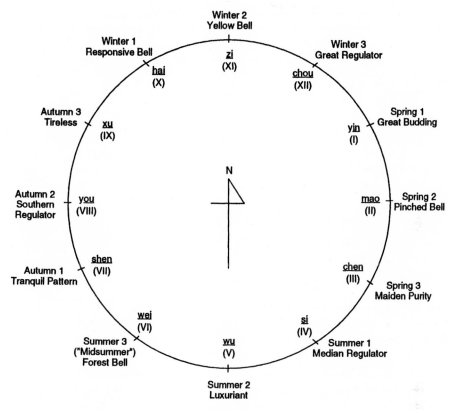

Figure 3.7. Diagram of the Xia sequence civil months and their associated pitch pipes. (Roman numerals in parentheses = the order of months as given in 3.XXVII and in *Huainanzi* 5, the "Treatise on the Seasonal Rules.")

2   One (alone), however, does not give birth.

3   Therefore it divided into yin and yang.

4   From the harmonious union of yin and yang, the myriad things were produced.

5   Thus it is said, "One produced two, two produced three, three produced the myriad things," and Heaven and Earth.

6   Three months make one season.

7   Thus a sacrifice of three [types or portions of] cooked grains are used in mourning rites.

8   The year continues for three shifts (of seasons) to make the seasonal nodes [complete their cycle].

9   Armies emphasize three signal-flags in order to maintain control.

10   Using three to examine matters:

11 3 × 3 = 9. Thus the Yellow Bell pitch pipe is nine inches long, and harmonizes with the note *gong*.

12 Furthermore, 9 × 9 = 81. Thus the number of the Yellow Bell is established therein.

13 Yellow is the color of the power of earth; the bell is that whereby the (seeds of) qi are sown.

14 At the winter solstice the accumulating qi produces Earth; the color of Earth is yellow.

15 Thus the (note of the winter solstice) is called Yellow Bell.

16 The number of pitch pipes is six, classified as female and male [for a total of twelve].

17 Thus it is said there are twelve bells to act as adjuncts to the twelve months.

18 Each of the twelve is based on three.

19 Thus if one sets up (the number) one and triples it eleven times [i.e., 3^{11}], the total is 177,147.

20 The Great Number of the Yellow Bell is thereby revealed.
    [3:21b:2]

Commentary to Section XXVIII

The opening lines of this section first paraphrase, and then quote, *Laozi* 42. The intent here is not really to deal in cosmogony, however, but simply to arrive at the number three, which forms the basis of the numerology of pitch pipes that is the real subject of this section.[47]

The text then gives three examples—from the realms of ritual, calendrical astrology, and military affairs—to illustrate the importance of three in human affairs. The reasoning here is typical of the microcosm-macrocosm rhetoric of Chinese numerology, of which many other examples are to be found in these three chapters of *Huainanzi*.

The text then multiplies 3 × 3 to get 9, the length of the pitch pipe Yellow Bell. The length of the next pipe in the series, Forest Bell, would be 9 inches × ⅔, or 6 inches. The juxtaposition of nine and six would seem to suggest the numerology of the *Book of Changes*; this is coincidental, however, and the numerology of pitch pipes and trigrams is not pursued in *Huainanzi*. In line 12 above, three is raised to the fourth power, that is, 9 × 9 = 81. That 81 is "the number of Yellow Bell" is reiterated in 3.XXIX.14 below; although we are told in this section that the Yellow Bell pitch pipe is nine inches long, the ratios in Section XXIX seem to imply a Yellow Bell pitch pipe 8.1 inches long. A secondary reason for deriving the number 81 is to return to the number one (just as, in 4.X below, multiples of nine are used to derive the integers 1 through 8 for numerological purposes.) Yellow Bell is taken as 1 in the series of ratios alluded to in lines 18–20 (for which see below).

Lines 13–15 here represent something of an anomaly in terms of standard five phase reasoning. Yellow Bell is first associated with phase earth (and the color yellow).

Yellow Bell always has the number 1, being first in the pentatonic scale; in other respects, however, it is normally correlated with the "direction" the center and the season "midsummer," both of which have the numerical correlate 5. This can be explained by noting that in line 14 the text shifts to a yin-yang perspective to say that "at the winter solstice the accumulating qi produces Earth." In five phase theory, winter is normally associated with phase water; here, however, the reference is to the yin-yang cosmogony of 3.I above. At the winter solstice, yin is at its maximum, and earth, in the dualistic analogy yin-yang/earth-heaven, is pure yin. This allows the pitch pipe Yellow Bell to have the correlates

yellow/yin/earth/winter,

instead of

yellow/balance/earth/midsummer,

as one normally would expect (as, for example, in the five phase correlates given in 4.XIV below).

Continuing with the numerology of three, the text here notes that there are two sets of six [2 × 3] pitch pipes, one female and one male set, for a total of twelve [4 × 3]. The twelve pitch pipes thus are correlated with the twelve months, as in 3.XXVII above. The statement in line 18 that "each of the twelve is based on three" refers to the method of generating the duodecatonic scale from a fundamental note. Both here and in the following section of text (3.XXIX), the "up-and-down" method is used, the fundamental being multiplied alternately by ⅔ and ⁴⁄₃, producing all of the notes from C to B (though not in that order) within a single octave. In 3.XXIX, the "number of Yellow Bell," i.e. 81, is taken as the fundamental, and rounding operations are performed to ensure that whole numbers result at every step. Here, quite a different procedure is used. The number of Yellow Bell is taken to be 1, and the rest of the notes in the series are expressed as fractions, each obtained by multiplying alternately by ⅔ and ⁴⁄₃.[48] The denominator of the fraction increases by one power of three at each step:

Yellow Bell = 1
Forest Bell = ⅔
Great Budding = ⁸⁄₉ [i.e. ⅔ × ⁴⁄₃]
Southern Regulator = ¹⁶⁄₂₇

* * *

Median Regulator = $\dfrac{131072}{177147}$

Thus the denominator of the fraction for the final operation in the series (prior to closing the scale one octave above the fundamental) is 3^{11}, or 177,147, the "Great

Number of the Yellow Bell." The ratios given here will, of course, yield an untempered chromatic scale regardless of what note is chosen as the fundamental.

The links among numerology, measures, cosmogony, and astronomy implied in this section are consistent with the rhapsodic description of the origin of music found in *Lüshi chunqiu* 5:

> That from whence music arose is in the far-distant past. It arose from measurement, and fundamentally from the Grand Monad (*taiyi*). The Grand Monad brought forth two instrumentalities (*yi*); the two instrumentalities produced yin and yang. Yin and yang underwent metamorphosis, one above and one below, and assumed forms.
>
> Chaotically drawing apart, they once again came together; coming together, they then drew apart. This is called the Heavenly Constant. The wheel of Heaven and Earth in the end reverts to the Original Ultimate, and then goes back again. There is nothing to which this process does not apply in equal measure.
>
> Of the sun, moon, stars, and planets, some hasten and some tarry. The sun and moon take unequal times to complete their orbital journeys. The four seasons arise in succession; some are hot, some are cold, some are of short days and some of long days, some are pliant, some are unyielding.
>
> With regard to the emergence of the myriad creatures, they are fashioned from the Grand Monad, transformed from yin and yang. Sprouts and shoots quicken, congeal, and assume form. . . .
>
> Music is that which ruler and minister, father and son, elder and younger desire and delight in. Desire is born from equanimity; equanimity is born from the Dao. The Dao: Looking, one does not see it; listening, one does not hear it; it cannot be given form. With knowledge, one cannot see it; even if one sees it, one cannot hear it; if one hears it, that still does not give it form. That which has form may be apprehended by knowledge. But the Dao is that which reaches the essence. One cannot give it shape, one cannot give it a name. If one insists, it may be called the Grand Monad. . . .

Having established some of these same themes in Section XXVIII, the *Huainanzi* text develops them further in the following three sections on mathematical harmonics and numerology.

Section XXIX: Harmonics of the Twelve Pitch Pipes

[3:21b:2]

1 There are twelve pitch pipes.
2 Yellow Bell makes the note *gong*.
3 Great Budding makes the note *shang*.
4 Maiden Purity makes the note *jue*.
5 Forest Bell makes the note *zhi*.

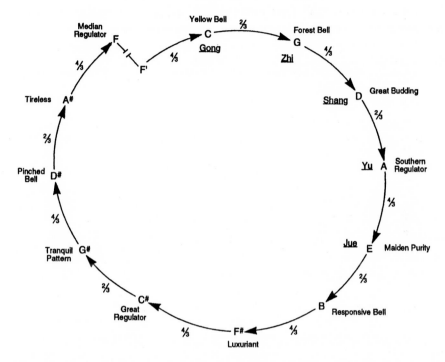

Figure 3.8. The pentatonic scale, and the generation of the chromatic scale (after Chen, "The Generation of Chromatic Scales in the Chinese Set-Bells of the 5th Century," p. 178).

6   Southern Regulator makes the note *yu*.

7   Matters are brought to completion by means of three;

8   Notes are established as (altogether) five.

9   3 + 5 = 8. Creatures born from eggs have eight bodily orifices.

10 This was the beginning of the pitch pipes.

11 (The ancients) recorded the sounds of the phoenix;

12 Therefore the notes are born from eight.

13 Yellow Bell makes the note *gong*; *gong* is the prince of the notes.

14 Thus Yellow Bell is established in *zi*; its number is 81, and it governs the eleventh month.

15 Descending, (Yellow Bell) produces Forest Bell.

16 The number of Forest Bell is 54 [81 × ⅔]; it governs the sixth month.

17 Ascending, Great Budding is produced.

18 Its number is 72 [54 × ⁴⁄₃]; it governs the first month.

19 Descending, Southern Regulator is produced.

20 Its number is 48 [72 × ⅔]; it governs the eighth month.

21 Ascending, Maiden Purity is produced.

22 Its number is 64 [48 × ⁴⁄₃]; it governs the third month.

23 Descending, Responsive Bell is produced.

24 Its number is 42 [≈ 64 × ⅔]; it governs the tenth month.

25 Ascending, Luxuriant is produced.

26 Its number is 57 [42 × ⁴⁄₃ + 1]; it governs the fifth month.

27 Ascending, Great Regulator is produced.

28 Its number is 76 [57 × ⁴⁄₃]; it governs the twelfth month.

29 Descending, Tranquil Pattern is produced.

30 Its number is 51 [≈ 76 × ⅔]; it governs the seventh month.

31 Ascending, Pinched Bell is produced.

32 Its number is 68 [51 × ⁴⁄₃]; it governs the second month.

33 Descending, Tireless is produced.

34 Its number is 45 [≈ 68 × ⅔]; it governs the ninth month.

35 Ascending, Median Regulator is produced.

36 Its number is 60 [45 × ⁴⁄₃]; it governs the fourth month.

37 (Beyond this) limit, nothing (further) is produced.
[3:22a:2] [3:24a:7]

38 Those pipes which descend are (created by multiplying the previous pipe's number) by ⅔.

39 Those pipes which ascend are (created by multiplying the previous pipe's number) by ⁴⁄₃.
[3:24a:7]

Commentary to Section XXIX

The section begins by making an explicit link between the notes of the pentatonic and duodecatonic scales, as follows:
Line 7 reiterates that the number three governs the generation of the duodecatonic notes (by means of the fractions ⅔ and ⁴⁄₃); line 8 states that there are five notes in the (pentatonic scale). The total thus is eight. Lines 9–12 repeat the common observation (as in 4.XI.1–2 and 10 below) that animals that have eight bodily orifices and are born from eggs are typified by birds, and link this observation to the myth that the musical notes entered the realm of human experience when ancient sages listened to the songs of phoenixes.

The remainder of this section is devoted to explaining the generation of the duo-decatonic notes by the "up-and-down" rule, which (as noted above) is a variant of the "ascending fifths" method, designed to keep all of the notes within the same octave. It is interesting to note that in this section the "numbers" of the duodecatonic notes are in every case rounded off to whole numbers, in place of the increasingly complex fractions yielded by the generation of the true chromatic scale. Clearly, for numerological purposes a number of 76 for Great Regulator is more meaningful, not to say more convenient, than the true figure of 2048/27. It also seems likely that such whole-number figures would have been used by metal founders in weighing out the amount of bronze, and calculating the size of molds, for the casting of bells, the fine-tuning of which would have been accomplished according to traditional specialized knowledge (of the sort "you need to add a little extra metal in casting this bell" or "you will need to file off some material from this bell after it has been cast").

Line 37 explicitly recognizes that the "up-and-down" method for generating the notes of the duodecatonic scale stops with the twelfth step (at F). From there, one must break symmetry in order to complete the octave, multiplying by ⅓ again instead of the expected ⅔. Because of the rounding operation applied at several steps along the way, the fundamental will not be produced in any case: ⅓ × 60 = 80, one short of the fundamental of 81.

Lines 38–39, which specify the "up-and-down" rule, have been moved from 3:24a below, where they are clearly out of place, to the end of this section, where they seem to belong.

There is a very extensive literature on mathematical harmonics in ancient China, for which the most convenient source is Joseph Needham's review of the field in *Science and Civilisation in China*.[49] For this section of *Huainanzi* 3, the best and most directly relevant work is that of Cheng-Yih Chen.[50] Chen compares the ancient Chinese chromatic scale as directly observed from studies of a set of bells from the tomb of Marquis Yi of Zeng (dated 433 B.C.E.) to the "Zhou method" of deriving the chromatic scale by means of mathematical ratios as found in the sixth chapter of *Lüshi chunqiu*, a text similar (and probably ancestral) to the present section. The highly technical analyses in Chen's article are too complex to summarize here but are drawn to the attention of the interested reader.

Section XXX: The Notes and the Seasons

[3:22a:2]

1   *Gong* produces *zhi*; *zhi* produces *shang*; *shang* produces *yu*; *yu* produces *jue*.
2   *Jue* produces Maiden Purity.
3   Maiden Purity produces Responsive Bell.
4   Responsive Bell is comparable to the fundamental note [i.e., Yellow Bell], and this produces harmony.
5   Responsive Bell produces Luxuriant.
6   Luxuriant is not comparable to the fundamental note, and thus produces discord.

7   At the winter solstice, the note is like Forest Bell immersed in turbidity.

8   At the summer solstice, the note is like Yellow Bell immersed in clarity.

9   The twelve pitch pipes respond to the changes of the twenty-four seasonal nodes.

10 At *jiazi*, Median Regulator moves to *zhi*.

11 At *bingzi*, Pinched Bell moves to *yu*.

12 At *wuzi*, Yellow Bell moves to *gong*.

13 At *gengzi*, Tireless moves to *shang*.

14 At *renzi*, Tranquil Pattern moves to *jue*.

[3:22b:11]

Commentary to Section XXX

The first line of this section gives the pentatonic notes in the "production order" as correlated with the five phases; this order appears again in 4.XIV.17 in the context of other five phase transformations. The effect is to produce a simple melody, that is, C-G-D-A-E.

The text next observes that *jue*, the last note (E) of this sequence, is identical to the tone Maiden Purity in the duodecatonic scale. Maiden Purity produces (by being multiplied by ⅔) Responsive Bell (B). Responsive Bell (times ⅘) produces Luxuriant. It is not clear, however, what is meant by the statement that Responsive Bell is comparable to the fundamental, and thus produces harmony, while Luxuriant is not comparable to the fundamental, and thus produces discord. It would appear that something more must be intended here than a statement about musical aesthetics (e.g., that C and B make a musically pleasing pair, while C and F# do not), but I am unsure what that something might be. Nor do the statements in lines 7–8 yield any readily comprehensible meaning; they appear to say something about the intervals C-G and F#-C, but the statement that F# is like C "immersed in clarity" would seem to contradict the earlier statement that those two notes produce discord.

On the other hand, the meaning of lines 9–14 is quite clear. The pentatonic notes are said to respond to the changes of the twenty-four seasonal nodes; the mechanism of their doing so is related to the five seventy-two–day "seasons" (as in 3.XXII above) designated by the cyclical characters *jiazi, bingzi*, etc. These lines demonstrate a recognition that any note (not just *gong*/Yellow Bell) can serve as the fundamental. As stated in 3.XXXI.36 below, "one pitch pipe produces five notes; twelve pitch pipes produce sixty notes." Here, for example, at *jiazi* Median Regulator moves to *zhi*, that is, F moves to G. G becomes the fundamental, from which a duodecatonic scale can be produced by the standard "up-and-down" method. Similar shifts yield a total of five (pentatonic) fundamentals, for a total of sixty notes. As Chen observes, citing 3.XXXI.36, the "early Chinese musicians were quite familiar with the . . . principle, according to which each note of a scale can in turn act as the fundamental."[51]

Section XXXI: The Numerology of Weights and Measures

[3:22b:11]

1   Anciently, weights and measures were created; lightness and heaviness were born from the Dao of Heaven.

2   The length of the Yellow Bell pitch pipe is nine inches.

3   All things are produced by (virtue of) three. [3 × 3 = 9.]

4   3 × 9 = 27. Thus the width of a standard bolt of cloth is two feet, seven inches [i.e., 2.7 *chi*].

5   There are shapes; thus there are also (musical) sounds.

6   The musical notes are mutually produced by (means of) the number eight.

7   Thus the length of a man's arm measures four feet.

8   A fathom is double (this length); thus eight feet make one fathom (*xun*).

9   A fathom is the height of an average man.

10 The number of the notes is five.

11 Using five to calculate in terms of eight, 5 × 8 = 40.

12 Thus four *zhang* [one *zhang* = ten feet] makes one *pi* [= 40 feet].

13 One *pi* is the measure of [i.e., the length of a bolt of silk produced by] a person of middling (skill.)

14 Therefore, one *pi* is used as (the unit in the cloth tax) administration.

15 At the autumn equinox, the beards of grain-husks are fully grown.

16 When the beards of the husks are fully grown, the grain ripens.

17 The number of the pitch pipes is twelve.

18 Thus (the width of) twelve husk-beards (laid side-by-side) equals one *su*. Twelve *su* make one inch.

19 The pitch pipes correspond to the chronograms.

20 The (pentatonic) notes correspond to the sun.

21 The number of the sun is ten.

22 Thus ten inches make one foot; ten feet make one *zhang*.

23 In terms of those units used to measure weight,

24 Twelve millet-grains make one *fen*.

25 Twelve *fen* make one *shu*.

26 Twelve *shu* make one half-ounce (*ban liang*).

27 The balance-beam has a left side and a right side.

28 Therefore, doubling the weight, twenty-four *shu* make one ounce.

29 Heaven has four seasons, completing one year.

30 Therefore, reckoning by fours, 4 × 4 = 16.

31 Therefore sixteen ounces make one catty (*jin*).

32 Three months make a season, and thirty days a month.

33 Therefore thirty catties make one *jun*.

34 Four seasons make one year,

35 Therefore four *jun* make one *shi*.

36 In terms of (units of) musical measurement:
37 One pitch pipe produces five tones; twelve pitch pipes produce sixty tones.
38 Therefore, reckoning by sixes, 6 × 6 = 36.
39 Therefore, 360 tones correspond to the days of one year.
40 Thus the number of (notes of) the pitch pipes and (days of) the calendar are in accord with the Dao of Heaven and Earth.
    [3:24a:7]

Commentary to Section XXXI

This passage moves from the rather technical mathematical harmonics of the immediately preceding sections to a set of assertions that weights and measures are derived from the numbers associated with the musical tones. The reasoning here is not mathematical but numerological, on the overall principle that "there are shapes; thus there are also (musical) sounds." The various arithmetical operations described here make no sense in terms of mathematical harmonics, but they make perfect sense as ingenious number-magic explanations (*post facto*) of the way things are, in this case, weights and measures. Similar numerological demonstrations are to be found below in 3.XLI.11–17 (microcosm/macrocosm) and 4.X in its entirety (gestation periods).

This type of numerology may seem, from a modern perspective, both mathematically trivial and antiscientifically superstitious. It is not insignificant philosophically, however; in its own terms, it constitutes a demonstration of the seamless unity of the cosmos and of the cosmological system employed to explain it. This is an important point in terms of the Huang-Lao political doctrine that underlies this treatise on astronomy and related subjects. The message to the royal reader of these pages is that nothing in the natural world is accidental; so too, therefore, must the ruler's every action conform to the patterns of the cosmic order.

The various assertions in this section, though surely wrong in terms of what they seek to explain (it is impossible to believe, for example, that a Chinese inch was derived from the width of the tips of twelve grain husk beards laid side-by-side), are clear enough in what they say, and need no particular explanation.

Section XXXII: The Twelve-Year Jovian Cycle

[3:24a:8]
1 The beginning of the Jovian Cycle is established in *jiayin*.
2 After one completion it (begins again), established in *jiaxu*.
3 After two completions, it (begins again) established in *jiawu*.
4 After three completions, it returns to its beginning in *jiayin*.
5 The year's annual shift is one chronogram.

6   After the (seasonal node) Beginning of Spring, it attains its (proper annual) location and shifts its position (away from the previous one).

7   It moves forward three places, and back five.

8   Thus all matters may be taken in hand.

9   Where *taiyin* is established, insects head for their burrows and stay quietly (therein); magpies nest in the countryside and make their homes.

10   (When) *taiyin* is in *yin*,

11   The Vermilion Bird is in *mao*,

12   The Angular Arranger is in *zi*,

13   The Dark Warrior is in *xu*,

14   The White Tiger is in *you*,

15   The Azure Dragon is in *chen*.

16   If *yin* is the establishing chronogram, then

17   *Mao* is Removal,

18   *Chen* is Fullness,

19   *Si* is Evenness, governing birth;

20   *Wu* is Fixedness,

21   *Wei* is Holding Firm, governing pitfalls;

22   *Shen* is Breaking, governing the balance-beam;

23   *You* is Danger, governing the ladle;

24   *Xu* is Completion, governing minor accretion;

25   *Hai* is Receiving, governing great accretion;

26   *Zi* is Opening, governing *taisui*;

27   *Chou* is Closing, governing *taiyin*.

[3:24b:6]

Commentary to Section XXXII

This section again relates to the use of the cosmograph, and gives a set of rules for reading astrological indications from the heaven plate juxtaposed with the earth plate on the basis of the position of *taiyin* counter-Jupiter. The section integrates two cycles: the twelve-year Jovian Cycle, and the sixty-year cycle of the Heavenly Stems and Earthly Branches.

The first rule is that *taiyin* shifts (on average, in the sky; but exactly, on the cosmograph) one chronogram (an Earthly Branch-denominated arc of 30° or ¹⁄₁₂ of the celestial circle) per year. A series of Jovian Cycles is said to begin properly in the seasonal node Beginning of Spring, corresponding to a year denoted by the sexagenary number *jiayin* (#51). The next cycle commences in *jiawu* (#31), the next one in *jiaxu* (#11); thus skipping by twenties, the cycle returns to *jiayin* after the third completion. The rule that "it moves forward three places, and back five" means that moving from *jiaxu* to *jiawu*, for example, comprises three cycles of the Heavenly Stems (i.e., *jia*

119

moves forward three places), while moving from *xu* to *wu* involves counting back five places in the list of Earthly Branches.

The general astrological rule given in line 9 is that where *taiyin* (here taken literally as "Great Yin") is located, yin is at its maximum, and the omens therefore are those of winter and quiescense. Compare, for example, the twelfth-month omen in 5.XII.13: "Magpies add to their nests." In this instance, an omen for the twelve months of the solar year is being transferred to the twelve-year Jupiter cycle for astrological purposes.

Lines 10–15 give rules for locating the directional gods (conceived of as asterisms) with respect to *taiyin*, an operation performed by moving the heaven plate of the cosmograph to the proper chronogram. The five are distributed unevenly among the twelve Earthly Branches:

1. *zi*	2. *chou*	3. *yin*	4. *mao*	5. *chen*	6. *si*
Angular Arranger		*taiyin*	Vermilion Bird	Bluegreen Dragon	
(-2)		(index)	(+1)	(+2)	
7. *wu*	8. *wei*	9. *shen*	10. *you*	11. *xu*	12. *hai*
			White Tiger	Dark Warrior	
			(-5)	(-4)	

A similar rule is repeated in 3.XXXIV.14–19 below, but with the locations being specified in terms of places ahead of or behind the position of *taiyin*, rather than by named chronograms. The place-values found in that section are different from those implied here (as noted by numbers in parentheses in the table above). Angular Arranger is associated with the center, being an asterism located in the central Purple Palace of circumpolar stars (3.XXXIV.19: "the Empty Star carries the Angular Arranger"); therefore it is not involved in calculations of the four seasons of the solar year. Here, however, the correlation is to a cycle of five (the five twelve-year Jovian Cycles in a sixty-year sexagenary cycle), and thus five "directional" asterisms are required.

The remaining lines of this section give a simple series of astrological "tags" for each of the twelve chronograms; the one in which *taiyin* is located is considered the "establishing chronogram." Presumably these astrological indications operate in a standard series, so that one could infer, for example, that if *wu* were the establishing chronogram, then *wei* would be Removal, *shen* Fullness, and so on.[52]

Section XXXIII: The Names of the Twelve Years of the Jovian Cycle

[3:24b:6]

1 When *taiyin* is in *yin*, the year is called *Shetige*.
2 The mate of *taiyin* is Jupiter.

3   It dwells in the (Lunar Lodges) Dipper and Ox-Leader.

4   In the eleventh month, it rises with them in the east at dawn.

5   (The Lodges) Eastern Well and Spirit-Bearer are opposite [i.e., setting in the west at dawn].

6   When *taiyin* is in *mao*, the year is called *Ming'e*.

7   Jupiter dwells in Serving-Maid, Emptiness, and Rooftop.

8   In the twelfth month it rises with them in the east at dawn.

9   Willow, Seven Stars, and Extension are opposite.

10   When *taiyin* is in *chen*, the year is called *Zhixu*.

11   Jupiter dwells in Encampment and Eastern Wall.

12   In the first month it rises with them in the east at dawn.

13   Wings and Chariot-Platform are opposite.

14   When *taiyin* dwells in *si*, the year is called *Dahuangluo*.

15   Jupiter dwells in Stride and Bond.

16   In the second month it rises with them in the east at dawn.

17   Horn and Neck are opposite.

18   When *taiyin* is in *wu*, the year is called *Dunzang*.

19   Jupiter dwells in Stomach, Pliades, and Net.

20   In the third month it rises with them in the east at dawn.

21   Root, Room, and Heart are opposite.

22   When *taiyin* is in *wei*, the year is called *Xiexia*.

23   Jupiter dwells in Turtle-Beak and Alignment.

24   In the fourth month it rises with them in the east at dawn.

25   Tail and Winnowing-Basket are opposite.

26   When *taiyin* is in *shen*, the year is called *Tuntan*.

27   Jupiter dwells in Eastern Well and Spirit-Bearer.

28   In the fifth month it rises with them in the east at dawn.

29   Dipper and Ox-Leader are opposite.

30   When *taiyin* is in *you*, the year is called *Zuo'o*.

31   Jupiter dwells in Willow, Seven Stars, and Extension.

32   In the sixth month it rises with them in the east at dawn.

33   Serving-Maid, Emptiness, and Rooftop are opposite.

34   When *taiyin* is in *xu*, the year is called *Yanmao*.

35   Jupiter dwells in Wings and Chariot-Platform.

36   In the seventh month it rises with them in the east at dawn.

37   Encampment and Eastern Wall are opposite.

38   When *taiyin* is in *hai*, the year is called *Dayuanxian*.

39   Jupiter dwells in Horn and Neck.

40   In the eighth month it rises with them in the east at dawn.

41   Stride and Bond are opposite.

42   When *taiyin* is in *zi*, the year is called *Kundun*.

43   Jupiter dwells in Root, Room, and Heart.

44   In the ninth month it rises with them in the east at dawn.
45   Stomach, Pliades, and Net are opposite.
46   When *taiyin* is in *chou*, the year is called *Chifenruo*.
47   Jupiter dwells in Tail and Winnowing-Basket.
48   In the tenth month it rises with them in the east at dawn.
49   Turtle-Beak and Alignment are opposite.
      [3:26a:11]

Commentary to Section XXXIII

It is obvious that the names of the years of the Jovian Cycle as given in this section (and in several other contemporary Chinese sources) are in a language that is not Chinese. A number of early scholars (both westerners and Chinese, the most prominent among the latter being Wen Yiduo) proposed theories to account for their origins,[53] but none of those theories is satisfactory. This is truly a neglected problem in Sinology; so far as I know, no one has been willing to tackle it in recent decades—perhaps because it is so intractable, involving as it does enormous problems in paleolinguistics. I have nothing to add to the solution of this mystery. It is, nevertheless, worth pointing out that these names imply sustained and serious intellectual contact between China and a non-Chinese culture (possibly India), a contact sufficiently strong to add some non-Chinese words to the Chinese astronomical vocabulary. What this signifies depends on the sort of guess one makes about the non-Chinese culture in question; the year names might come from a language spoken as nearby as the Huai/Yangtse region (i.e., within the state of Chu in late Warring States times) or as far afield as Southeast Asia, Central Asia, or India. See also 3.XLI below.

Other early sources (but not *Huainanzi*) also give a set of twelve "station names" (*ci*) for the years of the Jovian Cycle; these are equally fantastical and difficult to interpret.[54]

The Jovian Years are defined in terms of the location of *taiyin* among the lunar lodges inscribed on the cosmograph, so as to make astrological predictions about the year in question. It is obvious that the reference here is to the cosmograph rather than to the sky itself, because of the implication that the lodges are of equal angular extension and are distributed evenly around the celestial circle, as in Fig 3.9.

This assumption of equal angular extension of the twenty-eight lunar lodges bears no resemblance to reality; in fact, the lodges vary in angular extension from approximately 4° to 30°, as shown in the standard list of the lodges given in 3.XXXV.18 below. This shows that the cosmograph (as distinct from the "lodge dial" discussed in the commentary to 3.XXXV) was an abstraction and idealization of the observable universe, and thus suitable more for astrological than for astronomical purposes.

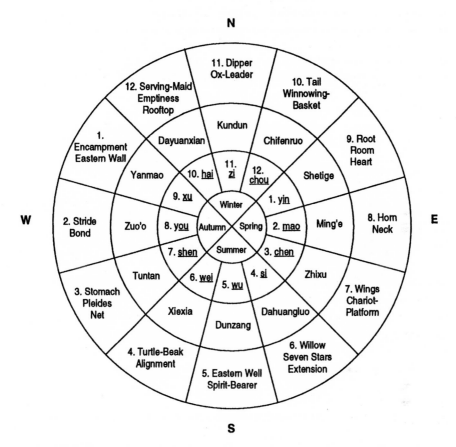

Figure 3.9. Diagram of the twelve chronograms, the twelve Jovian Years, and their associated lunar lodges.

Section XXXIV: Astrological Meaning of the Sixty-Year Jupiter Cycle

[3:26a:11]

1 When *taiyin* is in *jiazi* [#1], recision and accretion are harmoniously together in the Eastern (Celestial) Palace.

2 Invariably, the place toward which it [*taiyin*?] moves cannot obtain victory.

3 They are together for four years and then part.

4 They remain parted for sixteen years and then come together again.

5 As for the reason why they part,

6 Recision cannot enter the Central Palace, but moves into Wood.

7 The place where *taiyin* dwells is called accretion.

8 The chronograms govern accretion and recision.

9 The unyielding days being doubled, then there are the pliant days.

10 The place toward which it [*taiyin?*] goes is unable to overcome (the influence of) recision.

11 The chronograms (associated with) water move to wood.

12 The chronograms (associated with) wood move to water.

13 Metal and fire stay in their (designated) places.

14 Generally, (*taiyin*) moves through the directional gods (as follows):

15 The Vermilion Bird is one place ahead of *taiyin*.

16 The Angular Arranger is three places behind.

17 The Dark Warrior is five places ahead.

18 The White Tiger is six places behind.

19 The Empty Star carries the Angular Arranger, and Heaven and Earth follow in accord with this.

20 Of the Heavenly Stems, *jia*, is unyielding, *yi* is pliant, *bing* is unyielding, *ding* is pliant, and so on to *gui*.

21 Wood is born in *hai*, matures in *mao*, and dies in *wei*. These three chronograms together are wood.

22 Fire is born in *yin*, matures in *wu*, and dies in *xu*. These three chronograms together are fire.

23 Earth is born in *wu*, matures in *xu*, and dies in *yin*. These three chronograms together are earth.

24 Metal is born in *si*, matures in *yu*, and dies in *chou*. These three chronograms together are metal.

25 Water is born in *shen*, matures in *zi*, and dies in *chen*. These three chronograms together are water.

26 Thus there are five overcomings.

27 Birth occurs in step one, maturity in step five, and death in step nine [in any sequence of the Earthly Branches].

28 5 × 9 = 45. Thus the (directional) gods shift one place every forty-five days.

29 Taking three and responding with five, there are thus eight (such) shifts, and the year comes to an end.

30 In using *taiyin* (for prognostication), as a rule whatever is to its left, that is, ahead of it, suffers cutting-away; whatever is to its right, that is, behind it, obtains increase.

31 As to the chronogram suspended in the balance-beam of the Angular Arranger,

32 If there is war, it certainly will be victorious;

33 If there is an assault, it must succeed.
    [3:27a:4]

Commentary to Section XXXIV

The early lines of this section contain many obscurities, and the whole section has suffered substantial textual damage; some parts are quite garbled. The whole passage is open to varying interpretations. See, for example, the quite different punctuation (and textual emendations) in the *Shijie shuju* edition of the *Huainanzi*. Lines 5–11 seem particularly damaged, with sentences that are hardly more than fragments of whatever might have been there originally. Nevertheless the overall import of this section is clear enough; it has to do with day prognostications based on the movements of *taiyin* (counter-Jupiter) through the celestial circle as represented by the cosmograph or some analogous instrument, with the stem-branch designation of days being the controlling factor. Yang (odd-numbered) days are subject to the power of accretion (*dé*); yin (even-numbered) days to the power of recision (*xing*). This passage apparently belongs to what has become known as the "Yin-yang Militarist" school of philosophy, which specialized in calculating lucky or unlucky days for warfare on the basis of the positions of heavenly bodies.

What appears to be going on in the early lines of this section is the reconciliation of a number of calendrical periods, which can be visualized as a series of concentric circles (rather like those on a geomancer's compass), marked out with, successively, four, eight, five (each divided in two, for a total of ten), twelve, and sixty spaces (the last being subdivided into three groups of twenty).

Prognostications are based on correlations of movement through

1. the four seasons/directions (the first two of which, spring and summer, are yang and under the influence of accretion, the second two of which are yin and under the influence of recision);
2. eight shifts of the (directional) gods; these perhaps are connected to the eight "wind-seasons" of 3.XII above.
3. the ten days of the Heavenly Stems, which are either "unyielding" (yang) or "pliant" (yin);
4. the twelve chronograms, which for the solar year correspond to the twelve months, and for the Jovian Year to one solar year apiece;
5. five twelve-solar-year Jovian Cycles;
6. one *ganzhi* sixty-year cycle (encompassing the five Jovian Cycles), which is divided into three twenty-year periods (each of which thus moves through four of the twelve chronograms).

In general, this section continues the theme of the previous one, that is, rules for reconciling five twelve-year Jovian Cycles with the sixty-year sexagenary cycle. As the pointer of the Dipper revolves through the chronograms to mark the Jovian Year, other asterisms associated with it shift their places as well. This is the meaning of lines 14–19, which, as we have seen, give rules for locating the directional asterisms similar to those found in 3.XXXII.10–15 above.

Lines 3 and 4: Apparently this passage refers to asterisms governing accretion and recision, which move through five-fifths of a celestial circle over a twenty-year period; they are together for four years in the same fifth-of-a-circle (72°) arc, then apart for sixteen years. They then come together again.[55] This must occur three times during one sexagenary year cycle. But the general idea reflects that of Section XXXIX below, where the "male and female deities of the Northern Dipper" [= Jupiter and counter-Jupiter] move in opposite directions around the celestial circle, meeting in the eleventh and fifth months. The rules that govern why "recision cannot enter the Central Palace," and for associating the chronograms with the five phases and sorting the Heavenly Stems into categories of "pliant" and "unyielding," remain unclear. Presumably obdurateness is a yang characteristic, pliancy a yin one. The rules given in lines 21–27 for the "five overcomings," that is, the birth, maturity, and death of each of the five phases, are similar to those found in 4.XIV.6–10 below. These relationships are shown in Fig. 3.10, a diagram that appears in the *Huainanzi* text (on p. 3:31a) and is reproduced with Section LXII below.

The eight 45-day periods described in lines 28–29 are said by Qian Tang[56] to represent eight "palaces" correlated with the eight winds of the 360-day year. Each 45-day "wind-season" would, of course, encompass three seasonal nodes. In terms of the sexagenary cycle, the effect of these periods would be to divide the 60-day sexagenary cycle into eight (actually 2 × 4) periods, which would begin with *jiazi* (#1) at the winter solstice and continue with periods beginning on *jiyou* (#46), *jiawu* (#31), and *jimao* (#16), before recommencing with *jiazi* at the summer solstice. Presumably, then, a diviner using the complex cycles described in this section would also have to take account of the auspices associated with the wind season, the seasonal node, and the sexagenary day cycle. All of this is complicated further by the fact that some of the indications described in this section seem to refer to daily shifts in the direction of the Dipper (modeled by turning the cosmograph's heaven plate with respect to the earth plate) in the course of the solar year, and some to a sixty-year cycle involving five Jovian Years.

Whatever the exact meaning of all of these astrological operations with the cosmograph, the intent is clearly to predict military success or failure for states on the basis of the position of *taiyin*. This is made clear in line 30, which repeats the conventional principle (seen already in 3.XIX.9 above) that whatever state is to the left of *taiyin* suffers danger or defeat, and whatever state is to the right of it will gain victory. The final lines of this section give an additional principle, that whatever state is indicated (again, on the cosmograph) by the position of the Angular Arranger will be successful in both offensive and defensive warfare.

The Treatise on the Patterns of Heaven

Section XXXV: The Lunar Lodges

[3:27a:4]

1   If one wishes to know the Dao of Heaven, one takes the sun as the ruling factor.
2   In the sixth month, it matches the center.
3   Rotating leftwards, it moves, dividing (the celestial circle) and making the twelve months.
4   When they accord with (the movements of) the sun, Heaven and Earth are doubly in accord.
5   Thereafter, there can be no calamitous asterisms.
6   The first month is established in Encampment.
7   The second month is established in Stride and Bond.
8   The third month is established in Stomach.
9   The fourth month is established in Net.
10 The fifth month is established in Eastern Well.
11 The sixth month is established in Extension.
12 The seventh month is established in Wings.
13 The eighth month is established in Neck.
14 The ninth month is established in Room.
15 The tenth month is established in Tail.
16 The eleventh month is established in Ox-Leader.
17 The twelfth month is established in Emptiness.
18 The angular extensions of (the stars in the Lunar Lodges are as follows):

Horn:	12^d	Serving-Maid:	12^d	Net:	16^d
Neck:	9^d	Emptiness:	10^d	Turtle-Beak:	2^d
Root:	15^d	Rooftop:	17^d	Alignment:	9^d
Room:	5^d	Encampment:	16^d	Eastern Well:	30^d
Heart:	5^d	Eastern Wall:	9^d	Spirit-Bearer:	4^d
Tail:	18^d	Stride:	16^d	Willow:	15^d
Winnowing-Basket:	11.25^d	Bond:	12^d	(Seven) Stars:	7^d
Dipper:	26^d	Stomach:	14^d	Extension:	18^d
Ox-Leader:	8^d	Pliades:	11^d	Wings:	18^d
				Chariot-Platform:	17^d

19 The stars [= Lunar Lodges] are apportioned to territories, namely:

Horn and Neck to Zheng
Root, Room and Heart to Song
Tail and Winnowing-Basket to Yan
Dipper and Ox-Leader to Yue
Serving-Maid to Wu
Emptiness and Rooftop to Qi
Encampment and Eastern Wall to Wei[b]
Stride and Root to Lu

Stomach, Pliades and Net to Wei[a]
Turtle-Beak and Alignment to Zhao
Eastern Well and Spirit-Bearer to Qin
Willow, Seven Stars, and Extension to Zhou
Wings and Chariot-Platform to Chu.

20 When Jupiter dwells (in a lodge corresponding to a state, in that state) the five grains will be bountiful.

21 (The situation of the state corresponding to the lodge) opposite will be the reverse; the harvest will suffer calamity.

22 If Jupiter should dwell (in a lodge) and does not dwell there,

23 If it leaps and enters another place,

24 The ruler of the country (governed by that lodge) will die and his state will be extinguished.

[3:28a:2]

Commentary to Section XXXV

The first five lines of this section are introductory to what follows; they simply repeat standard rhetoric (aimed at the ruler who is the presumed audience for this treatise) about the harmonious consequences of the calendar (or the cosmograph) keeping synchronicity with the actual heavenly bodies.

Lines 6–17 give lunar lodges that begin each month, dealing now with the actual angular extensions of the lodges rather than their equal spacing as on the cosmograph. There was in fact a device to demonstrate these angular extensions; its original name is unknown, and it is now known by the descriptive name "lodge dial."[57] The lunar lodge extensions given here have been standard since around the time the *Huainanzi* was written; they are ascribed to the fourth century B.C.E. astronomer Shi Shen, though it is doubtful whether they are as old as that. The extensions given on the two lodge dials known from the beginning of the Former Han are different from these, and represent the so-called "old system" recorded in an appendix to the Shi Shen material quoted in the Tang *Kaiyuan zhanjing*.[58]

Likewise the territorial apportionments of the lunar lodges given here are fairly standard, though lists in other texts vary somewhat. Wang Yinzhi notes that most texts say "Dipper, Ox-Leader, and Serving-Maid to Wu and Yue," thus treating the territories of those two states as a single unit; perhaps the "southern orientation" of *Huainanzi* leads to greater discrimination in that respect. Jin is not in the *Huainanzi* list; most other texts eliminate Zhao. This affects the allotments of Lu and Wei[a].[59] As shown by the prognostication rules given in lines 20–24, all of the attention given here to the description and apportionment of the lunar lodges is for the purposes of the "Yin-yang Militarist" School, to indicate good or bad military fortune for the several states.

Section XXXVI: Seasonal Indications of Taiyin

[3:28a:2]

1　When *taiyin* controls the ordinances of spring, (the ruler) should act (in a way that is) pliant, kind, mild, and good.

2　When *taiyin* controls the ordinances of summer, (the ruler) should publish, bestow, proclaim, and make clear.

3　When *taiyin* controls the ordinances of autumn, (the ruler) should repair, put in order, and make ready his troops.

4　When *taiyin* controls the ordinances of winter, (the ruler) should be fiercely brave and resolute, and harden the frontier defences.

5　Every three years the season (governed by *taiyin*) shifts;

6　In a six year period there are changes from what is normal.

7　Thus within three years, there is a year of famine;

8　Within six years, there is a year of epidemic.

9　Twelve years brings a repose.

[3:28a:8]

Commentary to Section XXXVI

The seasonal ordinances referred to in lines 1–4 are standard; see the "Treatise on the Seasonal Rules" in its entirety, and more particularly 5.XIII, which gives a brief summary of the seasonal rules. Here, however, the reference is not to the ordinances of the four seasons of the solar year, but to the twelve (4 × 3) years of the Jovian Cycle. The reasoning is that each month of the solar year is correlated with one of the twelve chronograms, and has ordinances appropriate to it; the monthly ordinances can be grouped into four sets of seasonal ordinances, because the seasons are correlated with four of the five phases (spring = wood, summer = fire, autumn = metal, winter = water). Here those ordinances are transferred, in effect, to the chronograms themselves, disassociating them from the months of the solar year and transferring them to the years of the Jovian Cycle. Thus the ordinances of each month of the solar year become ordinances of the chronograms (= twelfths of a Jovian Year) as indicated by the position of *taiyin*. Three solar years thus become a Jovian "season"; each Jovian "season" has ordinances identical to those of a solar-year season. Thus, as line 5 says, the Jovian "season" shifts every three years.

Lines 6–9 are rather similar to a longer and more detailed passage from the *Jinizi*:

When *taiyin* is in phase metal for the first three years, there will be plentiful harvests. When it is in phase water, there will be damage to crops for the next three years. When it is in phase wood for the next three years, there will be prosperity. When it is in phase fire for the next three years, there will be drought.[60]

129

This clarifies the laconic (and textually damaged) text of *Huainanzi* here; the general sense of the *Jinizi* passage is that agricultural prosperity or dearth is governed by the Jovian "seasons," but that neither good harvests nor poor ones can be expected to last for more than three years at a time.

The text here is not as mechanical in its predictions as the *Jinizi* text, however. It allows the diviner more scope for natural annual variability in climate, and merely specifies that one should expect famine in one year out of three, and an epidemic in one year out of six. In *Huainanzi* 9:18a, the ruler is advised to set aside stores of famine-relief grain equal to one year's harvest out of three, which seems to respond to the prediction made here.

Section XXXVII: Stem-Branch Correlations

[3:28b:3]

1   (The territorial allotments of the celestial stems are as follows:)

jia with Qi	*ji* with Han
yi with Eastern Yi	*keng* with Qin
bing with Chu	*xin* with Western Yi
ding with Southern Yi	*ren* with Wei[b]
wu with Wei[a]	*gui* with Yue

2   (The territorial allotments of the earthly branches are as follows:)

zi with Zhou	*wu* with Qin
chou with Di	*wei* with Song
yin with Chu	*shen* with Qi
mao with Zheng	*you* with Lu
chen with Jin	*xu* with Zhao
si with Wei[b]	*hai* with Yan

3   (The stem and branch correlations of the five phases are as follows:)

(stems)	(branches)	(phases)
jia and *yi*	*yin* and *mao*	Wood
bing and *ding*	*si* and *wu*	Fire
wu and *chi*	the four seasons	Earth
geng and *xin*	*shen* and *you*	Metal
ren and *gui*	*hai* and *zi*	Water

[3:28b:7]

Using cosmology understood & literate at the time – political social...

Commentary to Section XXXVII

The correlations given here are all standard. Note that the only states that are correlated with both a Heavenly Stem and an Earthly Branch are Qi, Chu, Qin, and Wei[b]; this may be a measure of their perceived political importance at the end of the Warring States period, the time to which this set of correlates probably refers.

In the list of five phase correlations of the stems and branches, the branches called "the four seasons" are *chou, chen, wei,* and *xu*; they occupy the directions NE, SE, SW, and NW respectively, and thus usher in the four seasons of the year. (This grouping of course also provides a convenient means for correlating twelve branches with five phases.) The four seasons collectively are correlated with the center; see 3.III.6, "The four seasons are the officers of heaven," and 3.VI.16–18, "The Center is Earth. Its god is the Yellow Thearch. . . . He grasps the marking-cord and governs the four quarters."

All of these correlations serve the same purpose; they allow auspices derived from manipulations of the cosmograph to be assigned to the proper state (or, in the Han, territory of a former state) in order to make predictions about political and military affairs.

Section XXXVIII: Relations of the Five Phases

[3:28b:7]

1   Water produces wood, wood produces fire, fire produces earth, earth produces   *– how?*
    metal, metal produces water.
2   If the child gives birth to the mother, this is called righteousness.
3   If the mother gives birth to the child, this is called fostering.
4   If the mother and child mutually produce each other, this is called singleness of purpose.
5   If the mother vanquishes the child, this is called control.
6   If the child vanquishes the mother, this is called obstruction.
7   If one employs victory to smite and kill, the victory will be without recompense.
8   If one employs singleness of purpose to pursue affairs, there will be achievement.
9   If one employs righteousness to carry out fixed principles, one's fame will be
    established and it will not diminish.
10 If one employs fostering to nurture the myriad creatures, there will be luxuriant
    growth and prosperity.
11 If one employs obstruction to pursue affairs, there will be destruction, extermination,
    death, and extinction (of the state).
    [3:29a:1]

Commentary to Section XXXVIII

This passage has been analyzed illuminatingly by Derk Bodde[61] who regards it as an example of the ancient Chinese "moralistic view of nature"—rightly enough, because

131

the import of this section is rhetorical rather than cosmological, and has little to do with the cycles of the five phases as such. The rhetorical device consists of first listing the common "generation" cycle of the phases, then looking at variant forms of phase interactions (progenitor begetting offspring, offspring begetting progenitor, progenitor and offspring mutually bringing each other into existence, and so on) and finally assigning a moral quality to each of them. The text expands on the consequences for the ruler of behaving according to each of those moral qualities. Overall this section is more closely similar in tone and argumentation to *Huainanzi* 9, "The Art of Ruler-ship," than to the rest of *Huainanzi* 3. See for example *Huainanzi* 9:10b, "The Way of the ruler is to cultivate his person by dwelling in quietude and to lead his subjects with frugality and moderation. If he is quiet, his subjects are not disturbed; if he is frugal, his people will have no cause to complain."[62]

Section XXXIX: The Gods of the Northern Dipper

[3:29a:2]

1 The gods of the Northern Dipper are both female and male.
2 In the eleventh month, at the beginning (of the year), they are established (together) in *zi*.
3 Every month they shift by one chronogram.
4 The male goes leftwards, the female rightwards.
5 In the fifth month they coincide in *wu*, and devise recision.
6 In the eleventh month they coincide in *zi*, and devise accretion.
[3:29a:4]

Commentary to Section XXXIX

The principle here is the same as that developed above, in 3.XVII: Recision (*xing*, "paring-away") begins to control the year at the summer solstice, when the year begins to wane. Accretion begins to control the year at the winter solstice, when the year is reborn. This refers specifically to the paring away of the daily hours of daylight between the summer and winter solstices, and the accretion of the daily hours of daylight between the winter and summer solstices. The year is marked by the movement of the Dipper's handle through the chronograms on the cosmograph. The only new feature in this section is the introduction of the concept of two gods of the Dipper—a yang god, moving leftwards with the stars, and a yin goddess moving rightwards, meeting twice a year. This hints at the introduction of yin-yang/five phase correlations into the Dipper year cycle. It is a metaphor for, or visualization of, the movement of *taiyin*

132

(invisible counter-Jupiter) rightwards through the twelve chronograms on the heaven plate of the cosmograph, and the simultaneous but opposite movement of Jupiter left-wards through the heavens.

Section XL: Omens of the Stems and Branches

[3:29a:6]

1 The chronogram in which *taiyin* is located is called a "concealed day."
2 On concealed days one may not pursue (public) affairs.
3 Heaven and Earth move with slow dignity.
4 The male uses the (twelve) musical notes to know the female.
5 Thus (the chronogram in which *taiyin* is located) is known as the "singular chronogram."
6 The numbers (of the sexagenary cycle) begin with *jiazi*.
7 Offspring and mother mutually seek a harmonious place to come together.
8 Ten stems and twelve branches make a sexagenary cycle.
9 In all there are eight concurrences.
10 If the concurrence is (at a point in the cycle) prior (to the stem-branch combination in which *taiyin* is located), there will be death and destruction;
11 If the concurrence is later (in the cycle), there will be no calamity.
12 (The territorial allocations of the "eight concurrences" are as follows:)

jiaxu is Yan	*gengchen* is Qin
yiyou is Qi	*xinmao* is the Rong Tribes
bingwu is Yue	*renzi* is the Dai Tribes
dingsi is Chu	*guihai* is the Hu Tribes

13 (The territorial allocations of the "lesser conjunction" cyclical pairs are as follows:)

[*wuchen* is . . .]	*yiyou* is . . .
wuxu is . . .	*yimao* is Wei[a]
[*yisi* is . . .]	*wuwu* is . . .
yihai is Han	*wuzi* is . . .

14 The eight concurrences [together with the eight lesser conjunctions] (thus correspond to) All-Under-Heaven.
15 When *taiyin*, the Lesser Year, the asterisms [= lunar lodges], the branches, the stems, and the Five (directional) Gods all coincide on the same day, there will be clouds, vapors, and rain.
16 (The omen pertains to) the state and ruler (the stem-branch pair allotment of which) corresponds (to the day concerned).
[3:30a:1]

133

Commentary to Section XL

This section picks up on the theme of military prognostication from 3.XXXIII above, though given the sometimes extreme textual damage in this section (e.g., line 13) it is sometimes unclear to what states or territories the omens are intended to apply.

The text begins by defining a "concealed day," explained by Qian Tang[63] as follows: When *taiyin* and the sun are in the same chronogram (i.e., during the month of heliacal rising of the chronogram in which *taiyin* is located), *taiyin* "obscures" the sun. The month in which this occurs will shift one place annually through the twelve years of the Jovian Cycle.

Lines 3–5 are rather obscure; their general sense seems to be that the movements of the cosmos imitate the Dao in their stateliness; the transformations of the twelve pitch pipe notes harmonize the cycles of yin and yang. (The statement that the notes are related to maleness and femaleness goes back to the myth alluded to in 3.XXIX.20 that the ancients listened to the (mating) calls of the phoenix, which inspired them to discover the pitch pipe notes.) All of this is governed by the chronogram in which *taiyin* is located.

The "eight concurrences" of line 9 are explained as follows:[64] In the course of a sixty-year sexagenary cycle comprising five Jovian years (or, similarly, in each of the six sexagenary day cycles comprising a 360-day "lesser year") there will be eight instances in which the stem opposite the chronogram in which yang is established is paired in the sexagenary order with the branch opposite the chronogram in which yin is established. Thus, for example, in the eleventh month, both yin and yang are established in *zi*; *wu* is the chronogram opposite. The stem *bing* is linked with the branch *wu*, both opposite *zi*, so *bingwu* is a "concurrence." The eight concurrences thus derived are *bingwu* (#43), *yiyou* (#22), *jiaxu* (#11), *guihai* (#60), *renzi* (#49), *xinmao* (#28), *geng-chen* (#57), and *dingsi* (#54). These eight pairs are given territorial allocations in line 12, all of which are "outer" territories on the periphery of the central states of the North China Plain. Lines 10–11 supply the usual prediction that if the stem-branch pair for any given state or territory is to the left of *taiyin* the omen is unfavorable, if to the right, the omen is favorable.

The "lesser conjunctions" of line 13, also determined by yin-yang transformations relative to the *taiyin* cycle, take the same branches but different stems compared with the "eight conjunctions." The text here is badly damaged; it is possible to restore it to the extent of supplying the two missing stem-branch pairs, but there is no way to tell what states were correlated with the six that now lack territorial allocations. In any case, the eight "lesser conjunctions" are *wuchen* (#5), *wuxu* (#35), *yisi* (#42), *yihai* (#12), *yiyou* (#22), *yimao* (#52), *wuwu* (#55), and *wuzi* (#25). Each pair of binomes, in other words, is thirty units apart in the sexagenary cycle.

Lines 15–16 specify that when all pertinent celestial auspices coincide on the cosmograph in a stem-branch pair corresponding to one of the territories named here, there will be unusual meteorological manifestations.

Section XLI: Correspondences and Omens

[3:30a:1]

1 Of those honored by the gods of Heaven, none is more honored than the Bluegreen Dragon.
2 The Bluegreen Dragon is otherwise called the Heavenly Monad, or otherwise *taiyin*.
3 (The country corresponding to) the place where *taiyin* dwells cannot retreat, but can advance.
4 (The country corresponding to) the place beaten against by the Northern Dipper cannot withstand attack.
5 When Heaven and Earth were founded, they divided to make yin and yang.
6 Yang is born from yin, yin is born from yang; they are in a state of mutual alternation.
7 The four angles (of the celestial circle) penetrate (this alternating process).
8 Sometimes there is death, sometimes birth.
9 Thus are the myriad things brought to completion.
10 (Of all creatures that) move and breathe, none is more honored than man.
11 (The bodily) orifices, limbs and trunk all penetrate to [= have correspondences with] Heaven.
12 Heaven has nine layers; man also has nine orifices.
13 Heaven has four seasons, to regulate the twelve months;
14 Man also has four limbs, to control the twelve joints.
15 Heaven has twelve months, to regulate the 360 days;
16 Man also has twelve joints, to regulate the 360 bones.
17 Thus to attend to affairs while not being in accord with Heaven is to rebel against one's own nature.
[3:30a:8]

Commentary to Section XLI

The opening lines of this section continue the theme of Jupiter Cycle prognostications; but note here the interesting identification of *taiyin* Jupiter with the Bluegreen Dragon (as also in 3.VI.6 above), and the emphatic reiteration of the danger of *taiyin* portents. As Donald Harper has remarked about this passage, "The Dipper, not merely a passive marker of celestial time, has here been transformed into an awesome weapon, striking death-blows to whatever lies in its path."[65]

The larger import of this section, however, is to emphasize macrocosm/microcosm correspondences. In the heavens, nothing is more honored than the Bluegreen

Dragon; on earth, nothing is more honored than man. The heavens operate through the transformations of yin and yang; thus all is brought to completion. All of the features of the celestial frame are mirrored in the human body; thus human nature requires that the actions of man accord with those of the heavens.

Lines 11–16 here have an interesting parallel in *Huainanzi* 7:2a–3a:

> The external is manifest, the internal is concealed.
> The open and the shut, the extended and the contracted, each has its warp and weft.
> Thus the head is round, resembling Heaven;
> The feet are square [i.e., the two feet placed together occupy a square piece of ground], resembling Earth.
> Heaven has four seasons, five phases, nine sections, and 366 days;
> Man likewise has four limbs, five viscera, nine orifices, and 366 joints.
> Heaven has wind, rain, cold, and heat;
> Man likewise has receiving and giving, joy and anger.
> Thus the gallbladder equates to [*wei*, "makes"] clouds, the lungs equate to vapor [qi], the liver equates to wind, the kidneys equate to rain, and the spleen equates to thunder.
> Thereby they are in mutual interaction with Heaven and Earth; but the heart is the chief (of all the organs).
> For the same reasons, the ears and eyes equate to the sun and the moon;
> The blood and qi equate to the wind and the rain.

The identification of the gallbladder (phase metal) with clouds may be related to the notion of clouds as "metallic qi" as in 4.XIX. The equation of the five viscera with meteorological phenomena is an interesting reminder that for the early Chinese, everything that happened in the sky (and not just astronomical phenomena proper) belonged to the realm of heaven.

That all of this is of special interest to the ruler, as distinct from people in general, is made clear in *Huainanzi* 8:4a:

> Heaven, earth, and spacetime are the body of one man. All that lies within the six coordinates are under the rule of one man.

Section XLII: Prognostications for the Jovian Cycle

[3:30a:8]

1   Take the winter solstice as the starting-point for taking account of the coming harvest.

2   (If) fifty days after the first day of the first month, the people's food supply is adequate but not ample,

3   For fifty days reduce the ration by one pint (*sheng*) per day.

4   If there is a surplus, for fifty days increase the ration by one pint per day.

5   (For regulating these matters) there are the Masters of the Year.

6   The year *Shetige*: A year of early moisture and late drought. Rice-plants are sickly and silkworms do not mature. Legumes and wheat flourish. The people's food-ration is four pints. *Yin* in *jia* is called "impeded seedlings."

7   The year *Ming'e*: The year is harmonious. Rice, legumes, wheat, and silkworms flourish. The people's food-ration is five pints. *Mao* in *yi* is called "flag sprouts."

8   The year *Zhixu*: A year of early drought and late moisture. There is minor famine. Silkworms are obstructed, wheat ripens. The people's food-ration is three pints. *Chen* in *bing* is called "pliant omen."

9   The year *Dahuangluo*: A year of minor warfare. Silkworms mature in small numbers, wheat flourishes, legumes are sickly. The people's food-ration is two pints. *Si* in *ding* is called "strengthen the frontier."

10 The year *Dunzang*: A year of great drought. Silkworms mature, rice is sickly, and wheat flourishes but the crops do not yield. The people's food-ration is two pints. *Wu* in *wu* is called "manifestly harmonious."

11 The year *Xiexia*: A year of minor warfare. Silkworms mature, rice flourishes, legumes and wheat do not yield. The people's food-ration is three pints. *Wei* in *ji* is called "differentiate and separate."

12 The year *Tuntan*: The year is harmonious. The lesser rains fall in season. Silkworms mature, legumes and wheat flourish. The people's food-ration is three pints. *Shen* in *geng* is called "elevate and make manifest."

13 The year *Zuo'e*: A year of great war. People suffer illness, silkworms do not mature, legumes and wheat do not yield, crops suffer insect damage. The people's food-ration is five pints. *You* in *xin* is called "redoubled brightness."

14 The year *Yanmao*: A year of minor famine and warfare. Silkworms do not mature, wheat does not yield, legumes flourish. The people's food-ration is seven pints. *Xu* in *ren* is called "umbral blackness."

15 The year *Dayuanxian*: A year of great warfare and great famine. Silkworms rupture their cocoons, legumes and wheat do not yield, crops suffer insect damage. The people's food-ration is three pints. [*Hai* in *gui* is called. . . .]

16 The year *Kundun*: A year of great fogs rising up and great waters issuing forth. Silkworms, rice and wheat flourish. The people's food-ration is three bushels. *Zi* in *jia* is called "dawning brilliance."

17 The year *Chifenruo*: A year of minor warfare and early moisture. Silkworms do not hatch. Rice-plants are sickly, legumes do not yield, wheat flourishes. The people's food-ration is one pint. [*Chou* in *yi* is called. . . .]
    [3:32a:10]

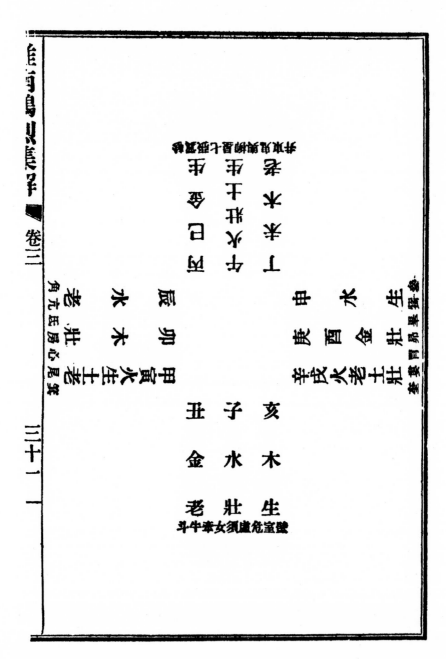

Figure 3.10. Diagram of the stems, branches, lunar lodges, and five phases, from *Huainanzi* 3:31a.

Commentary to Section XLII

On the names of the years of the Jovian Cycle, see Section XXXIII above. The miscellaneous prognostications for the Jovian Cycle (read from the position of *taiyin* on the cosmograph) given here are of a very automatic sort, reminiscent of vulgar zodiac prognostications in Western horoscopy; they assume the same set of conditions for each occurrence of each of the twelve years of the cycle. On the whole, this section is out of character with the rest of the chapter, and one wonders if there are hints here of a horoscopic astrological system as non-Chinese as the names of the years of the Jovian Cycle themselves. The concept of "the people's rations" seems to imply a utopian/totalitarian regime with Legalist or Mohist roots, in which people's basic diet is issued by the state from a central granary. This too seems inconsistent with the tone of the rest of the chapter, though the concept of economic forecasting implicit in this passage is of considerable interest.

In this section of the text, approximately between lines 5 and 6, a diagram[66] (which might or might not be contemporaneous with the text) is included in most editions of the *Huainanzi*, and is reproduced above as Figure 3.10.

Section LXIII: Appended Treatise on Gnomonics

See Appendix A, "A Chinese Eratosthenes of the Flat Earth" by Christopher Cullen.

Huainanzi Chapter 4: Dixingxun

୧ଠ

THE TREATISE ON TOPOGRAPHY

INTRODUCTION

The "Treatise on Topography" is a work of unusual importance for the study of early Chinese cosmology. It attempts to describe comprehensively the known world in Han times and the creatures that inhabit it, and to account for the interplay between living things and their environment. It is also of interest because it appears to continue the theories of the Zou Yan school of cosmology and cosmography in relatively pure form.

The treatise accords well with the overall Huang-Lao orientation of the *Huainanzi* in its attempt to enhance a reader's understanding (and presumably the intended reader would be an aspiring ideal ruler) of the world around him. It has much in common with *Huainanzi* 3 and 5, and it would seem likely (though this cannot now be verified) that all three chapters were written (or, if one likes, arranged and edited) by the same individual.

The "Treatise on Topography" draws heavily on a wide range of other early works, even to the extent of duplicating or closely paraphrasing long passages from them. The most important textual antecedents of the treatise are the "Yu gong" chapter of the *Shujing*, the *Shanhaijing*, *Lüshi chunqiu*, portions of the *Chu ci* (especially the "Tian wen"), and, presumably, the works of Zou Yan himself, though little of Zou Yan's writings survive to verify this contention.[1] It shares large blocks of material with the roughly contemporary—possibly slightly later—*Da Dai liji*, and also apparently had some influence on (and/or shared sources with) other subsequent Han works, including Dong Zhongshu's *Chunqiu fanlu*, the *Liezi*, *Kongzi jiayu*, *Bohutong*, and the chapters on geography and on the five phases in the *Shiji* and with relevant portions of the *Hanshu.* This is not to say, however, that the chapter is simply a compilation or re-statement of earlier sources, nor that the same information and point of view could be gotten from any of a number of pre-Han and Han works. The value of the treatise lies precisely in the clarity with which the Han understanding of cosmology is drawn from disparate sources, coherently rearranged, and supplemented with original material; the final product is a remarkably clear and cogent presentation of an understanding of how the universe works, an understanding that itself formed part of the most significant school of early Han philosophy, Huang-Lao Daoism.

According to the worldview presented in the treatise, all phenomena in the universe (whether "organic" or "inorganic" in modern, Western terms) can be analyzed and understood in terms of yin-yang/five phase categorical reasoning. The description of the visible cosmos in this treatise is consistent with *Huainanzi* 3, wherein earth is flat and "square," that is, defined by the solstitial and equinoctial nodes of the celestial equator, and heaven is "round," that is, defined by the celestial equator itself. The trea-tise follows Zou Yan in treating the earth as being divided into nine great continents. It takes one of these as the *oikoumene,* divided into nine subcontinents, one of which is China. China itself is further divided into nine provinces. China is seen as being an island of civilization surrounded by lands populated by barbarous or monstrous beings, and surrounded at a further remove by magical realms (such as Kunlun and the lands of the Fusang and Ruo sun-trees) hovering at the limit of physical reality where the edge of the earth meets the edge of the sky.

The cosmological point of view of the treatise is consistent with the famous cosmogonic passage at the beginning of *Huainanzi* 1 (itself derived directly from *Laozi* 42), whereby the Dao divides into yin and yang, which further divide into the five phases; from these, the "myriad things" are produced. But the cosmology here is also consistent with the cosmogony of the "Treatise on the Patterns of Heaven," *Huainanzi* 3, whereby the heavens and the earth separate out from primordial chaos, and qi itself becomes the fundamental stuff of phenomena, organized according to yin-yang/five phase principles. One of the most remarkable features of this treatise is that it shows how the "myriad things" are produced by a process of species differentiation of plants, animals, and minerals from first ancestors or progenitors within categories of five phase resonance. The treatise also mentions the "cosmic triad" of heaven, earth, and man (soon to become a key element in Dong Zhongshu's philosophy), and uses the numer-ology of three and nine to account for the gestation periods of various creatures.

In this translation, I have divided the "Treatise on Topography" into nineteen sections (no section divisions exist in the original text), as follows:

SYNOPSIS OF "THE TREATISE ON TOPOGRAPHY"

THE SHAPE OF THE EARTH
Section I: The Divisions of the Earth
  Introduction
  The nine continents.
  The nine mountains.
  The nine passes.
  The nine marshes.
  The eight winds.
  The six rivers.
Section II: Dimensions of the Earth

THE WORLD OF KUNLUN
Section III: The Kunlun Mountains
  Kunlun created by Yu the Great.
  The mountains of Kunlun and their characteristics.
Section IV: The Waters of Kunlun
  Four magical streams.
Section V: The Peaks of Kunlun and the Trees of the Sun
  Cosmic peaks and the *axis mundi.*
  The three sun-trees.

THE WORLD OF THE NINE CONTINENTS
Section VI: Beyond the Nine Provinces
  Eight distant regions and their marshes.
  Eight outlying regions and their terrors.
  Eight *terrae ultimae* and their cosmic gates.
Section VII: Treasures of the Nine Directions.
  Beautiful things from the nine provinces.

TOPOGRAPHY AND COSMOLOGY
Section VIII: Topographical Influences
  The qi of different terrains and waters produce different effects on living creatures.
Section IX: Diet and Disposition
  Yin-yang aphorisms.
  Different soils produce different human characteristics.
  Creatures that feed on different things have different dispositions.
Section X: Numerology and Birth
  The numerology of three governs the gestation periods of different creatures.
Section XI: Taxonomy
  Yin-yang characteristics create different types of creatures.

Taken together, the different sections of this treatise provide a remarkably clear and coherent description of the physical earth, the *axis mundi*, the magical regions on the periphery of China and at the margins of heaven and earth, the remarkable peoples and divinities that inhabit them, the habits and qualities of the earth's living creatures, and of the cosmic principles that govern the behavior of the entire world organism.

∾

THE TREATISE ON TOPOGRAPHY

Section I: The Divisions of the Earth

[4:1a:4]

1   Everything that exists on earth lies within the six coordinates and within the outer limits of the four directions.

2   The sun and moon illumine it; the stars and planets rule it.

3   The four seasons regulate it; the Great Year-star (*taisui*) controls it.

4   The world has nine continents and eight ultimate endpoints (of the eight directions).

5   The dry land has nine mountains; the mountains have nine passes.

6   There are nine marshes, eight winds, and six rivers.

7   What are the nine continents?

8   In the southeast is Shen Province, called the land of agriculture.

9   In the south is Zi Province, called the land of fertility.

10 In the southwest is Rong Province, called the land of abundance.

11 In the west is Yan Province, called the land of ripeness.

12 In the center is Ji Province, called the central land.

13 In the northwest is Tai Province, called the land of plenty.

14 In the north is Qi Province, called the land of consummation.

15 In the northeast is Bo Province, called the land of seclusion.

16 In the east is Yang Province, called the land of beginning again.

17 What are the nine mountains?

18 They are Mt. Guiji, Mt. Tai, Mt. Wangwu, Mt. Shou, Mt. Taihua, Mt. Qi, Mt. Taihang, Mt. Yangchang, and Mt. Mengmen.

19 What are the nine passes?

20 They are the Taifen Pass, the Min'ou Pass, the Jingruan Pass, the Fangcheng Pass, the Yaoban Pass, the Jingxing Pass, the Lingci Pass, the Gouzhu Pass, and the Juyong Pass.

21 What are the nine marshes?

22 They are The Juqu Marsh of Yue, the Yunmeng Marsh of Chu, the Yangyu Marsh of Qin, the Dalu Marsh of Jin, the Putian Marsh of Zheng, the Mengzhu Marsh of Song, the Haiyu Marsh of Qi, the Julu Marsh of Zhao, and the Zhaoyu Marsh of Yan.

23 What are the eight winds?

24 The northeast wind is called the intense wind.

25 The east wind is called the protracted wind.

26 The southeast wind is called the luminous wind.

27 The south wind is called the balmy wind.

28 The southwest wind is called the cool wind.

29 The west wind is called the lofty wind.

30 The northwest wind is called the elegant wind.

31 The north wind is called the cold wind.

32 What are the six rivers?

33 They are the Yellow River, the Vermilion River, the Liao River, the Black River, the Yangtse River, and the Huai River.
    [4:2b:1]

Commentary to Section I

The first paragraph of the "Treatise on Topography" (which is closely paraphrased from the opening paragraph of *Shanhaijing* 6) makes it immediately apparent that the scope of this chapter is cosmic as well as terrestrial. The world is defined as being within the "six coordinates"—not, however, as that term is used below in the "Treatise on the Seasonal Rules" (5.XVIII.1–7), to define six diametral chords lying across the celestial circle, but rather to mean what we would call the three dimensions: up and down, forward and backward, left and right. Thus the treatise takes as its subject all things that have shape and mass, and that also lie "within the outer limits of the four directions," that is, on the plane of the earth projected out into space, defined by the four seasonal "corners" of the celestial equator.

The earth does not exist in isolation from the rest of the universe; "the four seasons regulate it, the Great Year-star controls it." (The Great Year-star, *taisui*, is counter-Jupiter, usually called *taiyin* in *Huainanzi* 3, where it is discussed extensively; see for example 3.VII and 3.XIX, and the commentaries to those sections.) In other words, the earth is governed by time, and more particularly by the heavenly bodies that are the determinants of earthly time. This is consistent with the cosmogonic passage in Chapter 3, Section I, where spacetime—cosmos-as-it-extends and cosmos-as-it-endures—spontaneously emerges from primordial chaos. The subject of the "Treatise on Topography," then, is all things that exist in time and space on the face of the earth and in the margin between heaven and earth; and in fact the treatise is a systematic description of the configuration of the earth and a natural history of the creatures on it.

In this section the treatise presents the first of its several systematic (that is, categorical rather than geographical or situational) descriptions of the earth itself. It seems at first to promise a description of the entire face of the earth—"all under Heaven"—but then quickly narrows down to what is evidently a description of the provinces, mountains, marshes, etc., of China alone. The selection of the actual nine mountains, nine passes, nine marshes, and so on apparently has the weight of tradition behind it; the entire text of this section has been copied virtually unchanged from *Lüshi chunqiu* 13 (except for a section dealing with the heavens, which in *Huainanzi* has been moved to Chapter 3—further evidence of the editorial hand so frequently seen at work in *Huainanzi*, even when the text draws almost verbatim on earlier sources). Most of the place names in this section also appear in the *Shanhaijing* and other early geographical sources.

Many of the features named here remain famous places in China today, but others have fallen into obscurity with the passage of time or, in a few cases, were magical rather than terrestrial in the first place.[2]

The schematic nature of *Huainanzi's* cosmography, in which the shape of the earth is expressed as a 3 × 3 grid of nine squares, is apparent at the very beginning of this section and will form a dominant theme throughout the chapter.[3] On the other hand, the author (whoever he was) of this passage was unable to sustain that scheme uniformly. Mountains, passes, and marshes can readily be incorporated into a sche-

146

matic 3 × 3 grid cosmography—there are plenty to choose from, after all—but there are only eight cardinal points of the compass, and so only eight winds are given here. (A "wind of the center" would presumably have to fulfill a definition of "originating in the center and blowing nowhere.") Note that the names of the winds given here are quite different from those in 3.XII above and 4.XVIII.1–8 below.

It seems odd, however, to find only six rivers given here, especially as many more are named later in Section XVII of this chapter. The six given here include China's two greatest rivers, and two others, the Liao and the Huai, of some importance. But the final two, the Black and the Vermilion, are not even identifiable with confidence, and certainly are not among China's great rivers; if anything, they are identifiable only as two of the magical (and probably nonexistent on the face of the earth) rivers of Kunlun described in 4.IV below. One possible reason why there are only six, though this is no more than speculation, is based on numerology. In yin-yang/five phase numerology, nine is the number of pure yang, while six is the number of pure yin. To a writer steeped in that theory, a grouping of nine rivers might have seemed impossibly inharmonious; once a decision had been made to avoid the construction "nine rivers," "six rivers" would have suggested itself as the ideal number instead.

Section II: Dimensions of the Earth

[4:2b:2]

1 The expanse within the four seas measures 28,000 li from east to west and 26,000 li from south to north.
2 There are 8,000 li of watercourses, which pass through six valleys and 600 named streams.
3 There are 3,000 li of roads and paths.
4 Yu employed Tai Zhang to measure the earth from its eastern extremity to its western extremity.
5 It measured 233,500 li and 75 double-paces.
6 He also employed Shu Hai to measure from its northern extremity to its southern extremity.
7 It measured 233,500 li and 75 double-paces.
8 Concerning floodlands, deep pools, and swamps greater than 300 *ren* in area:
9 Within (the above-designated expanse of) 233,500 li, there are nine deep pools.
[4:2b:8]

Commentary to Section II

Having given a systematic description of the geography of China, the text goes on to give an estimate of the size of "the expanse within the four seas," and then of the entire area within the extreme projections of the four directions. The figures given for "the expanse within the four seas," 28,000 li from east to west and 26,000 li from south to north, are grossly too large for China itself, as a Former Han writer would have known. The reference here must therefore be to the *oikoumene*, the "known world." In fact, these distances are not a bad approximation of the size of the Eurasian continent, though that is not to say that our author had any knowledge of the size and shape of Eurasia. Rather we must assume that the *oikoumene* represented one of the nine "great continents" of Zou Yan[4] and that its dimensions were an expansion of a Han estimate of the size of China itself—which was taken to be one-ninth of the area of one "great continent." That is, the size of "the expanse within the four seas" would have been derived by computing an area roughly nine times that of China, in the same approximate shape, slightly greater east to west than south to north. According to this computation, the size of China, in the understanding of the author of this treatise, would have been about 9,300 li from east to west, and 8,250 li from south to north—not far wrong, considering that most of the area within the "natural borders" of China was known by the late Warring States and early Han periods.

Despite the oft-repeated assertion in early Chinese texts that "earth is square," the figures given here for the "expanse within the four seas" do *not* describe a square, being slightly larger in the east-west dimension than in the south-north dimension. A similar nonsquareness is implied in "Tian wen" 38:[5]

> Long are the spans from east to west, from south to
> north [which is longer?]

"Tian wen" 39 implies that the south-north dimension is greater—exactly the reverse of the picture given in *Huainanzi*:

> It is oblong, south to north [how much is the excess?]

It is interesting to compare the figures given here with those of Eratosthenes (276–296 B.C.E.), who estimated the size of the *oikoumene* as about 7,800 miles from east to west and 3,800 miles from south to north, apparently on the basis of reports and rumors of lands far removed from Greece. Eratosthenes, of course, is famous for having determined the sphericity of the earth by means of gnomon measurements, arriving at a surprisingly accurate figure of about 25,000 miles.

Having described the size of the known world, the passage goes on to give figures for the size of the entire plane of the earth—and these figures do make a square, as required by cosmological theory. Here the figures are represented as having been paced off by Tai Zhang and Shu Hai, of whom Gao You says, "They excelled at walking. Both were ministers of Yu." (A slightly fuller account of this surveying expedition is found in *Shanhaijing* 9.)

Ancient Chinese writers apparently were in great disagreement over what the true dimensions of the universe were, as measured between the extremes of the four directions. As Gu Jiegang noted,[6] figures given in various texts range from a low of the 233,500 li and 75 double paces of this passage, through the 597,000 li of *Lüshi chunqiu*, to the truly astronomical 50,109,800 li of *Shanhaijing*.[7] Nakayama has demonstrated that such figures were based on precise gnomonic and angular measurements and computed according to the (erroneous) hypotheses of the *gaitian* cosmological theory.[8] The figures thus are not random; the main variable is the set of assumptions applied to the gnomon measurements. As Nakayama notes, the seeming precision of the results betrays a lack of awareness of probable error—or, to put it another way, no awareness of the distinction between precision and accuracy. As Nathan Sivin has pointed out, no Chinese philosopher seems to have addressed this issue explicitly until the Song period.[9] This willingness to settle for what we would regard as false precision, together with assumptions and goals that were quite erroneous from the point of view of exact science, ensured that no Chinese Eratosthenes would emerge to demonstrate the sphericity of the earth and measure its circumference with fair accuracy. (These issues are explored at greater length by Christopher Cullen in Appendix A, below.)

In any case, such figures as are given in *Huainanzi* or *Lüshi chunqiu* for the dimensions of the plane of the earth out to the extremes of the four directions are vastly too large to fit the physical earth, and Chinese experience in the use of gnomons by the early Han would have been sufficient to make that clear to contemporary authors. What is measured by such figures, rather, is the ideal plane of the earth measured out to the sides of the square defined within the celestial circle by the equinoctial and solsticial nodes. As was noted earlier (Chapter 2, and commentary to 3.XVII), this is the true meaning of the early Chinese concept of a "square earth." In the "Treatise on Topography" and comparable texts, terrestrial and celestial topography meld readily into each other.

Lines 2 and 3 of this section present textual and conceptual difficulties that are explored in the "Textual and Technical Notes." If a somewhat emended version of the text is accepted as coming close to the intent of the (now-garbled) original, there would seem to be a link here with the six rivers of Section I: they flow through six valleys, along with six hundred "named" [the term is used literally here, rather than in its extended sense of "famous" or "illustrious"] streams that are presumably tributaries of the great rivers. Whatever the difficulties of the text, however, the impression given is clearly that of a world crossed and recrossed with many miles of waterways and land routes. This passage is one of several in the "Treatise on Topography" that come tantalizingly close to implying a grid mapping system, without being quite clear enough to allow one to conclude with certainty that that was what the writer had in mind. At the very least, the mapping techniques demonstrated in the celebrated maps from Mawangdui Tomb 3 are consistent with the understanding of the actual geography of China found in this passage.

Section III: The Kunlun Mountains

[4:2b:9]

1   Yu also took expanding earth to fill in the great flood, making the great mountains.
2   He excavated the wastelands of Kunlun to make level ground.
3   In the center (of the world) is a manifold wall of nine layers, with a height of 11,000 li, 114 double-paces, two feet, and six inches.
4   Atop the heights of Kunlun are tree-like cereal plants thirty-five feet tall.
5   (Growing) to the west of these are pearl trees, jade trees, carnelian trees, and never-dying trees.
6   To the east are found sand-plum trees and *lang'gan* trees.
7   To the south are crimson trees.
8   To the north are *bi* jade trees and *yao* jade trees.
9   Nearby are four hundred forty gates.
10 There are four li between each gate, and each gate is 15 *shun* broad. [One *shun* equals fifteen feet.]
11 Nearby are nine wells.
12 The jade vase [becomes filled with the elixir of immortality] only in the northwestern corner.
13 The north[west]ern gate opens to admit the wind from Mt. Buzhou.
14 Broad Palace, Revolving House, Hanging Garden, Cool Wind, and the Hedge Forest are within the Changhe Gate of the Kunlun Mountains.
15 This is (called) the Carved-Out Garden.
16 The pools of the Carved-Out Garden flow with yellow water.
17 The yellow water circulates three times and then returns to its source.
18 It is called cinnabar water; anyone who drinks it will not die.
    [4:3b:2]

Commentary to Section III

This section again takes as its point of departure some of the questions of the "Tian wen" (29–34):

> [Yu] inherited the work and completed his father's task;
> He kept to the prior plan, but his scheme was different [how could this be?].
> He filled in the floodwaters, fathoms deep [how?];
> He raised the nine regions of the square earth [how?].

The winged dragon laid the courses of the rivers and seas [how?]

. . .

Gun designed it and Yu completed it [what?]

Here again, we see the author (probably the same individual) of *Huainanzi* 3 and 4 carefully separating terrestrial and astronomical topics, for the next question in the "Tian wen" asks about cosmography: "Kang Hui [Gong Gong] was enraged, and the land leaned southeast [why?]." And as we have seen, that question was answered at the end of 3.I above.

The story of Yu's great engineering work is told in *Huainanzi* 8:8b:

> Shun employed Yu to drain the three rivers and the five lakes, to tunnel through Yujue Mountain and make channels for the Chan and Jian rivers. He levelled the land and conducted the waters, leading them to flow into the eastern sea. The flooding waters flowed away and the nine provinces became dry again. The multitudes recovered their peace of mind, and thus they considered Yao and Shun to be sages.

Yu's "expanding earth" appears first in *Shanhaijing* 18: "Gun [father of Yu] stole the Thearch's expanding earth and dammed the floods (with it)." Gao You comments on this line in *Huainanzi*, "The expanding earth does not diminish with use. The more one digs up, the more there is. Therefore it could be used to fill in the great flood." This seems to be the key to the statement in "Tian wen" that "He kept to the prior plan, but his scheme was different." Gun apparently stole the expanding soil and used it to make dams, not respecting the Dao of water, which is to flow; Yu, we see here, also used the magical earth, but in addition he excavated tunnels and channels for the water (following, "Tian wen" tells us, the track of a dragon that came to his aid), and so achieved success.

"Tian wen" (40–43) also contains an account of (and questions about) Kunlun:

> On Mt. Kunlun rests the Hanging Garden [where?];
> Its terraced walls are many-tiered [how many li high?].
> There are gates in the four directions [who passes through?];
> Open the Northwest Gate and a wind blows through [which one?].

The Hanging Garden is within the Changhe Gate; the walls are some 11,000 li high. This section of *Huainanzi* 4 does not say who passes through the gates, but they may be the sages and gods who climb the peaks of Kunlun to reach Heaven, as described in 4.V below (where the Hanging Garden is mentioned again). However, according to both Wang Yi's commentary to *Chu ci* and *Shanhaijing* 12, the answer is Yi the Archer; the same answer is implied by *Huainanzi* 6:16b: " . . . Yi the Archer requested the elixer of immortality from the Queen Mother of the West. Heng E stole it and fled to the moon."

The wind from Mt. Buzhou blows through the northwestern gate. (On Mt. Buzhou see 3.XII.16 and the commentary to that section.)

The wall with 440 gates is likely to be a celestial rather than a "topographical" feature; see for example the asterism called "Great Enclosure" (*taiwei*) in 3.VIII.1 above, a star group bounded by a "wall" (*yuan*) composed of stars in Virgo, Leo, and Coma Berenices. The figure of "11,000 li, 114 paces, two feet, and six inches" may have been extrapolated from some kind of measurements of angular extensions in the sky, but it falls into the category of false precision discussed above in connection with the measurement of the dimensions of the earth's plane.[10]

"Tian wen" 21–22 implies the existence of another wall with gates—a celestial counterpart to the walls and gates of Kunlun. It asks:

> Dark as it closes, bright when it opens [what is it?].
> Before the Horn rises, the Great Light hides [where?].

The Horn is one of the twenty-eight lunar lodges, and this passage says that the sun sets in the west before the Horn rises in the east. In Shang times (though no longer, because of the effects of precession), the lodge opposite Horn was (Eastern) Wall.[11] So the answer to "dark as it closes, bright as it opens [what is it?]" is the Eastern Wall, where the sun sets opposite the rising of Horn, and, of course, rises again the next morning as Horn is setting in the west. This would happen only once a year, as the sun made its daily shift of 1[d] along the ecliptic—but significantly, it would happen on the first day of Beginning of Spring (*li chun*) according to the the calendrical system of the twenty-four "solar nodes." As de Saussure explains, "It will be evident that the primordial role of the asterism Horn came from its being situated exactly opposite the siderosolar location of *li chun* [Beginning of Spring]."[12]

The essential principle in this case is that the position of the sun in the sky can be known by reference to the lunar lodges. If one observed the full moon in Horn, one could know by opposition that the sun had entered Beginning of Spring. That this corresponded to the lodge Eastern Wall in the Shang would have been, by the time "Tian wen" was written, very old wisdom indeed. But there is evidence from *Shanhaijing* 11:2a that a mythographical (not astronomical) equation was made between the calendrical role of Eastern Wall and the wall of Kunlun: "There are nine gates [of Kunlun]. One of them is called Opening Brightness; it is guarded by beasts." The Changhe Gate, as 4.V makes clear, is also a celestial gate, the Gate of Heaven itself that leads to the Purple Palace of the north circumpolar stars.

Broad Palace, Revolving House, Hanging Garden, Cool Wind, and the Hedge Forest, all located inside the Changhe Gate, are probably to be understood both as

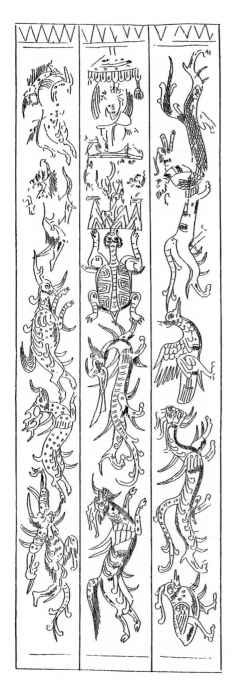

Figure 4.1. The peaks of Mt. Kunlun, resting on the back of a dragon and topped by the throne of the Queen Mother of the West, as depicted on a relief carved stone pillar from the Latter Han tomb at Yinan, Shandong (from Zeng et al., *Yinan gu huaxiang shimu fajue baogao*, Plate 66).

asterisms and as magical places at the edge of the cosmos. All of them are mentioned in the *Shanhaijing*; see for example the description of the Hedge (*fan*) Forest in *Shanhaijing* 12. One possible clue to the identity of the Revolving House is found in 3.XIV.1 above: "The Purple Palace governs the Dipper and turns to the left." Some of these mountains/asterisms are mentioned in other poems in the *Chu ci* anthology; see for example "Li sao" 40 and 55. "She jiang," the second of the Nine Songs ("Jiu zhang"), says,

> I rode with Zhong Hua in the Garden of Jasper,
> Climbed up Kunlun and ate the flower of jade,
> And won long life, lasting as heaven and earth.[13]

The second passage comes from "Ai shi ming," a poem roughly contemporary with the *Huainanzi*:

> I should like to go to the Hanging Garden of Kunlun,
> And pluck the flower of jade upon Zhong Mountain,
> To break off a branch of the precious tree,
> And gaze upon the mountains of Lang Feng [Cool Wind] and
>   Pan Tong [Hedge Forest].[14]

The nine wells of Kunlun are not mentioned in "Tian wen," nor is the northwest corner with its jade container of the elixir of immortality. The nine wells are mentioned in *Lüshi chunqiu* 14 and *Shanhaijing* 11, where they are described as having railings of jade. These wells may be grottos (*tong*) recirculating subterranean waters and/or sources of an elixir of immortality, as the reference to the jade container suggests.

The thrice-circulating yellow waters of Kunlun may be the same as the Weakwater, named in 4.IV below as one of the four rivers issuing from Kunlun. *Shanhaijing* 16 says of Kunlun, "The Weakwater pool surrounds it." These waters appear again in 4.IV below, where they are described as an elixir of immortality.[15] In any case, this circulating water is itself also a cosmic image, found in all versions of the Grand Origin Myth: the Maelstrom, a flood which swirls around the *axis mundi* in consequence of the cosmic disaster that broke the bonds of heaven and earth (= separated the ecliptic and the equator).[16]

It is not clear how one was intended to visualize the ninefold walls of Kunlun, but the most obvious image is of Kunlun as a peak of tremendous height, rising in nine steps like a ziggurat. Such a nine-tiered heaven (suggested also by the doubled and redoubled peaks within Kunlun in 4.V) makes little sense in terms of the overall *gaitian* cosmology of *Huainanzi*: might there be here a hint of weak and distant Indian influence to go along with the possibly Indian origin of the Jupiter Cycle names in *Huainanzi* 3.XXXIII? Certainly tiered-roof pagodas in later Chinese Buddhism reflect the

Indian nine-tiered cosmos; earlier influence of the same sort is unattested but hardly impossible.[17] The Ninefold Shade mountain (mentioned in *Shanhaijing* 8 and 17; see commentary to 4.XVI.29–31 below), associated with the Torch Dragon, is suggestive of a multitiered parasol of state of the sort found ubiquitously in Indic civilizations; it too may hint at an Indian-style ninefold heaven weakly impinging on early Chinese cosmology.

In general it is very difficult to identify the various gemstones or types of "jade" (remember the *Shuowen* definition of "jade" as "beautiful stone") found in Kunlun. The most troublesome of these stones is *lang'gan*, which, as Schafer has shown, most often means malachite.[18] Here it is tempting to use the more traditional interpretation of *lang'gan* as coral, especially in the context of "*lang'gan* trees," given the tree-like shape of some corals, such as the gem-quality red coral found in the Taiwan Straits. From a "rationalist" point of view, there could possibly be a reference here also to fossil corals found in mountain rocks, though there is no reason to take this passage so literally—this gem-studded paradise is mythical, not geographical.

This section, together with the following two, forms part of a very extensive pre-Han and Han literature on Kunlun, a full-scale treatment of which would require a lengthy monograph. But a few general remarks will be in order here to supplement the more specific textual comments above.

Kunlun has two closely related aspects: First, it is the world-mountain or *axis mundi*, the pillar that at once separates and connects heaven and earth. As such it is the highest of mountains, the terrestrial plane's closest approach, and stepping-stone, to the celestial vault. Section 4.V below deals more specifically with that aspect of Kunlun. Second, Kunlun is a paradise, a magical and beautiful land that is the home and kingdom of Xiwangmu, the Queen Mother of the West.

One problem that immediately arises in dealing with these two aspects of Kunlun is that the Kunlun Mountains are, and from early times have been known to be, an entirely real and terrestrial mountain range on China's northwestern frontier. The *Shanhaijing* (chap. 2 sect. 3, and chap. 11) shows an awareness of this problem by distinguishing between the Kunlun "beyond the Great Wasteland" and the Kunlun "within the seas." It then immediately clouds the issue again by describing the latter as "the earthly capital of the Supreme Thearch." In fact, it is not unusual for real but distant places to take on paradisical qualities; think of Serendip, or Shambala.

Thus in early China the name Kunlun attached to a geographical mountain and a mythical one, and the two soon were hopelessly conflated. Han descriptions of Kunlun emphasize loftiness, imperishability, and immortality. Loftiness is the dominant image latent in the ninefold walls of the *axis mundi*, however they are interpreted. Imperishability is the quality of the magical trees of paradise, most of them made of gemstones, perfect symbols of incorruptability; others are never-dying, are of marvellous size, or (according to commentators) confer immunity from disease or even death upon those who eat the fruit that grows upon them. Immortality is contained not only in those fruits, but also in the cinnabar or jade elixirs found in the springs of the carved garden.

Quite naturally such a paradise became closely associated with the "quest literature" of the Han. A western paradise—Kunlun—figures prominently in the magical journeys of the "Li sao" and other poems of the *sao* genre and in poems that describe the trysts of Emperor Wu of the Han with Xiwangmu or her handmaidens at the Turquoise Pool.[19] Kunlun was the goal of the Son of Heaven Mu, the record of whose mythical journey constitutes one of the most complete early descriptions of the western paradise and its mythology.[20] Not all ancient quests were mythical; the expeditions sponsored by Qin Shihuangdi in search of the eastern equivalent of Kunlun, the Penglai Islands, are well-attested in the historical record; and Kunlun itself was one of the goals of the expedition undertaken by Jiang Qian on behalf of Emperor Wu.

But such real-life journeys in search of paradise were futile, no matter how fervently people of the time believed in the reality of Penglai and Kunlun (and in the marvellous creatures to be found in their vicinity: as Schafer points out, "Even persons of broad experience and education often placed credence . . . in fantastic beings comparable to the kelpies and mermen of our world"[21]). Paradise was located elsewhere than on the physical earth.

As Hulsewé notes, the quest-journeys of the Son of Heaven Mu or the author-persona of "Li sao," like those of Odysseus or Gilgamesh, "give the impression of being coherent descriptions of travels" which a Han ambassador or a modern historian might be able to retrace. But "because many different representatives of the other world and its inhabitants have been combined into a colorful image . . . no attempts, even supported by a sound knowledge of ancient geography, can lead to a satisfactory solution to the enigmas of these journeys."[22] That such journeys were more appropriate for disembodied souls than for living persons is shown by the discovery of the text of the *Mu Tianzi zhuan*, which was found among the funerary offerings in a tomb of a prince of Wei dating from around 300 B.C.E. and excavated in 279 C.E. Hulsewé concludes that the text was included among the tomb furnishings to serve as a guide for the prince's journey to the next world.

Thus here and in a wide range of comparable texts, Kunlun appears as a place not located on the earth, but poised *between* heaven and earth, redolent with the jades and waters of immortality, magnificent in its loftiness, the fitting object of an adept's quest.

Section IV: The Waters of Kunlun

[4:3b:5]

1   The waters of the Yellow River issue from the northeast corner of the Kunlun Moun-

tains and enter the ocean, flowing (eastward) along the route of Yu through the
Piled-Stone Mountains.

2   The Vermilion River issues from the southeast corner and flows southwest to the
Southern Sea, passing to the east of Cinnabar Marsh.

3   The Weakwater (River) issues from the southwest corner; when it reaches Heli, its
overflowing waves pass through the Flowing Sands and flow south to enter the
Southern Sea.

4   The Yang River issues from the northwest corner and enters the Southern Sea south
of (the country of) the Winged People.

5   The four streams (originate in) the sacred springs of the (Yellow) Thearch, from
which can be concocted all kinds of medicinal substances to bring physical well-
being to the myriad creatures.
[4:4a:9]

Commentary to Section IV

This section contains numerous textual problems that are explored in the Textual and
Technical Notes below; the text translated above has been extensively reconstructed.
Note that the "Yellow River" here cannot be taken at face value as the river now known
by that name; in early Chinese texts that river is invariably known simply as *he*, The
River; the name "Yellow River" here is more likely to have cosmological than geographical significance (as shown by its obvious pairing with the Vermilion River—not
identifiable with certainty with any earthly river—in the same set of rivers flowing
from Kunlun). See also 4.XVII and the commentary on it below.

The Weakwater figures prominently in Warring States/Han works of mythical
geography. Allegedly nothing would float in it, not even a feather. Needham suggests a
petroleum seep; quicksand is also a possibility.[23] Those explanations might suffice to
account for the origins of the concept, but they are too literal to illuminate the real
meaning of Kunlun; by the time the Weakwater made its way into written literature, it
was firmly established as a magical river.

The idea that a great river issues from each of the four corners of Kunlun is shared
by the other cosmological/geographical texts—*Lüshi chunqiu, Shanhaijing, Chu ci*—
with which these sections of *Huainanzi* 4 have so much in common. We may assume
that it was a widely held view of the "landscape" of Kunlun. One might expect, then,
that the four rivers would flow to the four corners of the earth, but a second look shows
that all flow instead, by various routes, to the Southern Sea. (For more on the course of
the Yellow River, see below, 4.XVII.2 and the commentary to Section XVII.) This is
consistent with the cosmology of *Huainanzi* 3 and 4, for the myth of the tilting of the
earth's plane requires that all rivers should flow to the southeast. China's major rivers
do tend to flow roughly southeasterly, while the high mountains are in the northwest;

this geographical fact corroborates the cosmology and was the source of the imagery of the Chinese version of the myth of the ecliptic and the equator.

The place names here also reflect a mixture of geographical reality and cosmic mythology. The Flowing Sands might be the Gobi; Heli is a genuine place name; but the Winged People (cf. 4.XV.15 below) do not live in such real places—see *Chu ci*, "Yuan you" 39:

> I met the Winged Ones on the Hill of Cinnabar
> I tarried in the ancient land of Immortality.[24]

Thus one must approach this description of the rivers of Kunlun with caution and an open mind. Much effort has been expended by Chinese commentators and by such modern scholars as Erkes and Conrady in trying to identify these rivers with the real rivers of China and nearby lands. Such efforts are as doomed as those that have been made by other scholars to make a map of the Son of Heaven Mu's trip to Teheran.[25]

The final line of this section confirms that we are not dealing here with ordinary rivers. These rivers originate in the sacred spring of the Yellow Thearch and can be used to make a magical medicine. Their source is almost certainly the same as the thrice-circulating yellow waters described in 4.III above. The spring and the rivers that rise from it are thus aspects of the realm of a god, and so belong in the heavens as much as they belong on earth.

Section V: The Peaks of Kunlun and the Trees of the Sun

[4:4a:9]

1   If one climbs to a height double that of the Kunlun Mountains, (that peak) is called Cool Wind Mountain.
2   If one climbs it, one will not die.
3   If one climbs to a height that is doubled again, (that peak) is called Hanging Garden.
4   If one ascends it, one will gain supernatural power and be able to control the wind and the rain.
5   If one climbs to a height is that is doubled yet again, it reaches up to Heaven itself.
6   If one mounts to there, one will become a god.
7   It is called the abode of the Supreme Thearch.
8   The Fu [= Fusang] Tree in Yang Province is baked by the sun's heat.
9   The Jian Tree on Mt. Duguang, by which the gods ascend and descend (to and from Heaven), casts no shadow at midday.
10   If one calls (from that place), there is no echo.
11   It forms a canopy over the center of the world.
12   The Ruo Tree is to the west of the Jian Tree.
13   On its branches are ten suns; its blossoms cast light upon the earth.
     [4:4b:8]

Commentary to Section V

This section deals with cosmic pillars, first in the guise of the step-like ascending peaks of Kunlun, and then in the form of the trees of the sun. The problems raised by this section are surprisingly complex; I deal with them at length elsewhere[26] and will mention only a few points of interest here.

I noted in the commentary to 4.III above that Kunlun can in some respects be visualized as a ziggurat, rising in steps up to the dome of heaven itself. Here that image is made explicit; each peak of Kunlun is twice the height of the one before. The names of these peaks—Cool Wind, Hanging Garden, and the Abode of the Supreme Thearch—emphasize their mythical character. The image given in this section of a series of ever-higher peaks, the scaling of which imparts supernatural powers, emphasizes also the connections between Kunlun and the cult of immortality. The challenge of climbing peak after peak, each double the height of the last, may be seen as a metaphor for the spiritual journey towards enlightenment and the attainment of superhuman powers by the Daoist adept. Such a spiritual journey of course also recalls the "quest literature" poems of the *Chu ci*, such as the "Li sao." If one accomplishes the final stage in the journey one becomes a god, in full communication with the Supreme Thearch who dwells on the highest peak of Kunlun. (The identification of Kunlun as the "earthly capital of the Supreme Thearch" is found also in *Shanhaijing* 2).

The Fusang tree and the Ruo tree are well known from early Chinese mythology as the trees at the eastern and western edges of the world, where the sun-crow (or the sun-chariot) begins and ends its daily journey across the sky. One account of the sun's journey was given in *Huainanzi* 3.XXV above. The rich symbolism of these trees has been analyzed thoroughly by Sarah Allan.[27]

The Ruo tree is mentioned in "Tian wen" 45, and here as in many other instances the *Huainanzi* provides an answer to one of these "Heavenly Questions."

The Ruo Tree shines before Xihe has risen [how?]

The answer is, because there are ten sun-crows, not just one. The implication of line 13 is that the ten suns (or some of them, anyway) linger in the branches of the Ruo tree after sunset before making their way back to Fusang via an underground grotto before dawn. This is a poetic way of taking note of the fact that the glow of sunset continues to light the sky after the sun has descended below the horizon.

While the Fusang and Ruo trees are well known, the Jian tree is much less frequently mentioned in surviving mythological texts.[28] The Jian tree is described in *Shanhaijing* 10:

There is a kind of tree that resembles an ox. Its bark peels off like a sash, or like a yellow snake. Its leaves are gauzy, its fruits are like those of the jambu tree, and its

Figure 4.2. The Fusang tree, as depicted on a stone relief carving from the Wu Liang Shrine. Xihe hitches her dragon-horse to the sun chariot at the base of the tree; above, Archer Yi takes aim at the sun-crows. (After Chavannes, *Mission archéologique dans la Chine septentrionale*, vol. 2, plate 51, no. 107). Courtesy of Princeton University Libraries.

wood resembles that of the thorny elm. It is called the Jian tree, and it grows west of Yayu, near the Weakwater.

A passage in *Shanhaijing* 16, though not explicitly linked with the Jian tree, seems like a personification of it:

The land of Longevity Hemp is here. The god of South Peak married a woman from Zhou Mountain named Nü Qian. Nü Qian gave birth to Ji Ge, who begat Longevity Hemp. When Longevity Hemp stands upright he casts no shadow; when he calls loudly there is no echo. His land is terribly hot; humans cannot go there.

The Jian tree is the southern cosmic pillar, in the far south where the sun stands directly overhead at noon. It is thus a symbol of both the south and of centrality. In the commentary to 4.I above, I noted that if there were a wind of the center, it would have to originate in the center and blow nowhere. In 4.VI.33 below, the winds of the outlying regions are described as converging upon the central region. Thus the idea of "calling out but producing no echo" is more than a rhetorical device to match the idea of the equatorial sun at noon casting no shadow; it signifies that the exact center of the world is a place where qi converges and so from whence no sound could escape.

Section 4.XVIII.29,32 below seems to suggest that the Fusang, Jian, and Ruo trees were regarded as divine ancestors of ordinary trees and plants.

Section VI: Beyond the Nine Provinces

[4:4b:9]

1   The borders of each of the nine provinces encompass one thousand li.
2   Beyond the nine provinces are eight distant regions, each encompassing a thousand li.
3   The one to the northeast is called Impenetrable, (also) called Great Marsh.
4   The one to the east is called Great Island, (also) called Sandy Sea.
5   The one to the southeast is called Juqu, (also) called Misty Marsh.
6   The one to the south is called Great Dream, (also) called Vast Marsh.
7   The one to the southwest is called Island Wealth, (also) called Cinnabar Marsh.
8   The one to the west is called Nine Districts, (also) called Marsh of Springs.
9   The one to the northwest is called Bactria, (also) called Ocean Marsh.
10 The one to the north is called Great Obscurity, (also) called Frigid Marsh.
11 All of the clouds of the eight distant regions and eight marshes are rain clouds.
12 Beyond the nine provinces and the eight distant regions are eight outlying regions, each also encompassing one thousand li.
13 The one to the northeast is called Harmonious Hill, (also) called Wasteland.
14 The one to the east is called Thorn Forest, (also) called Mulberry Wilderness.
15 The one to the southeast is called Great Destitution, (also) called Horde of Women.
16 The one to the south is called Duguang, (also) called Reversed [i.e., north-facing] Doors.
17 The one to the southwest is called Scorched Pygmies, (also) called Fiery Earth.
18 The one to the west is called Metal Hill, (also) called Fertile Wilderness.
19 The one to the northwest is called One-Eye, (also) called Place of Sands.
20 The one to the north is called Amassing Ice, (also) called Abandoned Wings.
21 The qi of the eight outlying regions are those which put forth cold and heat.
22 In order to harmonize the eight proper (directional qi), there must be wind and rain.
23 Beyond the eight outlying regions are eight *terrae ultimae*.
24 The one to the northeast is called Square-Soil Mountain, (also) called Azure Gate.
25 The one to the east is called Extreme East Mountain, (also) called Opening-Brightness Gate.
26 The one to the southeast is called Mother-of-Waves Mountain, (also) called Yang Gate.

27   The one to the south is called Extreme South Mountain, (also) called Summer-Heat Gate.

28   The one to the southwest is called String of Colts Mountain and White Gate.

29   The one to the west is called Extreme West Mountain, (also) called the Changhe Gate.

30   The one to the northwest is called Non-Circumscribing Mountain, (also) called the Gate of Darkness.

31   The one to the north is called Extreme North Mountain, (also) called Winter-Cold Gate.

32   The clouds of the eight *terrae ultimae* are those that bring rain to the whole world; the winds of the eight gates are those that regulate seasonal heat and cold.

33   The clouds of the eight outlying regions, the eight distant regions, and the eight marshes bring rain to the nine provinces and produce harmony in the central province.
[4:6b:3]

Commentary to Section VI

Superficially this section seems to describe the nine provinces laid out by Yu the Great, and the lands lying beyond them, in a fairly straightforward manner. The provinces, each 1,000 li square, form a central territory 3,000 li square, arranged as a 3 × 3 grid. Beyond this central area, the distant regions, outlying regions, and *terrae ultimae* each extend outward for another 1,000 li. Thus the whole picture is of a square of 9,000 li, presumably one that could be envisioned as a set of nesting squares—a familiar figure from descriptions of China and its hinterlands found in the "Yu gong" and other early texts.[29] The area of 9,000 li square described here closely approximates the implied size of one-ninth of one of Zou Yan's "Great Continents" discussed in the commentary to Section II above.

The names of the eight gates of the *terrae ultimae* given in this section are of great interest. The names of the gates of the four cardinal points are all connected to directional attributes: Opening-Brightness Gate, the gate of sunrise, in the east; Summer-Heat Gate in the south; Changhe Gate, the heavenly portal associated with the cosmic pillar in the Kunlun Mountains, in the west; and Winter-Cold Gate in the north. The names of the other four gates illustrate the concept of process and coming-into-being characteristic of yin-yang/five phase cosmology. The northeastern gate is Azure Gate; Gao You comments, "In the northeast the phase Wood is about to be used (to govern) affairs. It is the beginning of the color bluegreen. Thus it is called the Azure Gate." The southeastern gate is Yang Gate. Gao You says, "When the moon [indicates the southeast], the force of yang is in effect. Therefore it is called the Yang Gate. Accordingly, the southeastern gate of every city under Heaven is called Yang Gate, because they fall into that category." The southwestern gate is White Gate. Gao You says, "When the moon [indicates the southwest], it is the beginning of the ascendance of the qi of Metal. Metal is white, thus it is called the White Gate." Finally, the northwestern gate is called Gate of Darkness. Gao You says, "[In the northwest], mysterious darkness begins to be ascendent, flowing yin collects. Thus it is called the Gate of Darkness." That the qualities of bluegreenness, yang, white, and yin appear at the "corners" rather than at the four cardinal directions indicates the importance of potentiality, that is, of coming-into-being, in *Huainanzi's* cosmology. This quality of potentiality can be visualized in Figure 4.3, in which the phases describe a clockwise circle, with earth at the center.

The names and attributes of the southern and northern "outlying regions" indicate something of the extent of geographical knowledge in early Han China. In China, all buildings were arranged so that their principal doors faced south, toward the sun (which, because China is north of the equator, always was south of the zenith at noon no matter what the season). "Reversed Doors," therefore, indicates a land south of the equator, where to catch the rays of the noonday sun, doors would have to face north. "Abandoned Wings," a name presumably of mythic significance, may never be completely understood now; it is difficult to decide even how to translate (or gloss) the name. *Weiyu* might mean "abandoned wings," but it could also mean "broken wings" or "shed feathers," and several other interpretations are also possible. In 4.XVI.30 below, it is said to be the hiding place of the Torch Dragon. Gao You simply says, "*Weiyu* is the name of a mountain," and comments, "in the shade of the northern limit, the sun cannot be seen." Together with other descriptions in the "Treatise on Topography" of the north as a gloomy, icebound place where the sun does not shine, this passage would seem to indicate that the Chinese either heard distant reports or rumors of the actual character of the arctic north, or else (perhaps) calculated on the basis of *gaitian* cosmology that the north *should* be such a place.[30]

This section also contains material of interest to the theory of meteorology in early China. Each of the distant, outlying, and ultimate "concentric squares" of the geographic/cosmographic model depicted in this section has weather attributes—wind, rain, or clouds. All interact to produce seasonal heat, cold, and rain. The implication is of a vortex action of climatic forces; the weather in a given area (here, the central nine provinces) is the product of forces originating externally and combining to work their effects in the place in question. The focus here is, of course, Sinocentric; the author is interested in forces that "bring rain to the nine provinces and produce harmony in the central province." But we see in this passage also the observational skills of Han natural philosophers, who understood that heat and cold and rain (or its absence) were produced by weather systems (thought of as clouds of qi) borne by winds from afar.

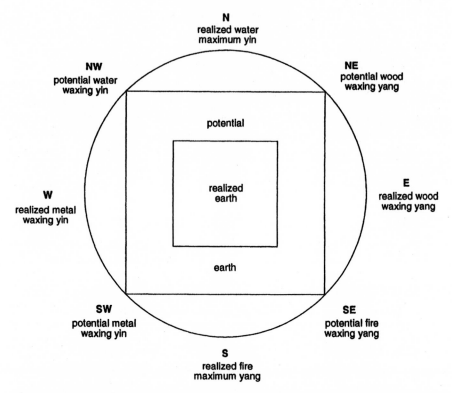

Figure 4.3. The cycle of yin, yang, and the five phases associated with the directions. In each case, the noncardinal direction (or, in the case of the center, outer center) represents potentiality, and the following cardinal direction (or the exact center) indicates realization.

Section VII: Treasures of the Nine Directions

[4:6b:3]

1 The beautiful things of the east are the *xun, yu,* and *qi* jades of Yimulu Mountain.
2 The beautiful things of the southeast are the arrow-bamboos of Mt. Guiji.
3 The beautiful things of the south are the rhinoceros and elephants of Mt. Liang.
4 The beautiful things of the southwest are the precious metals and jade of Mt. Hua.
5 The beautiful things of the west are the pearls and jade of Mt. He.
6 The beautiful things of the northwest are the *qiu, lin,* and *lang'gan* jades of the Kunlun Mountains.
7 The beautiful things of the north are the sinews and horn of Mt. Youdu.
8 The beautiful things of the northeast are the tiger and leopard skins of Mt. Zhi.
9 The beautiful things of the center are the five grains, mulberry, hemp, fish, and salt produced at Mt. Daiyue.
    [4:6b:11]

Commentary to Section VII

This section is in the tradition of the lists of "tribute" from each of the nine provinces in the "Yu gong" chapter of the *Shujing*, and of the closely related description of the nine provinces and their tribute articles in *Zhou li* 33. The language is also somewhat reminiscent of a passage in *Lüshi chunqiu* 14, in which Yi Yin instructs King Tang in the "beauties" of food and drink. However, the "beautiful things" of the nine directions listed here correspond only to a small degree with the tribute lists in "Yu gong" and *Zhou li* 33; the resemblance is largely thematic. The articles listed here contain few surprises, and describe accurately enough the provenance of various rarities that would have been sought after in early Han times, things that might well have captured the interest and imagination of a contemporary geographer. (Lists of rare and valuable products found in faraway places would continue to be a standard feature of Chinese geographical literature for centuries to come.)

It is interesting to note that this section, like the preceding one, blurs the distinction between mundane and magical geography. Although some of the mountains listed in this section, such as Mt. Guiji and Mt. Hua, and perhaps even the Kunlun Mountains, can be identified with actual mountains in or near China (or at least bear the same names as those mountains), it seems clear that here they are being used to suggest places at an indefinite but very great distance from the "central regions." Mt. Youdu, "Dark Capital," in the north, is associated with Wild Goose Gate, and in turn with the Torch Dragon that lights up the sunless north. Yimulu (or Yiwulu) Mountain in the east has a strange-sounding name, perhaps a transcription of a non-Chinese word. It is probably another version of Mt. Weilu of "Yuan you" 51, a mountain rich in mythic connotations: It is a jade mountain and also a great vortex that sucks in the waters of the Eastern Sea. The presence of both a mountain and a whirlpool marks this as one of the eight cosmic pillars that holds up the sky. Thus the unsurprising list of luxury products given in this section is projected onto a terrestrial/cosmic landscape that adds an extra, and extraordinary, dimension to the entire passage.

Most conspicuous among the "beautiful things" in this section are various sorts of precious stones. Such gems were prominent in the description of Kunlun in Section III above. Already by the time *Huainanzi* was written, it was clear from the "Li sao" and other early poems of the *Chu ci* that paradise, as conceived by the Chinese, was a gemmy place; and gemstones were to become a ubiquitous feature of Chinese descriptions of otherworldly fairylands—both Daoist and Buddhist—in the future. Because the eight outlying mountains of this section appear to stand not only for actual mountains but also for the eight pillars of heaven, it is quite natural to find a preponderance of precious stones among their famous products.

A wide variety of gemstones were known to and prized by the Han Dynasty

Chinese, as evidenced by the gem-encrusted bronze vessels and ornamental objects produced at the time. The question of just which precious stones are intended here is still a difficult one. As noted earlier, *lang'gan* has traditionally been understood to mean coral, but Schafer has argued convincingly the word often means malachite.[31] The "pearls and jade of Mt. He" in the west are fairly straightforward (and incidentally give evidence for long-distance trade in luxury goods; the pearls presumably came from India or the Persian Gulf). But as for the other "jades" of Mt. Yimulu in the east and the Kunlun Mountains in the northwest, it is no longer clear what their names signify. Neither Laufer, in his famous monograph on jade, nor Zhang Hongzhao, in his invaluable *Shi ya*, were able to solve all of the problems of nomenclature.[32] This problem of lapidary terminology will pose a challenging research topic for some future scholar of Schaferian diligence and imagination.

The rhinoceros and elephants of the south fall almost into the same category as gemstones, for they were prized for their horn and ivory. Both animals were known in China from early times, and their range must have extended well into central China; they appear, both in relief and modeled in the round, on Shang and Zhou bronzes. The Asian rhino is nearly extinct now, but a few elephants may still remain in the forests of extreme southern China. In Section XIII below, the south is described as being "full of rhinoceros and elephants."

Bamboo is one of the essential elements of Chinese civilization, and so it is somewhat surprising to find bamboo in this list of regional special products. We may suppose that the "arrow-bamboo" of the southeast, which still represented a frontier of expansion in Han times, was a special variety prized in, and imported into, the more northerly parts of China.

Archery also lies behind the mention of the sinew and horn of the north. Gao You's commentary says, "(The north's) domestic animals (include) cattle, sheep, and horses, (which) produce excellent sinew and horn which can be used for bows and crossbows." Sinew was used for bowstrings, and also for the outer sheathing of the short, powerful composite bows of laminated horn and wood that were adopted by the Chinese from their horse-riding "barbarian" neighbors to the north.

The "patterned skins" of the northeast of course come from the tigers and leopards that even today, in dwindling numbers, inhabit the far reaches of the northeastern provinces.

The beautiful things of the center stand in sharp contrast to the rarities of the eight directions. The stuff of food and clothing—grain, mulberry (for leaves to feed silkworms; not long after this passage was written, mulberry bark would also provide a raw material for paper, but that meaning is unlikely to have been intended here yet), hemp for cloth and cord, fish, and salt—indeed, the basic stuff of civilization, of which the Chinese saw themselves as the guardians and inheritors, is seen here as inextricably bound up with the *mana* of Mt. Tai, ancient China's most sacred place, the altar of kings.

Section VIII: Topographical Influences

[4:7a:1]

1   In the (fabric of) the earth's shape, east and west are the weft, north and south are the warp.

2   Mountains are the cumulative (result of) accretion, valleys are the cumulative (result of) cutting away.

3   High places govern birth, low places govern death.

4   Hills govern maleness, valleys govern femaleness.

5   Water (congealed) in round shape forms pearls; water (congealed) in square shape forms jade.

6   Clear water yields gold; the dragon's lair in the depths yields the quintescent beauty of jade.

7   Various sorts of earth give birth (to living creatures), each according to its own kind.

8   For this reason, the qi of mountains gives birth to a preponderance of men; the qi of low wetlands gives birth to a preponderance of women.

9   The qi of dikes produces many cases of muteness.

10 The qi of wind produces many cases of deafness.

11 The qi of forests produces many cases of paralysis of the legs.

12 The qi of wood produces many cases of spinal deformity.

13 The qi of seashores produces many cases of ulcerations of the lower extremities.

14 The qi of stone produces much strength.

15 The qi of steep passes produces many cases of goiter.

16 The qi of heat produces many cases of early death.

17 The qi of cold produces much longevity.

18 The qi of valleys produces many cases of rheumatism.

19 The qi of hills produces many cases of rickets.

20 The qi of low-lying places produces much human fellow-feeling.

21 The qi of mounds produces much covetousness.

22 The qi of light soil produces much haste.

23 The qi of heavy soil produces much sluggishness.

24 The sound of clear water is small, the sound of muddy water is great.

25 Men (who live near) rushing water are light; men (who live near) placid water are heavy.

26 The central region produces many sages.

27 All things are the same as their qi; all things respond to their own class.

28 Thus in the south there are plants that do not die; in the north there is ice that does not melt.

29   In the east there are countries of superior people.
30   In the west are tribes of crippled people, whose waking and sleeping are a constant
      dream; when such people die, they become ghosts.
      [4:8a:1]

Commentary to Section VIII

This section begins with a general statement, beautifully and elegantly phrased, that
the substance and shape of the earth conform in all respects to the influences of yin
and yang. The earth is part of the cosmos, and owes its particular characteristics to
cosmic forces. The products of earth and water—mountains and valleys in geological
terms, jade and pearls in quintessential terms—are to be seen here as paradigms for
physical manifestations of cosmic forces as a whole.

The imagery of precious stones here contains several points of interest. Of pearls
and jade, Gao You comments, "Round shapes are yang; pearls are the yang within the
yin. Square shapes are yin; jade is the yin within the yang." The commentary to the
similar line in *Guanzi* 39 explains that the pearl is yang within yin because it is found
in (yin) water but is luminous (a yang attribute); jade is yin within yang, because it is
formed in the (yang) mountains but is dark of itself (yin). The most important point
about pearl/jade imagery is its emphasis on the mutual, reciprocal presence of both yin
and yang in all things. Pearls are round (yang) in shape, and are luminous (yang), but
are congealed from and found in water (yin). Jade is assumed to be naturally square in
shape (yin) and dark, that is, with no internal luminosity (yin), but it is found in
(yang) mountains and is very hard (also yang). Thus even the most paradigmatic yin
substance contains a germ of yang, and even the most yang substance has its germ of
yin.

The association of clear water and gold in the following line is less obvious.
Perhaps it refers to the presence of gold dust in some fast-flowing streams; it may also
associate the purity of clear water with the incorruptibility of gold. The dragon's lair in
the depths yields *yu ying*, which I have glossed as "the quintessential beauty of jade,"
but which literally means something like "jade-gleam." This too is yang-within-yin
imagery. The dragon is yang, but lives in the (yin) depths as well as in the (yang) sky.
It usually is associated with the pearl, but "jade-gleam" in the murky depths seems to
point to another layer of yang-within-yin meaning. Perhaps there is a suggestion here
of natural alchemy like that found in Section XIX below; that is, the dragon's pearl
might transmute into a quintessential or highly rarified sort of jade.

Moving beyond general principles of yin and yang, this section of the "Treatise
on Topography" goes on to propose that the forces of yin and yang are embodied in

different types of human attributes and afflictions. This passage is closely analogous to one in *Guanzi* 39, in which the habits and character of people are correlated with the type of water near which they live. It is also related to the following section (Section IX) in this chapter, in which humans' characteristics are seen to correspond to various types of soil, and the habits of various sorts of creatures, including humans and immortals, are explained in terms of diet. Both this section and Section IX resonate with the long passage at the beginning of *Huainanzi* 7, where the human body is seen as a microcosm of heaven and earth—a common theme in early Chinese medical works.

Although no transmission of ideas is indicated here, it is interesting to note that Hippocrates, in his treatise "On Airs, Waters, and Places," also discusses the physiological effects of climate and topography.[33] His approach, however, was to deal with combinations of factors rather than with single forces acting alone, as here.

The notion that topography exerts specific influence on various types of physical characteristics clearly is related to ideas that gave rise to the Chinese pseudoscience of geomancy. The beneficial and harmful manifestations of yin and yang found in this passage are of exactly the same sort that Chinese geomancers sought to understand and manipulate in the siting of buildings and graves, in order to obtain the maximum advantage from auspicious yin-yang forces and to avoid inauspicious ones.

Line 27 of this section states that "all things are the same as (*tong*) their qi"; this recalls the principle, stated in Section 3.I, that everything is *made of* qi. Of the specific influences of yin and yang adduced here, the author particularly emphasizes the connections between yin and femaleness, and yang and maleness. We are told that "hills govern maleness, valleys govern femaleness," and this, in conjunction with the prior statement that "mountains are the cumulative (result of) accretion, valleys are the cumulative (result of) cutting away," has led some scholars, not entirely without reason, to see evidence of phallicism in the yin-yang imagery of Chinese cosmology. Certainly yin and yang are seen here in normative terms; if both are essential to the functioning of the universe, they are nevertheless not equally to be preferred: "High places govern birth, low places govern death." Phallocentric or not, the general preference for yang over yin by Han times (in contrast to the more neutral attitude toward these dualistic qualities in Warring States philosophical works) certainly extended to a preference for the male over the female; perhaps there is a hint here of growing Confucian influence on cosmological attitudes.

Other specific topographical influences mentioned in this passage seem to be based either on actual observation of the incidence of disease in various environments, or on sympathetic magic. For example, "the qi of steep passes produces many cases of goiter" may well be based on observations of the high incidence of goiter in the loess hills of northwestern China;[34] similarly, "the qi of hills produces many cases of deformity of the legs or spine" may represent observations of the incidence of beriberi or rickets in areas that lead to a vitamin-poor diet. On the other hand, such statements as "the qi of wood produces many cases of deformity of the spine" (meaning hunched backs) almost certainly is by a simple association of the gnarled quality of tree branches and a similarly gnarled spinal column. Even more obvious are the links between stone and strength, mounds and covetousness, and dikes (i.e., blockages) and muteness. The statement that "the qi of seashores produces many cases of ulceration of the lower extremities" might be based both on observation and sympathetic magic; on the one hand, seashore environments are likely to produce many cases of infected insect bites and other ulcerating wounds, but on the other hand there may be a simple mental association here between low-lying places and infirmities of the lower extremities. Similarly, the observation that "the qi of heat produces many instances of early death; the qi of cold produces much longevity" may reflect an awareness of the relatively greater danger of disease in hot climates; but here the yin-yang theoretical implications also cannot be ignored. Heat correlates with yang, activity, and intentionality, whereas cold is yin and passive—reminiscent of Zhuangzi's prescription for enhancing longevity through "uselessness," that is, avoidance of involvement in public affairs.

After going through a list of attributes associated with soils and topography, the text briefly alludes to the influence of different types of water, in lines reminiscent of the *Guanzi* 39 passage mentioned above.

Section VIII ends with a general statement of similar sorts of effects of the five directions on natural phenomena, anticipating a fuller statement of the same point in Section XIII below. The last part of Section VIII begins with the statement, typical of Chinese cultural self-congratulation, that the center produces many sages. It then generalizes that all things are the same as their qi. The text continues with what seem like observations remarkable only for the accuracy of the information they reveal about far-distant places. Thus we are told that in the north there is perennial ice and in the south there are plants that do not die—presumably tropical evergreens. Some scholars have taken *busi zhi cao* to mean "plants of deathlessness," that is, ingredients of an elixir of immortality.[35] Such a meaning might well be intended here, at least secondarily— Section XV below lists a land of Undying People in the south—but the straightforward botanical fact of perennial tropical forests in the south seems more germane. (In terms of sympathetic magic, plants that do not die seasonally would be good ingredients for an elixir of immortality, so both interpretations are possible.) On closer examination, the geographical facts presented here seem to be based as much on cosmological theory as on geographical knowledge. That is to say, according to the *Huainanzi*'s cosmology, there *should be* undying plants in the south, just as there should be unmelting ice in the far north. This becomes clear in the next two lines of text: we are told that in the east there are countries of superior beings, and in the west tribes of mutilated victims of war, who after death become ghosts. In every case—the center and the four cardinal directions—the concrete statement is an illustration of the general principle that all things respond to their dominant five phase qi.

The assumption that the east produces superior people would have been bolstered by the long-standing mythic tradition of the Penglai "islands of the blest" in the Eastern Sea, with their population of immortals and sages. In his commentary on this passage Zhuang Kuiji says, "The *Shuowen* reads, 'the barbarians of the east are large men; their customs are benevolent. The benevolent are long-lived (see *Analects* 6:21). Thus there is a land of immortal *junzi*.' This passage is the same as that." Similarly, the tribes of (from the Chinese point of view) war-like "barbarians" to the west of China could have provided inspiration for the race of cripples supposedly to be found there. Gao You's commentary here is of interest:

> The west is metal. Metal is for cutting. In times of warfare it produces mutilated corpses. . . . The qi of metal is steely. Therefore when they sleep they dream; when they are awake it is (still) like a dream. Therefore it says 'constantly a dream.' Their lives do not end. When they die they become ghosts that can cause prodigies and bring illness to people. It is said that the mutilated corpses use the two nipples as eyes and the navel as a mouth; they carry a shield and a spear and dance.[36] Heavenly spirits cut off their hands, and afterwards the Lord of Heaven cuts off their heads so that they will not dance. Thus it is said that their sleeping and waking is like a dream.

From the passages of commentary just quoted, it is obvious that the requirements of five phase theory are more important in these lines than any empirical observation. The ethical characteristic of phase wood, associated with the east, is *ren*, humaneness; thus in the east there *should be* countries of superior persons. Likewise, the phase of the west, metal, has associations of cruelty and of maiming caused by punishments and warfare; thus in the west there *should be* peoples ravaged by the consequences of violence. (Cf. 4.XIII.23: "The people [of the west] are daring but not benevolent.") For an early Han cosmologist, these correlations are as empirically based as unmelting ice in the north, tropical evergreen plants in the south, and sages in the wise and well-governed central region, that is, China itself.

This concluding passage of Section VIII thus is illuminating for two reasons. First, it illustrates that in some cases at least, accurate data gained from a knowledge of natural phenomena could be fitted easily into, and hence could be regarded as evidence for the essential accuracy and validity of, yin-yang/five phase cosmology. Second, predictive or presumptive statements about the unknown based on the known, in accordance with those cosmological principles, often were somewhat or even wildly at variance from the facts that might have been obtained through actual observations. But in the absence of contradictory data, the statements were part of a convincing whole, and could be accepted in their time as entirely reasonable.

The Treatise on Topography

Section IX: Diet and Disposition

[4:8a:3]

1 Lodestone flies up; mica draws water.
2 The earthen dragon brings rain; swallows and wild geese fly in succession.
3 Clams, crabs, pearl oysters, and tortoises flourish and decline with (the waxing and waning of) the moon.
4 Thus for the same reason,
5 People who live in regions of hard soil are hard and unyielding,
6 People who live on easily-worked soil are fat.
7 People who live on lumpy soil are large,
8 People who live on sandy soil are small.
9 People who live on fertile soil are beautiful,
10 People who live on barren soil are ugly.

[4:8b:1] [4:10a:8]

11 People who live on level ground are clever and are suited for eating the five kinds of grain.

[4:10a:8] [4:8b:1]

12 Creatures that feed on water excel at swimming and are able to withstand cold.
13 Creatures that feed on earth do not have hearts but are sensitive.
14 Creatures that feed on wood are very powerful and are fierce.
15 Creatures that feed on grass excel at running but are stupid.
16 Creatures that feed on (mulberry) leaves produce silk and turn into moths.
17 Creatures that feed on flesh are brave and daring but are cruel.
18 Creatures that feed on qi are sage-like and enlightened, and have great longevity.
19 Creatures that feed on grain are knowledgeable and clever but short-lived.
20 Creatures that do not feed on anything do not die; they are spirits.

[4:9a:2]

Commentary to Section IX

This section opens with two lines of doggerel, each with two balanced phrases, that are suggestive of proverbs or riddle verses: catchphrases to aid a magician's memory. They serve as an introduction to what follows, to emphasize that yin and yang are inherent in all natural things, and their actions and transformations govern natural processes.

"Lodestone flies up" (or, to give the verb a causative aspect, "lodestone makes [iron filings] fly up"), illustrates the well-known early Chinese interest in magnetic phenomena. Small fragments of magnetite will "fly up" to adhere to a piece of iron held just above them; similarly, iron filings will "fly up" to adhere to a piece of magnetite. The phenomenon is yang, because it is active. In contrast, the condensation of dew on a piece of mica (which, like any glassy substance, easily attracts water through condensation) is passive, and therefore yin.

172

The earthen dragon in line 2 is a reference to the well-known folktale of how Tang the Victorious brought rain by creating an earthen dragon effigy, a practice that continued into Han times.[37] Here too, as in several instances above, *Huainanzi* appears to be supplying an answer to one of the questions of the "Tian wen," which in verse 81 asks, "When Ping [Yi] cried out and brought forth the rain, how did he make it come?" The dragon, in its cloudy/abyssal aspect, is an ultimate embodiment of yin, and thus attracts yin rain. The second phrase of line 2 is less obvious, but Gao You explains, "The swallow is a dark bird. In spring it arrives [from the far south]. In the spring the wild goose departs and goes north to the midst of the wastelands. The swallow departs in the autumn. In the autumn the wild goose flies south [from Siberia] to Pengli Lake [Lake Poyang] in Jiangxi. Thus it is said they fly in succession." This empirical observation presumably also has yin-yang connotations, but it is no longer clear what they are.

All of the text beginning with line 3 here and continuing through Sections X and XI is nearly identical with part of Chapter 81 of *Da Dai liji*, with minor changes in wording and with the paragraphs in a different order.[38] It seems likely that both texts are quoting a now-lost earlier source.

The statement that clams, crabs, etc. (i.e., scaly and shelled creatures generally) are governed by yin, and thus are responsive to the waxing and waning of the moon, reflects a widespread belief in early China. Statements of this type are repeated over and over in early Chinese cosmological literature, with minor changes in the lists of yin creatures involved. Some examples are found in *Guanzi* 37 and *Da Dai liji* 58,[39] as well as in *Huainanzi* 3, Section II, lines 22–24: "The moon is the fundament of yin. Therefore, when the moon wanes, the brains of fishes shrink; when the moon dies, wasps and crabs shrivel up."

Line 4 in this passage prefaces the several statements that follow with the words "Thus for the same reason." The reason is the one stated in 4.VIII.27 above: "All things are the same as their qi." The present section thus continues the line of reasoning in that section, whereby human characteristics are related to the qi of particular environments of soil or water. Nevertheless, the correspondences given for the various types of soil in the present section seem to be intuitive or proverbial, rather than being based on the requirements of yin-yang/five phase reasoning. It does not require any cosmological theory to suppose that people who live on fertile soil will be affluent and well-nourished, and therefore comely, while people who live on barren soil will be correspondingly overworked, badly nourished, and ill-favored. Thus the correlations given in this section seem to be based either on actual observation of nature, on sympathetic magic, or on simple common sense. The observations are cast in the general cosmological framework of yin-yang/five phase resonance; things correspond to the qi of environment or diet. Nevertheless, specific yin-yang/five phase correlations, while present, are not stressed, nor does the author labor to conjure up data to suit the requirements of the theory.

It is not always obvious which creatures are meant that feed on the various substances mentioned here. "Creatures that feed on water" are fish, turtles, and the like. That such creatures excel at swimming and can withstand the cold is certainly true, but one would have expected Han natural philosophers to have known that fish did not feed on water. The statement may reflect an incorrect understanding of fishes' inhalation of water for gill breathing.

"Creatures that feed on earth" are earthworms, which do indeed ingest earth in order to derive nourishment from the microorganisms it contains. They are described as being *hui*, a word which in its two other occurrences in this section I translate as "clever," but which here must mean something like "sensitive" (or even "sentient"). "Creatures that feed on wood" are, according to Gao You, bears. Bears do not eat wood, of course, but this statement might reflect an incorrect conclusion from observation of a common feeding habit of bears, which often tear open (and seem to eat?) old trees and logs in search of honey or grubs. Pandas are bear-like, and they do eat woody plants—bamboo—but it would probably be overreaching to construe this line as referring to them. If pandas had been intended here, the text would probably have been more specific about it.

"Beings that eat qi" are sages; this refers to early Daoist yogic techniques of breath control as a path to immortality. Given the substantial influence of the *Zhuangzi* on the *Huainanzi*, it is not surprising to find such an allusion to "nourishing the vital essence" here. In a similar vein, *Huainanzi* 11 refers to the sages Wang Qiao and Chi Sungzi, who lived by "nourishing their breath." The classic reference to this type of breath control is in *Zhuangzi* 33: "There is a holy man who lives far away on Gu Yi Mountain. . . . He does not eat the five grains, but (rather) imbibes the wind and drinks the dew. . . ." The contrast between the diet of sages and that of ordinary mortals is made clear in the present passage in *Huainanzi*, which describes people who eat grain (the Chinese, that is, in contrast to "barbarians" as well as to sages) as clever but short-lived. A further contrast is made with spirits—pure, disembodied, numinous beings—who need eat nothing at all.

Section X: Numerology and Birth

[4:9a:2]

1 Concerning humans, birds, and beasts, the myriad creatures and tiny organisms, each has that which governs its birth.

2 Some are odd and some are even, some fly and some go on foot, but no one knows the nature of this.

3   Only one who knows how to trace the Dao can get to the source and root of it.

4   Heaven is one, Earth is two, man is three.

5    $3 \times 3 = 9$. $9 \times 9 = 81$. 1 governs the sun. The number of the sun is 10.

6   The sun governs man, so man is born in the tenth month (of pregnancy).

7    $8 \times 9 = 72$. 2 governs even numbers. Even numbers contain odd numbers. Odd numbers govern (the Branch) *chen. Chen* governs the moon.

8   The moon governs the horse, so horses are born in the twelfth month (of pregnancy).

9    $7 \times 9 = 63$. 3 governs the Dipper.

10   The Dipper governs the dog, so dogs are born in the third month (of pregnancy).

11    $6 \times 9 = 54$. 4 governs the seasons.

12   The seasons govern the pig, so pigs are born in the fourth month (of pregnancy).

13    $5 \times 9 = 45$. 5 governs the musical notes (of the pentatonic scale).

14   The musical notes govern the ape, so apes are born in the fifth month (of pregnancy).

15    $4 \times 9 = 36$. 6 governs the notes (of the pitchpipes).

16   The pitchpipe notes govern the deer, so deer are born in the sixth month (of pregnancy).

17    $3 \times 9 = 27$. 7 governs the stars.

18   The stars govern the tiger, so tigers are born in the seventh month (of pregnancy).

19    $2 \times 9 = 18$. 8 governs the wind. The wind governs insects, so insects undergo metamorphosis in the eighth month.
[4:9b:1]

Commentary to Section X

This section is similar in its general argumentation to Sections VIII and IX. It opens with a general statement to the effect that all creatures are governed by natural principles, and here adds that the principles are obscure and difficult to understand. They are accessible only to a (presumably sage-like) person who is attuned to the Dao. The statement that "Heaven is one, Earth is two, man is three" echoes the famous line from *Laozi* 42 that says, "The Dao begets one, one begets two, two begets three, three begets the myriad things." (This line was quoted verbatim in 3.XXVIII.5 above; it is the basis for the cosmogony of *Huainanzi* 1, and the concept is also related to the cosmogonic passage at the beginning of *Huainanzi* 7, wherein two deities transform into yin and yang, which beget the myriad things.) The triad of heaven, earth, and man in the present passage is related to, but is not the same as, this *Laozi*-influenced numerological cosmogony; the triad was emphasized by Dong Zhongshu a generation after *Huainanzi* was written, and its appearance here must represent one of the earliest occurrences of the concept.

Figure 4.4. An immortal embarking on a spirit journey through the sky. He rides on a dragon, accompanied by a crane (a symbol of immortality); above him is a parasol or canopy similar to the chariot-canopy that was a standard symbol for the heavens in *gaitian* cosmology, while beneath the dragon is a fish that recalls the giant Pang fish of 4.XVI.2 below. (Pencil drawing by Sandra Smith-Garcès of a silk painting from a Chu tomb at Changsha, after *Changsha Chumu bohua*.)

This section is principally concerned with giving reasons for the varying lengths of the gestation periods of various animals. While the actual gestation periods of the animals named are generally correct, the reasons given for them show none of the commonsense naturalism in the dietary correspondences found in Section IX just above. Instead, the explanations here depend on numerology. It has already become clear from various passages in *Huainanzi* 3 that in early China the line dividing mathematics from numerology was not only unclear, it was inconceivable. There was a natural tendency in early societies to regard numbers as magical; mathematical tricks and curiosities (such as the many remarkable properties of the numbers three and nine) were taken seriously indeed. This remained true even after computational mathematics had reached a high level of development, as was certainly true in Han China. Other societies yield similar examples; the parallels with Pythagorean mathematical philosophy are especially striking.

The numerology of gestation periods found here is strongly similar to the numerology of weights and measures found in Chapter III, Section XXXI above. The heart of this section is a mathematical trick: If one works the multiplication table for nine from the "high end"—$9 \times 9 = 81$, $9 \times 8 = 72$, etc.—the second digits of the products count from one to nine in order. Having observed this computational quirk, the author sets out to derive the number nine itself from first principles, taking the cosmic triad of heaven, earth, and man to reach three, and multiplying three times itself to get nine.

The difficulties of such numerological reasoning are obvious. In some cases, the system is very neat, for example in the case of $7 \times 9 = 63$. Three governs the Dipper, the Dipper governs the dog, so dogs are born in the third month of pregnancy. The reasons why three governs the Dipper, and why the Dipper governs the dog, are not obvious (see below), but at least the formula produces a quick and tidy result. Compare this with $8 \times 9 = 72$, whereby 12 governs the gestation and birth of the horse; the argument is very strained, and the equation of 2 with 12 is unexplained. Moreover, the necessary added steps produce a break in the prosodic parallelism that so often characterizes Chinese philosophical argumentation of this kind (compare Section XIX below). It is obvious from this that the author's primary aim was to derive the final number (the length of the gestation period, known from actual observation) in each case, and he was willing to manipulate his figures as much as necessary in order to obtain it. The process is neither satisfactory scientifically nor convincing rhetorically. This does not mean, of course, that the author of this passage was a charlatan; he undoubtedly believed in his own methods.

Some of the correspondences in this section can be identified with reasonable confidence. Ten is the number of the sun because of the ten suns that existed before Yi the Archer shot down nine of them, and also (which amounts to the same thing) because of the ten Heavenly Stems. That the sun governs man is less obvious cosmologically, though from a commonsense standpoint humans, perhaps especially in agrarian societies, are indeed governed—are wholly dependent upon—the seasonal round of the solar year.

That "two governs even numbers" is obvious; the notion that "even numbers contain odd numbers" may refer to the cosmological notion of yang-within-yin, or to the mathematical observation that two odd numbers summed produce an even number. It is not clear why the Earthly Branch (or chronogram) *chen* governs the moon; *Huainanzi* 3, where one might expect to find such astrological information, is silent on that point. As for the moon governing the horse, the moon is the essence of yin, and the horse was long known in China as a yin symbol.[40]

Despite all that is said about the Dipper in *Huainanzi* 3, nothing is mentioned there associating the Dipper with the number three. The connection may simply derive from the three conspicuous stars that make up the handle of the Dipper, though there may also have been a deeper reason that has long been forgotten. That the Dipper governs the dog may perhaps indicate a connection between the Dipper as a seasonal indicator, and the bright star Sirius—in China, as in western Asia, a dog (or in China's case, at least dog-like: it was known as the Wolf Star). There could also be a (rather farfetched) association between the Dipper as an indicator of the seasons and the dog, which is born in the third month of gestation—that is, within a single three-month season.

The association of pigs with four, apes with five, and deer with six appear to be simple instances of backward reasoning: those animals are born in the fourth, fifth, and sixth months of gestation, so those numbers must "govern" them. The links of four with the seasons, five with the pentatonic scale, and six with the pitch pipes are obvious.

Seven is the number of the stars in a twofold sense: there are seven stars in the Dipper, and also seven "stars" (properly, asterisms) that move through the sky, those being the sun, the moon, and the five naked-eye planets. For the same reasons, the link between seven and the stars is found throughout Eurasia; compare, for example, a line from an old English folk song: "Seven for the seven stars in the sky. . . ." It is not obvious why the stars should govern the tiger, though one might note that the tiger was one of the familiars of a celestial deity much admired in the Han: Xiwangmu, the Queen Mother of the West. (Directional number correlation does *not* work here; seven is the number of the east and the Bluegreen Dragon, not of the White Tiger of the west.)

Similarly, eight as the number of the winds is obvious, and in both *Huainanzi* 3 and *Huainanzi* 4 long passages are devoted to the eight winds. It is, however, not clear why the wind governs insects. Perhaps it is because their flight is weak and unable to contend against the force of the wind. It is also not clear whether this line refers to the normal metamorphosis of insects (into, or from, pupae), or to their transformation into other kinds of animals (see the "Technical and Texual Notes" for more on this point.)

This section of *Huainanzi* 4, which deals with gestation, has an interesting complement in *Huainanzi* 6:1b–2a dealing with embryology (with specific reference to humans):

> Thus one gives birth to two, two gives birth to three, three gives birth to the ten thousand things. The ten thousand things carry yin and enfold yang; the mingling of qi creates harmony. Thus it is said: In the first month there is a speck of fertile grease; in the second month there is a globule; in the third month, an embryo; in the fourth month, flesh; in the fifth month, sinews; in the sixth month, bones; in the seventh month, complete form; in the eighth month, quickening; in the ninth month, agitated movement, and in the tenth month, birth.

Section XI: Taxonomy

[4:9b:1]

1   Bird and fish are all born of yin, but are of the class of yang creatures.
2   Thus birds and fish are oviparous.
3   Fish swim through water, birds fly in the clouds.
4   Thus at the beginning of winter swallows and sparrows enter the sea and turn into clams.
5   The myriad living creatures are all born as different kinds.
6   Silkworms eat but do not drink.
7   Cicadas drink but do not eat.
8   Mayflies neither eat nor drink.
9   Armored and scaly creatures eat during the summer but hibernate in winter.
10   Animals that eat without mastication have eight bodily openings and are oviparous.
11   Animals that chew have nine bodily openings and are viviparous.
12   Quadrupeds do not have feathers or wings.
13   Animals that have horns do not have upper (incisor) teeth.
14   (Some) animals do not have horns and are fat, but do not have incisor teeth.
15   (Other animals) have horns and are fat, but do not have molar teeth.
16   Creatures born during the day resemble their fathers; those born at night resemble their mothers.
17   Extreme yin produces females, extreme yang produces males.
18   Bears hibernate, and birds vary seasonally.

[4:10a:1]

Commentary to Section XI

This section is a document of particular interest for the history of science in China. It is an attempt to create a systematic and consistent taxonomy of animals on the basis of data obtained mainly from the close observation of nature and then refined with reference to yin-yang principles. One is immediately struck by the high level of accuracy of the observations of anatomy and diet seen here, and by the sophistication with which various types of yin-yang classifications are used in combination to assign a specific taxonomic type to each creature. That this scheme did not in the end lead to a Chinese Linnaeus—for the familiar combination of reasons that drove Chinese natural philosophy in the direction of theoretically based generalization rather than observationally based exact science—does not detract from the intrinsic interest of the material here.

The basic approach of this section's taxonomy is to isolate various sorts of anatomical and behavioral features in such a way as to allow them to be grouped in classes of yin and yang. The different features described in this passage are as follows:

Feature	Yin	Yang
Birth mode	Oviparous	Viviparous
Locomotion mode	Flying/swimming	[Walking/running]*
Diet	(Unclear)	(Unclear)
Annual rhythm	Migration/hibernation	[Active year-round]
Diurnal rhythm	Born at night	Born during day
Mode of eating	Nonmastication	Mastication
Orifices	Eight orifices	Nine orifices
Bodily covering	Shell, scales, feathers	[Hair]
Forelimbs	Wings [& fins]	[Arms or forelegs]

* Items in square brackets are implied but not stated.

These nine separate categories of yin-yang dualism are then used in combinations of two or more to group animals into compatible classes. For example, birds and fish form a single class, because they are oviparous, have eight bodily openings (these two features really mean the same thing), do not chew, have a yang form of locomotion, and have a yin type of annual rhythm. In fact, as line 4 implies, because birds and fish are of the same class, they were thought to be able to metamorphose into one another. ("Fish" here is understood broadly as including shellfish; thus birds can be transformed into clams. Elsewhere, however, fish and shellfish are considered to belong to two different classes of creatures, the "scaly" and the "armored," respectively.) To take another example, mammals form a class, because they have nine bodily openings and are viviparous, they chew their food, they are usually quadrupeds, and (by implication from not having wings and feathers) they have hair. In some respects the yin-yang categories implied in this section are unclear, however; for example, it is not clear what the yin-yang implications are of the statement that silkworms eat but do not drink, cicadas drink but do not eat, and mayflies neither eat nor drink.

The latter part of this section shows an attempt to devise an even more sophisticated taxonomic scheme, one that defines subclasses within a taxonomic group on anatomical grounds. In an attempt to classify the mammals, the author of this section uses four criteria:

1. Presence or absence of horns;
2. Presence or absence of upper incisor teeth;
3. "Fat" (or "not fat");
4. Incisors vs. molars.

Using these criteria, the following taxonomic scheme is derived:

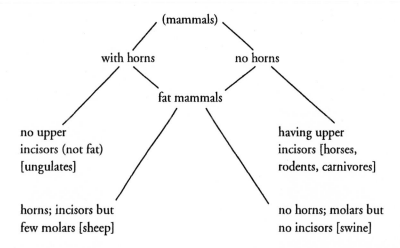

This system can be described as genuinely scientific, in that it makes use of valid data, is systematic, and is objective rather than normative. The observation that (most) horned animals do not have upper incisors apparently long predates the *Huainanzi*; as Erkes points out, it was commented upon in the Indian Vedas as well.[41] This fact of nature was sometimes used overtly to make a point about the coincidence of natural phenomena and human normative ones. For example, in *Lüshi chunqiu* 24, the fact that animals usually do not have both horns and upper incisors exemplifies the point that "the Former Kings knew that creatures could not have two kinds of greatness"; the statement appears in a political context, and is used to reinforce the idea that government should limit the power of officials. Similarly, in *Chunqiu fanlu* 8:3 Dong Zhongshu says, "Heaven does not bestow twice. Thus what has horns is not permitted to have [*bu de you*] upper teeth." This is another of many instances in which, in China as elsewhere in the ancient world, no distinction was made between what we now would consider the separate realms of religion and science (or at least "natural philosophy").

The *Huainanzi* as a whole takes the position characteristic of the Huang-Lao School that it was important for rulers to learn about natural phenomena in order to make their rule conform to universal principles. Nevertheless, the three chapters of the *Huainanzi* under consideration in this book tend more than most comparable texts to leave the normative messages unstated, and to present scientific knowledge as it was understood at the time in relatively undiluted form. This passage is a striking example of that tendency.

Section XII: The Qualities of Water

[4:10a:1]

1   For the same reasons,
2   White water is appropriate for (white) jade,
3   Black water is appropriate for black stone [slate?],
4   Bluegreen water is appropriate for azure jade,
5   Red water is appropriate for cinnabar,
6   Yellow water is appropriate for gold,
7   Clear water is appropriate for turtles.
8   The waters of the Fen River are turbid and muddy, and are suitable for hemp.
9   The waters of the Qi River flow harmoniously and are suitable for wheat.
10   The waters of the Yellow River are blended together and are suitable for legumes.
11   The waters of the Luo River are light and free-flowing, and are suitable for grains.
12   The waters of the Wei^c River are powerful and are suitable for panicled millet.
13   The waters of the Han River are heavy and calm, and are suitable for bamboo.
14   The waters of the Yangtse River are fertile and benevolent, and are suitable for rice.
[4:10a:8]

Commentary to Section XII:

Returning from biological to more purely geographical topics, the beginning of this section nevertheless states that "the same reasons" (i.e., resonance within yin-yang/five phase categories) govern the behavior of both the animate and the inanimate. This section is less easy to understand than the ones that immediately precede it. The text states that waters of certain colors, or the waters of certain rivers, are "appropriate for" or "suitable for" certain types of minerals or agricultural products. What this means is not obvious.

In the case of colored waters, the implication seems to be that the minerals in question are (or ought to be) found in or near the waters in question, or are congealed from such waters. Certainly it is the case that the waters of different rivers and swamps come in different colors—reddish if not really red, yellowish if not really yellow, and so on. One might be tempted to see here traces of a proto-mineralogy, and an apologist for early Chinese science might note that the process of crystallization is so slow that the Chinese could be excused for inferring it from five phase theoretical consider-ations of color rather than observing it directly. Still, this will not really do; any early Chinese mineral prospector would have known that the fact that a river's water was yellowish and muddy would not have been a reliable predictor of the presence of gold. Any natural science present at all in this passage is of the loosest sort. Rather, there seems to be here not much more than appears on the surface: that is, statements that red water and red minerals belong to the same resonance class. Similarly, black water is appropriate for black minerals because both are black, and likewise with the other colors. That principles of resonance, rather than observation, are at work here is appar-ent from the last statement in the series, that clear water is appropriate for turtles. In fact, turtles are most likely to be found in the rather cloudy water of ponds, but that is beside the point. Instead, clear water is appropriate for turtles because the clarity of limpid water is equivalent to the oracular clarity of turtles in rites of divination.

The same reasoning applies to the waters of particular rivers and agricultural crops of various sorts. The subjective qualities of the flow patterns of these rivers—turbid or free-flowing, powerful or calm—are associated with the subjective qualities attributed to the different sorts of plants. There is, however, also a trace of geographical realism here; the more northerly rivers are matched to hemp, wheat, millet, "grain" in general, and panicled millet, while the more southerly rivers (the Han and the Yangtse) are matched to warm-weather crops, that is, bamboo and rice.

This passage may represent, more than anything else, a distillation of contem-porary lore about which crops grow best in various river basins. The information pres-ented in this passage is not, in any case, derived directly from five phase theory, for the directional and crop correlations fit only approximately (because bamboo, and "grain" in general, have no standard five phase correlates:

River	Approximate Direction	Directional Phase	Product	Product Phase
Fen	North/West	Water/Metal	Hemp	Metal
Qi	East	Wood	Wheat	Wood
Yellow	Center?	Earth	Legumes	Fire
Luo	South/West	Fire/Metal	Grain	?
Wei	Center?	Earth	Panicled Millet	Earth
Han	South	Fire	Bamboo	?
Yangtse	South	Fire	Rice	Fire

Making allowances for the degree to which this section must have been more readily understandable to a Han intellectual than to a twentieth-century commentator, it seems to be, overall, a rather awkward and unsystematic mixture of five phase theory, Han agricultural data, and an attempt to establish a typology of waters analogous to the typology of soils found in Section IX above, together with an effort to fit it all into the larger cosmological picture.

Section XIII: Peoples of the Five Directions

[4:10a:8]

1   The east is where streams and valleys flow to, and from whence the sun and moon arise.

2   The people of the east are heavy-bodied, and have small heads, prominent noses, and large mouths.

3   They have raised shoulders like hawks, and walk on tiptoe.

4   Their bodily openings are all channelled to their eyes.

5   The nerves and (bodily) qi belong to the east.

6   The color green governs the liver.

7   The people there are tall and large, and mature early; they are knowledgeable but not long-lived.

8   The land there is suitable for wheat; it is full of tigers and leopards.

9   The south is where yang qi gathers. Heat and damp reside there.

10   The people of the south have long bodies, and are heavy above.

11   They have large mouths and prominent eyelids.

12   Their bodily openings are all channelled to their ears.

13   The blood and the blood vessels belong to the south.

14   The color red governs the heart.

15   The people there are strong in their youth but die young.

16   The land there is suitable for rice; it is full of rhinoceros and elephants.

17   The west is a region of high ground.

18   Rivers issue forth from there, and the sun and moon set there.

19   The men of the west have ill-favored faces and misshapen necks, but walk with dignity.

20   Their bodily openings are all channelled to their noses.

21   The skin belongs to the west.

22   The color white governs the lungs.

23   The people there are daring but not benevolent.

24   The land there is suitable for millet; it is full of yaks and rhinoceros.

25   The north is a dark and gloomy place, where the sky is closed up.

26   Cold and ice are gathered there.

27   Insects in their larval and pupal stages lie concealed there.

28   The bodies of the people of the north are tightly-knit, with short necks, broad shoulders, and low-slung buttocks.

29   Their bodily openings are all channelled to their genitals.

30   The bones belong to the north.

31   The color black governs the kidneys.

32 The people there are stupid as birds or beasts but are long-lived.

33 The land there is suitable for legumes, and is full of dogs and horses.

34 The center is where the rains and qi come together from all directions, and is the place of confluence of the rains and the dew.

35 The people of the central region have large faces and short chins. They like beards and dislike obesity.

36 Their bodily openings are all channelled to their mouths.

37 Flesh and muscle belong to the center.

38 The color yellow governs the stomach.

39 The people of the center are clever and sage-like and are good at government.

40 The land there is suitable for grain, and is full of cattle and sheep and the various domestic animals.

[4:11a:4]

Commentary to Section XIII

This section presents a more elaborate version of the five phase directional influences on human inhabitants than that given in Section VIII above, but the fundamental principles are the same. The most important difference between Sections VIII and XIII is that the directional correlates of the five phases are given in considerably greater detail here. These correlations may be tabulated as follows:

Direction	Phase	Color	Sensory Organ	Structural Organ
East	Wood	Bluegreen	Eyes	Nerves and Channels of Qi*
South	Fire	Red	Ears*	Blood and Blood Vessels
West	Metal	White	Nose	Skin
North	Water	Black	Genitals*	Bones
Center	Earth	Yellow	Mouth	Flesh and Muscle

Visceral Organ	Attributes	Agricultural Products	Animals
Liver*	Knowledgeable, not Long-lived	Wheat	Tigers, Leopards
Heart*	Early Strength, Short-lived	Rice	Elephants, Rhinoceros
Lungs*	Daring, not Benevolent	Millet	Yaks, Rhinoceros
Kidneys*	Stupid, Long-lived	Legumes	Dogs, Horses
Stomach*	Clever, Sage-like	Grain*	Domestic Animals

* The correlations given here differ in some respects from the standard list given in Needham, SCC II:262–263. Cases of difference are marked with an asterisk. Needham's list does not include a category of health and personality attributes. The animals given in the table above were probably chosen on the basis of actual habitat rather than on five phase principles.

The direction/phase correlates of the visceral organs given here differ completely from the usual list, that is, east: spleen; south: lungs; west: kidneys; north: liver; center: heart. In some respects the list in this section makes more sense by the standards of five

185

phase logic: liver is appropriate for the east because of the greenish color of bile; the heart for the south because of red blood; the kidneys for the north because the phase of north is water; the stomach for the center possibly because of its central location in the torso, and because the Chinese regarded it as the seat of sensation; and the lungs for the west because the lungs are conspicuously whitish compared with the rest of the internal organs.

It is worth noting that while the author seems to be trying to describe natural phenomena in the objective terms of a scientific system, the terms of that system itself are value-laden; thus here as elsewhere it is no accident that the center—China—comes out looking rather well in comparison with the rest of the world.

Section XIV: Cycles of the Five Phases

[4:11a:4]

1. Wood overcomes Earth, Earth overcomes Water, Water overcomes Fire, Fire overcomes Metal, Metal overcomes Wood. Thus:
2. Grain is born in the spring and dies in the fall.
3. Legumes are born in the summer and die in the winter.
4. Wheat is born in the autumn and dies in the summer.
5. Green vegetables are born in the winter and die in midsummer.
6. When Wood is in its prime, Water is old, Fire is about to be born, Metal is paralyzed [imprisoned], and Earth is dead.
7. When Fire is in its prime, Wood is old, Earth is about to be born, Water is paralyzed, and Metal is dead.
8. When Earth is in its prime, Fire is old, Metal is about to be born, Wood is paralyzed, and Water is dead.
9. When Metal is in its prime, Earth is old, Water is about to be born, Fire is paralyzed, and Wood is dead.
10. When Water is in its prime, Metal is old, Wood is about to be born, Earth is paralyzed, and Fire is dead.
11. In music there are five notes, of which the chief is *gong*.
12. There are five colors, of which the chief is yellow.
13. There are five flavors, of which the chief is sweet.
14. For positioning there are five materials (*wucai*), of which the chief is Earth.
15. This is why Earth when refined [subjected to change] produces Wood, Wood when refined produces Fire, Fire when refined produces clouds (of metallic qi), clouds when refined produce Water, and Water when refined reverts to Earth.
16. Sweet when refined produces sour, sour when refined produces acrid, acrid when refined produces bitter, bitter when refined produces salty, and salty when refined reverts to sweet.
17. *Gong* [note #1] when changed produces *zhi* [note #4]; *zhi* when changed produces

shang [note #2]; *shang* when changed produces *yu* [note #5]; *yu* when changed produces *jue* [note #3]; *jue* when changed produces *gong*.

18 Thus one uses Water to harmonize Earth, Earth to harmonize Fire, Fire to transform Metal, and Metal to rule Wood; Wood reverts to Earth.

19 The five phases interact together, and so useful things are brought to completion. [4:11b:6]

Commentary to Section XIV

This section of *Huainanzi* 4 is a remarkably cogent, compact, and powerful presentation of how the five phases act in different sequences to affect (and reflect, and effect) natural processes of all kinds. Virtually every instance of five phase cosmology that one encounters in *Huainanzi* 4 is grounded in the theoretical summary presented here. For general remarks on the five phases and their role in Huang-Lao cosmology, see Chapter 2 above.[42]

The first sequence of the five phases given here is the familiar "mutual overcoming order," E-Wa-F-M-Wo-E. Earth overcomes water (by damming); water overcomes fire (by extinguishing it); fire overcomes metal (by melting it); metal overcomes wood (by cutting it); and wood overcomes earth (by growing out of it, or perhaps by people tilling the earth with wooden plows).

The author demonstrates that natural processes do conform to this order by pointing to the germination and maturation of food crops:

Legumes = fire = summer; winter = water. Water overcomes fire, so legumes sprout in the summer and die in the winter.

Wheat = metal = autumn; summer = fire. Fire overcomes metal, so wheat sprouts in the autumn and dies in the summer.

Green vegetables = water = winter; midsummer = earth. Earth overcomes water, so green vegetables sprout in the winter and die in midsummer.

A gardener might have some doubts about the details of this seasonal data, but it is close enough to actual observation to be generally convincing as an example.

This "mutual overcoming order" is closely associated with the political theories of Zou Yan, who applied it to the historical succession of dynasties; it was adopted by Dong Zhongshu as a key element in the Han Confucian synthesis, which in this respect as in many others drew heavily on Huang-Lao theory.[43]

Lines 6–10 in this section recall (and amplify) *Huainanzi* 3, Section XXVI, line 9: "Thus it is said that when the compass is born, the T-square dies, the level-beam is growing, the plumb-weight is hidden away, and the marking-cords dwell in the center as the root of the four seasons." Substituting the five phase seasonal correlates for the names of construction implements in this passage, this line says that when spring is born, summer is growing, autumn is (still) dead, and winter, having preceded spring, is now buried away. The phase earth plays no direct role in the seasonal sequence given in *Huainanzi* 3, but dwells in the center and regulates the other four. The passage from *Huainanzi* 3, in other words, is a special-case adaptation for the four seasons of the more general five phase cycle given here.

The sequence given in these lines is the "mutual production order," E-M-Wa-Wo-F-E. Earth produces metal (from ores); metal produces water (by melting); water produces wood (irrigation produces vegetative growth); wood produces fire (by combustion); and fire produces earth (ash). The mutual production order was applied to cyclical phenomena such as seasons and directions (moving clockwise around the compass, with earth at the center).

The sequence is presented here in the form of a rhythmic series of five ten-character lines, emphasizing the cyclical nature of the series. The lines read almost as a chant, and perhaps were intended as an aid to memorization. The sequence is completely circular; at any stage, one phase is dominant, the previous one has grown old, the following one is quickening, the phase two stages back has entered a dormant state, and the one two stages forward is still moribund.

Lines 11–14 establish the general rule that in any five phase cycle, the starting point is phase earth or its correlate, thus emphazing the psychological and cosmological importance of the center.

In line 15 we find a variant of the mutual production order, which the text applies especially to processes of physical transformation; it might be called the "smelting sequence" or the "alchemical sequence." The sequence is E-Wo-F-M-Wa-E. Earth produces wood (growth of plants from the soil); wood produces fire (combustion); fire produces metal (clouds of acrid qi in the smelting of metals); metal produces water (melting); water produces earth (perhaps as the residue from distillation operations, or as the precipitation of solids from supersaturated solutions). Significantly, the famous alchemical passage in 4.XIX below follows this sequence.

The order in line 16 might be called the "taste sequence": E-Wo-M-F-Wa-E. It is a restatement in the passive voice of the mutual overcoming order, reading that order in the opposite direction and using the passive "is overcome by" rather than the active "overcomes." The alchemical term "refined" is used here, and the sequence resembles the "smelting sequence," but the rationale behind the order is less easy to establish. Perhaps there is a hint here of yin-yang dualism, with sweet going by stages to its opposite, salty, and then suddenly reverting to sweet (recalling Laozi's famous dictum that "reversal is the movement of the Dao").

The sequence in line 17 might be called the "harmonic sequence." It represents the first five stages in the process of generating the chromatic scale described in 3.XXIX above, using the rule "down by ⅔, up by ⅓." The result of this sequence is to produce a pleasant little melody, C-G-D-A-E-C.

Section XIV ends with an order that is unusual both because it begins with a phase other than earth, and because it is a noncyclical order: earth follows water at the beginning of the sequence but follows wood (by "reversion") at its end. The sequence is Wa-E-F-M-Wo-E. The reasoning here seems slightly arbitrary. Water "harmonizes" earth (by being absorbed into it?); earth harmonizes fire (by controlling it in earthen or brick stoves?); fire transforms metal (by smelting and casting); metal rules wood (by cutting and shaping); wood "reverts" to earth (decay).

Thus, says the text, through these various processes useful things are brought to completion—not randomly or by accident, but through the systematic operation of knowable and exploitable principles inherent in the natural order.

Section XV: The Thirty-Six Countries Beyond the Seas

[4:11b:6]

1 Beyond the seas there are thirty-six countries.
2 In the region stretching from the northwest to the southwest, there are:
3 The Long-thighs;
4 The Sky People;
5 The People of Sushen;
6 The White People;
7 The Fertile[-land] People;
8 The Female People;
9 The Male People;
10 The One-legged People;
11 The One-armed People;
12 The Three-bodied People.
13 In the region stretching from the southwest to the southeast, there are:
14 The Bound-breast People;
15 The Winged People;
16 The People of Huantou;
17 The Naked People;
18 The Three Miao Tribes;
19 The Cross-legged People;
20 The Undying People;
21 The Pierced-breast People;
22 The Tongue-tied People;
23 The Hog-snouted People;
24 The Chisel-toothed People;

25   The Three-headed People;

26   The Long-armed People.

27   In the region stretching from the southeast to the northeast, there are:

28   The Land of Giants;

29   The Land of Superior People;

30   The Black-toothed People;

31   The Dark-legged People;

32   The Hairy People;

33   The Hardworking People.

34   In the region stretching from the northeast to the northwest, there are:

35   The Tiptoe-walking People;

36   The People of Juying;

37   The Deep-eyed People;

38   The People Without Anuses;

39   The People of Rouli;

40   The One-eyed People;

41   The People of Wuji.

[4:12a:10]

Commentary to Section XV

Geographical texts of Warring States and Han date (and later as well) commonly contain lists of strange countries beyond China's borders. Those lands have exerted a powerful fascination on many Sinologists, and an extraordinary amount of effort has been expended in an attempt to identify them with actual places and tribes on the periphery of China. This has led to such Sinological curiosities as the work of Wei Tingsheng, who would have "the Son of Heaven Mu" of the *Mu Tianzi zhuan* journeying along a carefully traced route to the shores of the Caspian Sea.[44]

Such undertakings seem increasingly to be a thing of the past; most scholars share Hulsewé's opinion that "to try and identify the names of these places on a map of China is an unprofitable exercise, for the traveler is not exploring the world of man."[45] This of course does not exclude the possibility that some of the countries do in fact refer to real peoples on the periphery of China: for example, people known as the Miao have lived in southwestern China since antiquity, and still live there (though whether they have anything to do with the "Three Miao Tribes" expelled from the central realm by the Sage-emperor Shun is another matter); the "Hairy People" mentioned in this section of *Huainanzi* 4 are quite probably the Ainu or some related group in ancient Japan. Nevertheless, these strange lands must always be treated with great care, for they belong to a type of literature in which terrestrial and mythical geography blend together.

190

Of the thirty-six countries listed in this section of *Huainanzi* 4, most also appear in the *Shanhaijing* and various other early texts, along with hundreds of countries besides.[46] A more conventional use of the phrase "thirty-six countries" refers only to the countries to the west of China; Ying-shih Yü has summarized the evidence on this problem, citing the opinion of Ise Sentarō and others that the number thirty-six (selected for astrological and numerological significance) is to be understood to mean "a large number" rather than taken literally.[47] Perhaps then the thirty-six countries listed here are simply a sample—possibly designed to stimulate the memories of contemporary scholars who would have been familiar with the relevant literature and oral traditions—of a larger number of "countries" thought to exist beyond China's frontiers; no obvious process can be discerned whereby these particular ones were selected from a much larger pool of possibilities. There appears to be no connection between the countries mentioned here and the various "outlying regions" and so on of Section VI above. Moreover, the regions in Section VI are listed in a clockwise order while the thirty-six countries here are listed counter-clockwise around the map.

The thirty-six countries named here can be grouped into several broad categories: known peoples; possibly real but unidentified peoples or places; terata and other fabulous monsters; immortal or celestial beings; and a few miscellaneous unclassifiables.

Known peoples, or peoples identifiable with reasonable certainty, include the Three Miao Tribes (though again, the Miao of myth may share nothing but a name with the actual Miao people), the Ainu "Hairy People,"[48] and the People of Sushen—a northern tribe mentioned often in Zhou literature. For example, the *Bamboo Annals* describes the Sushen as paying a visit of homage in the ninth year of King Cheng of Zhou, after the latter had subdued the "northern barbarians." Guo Pu's commentary to *Shanhaijing* 17 adds,

> The land of Sushen is 3,000 li north of Liaodong Commandery. The people live in caves and wear only pig hides for clothing. In winter they smear grease on their bodies to a thickness of several inches to protect themselves from the wind and the cold. They are good archers. . . .

Unidentifiable but possibly real countries include the Naked People, perhaps any one of many primitive peoples of Southeast Asia, and the Black-toothed People—tooth blackening was widely practiced in East and Southeast Asia, and persisted in Japan until early modern times. The likelihood that the Black-toothed People really existed is reinforced by the *Chu ci* poem "Zhao hun," line 15: "Oh soul, come back. In the south you cannot stay. There the people have tattooed faces and blackened teeth."[49] Schlegel identifies the Dark-legged People as the Giliak of Siberia,[50] on the basis of Shanhaijing 9: "Dark-leg Land is in the north. The people there dress in fish-skin clothing." Three other countries—the lands of Juying, Rouli, and Wuji—may refer to

real but unidentified places, because their names, which all are written in several variant forms in Chinese, are apparently phonetic approximations of non-Chinese words.
It is not always easy, however, to decide whether to regard such terms as meaningful or
as merely phonetic. In the case of the Wuji, Gao You says that the word means "without heirs"; the term appears in *Shanhaijing* 8 as Wubi, "No-calves." The variation
would seem to imply that the terms are being used phonetically, but one cannot be
entirely sure. In either reading, the names of these northwestern lands seem to resonate
at least faintly with the notion, derived from five phase directional correlation, of the
slaughtered or mutilated tribes of the metallic west; see Section VIII above. Rouli
appears in *Shanhaijing* 8 and 17 in the alternate forms Liuli and Niuli; *rouli* means
"soft-pliant," which accords with the description of the people themselves, who are said
to be boneless, to have only one hand and one foot, and to be able to bend their single
leg backwards. (These people sound more like dragons or demi-serpents rather than
human beings of any kind.)

These examples show how rash it would be to apply too much rationality to
identifying these peoples. Chavannes, on uncertain grounds, located the Cross-legged
People in Annam; Schlegel identified the "White People" with the Ainu, but Conrady
saw them instead as the Pandya of northern India;[51] each was merely pursuing his own
ethnographical enthusiasm. Any of several light-skinned western peoples might fit the
bill, but the name more probably derives from the identification of the west with the
phase metal and the color white. Yet again one might identify the "Sky People" with
sky-worshipping, horse-riding nomads of Central Asia, but the reference is more
probably to the immortals associated with the Kunlun Mountains.

Lands of terata and monsters form the largest category among the thirty-six
countries listed here. One such land is that of the "Chisel-toothed People." At first
glance it might be tempting to see hints of the Southeast Asian practice of tooth filing
in the name of this people, until one notes in Gao You's commentary to this passage
that they are supposed to have a single rodent-like tooth projecting downward. In fact
the origin of the Chisel-toothed People is unquestionably mythical; Chisel-Tooth is
personified in both *Shanhaijing* 6 and *Huainanzi* 8:7ab as a monster with long,
chisel-like teeth who did harm to the people and who was subdued by Yi the Archer
(on orders from Sage-emperor Yao) in the Field-of-Flowers Wilderness. Other lands of
monsters include the Long-thighed People, the Long-armed People, the Female People
and the Male People, the One-legged, One-armed, Three-bodied, and Three-headed
Peoples, the Pierced-breasted People, the Tongue-tied People (who are mute because
their tongues are inserted backward in their mouths), the Tiptoe-walking People (who
appeared also in Section XIII above; their heels do not reach the ground, and they have
stooped shoulders and hawk-like shoulder blades), the Hog-snouted People, the One-
eyed People, and the People Without Anuses.

Needham has considered the question of the prevalence of terata and monsters in the myths of all Eurasian peoples, and has summarized the evidence for the transmission of specific types. To this he adds,

> To an embryologist it seems obvious that most of the different abnormalities that form the basis of the corpus of legend could have been derived from human and animal monstrosities naturally occurring. . . . If this point of view should prevail, there would be no reason to assume any transmission at all, at any rate to account for origins.[52]

One might plausibly see the origins of some of these beings in oft-told tales of strange animals in distant places: the Long-armed People (or the Hairy People, for that matter) could have originated in accounts of orangutans in the far south. Such a rationalist point of view might perhaps contribute something to our understanding of how particular monsters emerged into people's imaginations; however, it ignores the mythic, supernatural, and extraterrestrial qualities that were invariably attributed to such creatures, and which constitute their real importance in understanding the worldview of the people who believed in them.

Monsters such as these figure very prominently in Han art motifs, most spectacularly on the Chu Silk Manuscript. The monsters depicted thereon apparently represent beneficent calendrical/directional deities; they include a three-headed figure and a figure tentatively seen as having one arm and one leg (though the severely damaged fabric of that portion of the manuscript makes the reconstruction doubtful).[53] Generally speaking, it seems probable that many of the monsters and human-animal hybrid figures found in early Chinese art, from Shang to Han, represent visualizations of beings of the sort described in *Huainanzi*, *Shanhaijing*, and similar texts, even if we now can only tentatively (or not at all) match the texts to the figures.

Very probably the supernatural or cosmological connotations of many of the fabulous creatures described in this section will never be fully understood, but in some instances they can repay further study. Five phase correlations might play a role in some cases; for example, the One-legged and One-armed peoples might plausibly be related to the tribes of people crippled by warfare mentioned in Section VIII above. A structuralist approach to myth has also proven to be useful in dealing with these motifs; Girardot has written illuminatingly of the "Woman People" and the "People Without Anuses" in connection with the "sack of flesh/deformed child of incestuous union" motif in the Huntun creation myths.[54] The strange creature called "Viewflesh" in 4.XVI.7 below is another example of this "lump of flesh" motif. Other monstrous people also figure in cosmogonic or ancestral myths; for example, in *Shanhaijing* 15, the Three-bodied People are said to be surnamed Yao, and to have been begotten by Lady E Huang, wife of Di Jun.[55]

Figure 4.5. Depiction of a humanoid figure covered with feathers and with small wings projecting from his arms; from the Latter Han tomb at Yinan, Shandong, possibly representing one of the Winged People as in *Huainanzi* 4.XV.15. (From Zeng et al., *Yinan gu huaxiang shimu fajue baogao,* Plate 65.)

Some of the thirty-six countries here are clearly lands of immortals, and belong in the cloudscape of mythical journeys. They include one race of outright immortals—the Undying People—who perhaps are identical to the beings mentioned in Section IX above: "Creatures that do not feed on anything do not die; they are spirits."[56] Several others are lands of people who are associated with flight, a noted characteristic of immortals; these include the Sky People, the Winged People (see Fig. 4.5), and perhaps the people of Huantou.

The Huantou are found in *Shanhaijing,* chapters 6 and 15 (in nearly identical language): "Gun married Shi Jing; Shi Jing's son Yen Yong brought forth the Huantou. The Huantou have human faces, bird beaks, and fins. They eat ocean fish, and lean on their fins to walk." Guo Pu describes them as having bird heads and wings. On the basis of this description, from a "rationalist" point of view one might also see the Huantou as the product of distant rumors of the dugongs of the Yangtse delta; similar creatures in quite different waters apparently had a powerful impact on the imaginations of early Western mariners. On the other hand, *Shanhaijing* 17 gives a quite different explanation for the Huantou:

> Beyond the northwestern sea, north of the Black River, are people with wings, called the Miao People. Zhuan Xu gave birth to Huantou; Huantou gave birth to the Miao People. The Miao People are surnamed Xi; they eat meat.

This passage, incidentally, is a nice example of the characteristic confusion in early Chinese texts about the geographical location of the Miao; in different texts, they are placed anywhere from the northwest to the southwest.

The Land of Giants and the Land of Superior People also have connotations of sagehood or immortality; see the commentary to Section VIII above. The Fertile-land People are described at length in *Shanhaijing* 16:

> Fertile Land is west of [Queen Mother of the West Mountain]. The Fertile-land People dwell in the Fertile Wilderness, eat the eggs of *feng* phoenixes, drink sweet dew, and have all they desire. Here are sweet flowers, sweet haw-berries, white willows, [various precious stones, etc.], and much silver and iron. The *luan* and *feng* birds sing, and the *feng* bird dances. Animals of all kinds dwell together here. Thus it is called the Fertile Wilderness.

A few unclassifiable countries remain. They include the Bound-breasted People—a monstrosity of some kind, or simply a tribe whose native dress is characterized by a tight bodice? The identifying characteristic of the "Hardworking People" is mundane enough; they could be almost anyone (though the sense here could be pejorative, if *lao min* were understood as "toilsome people"). Finally, the land of the Deep-eyed People in the north may refer to some ethnic group characterized by "round" eyes, that is, without the Mongoloid opthalmic fold. On the other hand, they might be an obverse counterpart to the people of the south with prominent eyes mentioned in Section XIII above.

However one regards these figures (and the many others like them in the literature of the time)—as barbarians, monsters, immortals, or bizarre cosmogonic figures in the genealogies of antediluvian culture heroes—the overall impact of this section is clear: China, the quintessential land of civilization—the land of rulers to whose attention the information in the *Huainanzi* is drawn—is surrounded on all sides by lands that are uncivilized, precivilized, or unworldly. Ultimately, the message is a moral one.

Section XVI: Magical Landscapes

[4:12a:10]

1 Luotang Mountain and Warrior Mountain are in the northwest corner.

2　The Pang Fish is (found) to the south of them.

3　Twenty-eight gods link their arms and serve the Thearch by watching over the night to the southwest of them.

4　Three pearl trees are northeast of them.

5　Jade trees are (found) along the banks of the Vermilion River.

6　The Kunlun Mountains and Floreate Hill are to the southeast.

7　There are found precious jade and (the countries of) Greyhorse and Viewflesh;

8　In that place carambola trees, sweet *cha* trees, and the hundred kinds of fruit are produced.

9　Harmonious Hill is in the northeast corner.

10　The three mulberry trees without branches are to its west.

11　Bragging Father and Hanging Ears dwell northeast of it.

12　Bragging Father cast aside his staff, which grew into the Forest of Deng.

13　The Hill of Kun Wu is in the south.

14　Chariot Pole Hill is to its west.

15　Shaman Xian dwells to its north, standing on Dengbao Mountain.

16　Sunrise Valley and the Fusang Tree are to the east.

17　The land of You Song [or You Rong] is north of Mount Buzhou.

18　The older sister was Jian Di, the younger sister was Jian Ci.

19　The Queen Mother of the West dwells at the edge of the Flowing Sands.

20　The Music People and the Nalü People live on an island in the Weakwater in Kunlun.

21　Three Dangers Mountain is to the west of the Music People.

22　Lighting Darkness and Candle-Gleam are on an island in the Yellow River; they illumine an area of one thousand li.

23　The Dragon Gate is in the depths of the Yellow River.

24　The Torrential Pool is in Kunlun.

25　Dark Smelting (is near) Mount Buzhou.

26　Shen Pool is in the Haiyu Marsh.

27　The Mengzhu Marsh is in Pei.

28　The Lesser and Greater Mansions are in Ji Province.

29　The Torch Dragon dwells north of Wild Goose Gate.

30　He hides himself in Abandoned Wings Mountain and never sees the sun.

31　This god has a human face and a dragon body, but no feet.

32　The grave-mound of Lord Millet is to the west of the Jian Tree.

33　The people there come to life again after they die.

34　There are demi-fish in their midst.

35　Flowing Yellow and the Fertile-Land People are three hundred li to the north.

36　Dogland is to the east.

37　In Thunder Marsh there are gods with dragon bodies and human heads. They drum upon their bellies to amuse themselves.

[4:13b:10]

The Treatise on Topography

Commentary to Section XVI

This section, in general terms, is a continuation of the theme of Section XV; but whereas that section presented a straightforward list of fabulous countries on China's periphery, this one differs slightly in approach by placing various mythical figures into their appropriate mythical landscapes. This section resembles the description of Kunlun in Sections 3–5 above, and like those sections, this one has close links to the *Shanhaijing*. Much of the material here is derived from *Shanhaijing* 8 and 9, respectively "Haiwai beijing" ("Northern Lands Beyond the Sea") and "Haiwai dongjing" ("Eastern Lands Beyond the Sea"). These chapters deal generally with mythical places and beings at the edge of the *oikoumene*, but it is immediately apparent that, despite the chapter titles, the places are not confined to those that are north and east of China. Prominent among the places mentioned are some that are already familiar from earlier sections of *Huainanzi* 4—Kunlun, Floreate Hill, Harmonious Hill, the Jian tree, and so on—and they are located all around the periphery of the known world. Many of the magical personages mentioned here are also familiar from a wide range of late Zhou and Han sources.

Specific identifications of and comments on places and personages mentioned in this section follow:

Line 1: Gao You says that "Luotang Mountain and Warrior Mountain are mountains in the northwest, where the sun sets." Neither is clearly identifiable with an actual mountain, nor would one expect them to be, given the mythographical context of this section.

Line 2: Gao You says, "The Pang Fish is like a carp; gods and sages mount upon it and travel to the nine fields [of heaven]. It is found to the south of the Wuji [People; see Section XV, line 41 above]." Compare the giant fish depicted in Fig. 4.4, and also the Kun Fish ("Leviathan") in 4.XXVII.18–19 below.

Line 3: The twenty-eight gods here may be taken as personifications of the twenty-eight lunar lodges, ringing the ecliptic like a chain and regulating ("watching over") the positions of other heavenly bodies. Their location—south of mountains in the northwest corner of the cosmos—is consistent with a view of them as being ranged along the ecliptic among the stars.

Lines 4–8: Gemstone trees as attributes of the Kunlun Mountains and its environs are familiar from earlier sections of this chapter, as well as from a wide range of other sources. *Shanhaijing* 2, section 1 describes a Great Floreate Mountain and a Lesser Floreate Mountain, which perhaps is the same as the Floreate Mountain in 4.VII:4 above (although *Huainanzi* locates it in the southwest, *Shanhaijing* in the west). But the "Floreate Hill" (*huaqiu*) here may perhaps be the same as the "Level Hill" (*pingqiu*) in *Shanhaijing* 8 and 9. Guo You appears to take Greyhorse and Viewflesh as names of countries. Of the latter, he says, "the people (there) do not know speech." Guo Pu, in his commentary to *Shanhaijing* 6, takes *shirou* as "seeing flesh," that is, a lump of flesh with two eyes in it. Thus "Viewflesh" would appear to fit into the "lump of flesh" motif connected with the Hundun cosmogonic myth of the south; compare the "People Without Anuses" mentioned in 4.XV.38 above.

Lines 9–10: Harmonious Hill appears above in Section VI, line 13, as the name of the "outlying region" of the northeast. Gao You identifies it as a place where the *feng* (male "phoenix") sings and the *luan* (female "phoenix") dances, that is, a place where yin and yang blend harmoniously in the northeast at the beginning of the solar year. The same birds were associated with the Fertile-land People in Section XV above. The three mulberry trees without branches appear also in *Shanhaijing* chapter 3, section 2, and in chapter 8, where they are variously described as being 100 or 250 *ren* tall. (One *ren* = seven feet).

Lines 11–12: Of Hanging Ears, Gao You says, "The ears of Hanging Ears hang to his shoulders. . . . He uses his hands to hold up his ears. He lives in the middle of the sea." Hanging Ears is also mentioned in *Shanhaijing* 17, and is perhaps the same as the "Split Ears" of *Shanhaijing* 10. The commentary *Shanhaijing* 10 quotes Zhang Yan's commentary to *Han shu*: "The Hanging Ears (people) carve the skin of their cheeks and ears into several strips that hang down like chicken guts."

Of Bragging Father Gao You says,

> Bragging Father was a spirit-creature [*shen shou*, "divine bestial creature"]. He drank the Yellow River and the Wei^c River, but they were insufficient. He was going to drink the western ocean, but did not know the way there, and died of thirst. . . . Others say that he was a (Daoist) adept.

Another version of the story appears in *Shanhaijing* 8:

> Bragging Father tried to walk faster than the sun. At sunset he grew thirsty and wanted to drink, so he drank the Yellow River and the Wei River. They were not enough, so he headed north to drink from the Great Marsh, but on the way he died of thirst. He threw away his staff, and it turned into the Forest of Deng.

Shanhaijing 17 adds,

> At the mountain called Walled Capital-City Embracing Heaven is a person wearing two yellow snakes as ear ornaments and holding two more yellow snakes in his hands. His name is Bragging Father. Hou Tu [son of Gong Gong] gave birth to Xin, who gave birth to Bragging Father. Bragging Father's strength was beyond measure; he chased the sun and caught up to it when it reached the Vale of Obscurity. . . .

Lines 13–14: For the Hill of Kun Wu, see above, 3.XXV.15, where the "astral projection" of Kun Wu, ancestor of the state of Chu, is named as the center point of the sun's journey across the sky. Chariot Pole is another name for Huangdi; Chariot Pole Hill thus means "The Hill of the Yellow Thearch." There is a Chariot Pole Hill in Henan, near Kaifeng, venerated as Huangdi's birthplace. Guo Pu's commentary in *Shanhaijing* 2 says, "This is where the Yellow Thearch married the daughter of Western Tumulus, giving this place the name Chariot Pole." And *Shanhaijing* 7 says,

> The land of Chariot Pole is next to Poverty Mountain. A life of eight hundred years is considered short here. This land is north of the Country of Women. (The people there) have a human face, the body of a snake, and a tail that encircles their heads. Poverty Mountain is north of there. No one dares shoot (arrows) to the west of Poverty Mountain, for fear of Chariot Pole Hill.

Guo Pu comments, "This means that for fear of the powerful aura of the Yellow Thearch, it is taboo to shoot to the west." The linking of Kun Wu and the Yellow Thearch here might indicate a subtle bit of Chu chauvinism.

Line 15: Shaman Xian is one of the best-known of late Zhou/Han divine personages. Gao You says, "He knew the Dao of Heaven and could foresee happiness and sadness." *Lüshi chunqiu* 22:4a mentions "Dao-eating and qi-imbibing immortals at the feet of Shaman Xian." *Shanhaijing* 7 says,

> Shaman Xian is north of Woman Chou [*nü chou*, "second woman"] Mountain. In his right hand he grasps a bluegreen snake, in his left hand he grasps a vermilion snake. He dwells on Dengbao Mountain, where the assembled shamans ascend and descend.

See also *Chu ci*, "Li sao" 141–143. There is a Shaman Xian Mountain in present-day Shanxi, known in legend as the original home of Yu the Great.

It is not clear what connection there might be between Shaman Xian (and his mountain) and the Pool of Xian, one of the "six departments" of heaven (3.IV.5 above). The Pool of Xian is described in 3.XII.12 as "a park of water and fishes," and in 3.XIX.3 and 10 as being connected with the Jovian Year. *Xian* means "broad," so the Pool of Xian could also be translated as "Broad Pool," with no connection to Shaman Xian implied at all. It seems more likely, however, given the tendency of *Huainanzi* 4 and similar texts to locate the homes of mythic personages both in far-distant terrestrial places and among the stars, that the Pool of Xian is an astral projection of Shaman Xian Mountain.

Line 16: Sunrise Valley is an alternative name for the Valley of Tang the Victorious, founder of the Shang. For Fusang, see Section V above. See also *Shanhaijing* 9:

> Above Tang Valley is the Fusang tree, where the ten suns were bathed. It is north of Black-tooth Land. In the water is a large tree bearing nine suns in its lower branches and one in its upper branches.

Shanhaijing 15 adds,

> On the other side of the southeastern ocean, near the Sweet River, is the land of Xihe. There a woman named Xihe bathes the sun in the Sweet Pool. She is the wife of Di Jun, and she bore ten suns [as sons].

Huainanzi 7:3a adds, "In the sun there is a lame [three-legged] crow"; the suns are visualized as perching in the branches of the Fusang tree like birds (as in the funerary banner from Mawangdui Tomb 1; see Figs. 2.9 and 4.2 above). For a thorough study of the Fusang myths, see Sarah Allan, "Sons of Suns."[57]

Lines 17–18: You Song [or Rong] is the name of a country, or perhaps of its ruler ("The possessor of Song"). Jian Di, the "older sister" of line 18, is described in *Shiji* 3:1a as follows: "Jian Di, the mother of Xie, was a woman of the You Song clan."[58] Jian Di was the ancestress of the ruling house of Shang. While she was imprisoned in a tower, the first ancestor of Shang, Di Ku, sent her a "dark bird," and she became pregnant by eating its egg. She later gave birth to Xie, a minister of the Sage-emperor Shun. He was the "dark king," ancestor of the Shang. The story is found often in early Chinese literature; see for example *Shijing*, "Dark Bird" (Mao Ode #303) and "Extending Forth" (Mao Ode #304); *Chu ci*, "Li sao" 119, "Tian wen" 107–8; *Lüshi chunqiu* 6:6b, and *Shiji* 3.[59] The theme of the two sisters appears only here and in *Lüshi chunqiu*. The name of the younger sister here (she is the elder sister in *Lüshi chunqiu*), Jian Ci, is inauspicious (*ci* means "blemish, mole"), and perhaps hints at a now-lost version of the myth which incorporates the theme of "unsuccessful offspring of first mating."[60]

For Mt. Buzhou, see above, 3.I.24, 3.XII.8, 4.III.13, and 4.VI.30. The name of this "Non-Circumscribing Mountain" suggests that it is the pivot of the heavens, unmoving while all of the heavenly bodies describe circles around it—in other words, an *axis mundi*. But it is also one of the eight pillars separating heaven and earth—the northwestern one that was knocked over in the fight between Gong Gong and Zhuan Xu.[61]

Line 19: There is a very extensive literature on Xiwangmu, the Queen Mother of the West,[62] of which only a brief summary need be given here. (See also Fig. 4.1.) Xiwangmu appears in both the *Mu Tianzi zhuan* and the *Bamboo Annals* as the name of a country in the west, with no particular attributes of magic or immortality. Perhaps the earliest reference to the Queen Mother of the West as a Daoist cult figure is in *Zhuangzi* 6, where she is listed among many sages and immortals who obtained the Dao: "The Queen Mother of the West obtained [the Dao] and retired to her place in Shaoguang; no one knows her beginning, and no one knows her end." She appears twice in *Huainanzi* 6:

> This [the futility of obtaining things rather than comprehending their Dao] may be compared to Yi the Archer requesting the elixer of immortality from the Queen

Mother of the West, or to Heng E's stealing it and fleeing to the moon. [6:16b]

The Old [Mother] of the West broke her *sheng* hair ornament, and the Yellow Thearch moaned. The wings of flying birds were injured, and four-footed animals became lame. Mountains were denuded of trees, and the flatlands were devoid of fresh water. Foxes and raccoons headed for their dens, horses and oxen escaped and wandered away. Fields were bare of growing grain, and roadsides of sedges and reeds. Gold bars were chipped at their edges, and jade discs had their surface decorations worn away. Shells of tortoises were pierced until they no longer yielded responses; divining-stalks were cast repeatedly. [6:13ab]

One sees in these passages a characterization of Xiwangmu as a sage: the dispenser, from her western axial realm, of the elixir of immortality, but also as a figure of potential danger, one who (when breaking her hair ornament in anger) can bring disaster to the human world. This fearsome aspect of the Queen Mother of the West is emphasized in several famous passages from the *Shanhaijing*:

350 li further west is Jade Mountain, where the Queen Mother of the West dwells. Xiwangmu resembles a human, (with) a leopard's tail and tiger's teeth; she is good at whistling.[63] In her disordered hair (she wears) a *sheng* hair ornament. She controls [the asterisms?] Calamity and Five Destructions. [*Shanhaijing* 2]

The Queen Mother of the West leans on a small table and wears a *sheng* headdress. To the south are the three bluegreen birds that bring food to the Queen Mother of the West. This is north of Mt. Kunlun. [*Shanhaijing* 12]

To the west is [Xi]wangmu Mountain, Ravine Mountain, and Ocean Mountain. The Fertile Land is here. . . .
South of the West Sea, on the edge of the Flowing Sands, behind the Vermilion River and in front of the Black River, is a large mountain called the Hill of Kunlun. There is a demigod there with a human face, a striped tiger body, and a tail with white spots. Below, the Weakwater Pool surrounds it. Beyond it is Blazing Fire Mountain; anything thrown onto it spontaneously bursts into flame. There dwells a person wearing a *sheng* hair ornament, who has tiger teeth and a leopard's tail and who lives in a grotto; this is Xiwangmu. All of the myriad things can be found on this mountain. [*Shanhaijing* 16]

Fracasso interprets these passages as depicting the Queen Mother of the West as a goddess of epidemics, and as a protectress against epidemics; he sees traces of Tibetan influence here.[64] There is of course no contradiction between these two attributes,[65] nor with her role as the keeper of the elixir of immortality—which may be regarded as a medical cure for death. Loewe notes that in the last years of the Former Han there were several instances of public hysteria over a coming disaster, when only those who wore the talisman of the Queen Mother of the West would be saved from destruction.[66]

The Queen Mother of the West became a signficant cult figure during the late Former Han, and later gradually evolved away from her ferocious appearance to be regarded as a beautiful seducer of emperors and a goddess of immortality, patroness of the peach orchard that produced elixir-fruit. As such she became known as an object of spiritual quests, such as that described by the noted astronomer Zhang Heng in his "Rhymeprose on the Western Park."

Line 20: The Weakwater is a magical river surrounding or flowing out from Kunlun; see 4.IV.3 above, as well as the passage from *Shanhaijing* 16 just quoted. The Music People (*yue min*, but also, with the same characters, possibly "Happy People," *le min*) are perhaps connected with the Great Music Wilderness described in *Shanhaijing*:

Great Music Wilderness is where Hou Qi (or Kai) of Xia danced the nine *dai* dances. Riding two dragons (above) three layers of clouds, grasping the (chariot's) feather-screen in his left hand, holding a *bi* jade disc in his right hand and with a *huang* jade half-disc in his belt, he rode north of Great Turning Mountain. Some say Great Turning Wilderness. [*Shanhaijing* 7]

Beyond the Southwestern Sea, south of the Vermilion River and west of the Flowing Sands, there is a person who wears two bluegreen snakes as ear ornaments and rides two dragons. His name is Hou Kai of Xia. He presented three slave-women to Heaven, after which he received the nine *bian* songs and the nine *ge* songs and descended again. This is the Tian Mu Wilderness, 2,000 *ren* high. There Kai first sang the nine *zhao* songs. [*Shanhaijing* 16]

Nalu ("graspgate") is virtually meaningless, perhaps a transliteration of a non-Chinese word.

Line 21: Gao You says that Three Dangers Mountain is another name for the Extreme Western Mountain, that is, the westernmost of the eight cosmic pillars. Three Dangers Mountain appears very widely in early Chinese texts, often in connection with the Queen Mother of the West, and always with magical associations.[67] In *Shujing* II, 1.12 (and also *Zhuangzi* 2, *Shiji* 1, etc.), it is the place to which the Three Miao Tribes were banished by Shun. *Chu ci*, "Tian wen" 53–54 links it to the Blackwater and the cult of immortality:

Three Dangers Mountain is there, and the Blackwater
   that darkens the feet [where?]
Life is long there, and there is no death [what limit?]

Shanhaijing 2 links Three Dangers Mountain to Xiwangmu's familiars:

220 li further west is Three Dangers Mountain, where three bluegreen birds live. It covers an area 100 li square. Atop it is an animal like a cow; it is white, has four horns, and its body is covered with hair like a coconut-husk raincoat. It is called the *aoye*; it eats people. There is a bird there with one head and three bodies, resembling an eagle; (but) it is called an owl. [*Shanhaijing* 2]

Line 22: Lighting Darkness and Candle-gleam are identified in *Shanhaijing* 12: "A wife of Shun, Lady Dengbi, gave birth to Lighting Darkness and Candle-gleam. They dwell in a big marsh by the Yellow River. Their numinous power is able to light up that place to a distance of 100 li."

Line 23: Dragon Gate refers to an actual place—the pass where the Yellow River descends from the loess highlands onto the plains—but one with a magical origin. According to *Huainanzi* 8:8a,

In the time of Shun, Gong Gong stirred up the flood; the waters came up to the Hollow Mulberry (Tree). The Dragon Gate was not yet opened, nor had the Luliang (Canal) been excavated. The Yangtse and Huai Rivers flowed together, and the four seas were unbounded.[68]

The Dragon Gate was opened as part of Yu the Great's engineering works, which also included piling up Mt. Kunlun, as detailed in the commentary to 4.III above.

Line 24: The Torrential Pool is probably the same as the pool of thrice-circulating water at Kunlun mentioned in 4.II.16–18 above.

Line 25: Dark Smelting is otherwise unknown. The text could also be construed to mean "Dark Smelting is [the same as Mt.] Buzhou."

Lines 26–27: The Shen Pool is unidentified. For the Haiyu and Mengzhu marshes, see 4.I.22 above; they apparently are real places, but of uncertain location.

Line 28: The Greater and Lesser Mansions are, according to Gao You, "another name for a high mountain in Yangcheng" (in Shanxi). Ji is the central province in the list of nine provinces given above, 4.I.12.

Lines 29–31: The Torch Dragon is well-known in early Chinese mythology. *Chu ci*, "Tian wen" 42, asks,

The Torch Dragon flares where the sun does not reach
[where? how?]

"Da zhao" 18 answers the question:

In the north is the Frozen Mountain,
and the red-glowing Torch Dragon.

Shanhaijing 17 amplifies:

Beyond the northwestern sea, north of the Vermilion River, is Varigated-tail Mountain. There is a god there with a human face and a serpent's body, colored red.

(Its body is 1000 li in length.) It has vertical eyes, and rides upright [?]. When it closes its eyes it makes darkness, and where it looks it becomes light. It summons the wind and rain, and lights up Ninefold-Shade Mountain. It is called Torch Dragon.

There is a similar passage in *Shanhaijing* 8. The Torch Dragon seems to me very probably to be a mythical interpretation of the aurora borealis.

Abandoned Wings Mountain was encountered above, 4.VI.20, as another name for Amassing Ice, the "outlying region" of the far north. Gao You's commentary on Dark Capital Mountain (4.VII.7 above), another name for Mt. Buzhou, says that it is "north of Wild Goose Gate."

Guo Pu's commentary to *Shanhaijing* 17 quotes a commentary to the *Shijing* that says, "The sky is insufficient to cover the northwest, so there is no ebb and flow of yang and yin. Therefore a dragon carries a torch in its mouth to light up the sky."[69]

Lines 32–35: In 4.V.9 above, the Jian Tree is said to be located on Mt. Duguang, which in turn is identified in 4.VI.16 as the name of the "outlying region" of the far south. The Jian tree, a sun-tree lying beneath the sun's apogee on its most southerly arc across the sky, is also a cosmic-pillar image associated with immortality; the *zhong jun di* ("many gods") use it to ascend to and descend from heaven.[70] The association between Duguang and the tumulus of Hou Ji is made explicit in *Shanhaijing* 13:

> In the southwest, where the Black River flows, is Duguang Wilderness and the tomb of Hou Ji. There are found excellent legumes, rice, and millet. Grain of all sorts grows during summer and winter. The *luan* (simurgh) spontaneously sings, and the *feng* (phoenix) spontaneously dances. The staff-bamboo, fruit, flowers, plants and trees all grow there. Plants live during winter and summer, and do not die.

Flowing Yellow appears in *Shanhaijing* 11 as a place west of the tomb of Hou Ji, but without any further hint as to what it might be. For the Fertile-land People, see 4.XV.7 above.

The association of longevity or immortality with the tombs of Chinese culture-heroes was noted above in connection with the tumulus of the Yellow Thearch. Here, the assertion that the people around the tomb of Hou Ji come to life again after death, presumably as the demi-fish that are in their midst, has a striking visual parallel in the Mawangdui funerary banner (see Fig. 2.9), where the the Lady Dai after her apotheosis is shown with a long serpent's body.[71]

Line 36: Dogland appears in *Shanhaijing* 17:

> In the Great Wasteland is a mountain called Smelt-Father Mountain. The Xun River enters there. The people called the Dog Rong live there. The Yellow Thearch gave birth to the Miao Dragon, who gave birth to Yongwu, who gave birth to Nongming, who gave birth to White Dog. White Dog was a hermaphrodite. (Its offspring) became the Dog Rong People. They eat meat.

Shanhaijing 12 adds, "Dog Altar [or Dog Tumulus: *feng*] Land is called the Land of the Dog Rong (People). The people resemble dogs." In texts of the immediate post-Han period, these Dog People are associated with the birth of the primordial ancestor Pan Gu.[72]

Line 37: This passage has a close parallel in *Shanhaijing* 13, where the thunder dragons are depicted as having distended, drum-like bellies. Granet remarked that "fools in the *Huainanzi* seem to be possessed by the spirit of thunder";[73] Girardot analyzes the theme of drumming in connection with shamanic ecstasy and divine possession.[74] Thunder Marsh is perhaps the same as the Thunder Chasm of *Chu ci*, "Zhao hun" 20. The thunder dragons here recall another thunder god of Chinese myth, described in *Shanhaijing* 14: "In the Eastern Ocean is Flowing Wave Mountain, 7000 li in the midst of the sea. On it is an animal like an ox that has a dark bluegreen body, no horns, and one leg. Whenever it enters and emerges from the water there is a storm. It shines like the sun and the moon and makes a sound like thunder. Its name is the Kui. The Yellow Thearch caught one, made a drum from its skin, and beat upon it with the bone of a thunder beast. The sound could be heard for 500 li, terrifying the world."

The image of the storm-and-thunder god as a demi-serpent or uniped is shared by a great many cultures; it is as widespread, and probably as ancient, as the Grand Origin Myth itself. (One striking example is the Mesoamerican god Hunrakan, from which is derived the English word hurricane.)[75]

This section of *Huainanzi* 4 is subtly different from, though obviously related to, the previous section. Whereas Section XV dealt extensively in mythical or monstrous beings, they were represented as being tribes of "people" on China's periphery. Here in contrast we are firmly in the dreamscape of myth and cosmogony. Despite the terminology of mountains, marshes, and so on (some of which have clearly identifiable terrestrial counterparts), these are not in this context really physical features of the earth, but rather places in the shadowy region where the terrestrial plane meets the dome of the heavens, the realm of the cosmic pillars and the gods that dwell among them.

That this is so can be seen not only in the preponderant references here to Kunlun, Fusang, the Jian tree, and other features of the mythographic landscape, but also from the notable presence here of scaly bodied divinities. The early Chinese shared with many other ancient cultures a tendency to see some of their cosmic deities as serpent-bodied.[76] The fish-bodied immortals near the tomb of Hou Ji, the dragon-bodied Torch Dragon, and the gods of Thunder Marsh, are of a kind with the sky-repairing goddess Nü Gua and her consort Fu Xi, and with the immortalized *hun* soul of the Lady Dai. Many explanations of this phenomenon have been put forward; de Santillana sees them as representing the serpentine motions (a pre-Copernican European might have said, epicyclic motions) of the five visible planets through the sky, while others point to the ability of reptiles to revive in the springtime from a death-like hibernation as an emblem of rebirth and immortality. It may never be possible to find a way of choosing a "right answer" from among many plausible speculations in this case. Nevertheless it is worth noting that even the most sober of early Chinese intellectuals would routinely have thought of the world as including mythical landscapes inhabited by a plenitude of scaly bodied divinities.

Section XVII: The Rivers of China

[4:13b:11]

1   The Yangtse issues from Mt. Min and flows eastward, passing through Han and entering the ocean. It (then) turns left and flows north to (a point) north of Kaimu Mountain. Then it turns right and flows eastward to the Eastern Pillar.

2   The Yellow River issues from the Piled-Stone Mountain.

3   The Qu River issues from Mt. Jing.

4   The Huai River issues from Mt. Tongbo.

5   The Sui River issues from Feather Mountain.

6   The Clear Zhang River issues from Mt. Jieli.

7   The Turbid Zhang River issues from Mt. Fabao.

8   The Qi[a] River issues from Mt. Wangwu.

9   The Shi River, the Si River, and the Yi River issue from Mt. Tai[a], Mt. Tai[b], and Mt. Shu.

10 The Luo[a] River issues from Mt. Lie.

11 The Wen River issues from Mt. Fuqi and flows westward to join the Qi[a] River.

12 The Han River issues from Mt. Bozhong.

13 The Jing River issues from Mt. Boluo.

14 The Wei[c] River issues from Bird-and-Rat Cave.

15 The Yi River issues from Mt. Shangwei.

16 The Luo[b] River issues from Bear Ear Mountain.

17 The Jun River issues from Flower Hole.

18 The Wei[d] River issues from Mt. Fuzhou.

19 The Fen River issues from Mt. Yanjing.

20 The Ren River issues from Mt. Fenxiong.

21 The Zi River issues from Mt. Muyi.

22 The Cinnabar River issues from Mt. Gaochu.

23 The Pan River issues from Mt. Qiao.

24 The Hao River issues from Mt. Xianyu. [Read: The Hao River issues from. . . . The Bo River issues from Mt. Xianyu.]

25 The Liang River issues from Mt. Maolu and Mt. Shiliang.
26 The Ru River issues from Mt. Meng.
27 The Qi[b] River issues from Mt. Dahao.
28 The Jin river issues from Mt. Jiezhu [also called Dragon Mountain.]
29 The He River issues from Mt. Fengyang.
30 The Liao River issues from Grindstone Mountain.
31 The Fu River issues from Mt. Jing.
32 The Qi[c] River issues from Stone Bridge Mountain.
33 The Hutuo River issues from Mt. Luping.
34 The Nituyuan River issues from Mt. Man.
35 The Wei[d] River and the Shi River flow north into Yan.
   [4:15b:10] [4:3b:7]
36 The Weakwater issues from Exhausted Stone Mountain and enters the Flowing Sands.
   [4:3b:7] [4:15b:10]

Commentary to Section XVII

This section returns, with few exceptions, from the landscape of myth to the ordinary topography of China proper. Nearly all of the rivers and mountains mentioned here exist in fact, and can readily be found in standard reference works on Chinese historical geography.[77] Most of them also can be found in such early geographical works as *Shanhaijing* 1–4 and the *Shuijingzhu*.

The course of the Yangtse River as given here is of some interest, because the river is considered to retain a discrete identity even after it enters the sea. Gao You identifies Mt. Kaimu as a mountain in the midst of the ocean, and the river is depicted as flowing to the north of that mountain and then turning east to flow all the way to the eastern cosmic pillar. The world's oceans are in fact, of course, traversed by numerous "rivers," the great oceanic currents, and this description of the Yangtse's course after it enters the ocean perhaps reflects early knowledge of such currents. Needham and others have suggested[78] that early Chinese seafarers might occasionally have become caught in the Kuroshio and North Pacific currents that flow northeastward from the east coast of China and along the southern coast of Japan, thence in a great arc across the north Pacific and down the west coast of North America. Tales of seafarers who had experience (whether voluntary or not) of those currents could account for the description given here. On the other hand, one need not rely on such rationalistic interpretations to account for the phenomena of early myths.

The course of the Yellow River given here is an abbreviation of the one given above, 4.IV.1. *Shanhaijing* 2, section 1, says "The Yellow River flows south from [the northeast corner of Kunlun], then east to Wuda." *Shanhaijing* 11 says, "The Yellow

River flows from the northeast corner, passes northward, and then enters the Sea of Bo to the west. Then it flows out of the sea, flows westward, and to the north enters Piled Stone Mountain, where Yu excavated." *Shanhaijing* 17 says, "In the Great Wasteland is a mountain called Great Altar of Xian Kan Mountain. There the Yellow and Ji Rivers enter the sea. To the west is a mountain called Piled Stones, where Yu excavated." There was considerable confusion in early China about the source and course of the Yellow River.[79] "Yu gong" II, 7 for example, names the Piled Stone Mountain as its source; more mythologically inclined texts place its source in Kunlun. *Huainanzi* 6:16a implies that the Yellow River owes its powerful flow to the fact that it descends from the great heights of Kunlun: "That the Yellow River makes nine turns while flowing to the sea, yet flows without obstruction, is due to its being propelled by Kunlun."

Briefly stated, there seems to have been an early terminological confusion between what we now call the Yellow River—which the early Chinese simply called *he,* "The River," and the Yellow River so-named, which was a mythical river flowing out of Kunlun. The confusion was resolved by positing that the Yellow River flowed from the northeastern corner of Kunlun, as stated in many texts, but then at some point entered a western ocean, or perhaps flowed underground (according to some commentators, beneath the "sand ocean" of the Gobi; but in any case in one of the subterranean channels of the Yellow Springs[80]), emerging again at Piled-Stone Mountain (formed of debris excavated by Yu in his river-channeling labors), whence it took its true terrestrial course to the eastern sea.

The last line of this section, about the Weakwater, has been transposed from 4.IV.3 above, where it appears to be superfluous, to here, where its syntax suggests that it belongs.

Section XVIII: Evolution of Animals and Plants

[4:15b:11]

1 Zhu Ji and She Ti were born from the *tiao* [northeast] wind.
2 Tong Shi was born from the *mingshu* [east] wind.
3 Chifenruo was born from the *qingming* [southeast] wind.
4 Gong Gong was born from the *jing* [south] wind.
5 Zhu Bi was born from the *liang* [southwest] wind.
6 Gao Ji was born from the *Changhe* [west] wind.
7 Yu Qiang was born from the *Buzhou* [northwest] wind.
8 Qiong Qi was born from the *guangmo* [north] wind.
9 Downyhair gave birth to Oceanman. Oceanman gave birth to Ruojun.
10 Ruojun gave birth to sages; sages gave birth to ordinary people.
11 Thus creatures with scanty hair are born from ordinary people.

208

12   Winged Excellence gave birth to Flying Dragon. Flying Dragon gave birth to the phoenix (*fenghuang*).

13   The phoenix gave birth to the simurgh (*luan*). The simurgh gave birth to ordinary birds.

14   Feathered creatures in general are born from ordinary birds.

15   Hairy Heifer gave birth to Responsive Dragon. Responsive Dragon gave birth to Establish-Horse.

16   Establish-Horse gave birth to the *qilin*. The *qilin* gave birth to ordinary beasts.

17   Hairy animals in general are born from ordinary beasts.

18   Scaly One gave birth to Scaly Dragon. Scaly Dragon gave birth to Leviathan.

19   Leviathan gave birth to Establish-Apotrope. Establish-Apotrope gave birth to ordinary fishes.

20   Scaly creatures in general are born from ordinary fishes.

21   Armored Abyss gave birth to First Dragon. First Dragon gave birth to Dark Sea-Turtle.

22   Dark Sea-Turtle gave birth to Divine Tortoise. Divine Tortoise gave birth to ordinary turtles.

23   Armored creatures in general are born from ordinary turtles.

24   Warm Damp gave birth to Countenance. Warm Damp was born from Hair Wind.

25   Hair Wind was born from Damp Darkness. Damp Darkness was born from Feather Wind.

26   Feather Wind gave birth to Mild Armored-Creature. Mild Armored-Creature gave birth to Scaly Meager.

27   Scaly Meager gave birth to Warm Armored-Creature.

28   The five classes (of animals) in their various manifestations flourished in the outside world and multiplied after their own kind.

29   Sun-Climber gave birth to Brightness-Blocker. Brightness-Blocker gave birth to Lofty Ru.

30   Lofty Ru gave birth to Trunktree. Trunktree gave birth to ordinary trees.

31   All plants with quivering leaves are born from ordinary trees.

32   Rooted Stem gave birth to Chengruo. Chengruo gave birth to Dark Jade.

33   Dark Jade gave birth to Pure Fountain. Pure Fountain gave birth to Sovereign's Crime.

34   Sovereign's Crime gave birth to ordinary grasses.

35   All rooted stems are born from ordinary grasses.

36   Ocean Gate gave birth to Swimming Dragon. Swimming Dragon gave birth to Lotus Flower.

37   Lotus Flower gave birth to Duckweed. Duckweed gave birth to Aquatic Plant. Aquatic Plant gave birth to seaweed.

38   All rootless plants are born from ordinary seaweed.
     [4:17a:8]

Commentary to Section XVIII

This section opens with a list of deities who are said to be "born from" the eight winds.[81] The association of these gods with the winds has both directional and calendrical significance; the northeast, for example, marks the beginning of both the solar and the Jovian Years, and She Ti (or Shetige) is the name of the first year of the Jovian Cycle. But the association does not hold true in the case of Chifenruo, the name of the last year of the Jovian Cycle; one would expect Chifenruo to be correlated with the twelfth month and the twelfth year, and thus the direction north, but he (it?) is said here to be born of the southeast wind. The reason for this discrepancy is obscure. The correlation of the giant (and cosmic rebel) Gong Gong with the south is consistent with suggestions in *Shanhaijing* that Gong Gong (who had a human face and a serpent's body) was a southern deity. The rest of the deities named here are otherwise unknown; Gao You's commentary gives no help, for he simply identifies them as "heavenly deities." The only exception is Qiong Qi of the north, of whom Gao You says, "Qiong Qi is a heavenly deity in the north, said to be sufficient (in strength) to overcome two dragons. His appearance is like a tiger."

The rest of this section consists of a set of remarkable evolutionary schemes for different types of animals and plants. In several passages in *Huainanzi* 3 and 4 we have encountered cases of creatures being transformed into other creatures (e.g., swallows and sparrows into clams in 4.XI.4), but the argument made here is much more systematic. Each section follows the same formula: a primordial ancestor begets a series of mythical/magical forms within the category of animal or plant in question; these finally give birth to "ordinary people" (or "ordinary scaly creatures," "ordinary rooted plants," etc.). The names of the mythical creatures include some that are well known—such as the *qilin*, the *feng* and *huang* "phoenixes," and *luan* "simurghs" (which feature prominently in the haunts of gods and immortals in the *Shanhaijing*), the *qiao* and *long* dragons (used here as a compound, *qiaolong*, which I translate as "Scaly Dragon"), and Leviathan (*kun'geng*), which presumably is the same as the giant Kun fish in *Zhuangzi* 1.[82]

The prevalence of dragons and phoenixes here takes on additional significance in light of an observation made by Jean-Pierre Diény, who notes that the graphs for *long* and *feng* in early oracle-bone inscriptions are partly identical, and suggests that the identical elements may "designate these two animals as the chiefs of their respective families, in anticipation, thus, of the first zoological classifications of the Chinese."[83] Diény's analysis of this passage from *Huainanzi* 4, together with passages from other works depicting other dragons (such as the Torch Dragon) and mythical personages with serpentine characteristics (such as Pan Gu) is of exceptional interest in explicating the complex dragon lore of the early Han.[84]

Some of the figures in these genealogies, on the other hand, are quite obscure. My odd-looking phrase "Establish-Apotrope" is based on the assumption that *xie* is the same as the *bixie* apotropaic monster often used as a tomb-guardian figure. *Huanggu* means something like "sovereign's crime," but how that fits as an ancestor of grasses is completely opaque. *Pingcao*, another plant ancestor, is also obscure; my rendering of "Aquatic Plant" is a gloss, not a translation. The use of *ru* or *ruo* in several of these names (*ruojun, chengruo, qiaoru*) leads me to suspect that some of them might be transliterations of non-Chinese words, in which case attempts at translation would be doomed. There may be a vague reference in some of these vegetative-ancestor names (Sun-Climber, Brightness-Blocker, Chengruo ["Establish-Ruo"?]) to the Fusang, Jian, and Ruo sun-trees mentioned in Section 4.V above.

Lines 24–27 are garbled beyond recovery, and seem like hardly more than the detritus of some broken bamboo slips from an early copy of the book, inserted here for lack of a better place to put them. The commentators ignore them.

That those lines should not be here at all is suggested by line 28, which refers to the "five classes (of animals)"—that is, those described in lines 9–23. The five classes, with their five phase correlates, are as follows:

Creatures with scant body hair: humans	Earth
Hairy creatures: mammals	Metal
Feathered creatures: birds	Fire
Scaly creatures: fish, reptiles, dragons	Wood
Armored creatures: shellfish, turtles	Water

This five phase classification of animals complements the yin-yang classification found above in 4.XI, on taxonomy.

The treatment of plants here is generally similar to that of animals, though there is no attempt to create a five-category classification of plants parallel to that of the animals. The text in these lines also is somewhat damaged (see "Textual and Technical Notes").

These evolutionary schemes are, so far as I know, unique in early Chinese literature; the only clear but partial parallel is the famous (and notoriously difficult) "evolutionary" passage in *Zhuangzi* 18.[85] But these passages, in contrast to the one in *Zhuangzi*, are models of clarity; and though it would be absurd to suggest that one is dealing here with an ancient Chinese anticipation of Darwin, the material does betray some disposition toward the scientific investigation of natural phenomena. There is a big gap in the cosmogonic process in *Laozi* 42, *Huainanzi* 1–3, and cognate texts, wherein the Dao divides into yin and yang (or into one, two, and three), yin and yang produce the five phases, and the five phases produce the "myriad creatures." If one asks, "How are the myriad creatures produced," those cosmogonic narratives are silent;

this section provides an answer. From primordial first ancestors, each of which has specific yin-yang/five phase characteristics, various classes of creatures evolve, and so it is through the working of yin and yang and the five phases within taxonomic groups that species differentiation takes place. Thus the gap between the Dao, yin-yang, and the five phases, on the one hand, and the "myriad creatures," on the other, is bridged, making this section of *Huainanzi* 4 a most interesting and important document for the development of Chinese natural philosophy.

Section XIX: Natural Alchemy

[4:17a:10]

1 The qi of balanced earth is received into the yellow heaven, which after 500 years engenders a yellow jade [realgar? amber?].

2 This after 500 years engenders a yellow quicksilver, which after 500 years engenders gold ["yellow metal"].

3 After 1000 years, gold engenders the yellow dragon.

4 The yellow dragon, going into hiding, engenders the yellow springs.

5 When the dust [vapor?] from the yellow springs rises to become a yellow cloud, the beating together of yin and yang makes thunder; their rising to a crescendo makes lightning.

6 What has ascended then descends as a flow of water which collects in the yellow sea.

7 The qi of unbalanced earth is received into the bluegreen heaven, which after 800 years engenders a bluegreen malachite.

8 This after 800 years engenders a bluegreen quicksilver, which after 800 years engenders lead ["bluegreen metal"].

9 After 1000 years, lead engenders the bluegreen dragon.

10 The bluegreen dragon, going into hiding, engenders the bluegreen springs.

11 When the dust [vapor?] from the bluegreen springs rises to become a bluegreen cloud, the beating together of yin and yang makes thunder; their rising to a crescendo makes lightning.

12 What has ascended then descends as a flow of water which collects in the bluegreen sea.

13 The qi of vigorous earth is received into the vermilion heaven, which after 700 years engenders a vermilion cinnabar.

14 This after 700 years engenders a vermilion quicksilver, which after 700 years engenders copper ["vermilion metal"].

15 After 1000 years, copper engenders the vermilion dragon.

16 The vermilion dragon, going into hiding, engenders the vermilion springs.

17 When the dust [vapor?] from the vermilion springs rises to become a vermilion cloud, the beating together of yin and yang makes thunder; their rising to a crescendo makes lightning.

18 What has ascended then descends as a flow of water which collects in the vermilion sea.

19 The qi of weak earth is received into the white heaven, which after 900 years engenders a white arsenolite.

20 This after 900 years engenders a white quicksilver, which after 900 years engenders silver ["white metal"].

21 After 1000 years, silver engenders the white dragon.

22 The white dragon, going into hiding, engenders the white springs.

23 When the dust [vapor?] from the white springs rises to become a white cloud, the beating together of yin and yang makes thunder; their rising to a crescendo makes lightning.

24 What has ascended then descends as a flow of water which collects in the white sea.

25 The qi of passive earth is received into the black heaven, which after 600 years engenders a black slate.

26 This after 600 years engenders a black quicksilver, which after 600 years engenders iron ["black metal"].

27 After 1000 years, iron engenders the black dragon.

28 The black dragon, going into hiding, engenders the black springs.

29 When the dust [vapor?] from the black springs rises to become a black cloud, the beating together of yin and yang makes thunder; their rising to a crescendo makes lightning.

30 What has ascended then descends as a flow of water which collects in the black sea.
    [4:18b:6]

Commentary to Section XIX

This is without doubt the best-known and most-studied passage in *Huainanzi* 4. As a document of great importance for the early history of Chinese alchemy, it has been translated and analyzed by, among others, Dubs, Needham, Sivin, and Ho.[86]

It is immediately obvious that this passage is filled with five phase symbolism, applied with rigorous consistency to the problem of the evolution and growth of ores and minerals in the earth. So consistent is the symbolism, in fact, that each subsection of the passage can be reduced to a formula together with an explanatory table (as suggested by Sivin) as follows:

The qi of X earth ——Y years——> Z mineral ——Y years——> Z
quicksilver ——Y years——> Z metal ——1000 years——> Z dragon
——concealment——> Z springs.

X is an attribute, Y is a number of years, and Z is a color:

X	Y/100	Z	mineral	metal	Phase
balanced	5	yellow	yellow jade	gold	earth
unbalanced	8	bluegreen	malachite	lead	wood
vigorous	7	vermilion	cinnabar	copper	fire
weak	9	white	arsenolite	silver	metal
passive	6	black	slate	iron	water

The minerals and metals included in the formula obviously have been chosen on the basis of color in accordance with five phase theory. This is most obvious in the cases of gold, silver, and copper, but applies to lead and iron as well. Lead has a slightly bluish or iridescent sheen; iron, especially as powder or filings, or as a reduced glaze on ceramics, is dark grey or black. The mineral correlates cannot be determined with equal certainty, especially in the cases of "yellow jade" (for which realgar and amber seem like good candidates, though realgar lacks the translucence of jade) and slate, but it is obvious nevertheless that color was the main consideration. The notion of different colors of mercury belongs, however, to the world of magic rather than the world of chemistry, and for that reason I have used the colloquial "quicksilver" rather than the proper chemical term "mercury."

The Yellow Springs is a meaningful term of long standing in Chinese mythical cosmology. Springs of other colors have no such status; still, the Chinese subterranean world was laced through with springs and channels of all sorts (all of which, Allan suggests, were branches of the Yellow Springs[87]), such as the watery tunnel through which the sun returned nightly from the Ruo tree to the Fusang tree, the magical grotto that was believed to lie beneath Tongting Lake, and—less certainly—the underground sources of the various colored rivers that sprang from Kunlun. There is no strong reason to think that the "yellow spring" of this passage is explicitly the Yellow Spring that lay beneath Kunlun, but to a Han Chinese the question of whether or not they were the same probably would not arise at all. The important point here is that an appropriately colored spring (engendered by a dragon, the symbol of water) was available in each case for a process of vaporization to take place. The assertion that "the dust from Z springs rises to become a Z cloud" is perhaps a recognition that both dust and vapor are particulate; one kind is earth, the other water, but both represent suspension of minute particles of one substance in another.

The five phase symbolism here does not include any explicit reference to directions, but the directional correlations of the five phases were already established earlier in this chapter (see Section XIII). This section, as quoted in the *Taiping yulan*, includes a commentary that is omitted from most editions of *Huainanzi* that makes the directional correlations explicit; for example, the commentary for the first of the "earths" here says, "'balanced earth' is the center. The celestial correspondent to its qi is called 'dusty.' It is the central [circumpolar] portion of the heavens."

The order in which the five subsections of this text is presented is Earth-Wood-Fire-Metal-Water, akin but not identical to the normal "production order" of the five phases, that is, Earth-Metal-Water-Wood-Fire. The order here is, in fact, the "smelting order" given in 4.XIV.15 above, and shows concretely that the chemical processes described there were applied to alchemical theory. Three of the processes mentioned in 4.XIV.15 can be identified with certainty here—growth of ores in the earth, vaporization, and condensation—while the reference to lightning may imply combustion, and the "engendering of the Z spring by the Z dragon" may imply precipitation.

It is also noteworthy—especially because this section immediately follows a section on the evolution of animals and plants begotten from various ancestors—that there is a great deal of sexual symbolism in the images employed here. The word *yu*, which I translate as "is received into," could be taken more literally to mean "copulates with." The earths of the south and the north, which I translate as "vigorous" and "passive," similarly could be expressed directly as "male" and "female." Finally, the last stage in the process of producing the metals of the five different colors is a sexual union: yin and yang blend into and draw apart from each other, accompanied by a thundrous orgasmic climax, producing a liquid emission that collects in a coital ocean. (See also 3.II.13–14 above.) This appears to provide a link even at the very earliest stages of Chinese alchemy between the metallurgy of *waidan* practice and the macrobiotics and sexual yoga of *neidan*.

The broad significance of this passage is quite striking. Just as animals and plants evolved into different species within taxonomic classes from primordial ancestors, so minerals and metals slowly change, transform, and differentiate underground from different types of primordial "earths." It is hardly necessary to point out that early Chinese cosmologists would have considered meaningless the kinds of distinctions that we now make between the "organic" and the "inorganic." As Sivin has put it,

> Like thinkers in the other great civilizations, the Chinese alchemists believed that, since everything had a life cycle, minerals and metals also grew inside the earth, slowly developing along a scale of perfection over immense stretches of time. (This point . . . was first established as generally valid by Mercea Eliade in *Forgerons et alchemistes*.)[88]

This belief was of crucial importance in the development of alchemy, because

> In extracting a metal from its ore, or making strong steel from brittle cast iron [the alchemist or metallurgist] was demonstrating that man can imitate natural process, that he can stand in the place of nature, and bring natural changes about at a rate immensely faster than nature's own time. The discovery that the speed of mineral growth processes, unlike those of plants and animals, can be controlled by man, is apparently what led to the beginning of what I have called scientific alchemy. For the

alchemist went on to design processes for reproducing at a much faster rate the cyclical rhythms of nature which controlled the maturing of minerals and metals in the first place.[89]

It is important, finally, to view this section of *Huainanzi* 4 in a dual perspective—on the one hand to recognize and appreciate it for the important document in the history of science that it undoubtedly is, and on the other hand to remember its context of Huang-Lao Daoism, as a passage included in a compendium of "what the modern ruler needs to know." In the early Chinese cosmology represented by the *Huainanzi*, the world was subject to the critical scrutiny of natural philosophy, which could bring to bear remarkable powers of observation and deduction about the nature of the physical world; but all such observations and deductions had moral values that could be applied in the world of human affairs. The cosmos itself "had the property of bringing to birth moral values and ethical behavior when that level of organization had been reached at which it was possible that they should manifest themselves."[90] The message here would be—among other things—that the same universal yin-yang/five phase principles that governed the ruler's choice of ritual garments and his application of mercy and controlled violence according to the seasonal round also governed the nonhuman world over periods of time immensely longer than the life span of any single human. Those principles, in other words, were so deeply embedded in the structure of the cosmos itself that no governor of human affairs could afford to ignore them.

Huainanzi Chapter 5: Shicixun

ᘒ

THE TREATISE ON
THE SEASONAL RULES

INTRODUCTION

The *Huainanzi* "Treatise on the Seasonal Rules" belongs to a genre of early Chinese almanacs that give astronomical, stem-branch and five phase correlations for each of the twelve months and prescribe appropriate ritual and administrative behavior for the ruler throughout the year. The *Huainanzi* text is one of three versions of a text usually known as "Yueling," "Monthly Ordinances." The earliest of these versions is found as the first section of each of the first twelve chapters of the *Lüshi chunqiu*; collectively these chapters are known as the "Shiji," "Monthly Records."[1] Another version, substantially identical to and clearly derived from that in the *Lüshi chunqiu* but collected into a single chapter, is found in the *Liji*, "Record of Rites."[2] These texts also have affinities with the "Months of Zhou" ("Zhou yue") chapter of the *Yizhou shu*; the "You guan" ("Dark Palace"), "Sishi" ("Four Seasons"), "Wu xing" ("Five Phases"), and "Qing zhong ji" ("Light and Heavy") chapters of the *Guanzi*;[3] the "Lesser Annuary of Xia" (*Xia xiaozheng*), which is usually published with the *Da Dai liji* as an appendix to that text;[4] and also with the Chu Silk Manuscript.[5] Several sections of Huainanzi 3, the "Treatise on the Patterns of Heaven"—notably 3.XVI, 3.XVII, 3.XXII–XIV, and 3.XVI—are also closely related to this cluster of texts dealing with calendrical astrology. All of these texts prescribe behavior for the ruler in accordance with the seasons and the months, based on the concept of *ganying* "resonance" between the cosmos as a whole and the actions of humans. In the case of the various versions of the "Yueling" the prescriptions are based explicitly on five phase correlative thinking.[6]

217

The "Treatise on the Seasonal Rules" follows the Xia sequence calendar, wherein the first civil month is correlated with the Earthly Branch *yin*, and begins with the second lunar month following the month in which the winter solstice occurs. The month of the winter solstice, the first "astronomical month," is therefore numbered month eleven in the Xia sequence. For a review of the difficulties encountered in reconciling the astronomical and civil calendars for astrological purposes, see Chapter one, pp. 19–21, and also the commentary to *Huainanzi* 3.XVI above.

The *Huainanzi* "Treatise on the Seasonal Rules" is a variant of the "Yueling"; it contains some information not found in the *Lüshi chunqiu/Liji* versions of that text, and also lacks some information that is found in those versions. It is possible but unlikely that *Huainanzi* 5 was originally essentially identical to the *Lüshi chunqiu/Liji* versions of "Yueling" but later departed from that text because of the random drift of errors introduced by copyists and editors. This is unlikely because the differences between the *Huainanzi* 5 version and the *Lüshi chunqiu/Liji* versions tend to be large and systematic rather than minor and random. It is also possible that the *Huainanzi* 5 version was reproduced from memory from the *Lüshi chunqiu* version by one of the scholars at Liu An's court at Huainan; a systematically flawed memory could account for both the missing and the added material. However, the most likely explanation is that the *Lüshi chunqiu* version was well known to, and perhaps even available in a manuscript copy to, the scholars at Liu An's court, and that when it was incorporated into the *Huainanzi* it was systematically edited and revised to suit the beliefs and preferences of Liu An and his circle.

The systematic variations in the text (e.g., "*zhaoyao* points to branch X" instead of "the sun is in Lunar Lodge X") tend to indicate an active editorial hand. (In this instance, the substitution probably represents a tendency in the second century B.C.E.—the time of Liu An and his circle—to make use of the *shi* cosmograph for determining astronomical place locations, instead of the direct visual observation that would have been employed a century or so earlier in the time of Lu Buwei. *Zhaoyao*, "Far-Flight," is a bright star in Bootes that was often, in China, taken to be an extension of the "pointer" of the handle of the Northern Dipper.[7]) An active editorial hand is also suggested by the systematic amplification of certain types of material, such as additional seasonal correlations including weapons, domestic animals, fuel for the ruler's ritual cooking fire, etc., and monthly correlations, including offices and trees. The same may be said of *Huainanzi* 5's omission of a thearch (*di*) and a god (*shen*) for each month; instead, thearchs (gods) and their "assistants" (similar but not quite identical to the planetary deities of *Huainanzi* 3.VI) for the five directions are given in the first of the chapter's supplementary sections (*Huainanzi* 5.XIII). It is also possible that the additional material in the *Huainanzi* 5 version of "Yueling" was originally also included in the *Lüshi chunqiu/Liji* version, but was omitted in those texts by later editors. Other changes, too, might have crept into the *Lüshi chunqiu/Liji* version of the text, causing it to diverge over time from the *Huainanzi* 5 version. While the *Huainanzi* 5 and the *Lüshi chunqiu/Liji* versions of the "Yueling" are all, in effect, the same text in the sense that what they have in common is far more substantial than the ways in which they differ, the *Huainanzi* 5 version deserves more attention than it has received from scholars for two reasons.

The first is simply the fact of its inclusion in the *Huainanzi*. If one accepts the assumption that the entire *Huainanzi* text was deliberately put into something like its present form by Liu An and his court scholars, then the incorporation of the "Yueling" into the *Huainanzi* means that its seasonal rules were an integral part of the Huang-Lao Daoist program advocated by the Huainan academicians. (The many parallels between *Huainanzi* 3 and *Huainanzi* 5 reinforce this impression.) The second reason is that the additional material in the *Huainanzi* 5 version of the "Yueling" makes a substantial contribution to our present understanding of early Han correlative thinking.

The variant materials in the *Huainanzi* 5 version include the following, in addition to those mentioned above.

1. The treatment of the artificial fifth season of "midsummer." Very early ritual calendars, such as the *Guanzi* "Four Seasons," proceed on the basis of the self-evident fact that the year contains four and only four seasons. These are correlated in the customary fashion with the phases wood, fire, metal, and water; phase earth and its correlates play little or no role. In the *Lüshi chunqiu/Liji* "Yueling", the section for the sixth month treats that month basically as the third month of summer, and all correlations for that month are to phase fire; but it also contains a short supplementary section that gives phase earth correlations for a midsummer season of unspecified date and duration. In *Huainanzi* 5, however, phase earth correlations are substituted for phase fire ones throughout the sixth month; in other words, in *Huainanzi* 5 the sixth month is treated as a separate midsummer "season," in defiance of astronomical reality but incorporating fully the theoretical resonances of the five phase system.

2. Sections additional to the twelve-month calendar. After the sections on the twelve months—material closely related to the "Yueling"—*Huainanzi* 5 adds three more chapter sections, which are neither found in nor closely related to *Lüshi chunqiu/Liji*. They do not seem to be derived from any extant Warring States or early Han text, either, and so may be regarded (pending the possible archaeological discovery of such a text) original to *Huainanzi*. These sections are:

a. The "Five Positions" (*wu wei*). This section provides information, partly geographical and partly mythographical, about five regions: east, south, the center, west, and north, with rules governing each. These rules are prescriptions for the conduct of government; they are similar but not identical to those for the five "seasons" contained in the twelve monthly sections of the text.

b. The "Six Coordinates" (*liu he*). These are six diagonals drawn across the celestial circle, similar to the "Six Departments" found in *Huainanzi* 3.XIII.8. The pairs, in this instance, are of months, for example, first month of spring–first month of autumn, and middle month of summer–middle month of winter. (Note that in this scheme the third month of summer is not singled out as a special "midsummer" season.) The twelve months are each characterized in a phrase or two, following which formulae are given for the pairs, for example, "If government fails in its duties in month N, in month N + 6 there will be bad consequence X." The section ends with a set of prognostications similar to those that conclude each of the twelve monthly sections of the text, but keyed to the season rather than to the month: "If in season A the ordinances of season B (C, D) are carried out, there will be bad consequence X (Y, Z)."

c. The "Six Regulators" (*liu du*). This section describes six measuring instruments—the marking cord, the level, the compass, the balance beam, the square, and the plumb bob—which are correlated with heaven, earth, spring, summer, autumn, and winter, respectively. Each instrument is the subject of a poetic paean to its virtues as a standard, and further lines tell how each should be applied "in the regulation of the Mingtang," or in other words, to the annual calendar of ritual observances.

In all versions of the "Yueling," material is presented in a rigid and formulaic manner. For comparison with the twelve monthly sections of the *Huainanzi* "Treatise on the Seasonal Rules" translated below, the following is a schematic outline of the twelve monthly sections of the *Lüshi chunqiu/Liji* version; paragraph numbers follow the numbering in James Legge's translation of the *Liji* version:

"Yueling," General Outline of the Monthly Ordinances

1. In the Nth month, the sun is in Lunar Lodge A. Lodge B culminates at dusk, Lodge C culminates at dawn.
2. The cyclical characters [seasonal, not monthly] are XY.
3. The god is AA, his assistant is BB.
4. The class of creatures is CC [seasonal, not monthly].
5. The pentatonic note is DD [seasonal], the pitchpipe is EE [monthly].
6. The number is FF, the taste is GG, the smell is HH [all seasonal].
7. Sacrifices are made to the II household god; organ JJ is offered first [seasonal].
8. Omens and portents from the world of living creatures; signs of the changing year [monthly].
9. Son of Heaven occupies chamber KK of the Mingtang. He rides in a chariot with

LL bells, drawn by horses of seasonal color MM, with a MM banner. Wears MM robes and an MM jade pendant. He eats grain NN and meat OO (for ritual meals). His food vessels are of PP shape [all seasonal, not monthly].

10. Inauguration of season QQ [first month of each season only]. Three days before the ceremony, the Grand Astrologer makes an announcement, saying that such-and-such a day marks the inauguration of season QQ; the qi of the season is in phase RR. The thearch undergoes purification. On the appointed day, he person-ally leads the three sires, nine lords, and the feudal princes and great officers to meet the QQ season at the altar in the (direction SS) suburb. Returning, he dis-tributes rewards at court.

11. The Son of Heaven issues charges to the officials.

12. He also issues injunctions that proper behavior according to the season and month be observed.

13. Statement of ritual actions of the Son of Heaven appropriate to the season and month.

14. Indications from the natural world that it conforms to the correlative values of the season and month.

15. The Son of Heaven issues orders regarding husbandry, etc.

16. The Son of Heaven issues orders regarding music and sacrifices.

17–23. Various prohibitions appropriate to the season and month.

24. Portents and warnings of the ill consequences of using, during the current sea-son, ordinances appropriate to the other three seasons.

As will readily be seen from the translation below, the *Huainanzi* 5 version of the "Yueling" closely conforms to this scheme, with certain consistent differences as previ-ously mentioned. Because of the highly schematic nature of the text of the first twelve sections of the "Treatise on the Seasonal Rules," it has been possible to compress much of the necessary commentary on those sections into this introductory essay. Conse-quently the commentaries on the first twelve sections of the treatise below will be rela-tively brief, concentrating on features peculiar to each individual section.

Because the format for each month's section of the text is so stereotyped, it is easy to extract from the text lists of twelve-branch and five phase (that is, monthly and seasonal) correlates. These may be tabulated as on pages 222–223.

The seasonal rules call for the Son of Heaven to preside over certain ceremonies each month in one or another chamber of the Mingtang, a ritual building of nine rooms laid out as a 3 × 3 grid.[8] This requires reconciling incommensurables; there are twelve months but only nine chambers. The solution given in *Huainanzi* 5 is for three of the chambers—the northeastern, southeastern, and northwestern ones—to be used twice. The Son of Heaven begins the year in the northeastern chamber. He moves next

EARTHLY-BRANCH CORRELATES IN HUAINANZI 5

Month	Branch	Dawn-Culminating Asterism	Dusk-Culminating Asterism	Pitch Pipe	Room of Mingtang	Office	Tree
1	yin	Array	Tail	Great Budding	NE Corner	Master of Works[e]	Willow[f]
2	mao	Bow[a]	Establishing Stars[b]	Pinched Bell	Eastern Chamber	Granary	Almond
3	chen	Seven Stars	Ox-Leader	Maiden Purity	SE Corner	Villages	Pear
4	si	Wings	Widow[c]	Median Regulator	SE Corner	Tilled Fields	Peach
5	wu	Neck	Rooftop	Luxuriant	Southern Chamber	Functionaries	Elm
6	wei	Heart	Stride	Hundred Bell[d]	Central Palace	Lesser Ingathering	Hazel
7	shen	Dipper	Net	Tranquil Pattern	SW Corner	Armory	Tung-tree
8	you	Ox-Leader	Turtle-Beak	Southern Regulator	Western Chamber	Military Officers	Cudrania
9	xu	Emptiness	Willow	Tireless	NW Corner	Archer-Lords	Sophora
10	hai	Rooftop	Seven Stars	Responsive Bell	NW Corner	Master of Horses	Sandalwood
11	zi	Eastern Wall	Chariot Platform	Yellow Bell	Northern Chamber	Metropolitan Guards	Jujube
12	chou	Bond	Root	Great Regulator	NE Corner	Prisons	Chestnut

a. Bow (hu) is a constellation south of the Lunar Lodge Spirit-Bearer.

b. Establishing stars (jian xing) is a constellation of six stars north of the Lunar Lodge Dipper.

c. Widow (wunü) is a constellation north of the Lunar Lodge Serving-Maid.

d. Hundred Bell = Forest Bell.

e. The monthly offices (or, more broadly, functions of government) are not terribly systematic, but tend to derive in a general way from the content of each month's ordinances.

f. The monthly trees generally follow a natural seasonal progression, from the early-greening willow and early-blooming almond of spring to the jujube (the fruit of which is usually eaten dried) and the long-keeping chestnut of winter.

FIVE PHASE CORRELATIONS IN HUAINANZI 5

Season	Direction	Heavenly Stem	Phase	Class of Beast	Note	No.
spring	east	*jia, yi*	wood	scaly	*jue*	8
summer	south	*ping, ding*	fire	feathers	*zhi*	7
midsummer	center	*wu, ji*	earth	naked	*gong*	5
autumn	west	*geng, xin*	metal	hairy	*shang*	9
winter	north	*ren, gui*	water	armored	*yu*	6

Flavor	Smell	God	Organ First Offered in Sacrifice	Son of Heaven's Food	Ritual Fuel
sour	musty	door	spleen	wheat, mutton	fern stalks
bitter	burnt	stove	lungs	legumes, chicken	Cudrania branches
sweet	fragrant	drain	heart	millet, beef	Cudrania branches
pungent	rank	door	liver	hempseed, dog meat	Cudrania branches
salty	putrid	well	kidneys	millet, pork	pine branches

Color	Music	Weapon	Animal	Thearch	Assistant
bluegreen	strings	spear	goat	Tai Hao	Gou Mang
vermilion	pipes	glaive	chicken	Chi Di	Zhu Rong
yellow	[none]	sword	bovine	Huang Di	Hou Tu
white	bells	halberd	dog	Shao Hao	Ru Shou
black	chimes	partisan	pig	Zhuan Xu	Xuan Ming

to the eastern chamber, then to the southeastern one, which is used for the third and fourth months in succession. Then he moves to the southern chamber, the central chamber, the southwestern chamber, and the western chamber, for one month apiece. In the ninth and tenth months he occupies the northwestern chamber. In the eleventh month he occupies the northern chamber; in the twelfth month, he is back in the northeastern chamber, where the ritual cycle for the year ends.

Five of the Mingtang's nine chambers have specific names. The named chambers of the Mingtang are as follows: East, *qingyang*, "Bluegreen Yang"; South, *mingtang*, "Bright Hall," from which the building as a whole takes its name; Center, *zhonggong*, "Central Palace"; West, *zongzhang*, "Comprehensive Template"; and North, *xuantang*, "Dark Hall." The corner chambers are designated simply by position, so that, for example, northeastern chamber takes its name from the eastern chamber and is called the "Bluegreen Yang corner chamber".

The plan of the *Huainanzi* 5 Mingtang, and the Son of Heaven's movements through it during the course of a year, are summarized in the following figure:

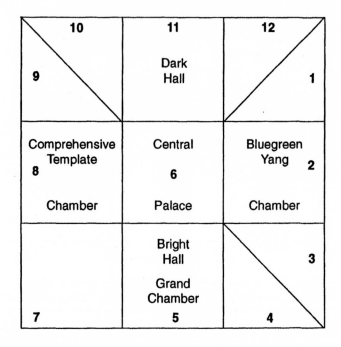

Figure 5.1. Diagram of the Mingtang, showing how the chambers are employed by the ruler in the twelve-month ritual rotation described in *Huainanzi 5.*

❧

THE TREATISE ON
THE SEASONAL RULES

Section I: First Month

[5:1a:4]

1   In the first month of spring, *zhaoyao* points to *yin.*
2   (The Lunar Lodge) Array culminates at dusk; Tail culminates at dawn.
3   (Spring) occupies the east. Its days are *jia* and *yi.*
4   The fullness of power is in Wood.
5   Its beasts are (those of the) scaly (class).
6   Its (pentatonic) note is *jue.*

7   The pitchpipe (of the first month) is Great Budding.

8   The number (of spring) is eight.

9   Its flavor is sour.

10   Its smell is musty.

11   Its sacrifices are made to the door-god.

12   From the body of the sacrificial victim, the spleen is offered first.

13   The east wind dispels the cold. Hibernating creatures begin to stir and revive.

14   Fish rise and (rub their) backs (against) the ice. Otters sacrifice fish. Look for the geese (to return) north.

15   The Son of Heaven wears bluegreen clothing. He mounts (a carriage drawn by) azure dragon(-horses). He wears azure jade (pendants) and flies a bluegreen banner.

16   He eats wheat with mutton. He drinks water gathered from the eight winds, and cooks with fire (kindled from) fern-stalks.

17   The imperial ladies of the Eastern Palace wear bluegreen clothing with bluegreen trim. They play lutes and zithers.

18   The weapon (of spring) is the spear.

19   The domestic animal (of spring) is the goat.

20   (The Son of Heaven) holds the dawn session of court in the corner (chamber of the Mingtang) to the left [i.e., counterclockwise from] of the Bluegreen Yang Chamber.

21   He promulgates the spring ordinances, extends his virtue, bestows favor, carries out (rites of) celebration and praise, and reduces corvée exactions and tax levies.

22   On the first day of spring, the Son of Heaven personally leads the Three Sires, the Nine Lords, and the great nobles to welcome the year at (the altar of) the eastern suburbs.

23   He repairs and cleans out the place of sacrifice and (employs) wealth-offerings to pray to the ghosts and spirits. Only male animals are used as sacrificial victims.

24   It is prohibited to cut trees. Nests must not be overturned nor the unborn young killed, likewise neither young creatures nor eggs.

25   People must not be assembled (for labor duty) nor fortifications erected.

26   Skeletons must be reburied, and corpses interred.

27   If in the first month of spring the ordinances of summer were carried out, then there would be unseasonable winds and rain; plants and trees would wither early, and the state would suffer anxiety.

28   If the ordinances of autumn were carried out, the people would suffer epidemics; violent winds and torrential rains would arrive at the same time, and thorns, weeds, briars, and overgrowth would spring up together.

29   If the ordinances of winter were carried out, floods would create ruin; there would be rain, frost, and great hailstones. The first-sown seeds would not sprout.

30   The first month governs the Master of Works.

31   Its tree is the willow.

[5:2b:4]

Commentary to Section I

The first month marks the beginning of the accretion of yang (as described, for example, in the eastern-horizon solar calendar of 3.XVII above) in the annual round of waxing and waning of yin and yang; the season of spring is linked to the vegetative growth of the phase wood in five phase correlative cosmology. Here, as throughout the "Treatise on the Seasonal Rules," the astronomical/astrological, directional, and other ritual correlates prescribed for the month and the season are entirely consistent with those of standard Han five phase and duodenary correlative thinking.

Indications from the natural world are adduced to demonstrate the correctness of the schematic and systematic prescriptions derived from cosmological theory. The tree of spring is the willow, the branches of which turn a delicate yellow-green in the waning weeks of winter. The animal kingdom, too, is in accord with the ascending influence of yang; fish revive from their winter torpor, and otters begin to feed upon them. Observations of the migration patterns of geese, such as the one mentioned here, are ubiquitous in early Chinese texts, proof that this obvious indicator of seasonal change was an established part of Chinese folk wisdom.

In lines 15–16, the thearch's steed is described as a "dragon." This is glossed by Gao You (citing *Liji*) as a particularly large horse. Given the aura of ritual magic that pervades this text, however, we may assume that the ruler's subjects were supposed to envision his horses as being literally dragon-like, perhaps on the order of the equine-looking dragons that draw the carriage in the famous "musical banquet" scene from the Yinan tomb reliefs.[9] Symbolically the thearch's steed is the Bluegreen Dragon of the Eastern Palace of Heaven, the living celestial symbol of spring, ascendant yang, and all of the correlates of phase wood. The thearch is said in the *Huainanzi* text to "mount" this beast; presumably what he mounts is a carriage (a "phoenix carriage", as in the *Lüshi chunqiu*/*Liji* version) drawn by a team of dragon-horses. In the Han, a ruler traveling in state would more likely be in a luxurious vehicle than riding astride.

The thearch is said also to drink water "gathered from the eight winds." Gao You says that this is dew drawn from a bronze vessel—presumably the magical, square, dew-collecting *fangju* mentioned in 3.II.31. The ritual fire for the thearch's sacrifical offerings is kindled from fern stalks, the fern being among the earliest herbs to sprout in the softening soil of spring.

Here as throughout the treatise, the acts undertaken or encouraged by the ruler conform to the ethical implications of yang and yin, the former requiring forebearance and generosity, the latter sternness and punishment. Thus at the beginning of spring the ruler is especially solicitous of young animals and the nests and eggs of birds. People may not be employed for corvée labor, but must be left free to attend to the planting of their fields. Anything connected with killing or death must be avoided so as to conform to the natural rhythm of the cosmos. Thus trees may not be cut, and any disinterred skeletons must be reburied and fresh corpses committed to the ground (in order, as Gao You explains, to ward off the malignant qi that would arise from them).

Likewise during any given season the employment of the regulations of another season would be a prescription for disaster. In the case of spring, the adverse consequences arise as follows:

Summer in spring = fire imposed upon wood; crops sprout too quickly and wither too soon, tempestuous winds replace springtime zephyrs. A successful harvest would be in doubt.

Autumn in spring = metal imposed upon wood; yin where there should be yang engenders disease and violent storms. Weeds crowd out and overwhelm beneficial plants.

Winter in spring = water imposed upon wood; floods, frost, and ice prevent plants from sprouting, and disaster ensues.

Section II: Second Month

[5:2b:5]

1   In the middle month of spring, *zhaoyao* points to *mao*.
2   (The constellation) Bow culminates at dusk; Establishing-Stars culminates at dawn.
3   (Spring) occupies the east.
4   Its days are *jia* and *yi*.
5   Its beasts are (those of the) scaly (class).
6   Its (pentatonic) note is *jue*.
7   The pitchpipe (of the second month) is Pinched Bell.
8   The number (of spring) is eight.
9   Its flavor is sour.
10   Its smell is musty.
11   Its sacrifices are made to the door-god.
12   From the body of the sacrificial victim, the spleen is offered first.
13   The rains begin. Peaches and pears begin to blossom.
14   The oriole sings. Hawks metamorphose into pigeons.
15   The Son of Heaven wears bluegreen clothing. He mounts (a carriage drawn by) azure dragon(-horses). He wears azure jade (pendants) and flies a bluegreen banner.
16   He eats wheat with mutton. He drinks water gathered from the eight winds, and cooks with fire (kindled from) fern-stalks.
17   The imperial ladies of the Eastern Palace wear bluegreen clothing with bluegreen trim. They play lutes and zithers.
18   The weapon (of spring) is the spear.
19   The domestic animal (of spring) is the goat.

20   (The Son of Heaven) holds the dawn session of court in the Bluegreen Yang (chamber of the Mingtang).

21   He orders those in authority to ameliorate penal servitude and to cause manacles and fetters to be struck off. (There is to be) no flogging, and criminal trials are halted.

22   The young and the small are to be nourished, the orphaned and childless protected, in order that (these policies) may communicate (their efficacy) to the growing sprouts.

23   He chooses an auspicious day and orders the people (to sacrifice) at shrines.

24   In this month, the days and nights are equally divided. The sound of thunder begins to be heard. Hibernating insects all stir and revive.

25   Anticipating the thunder by three days, (he sends messengers to) strike bells with wooden clappers, proclaiming among the people,

26   "The thunder is about to sound forth. Those who are not careful of their demeanor (and) who give birth without taking (appropriate) precautions will surely suffer catastrophes."

27   He orders the Master of Markets to make uniform all weights and measures: the *jun*, the steelyard, the *shi*, the catty, the peck and the pail.

28   (In this month, one must) not drain rivers and marshes, nor draw off water from embanked ponds, nor set fire to the mountain forests, nor undertake any large-scale works such as would impede the efficiency of farming.

29   In sacrifices, animal victims are not used; (rather) one uses (jade) scepters and discs, fur pelts and rolls of (silk) cloth.

30   If in the second month of spring the autumn ordinances were carried out, the country (would suffer) great floods and cold winds at the same time. Bandits and barbarians would attack.

31   If the ordinances of winter were carried out, the yang qi would not prevail, wheat would not ripen, and the people thereby would suffer great ruin.

32   If the ordinances of summer were carried out, the country (would suffer) great drought; hot qi would arrive prematurely. Insect pests would wreck havoc.

33   The second month governs the granary.

34   Its tree is the almond.

     [5:3b:10]

Commentary to Section II

In the second month of spring, the seasonal correlates of course remain the same as in the first month, while the monthly correlates change. Folk wisdom again predicts the normal progress of events as spring weather takes hold: the rains begin, fruit trees begin to flower, and the oriole sings (in what we would now recognize as the onset of territorial nesting behavior).

In another of the many instances of the metamorphosis of one animal into another in these cosmological chapters of *Huainanzi*, hawks are said to change into pigeons

228

during the second month. Because this type of metamorphosis seems more likely to reflect folk belief than the "high" intellectual tradition of formal cosmology, it would seem appropriate to seek an explanation for it in the perceived natural world rather than in the workings of yin-yang/five phase systematics. In this instance, one may note that hawks migrate over relatively short distances, from cold northern regions to temperate midlatitude ones; in winter, hawks would have been a conspicuous sight perched in the leafless trees of central China. In the spring the hawks become less conspicuous, both because some of them migrate northwards again and because others are less visible in the foliated trees, while pigeons, returning from their more southerly migrations, become more noticeable. Hawks and pigeons being of about the same size, it is perhaps unsurprising that people believed that the former changed into the latter. (Hawks eat pigeons, too; perhaps this is an early Chinese example of "you are what you eat.") However, one could also infer a yin-yang/five phase explanation for this: the carnivorous, rapacious hawks of winter yield to the peaceable, herbivorous doves of spring.

The onset of thunder is associated with the awakening of dormant insects, not merely by coincidence but because thunder apparently was thought to revive the insects by some resonant correlative relationship. We see here that thunder is also linked in folk belief with the hazards of childbirth; the thearch sends messengers into the countryside to warn those about to give birth to take precautions.

The vernal equinox occurs during the second month. As yang continues to wax and yin to diminish, the ruler's actions reflect benevolence and concern. Weights and measures are inspected, reflecting the kind of regulatory justice that the common people of China were led to expect from their government. The attention to these matters no doubt reflects *ganying* resonance with the "balance" implied by the equality of day and night at the equinox; a similar regulation of weights and measures occurs during the eighth month, at the time of the autumn equinox.

Public works involving what now would be termed environmental destruction are banned, as are activities that would distract farmers from their tasks. In criminal matters, amnesties or at least postponements of trials and punishment are decreed. In one case this requirement of royal benevolence leads to contradictory prescriptions in this section; in line 12 we are told that in sacrificial rituals the spleen of the victim is offered first (as is true throughout the spring), while in line 29 we learn that luxury articles are substituted for living victims in sacrifices. It is hard to know how to reconcile these contradictory prescriptions; perhaps the avoidance of living victims was intended to apply only to routine rituals and not to the most important imperial sacrifices.

The consequences of using inappropriate seasonal ordinances in this second month of spring reflect the intensification of the force of yang as spring proceeds. Thus in the cases of using the (yin) ordinances of autumn and winter in the second month of spring, the conflict between yang and yin is greater than in the previous month, with exaggerated consequences; in the case of using the ordinances of summer, the additive effect of too much yang brings drought, heat, and plagues of insects.

Section III: Third Month

[5:4a:1]

1 In the final month of spring, *zhaoyao* points to *chen*.
2 (The Lunar Lodge) Seven Stars culminates at dusk; Ox-Leader culminates at dawn.
3 (Spring) occupies the east.
4 Its days are *jia* and *yi*.
5 Its beasts are (those of the) scaly (class).
6 Its (pentatonic) note is *jue*.
7 The pitchpipe (of the third month) is Maiden Purity.
8 The number (of spring) is eight.
9 Its flavor is sour.
10 Its smell is musty.
11 Its sacrifices are made to the door-god.
12 From the body of the sacrificial victim, the spleen is offered first.
13 The tung tree begins to bloom. Field-mice turn into quail.
14 Rainbows first appear. Duckweed begins to sprout.
15 The Son of Heaven wears bluegreen clothing. He mounts (a carriage drawn by) azure dragon(-horses). He wears azure jade (pendants) and flies a bluegreen banner.
16 He eats wheat with mutton. He drinks water gathered from the eight winds, and cooks with fire (kindled from) fern-stalks.
17 The imperial ladies of the Eastern Palace wear bluegreen clothing with bluegreen trim. They play lutes and zithers.
18 The weapon (of spring) is the spear.
19 The domestic animal (of spring) is the goat.
20 (The Son of Heaven) holds the dawn session of court in the corner (chamber of the Mingtang) to the right of the Bluegreen Yang Chamber.
21 The Master of Boats turns over the (imperial) boats (to inspect them), five times over and five times back, and then delivers a report (on their condition) to the Son of Heaven.
22 The Son of Heaven thereupon boards his boats for the first time (in the new year).
23 A sturgeon is offered in the inner chamber of the (ancestral) temple, and prayers are made that the wheat should bear grain.
24 In this month the production of qi reaches its fullest; yang qi spreads abroad.
25 Young plants grow no more and the sprouting plants attain their maximum growth, but they cannot (yet) be gathered in.
26 The Son of Heaven orders those in authority to open the granaries and storehouses to assist the impoverished and the bereft, to relieve the exhausted and (those who are)

cut off (from their families); and to open the strong-rooms and treasuries to distribute rolls of silk.

27　He sends embassies to the nobles, enquires after eminent scholars, and performs courtesies to the worthy.

28　When the seasonal rains are about to descend he orders the Minister of Works to mount and, following all of the roads from the capital city, make a tour of inspection of the plains and uncultivated fields, repairing the dikes and embankments, channeling the ditches and watercourses, following to its end every road and exhausting every byway, beginning at the metropolis and stopping only upon reaching the frontier.

28　Those who hunt, (whether with) nets or with arrows, with rabbit-snares or bird-nets, or by putting out poisoned bait, are prohibited from going out from the nine gates (of the city).

30　(The Son of Heaven) also (issues) a prohibition to the foresters in the wilderness, (saying that there must be) no cutting of mulberry trees or Cudrania trees.

31　The turtledove spreads its wings; the crested hoepoe lands in the mulberry tree.

32　Preparing plain cocoon-frames, round baskets and rectangular baskets, the royal consort and the royal concubines fast and perform austerities. Then they go to the mulberry (groves) in the eastern suburbs where the ladies initiate and oversee (the work of) sericulture.

33　(He) commands (those in charge of) the five storehouses to order the workmen to inspect the gold and iron, the pelts and hides, the sinew and horn, the arrowshaft bamboo and the bow-wood, the grease and glue, the cinnabar and lac (seeing to it that) there is none that is not excellent.

34　Selecting an auspicious day in the last ten-day period of the month, (he holds) a great musical performance, which brings jubilation.

35　Moreover (he orders) bulls to be mated with cows, and stallions with mares; afterwards the female animals are driven out to their herdsmen.

36　He orders on behalf of the kingdom an exorcism at the nine gates (of the capital city, in which) sacrificial (animal victims) are torn apart in order to bring an end to the qi of springtime.

37　If the ordinances for this month are observed, sweet rain will fall during the three ten-day periods of the last month of spring.

38　If the ordinances of winter were carried out, then cold qi would from time to time issue forth; the plants and trees would all wither, and the state would (suffer) great anxiety.

39　If the ordinances of summer were carried out, the people would (suffer) epidemics, the seasonal rains would not fall, and nothing would grow on the mountains and tumuli.

40　If the ordinances of autumn were carried out, Heaven would drown in a flood of yin. Rains would fall (unseasonably) early; military rebellions would break out.

41　The third month governs villages.

42　Its tree is the pear.
　　[5:5b:6]

Commentary to Section III

In the third month, the accretion of yang continues; the natural world responds by producing a balancing flow of yin rain. The imagery of this month is conspicuously watery. The royal boats are inspected and prepared for the ruler's use, presumably in a formal ritualized fishing expedition designed to produce the great sturgeon that will be offered in the inner chamber of the ancestral temple. In anticipation of the rains water control facilities are inspected and repaired. Rain falls throughout the month, and as the sun cuts an ever-higher arc across the sky rainbows are frequently observed. Duckweed sprouts as seasonal ponds fill with water and are warmed by the sun.

The section for this month again gives us a certain amount of folk wisdom about the animal kingdom. Turtledoves and hopoes are sighted, presumably nesting in trees. In yet another example of metamorphosis, we are told that field mice turn into quails. Chinese country folk must surely have known that quail hatched from eggs, yet the similarity of scurrying mice to quail chicks, newly hatched and running after their mothers in the late spring, gives this image both charm and intuitive appeal.

Another conspicuous feature of this month's activities is the amount of attention paid to sericulture. The implements of sericulture are made ready; the women of the palace fast and perform rituals before going to the mulberry groves to begin their work. It is prohibited to cut down mulberry and Cudrania trees. (The Cudrania is the *zhe* tree, *Cudrania tricuspidata*, a small, thorny tree or bush, sometimes known as the false paper-mulberry. Its leaves were used in China to feed silkworms if true mulberry leaves were unavailable.)[10] The Cudrania seems to have been held in particularly high esteem by the authors of the "Treatise on the Seasonal Rules," no doubt because of its importance for sericulture. Its branches provide the fuel for the royal sacrificial cooking fire in three of the five "seasons," namely summer, midsummer, and autumn.

The thearch's role continues to be one of yang benevolence; courtesies are shown to notables and alms distributed to the needy. Living things come under royal protection: hunting and tree cutting are prohibited. Perhaps as much to encourage the production of yang qi as to attend to the needs of animal husbandry, the ruler gives orders for cattle and horses to be bred. For the first time, however, a note of sternness enters into the royal decrees; people are prohibited from traveling outside the city (perhaps to ensure that urban folk will stick to their appointed tasks, or to avoid disruption of the work of the countryside), while the inspection of goods in the royal storehouses hints that the time will soon come to prepare weapons and chariots for use in hunting and warfare.

Again, the consequences of using the wrong seasonal ordinances during this month reflect the effects of piling yang upon yang, or of opposing yang with yin.

Section IV: Fourth Month

[5:5b:7]

1   In the first month of summer, *zhaoyao* points to *si*.
2   (The Lunar Lodge) Wings culminates at dusk; (the constellation) Widow culminates at dawn.
3   (Summer) occupies the south. Its days are *ping* and *ding*.
4   The fullness of power is in Fire.
5   Its beasts are (those of the) feathered (class).
6   Its (pentatonic) note is *zhi*.
7   The pitchpipe (of the fourth month) is Median Regulator.
8   The number (of summer) is seven.
9   Its flavor is bitter.
10 Its smell is burnt.
11 Its sacrifices are made to the stove-god.
12 From the body of the sacrificial victim, the lungs are offered first.
13 Crickets and tree-frogs sing on the hillsides; earthworms emerge.
14 The royal-melon (begins to) set fruit. Bitter herbs flourish.
15 The Son of Heaven wears vermilion clothing. He mounts (a carriage drawn by) black-maned vermilion horses. He wears vermilion jade (pendants) and flies a vermilion banner.
16 He eats legumes with chicken. He drinks water gathered from the eight winds, and cooks with fire (kindled from) Cudrania branches.
17 The imperial ladies of the Southern Palace wear vermilion clothing with vermilion trim. They play reed-pipes and mouth-organs.
18 The weapon (of summer) is the glaive.
19 The domestic animal (of summer) is the chicken.
20 (The Son of Heaven) holds the dawn session of court in the corner (chamber of the Mingtang) to the left of the Mingtang Chamber.
21 He promulgates the summer ordinances.
22 On the first day of summer, the Son of Heaven personally leads the Three Sires, the Nine Lords, and the great nobles to welcome the year at (the altar of) the southern suburbs.
23 Returning (from this ceremony), he bestows favors, enfeoffs nobles, rectifies ceremonials and music, and gives a feast for (the officials of) the left and the right.
24 He commands the Intendant-General to single out for praise the heroic and meritorious, to select the eminent and excellent, and to raise up the filial and fraternal.
25 He carries out (ceremonies of) ennoblement and issues official emoluments; assisting (the work of) Heaven, he increases the nurture (of the people), lengthens that which is long, piles up that which is high.
26 (There must be) no destructive or vicious (behavior), no raising up of earthenwork (fortifications), no cutting of great trees.

27   He orders the foresters to travel (through) the cultivated fields and the plains, to encourage the practices of agriculture and to drive away (both) wild and domestic animals so as not to permit them to harm the (growing) grain.

28   The Son of Heaven takes a pig (together with) sacrificial wheat, and presents them as the first offerings in the inner chamber of the (ancestral) temple.

29   Domestic animals are rounded up. Medicinal herbs (begin to) wither, and grassy plants die.

30   (So that) the wheat will mature in autumn, minor criminal cases are decided, and petty punishments are carried out.

31   If in the first month of summer the autumn ordinances were carried out, then bitter rains would come on numerous occasions. The grain would not be nourished (thereby). Neighboring peoples on four sides would penetrate (the country's) defensive fortifications.

32   If the ordinances of winter were carried out, the plants and trees would dry up early; thereafter there would be floods, destroying the city walls and outer fortifications.

33   If the ordinances of spring were carried out, grasshoppers and locusts would cause devastation; scorching winds would come and attack (the fields, so that) the flourishing plants would not bear seed.

34   The fourth month governs the tilled fields.

35   Its tree is the peach.
[5:6b:8]

Commentary to Section IV

In the fourth month summer begins, spring having been ritually brought to an end—in fact, destroyed—through a sacrificial rending of animal victims at the end of the third month. All five phase correlates thus shift from wood to fire, while all duodenary correlates shift to those appropriate to the fourth month. These correlates are standard and familiar, except perhaps for the seasonal weapon. The weapon of summer is the *ji*, a pole-mounted weapon with a crescent-shaped blade. Unlike the *ge*, the common ancient Chinese pole-mounted dagger-axe (often translated as "halberd"), the *ji* could be used with either a thrusting or a sweeping motion. The Japanese *naginata* is of a generally similar type; the closest equivalent in the English language is *glaive*.[11]

Seasonal indicators from the natural world hold no surprises. Crickets and tree frogs sing in the evening, as summer heat succeeds the late spring rains, and earthworms are plentiful. Leafy herbs reach full growth and show the first signs of withering; grass turns from green to gold. Melons, having flowered in the spring, begin to set fruit.

The ritual color of summer is vermilion. The thearch's carriage is drawn by vermilion black-maned horses—an equine equivalent of the Vermilion Bird of the Southern Palace of Heaven.

With the onset of summer, yang is clearly ascendant over yin, and the ruler conducts himself accordingly. Praise and honors are freely bestowed; to those who have, more is given. Destructive (yin) activities of all kinds are prohibited. Yet punishments appear in the cycle of seasonal activities for the first time, in anticipation of the coming months of waxing yin; care is taken, however, that this should be done in an appropriately low-key fashion, with court cases being limited to minor matters, and punishments to those of small severity.

If in this month the ordinances of autumn were carried out, lesser yin would oppose greater yang, producing not only cold rains devoid of nourishing power, but (because of the influence of autumn's phase, metal) also invasions from neighboring countries. If the winter ordinances were carried out, greater yin would oppose greater yang, producing first drought (as yin overcame yang) and then floods (as yin raged unrestrained). If the ordinances of spring were carried out, lesser yang would impinge upon greater yang; plants that had begun to grow would not reach maturity, whether because of destructive insect pests or because hot winds (yang added to yang) would cause the crops to wither before bearing seed.

Section V: Fifth Month

[5:6b:9]

1   In the second month of summer, *zhaoyao* points to *wu*.

2   (The Lunar Lodge) Neck culminates at dusk; (the Lodge) Rooftop culminates at dawn.

3   (Summer) occupies the south.

4   Its days are *ping* and *ding*.

5   Its beasts are (those of the) feathered (class).

6   Its (pentatonic) note is *zhi*.

7   The pitchpipe (of the fifth month) is Luxuriant.

8   The number (of summer) is seven.

9   Its flavor is bitter.

10   Its smell is burnt.

11   Its sacrifices are made to the stove-god.

12   From the body of the sacrificial victim, the lungs are offered first.

13   The Lesser Heat arrives; mantids are born.

14   The shrike begins to cry; the turn-tongue is not heard.

15   The Son of Heaven wears vermilion clothing. He mounts (a carriage drawn by) black-maned vermilion horses. He wears vermilion jade (pendants) and flies a vermilion banner.

16   He eats legumes with chicken. He drinks water gathered from the eight winds, and cooks with fire (kindled from) Cudrania branches.

17 The imperial ladies of the Southern Palace wear vermilion clothing with vermilion trim. They play reed-pipes and mouth-organs.

18 The weapon (of summer) is the glaive.

19 The domestic animal (of summer) is the chicken.

20 (The Son of Heaven) holds the dawn session of court in the Mingtang Great Chamber.

21 He commands the Music Master to repair the hand-drums and kettle-drums, the lutes and zithers, the flutes and pan-pipes, to polish the bells and lithophones, and to attend to the (ceremonial) shields, battle-axes, haldberds, and feather plumes (used in war-dances).

22 (He) commands those in authority to pray and sacrifice to the mountains, rivers, and the hundred [= all] river sources.

23 In the great prayer to the gods for rain, a full panoply of music is employed.

24 The Son of Heaven takes a chicken (together with) the sacrificial panicled millet, along with a sacrifical offering of ripe peaches, and presents them (all) as first offerings in the inner temple of the (ancestral) temple.

25 (He) issues prohibitions to the people, (saying that they must) not reap indigo for dyeing, nor bake charcoal, nor dry bolts of cloth in the sun.

26 City and village gates must not be closed up; tax exactions must not be levied on markets.

27 Serious criminal cases are put off, and (the prisoners') rations are increased. Widows and widowers are preserved (from want), and relief is distributed for (those incurring) funeral expenses.

28 The (pregnant) female animals are separated out from the herds; stallions and colts are tied up. (The ruler) promulgates regulations for (the raising of) horses.

29 When the day reaches its maximum length, yin and yang contend; life and death reach a dividing-point.

30 The nobles fast and perform austerities. They display no angry emotions, refrain from music and sex, and eat meagerly.

31 All officials rest in tranquility from their duties and do not travel abroad; (all this), in order to make definite the establishment of the serene (forces of) yin.

32 Deer shed their antlers; cicadas begin to cry.

33 The Half-summer plant begins to grow; the hibiscus tree blooms.

34 A prohibition is issued to the people, (saying) they must not set fires. (But) it is permitted to dwell in high places (so as to) see clearly into the distance, to climb on hills and mounds and to stay on estrades and towers.

35 If in the middle month of summer the ordinances of winter were carried out, hail and sleet would damage the grain, the roads would be impassable, and fierce armies would invade.

36 If the ordinances of spring were carried out, the five kinds of grain would not ripen; all kinds of destructive insects would spring up during the season, and the country would suffer famine.

37 If the ordinances of autumn were carried out, the plants and trees would droop and
fall, fruits and grains would ripen prematurely, and the people would suffer calamities of pestilence.

38 The fifth month governs functionaries.

39 Its tree is the elm.

[5:8a:8]

Commentary to Section V

The seasonal correlates of summer remain unchanged; duodenary correlates are those of the fifth month. Seasonal indicators from the natural world are those of high summer; mantids hatch from their egg cases, and late-growing or late-flowering plants are conspicuous. The late-nesting shrike calls conspicuously, while the blackbird, having completed its nesting, falls relatively silent. The bird name here translated as "turn-tongue" is *fan-she*, described by Gao You as "a bird which is able to change its song to mimic other birds." Most sources say that this is the same as the *bai-she*, "hundred tongues," which is a common name for the Chinese blackbird, *Turdus merula*. That bird, a thrush, is an excellent songster, though not notably a mimic. This identification is probably correct, though some room for doubt remains. The crested myna, the range of which extends into south-central China, is a another possibility, as is the common Eurasian jay, which is famous as a mimic.

The comment that deer shed their antlers is puzzling; most species of deer shed their antlers earlier in the year, and by midsummer should have begun to grow new ones. In his commentary on a similar line in 3.II.21, Gao You says that *mi* deer shed their antlers at the winter solstice, and *lu* deer shed their antlers at the summer solstice. This does not seem entirely convincing. On the other hand, the remark that "cicadas begin to cry" is clearly based on observation; anyone who has spent a summer in East Asia will testify that the shrilling of cicadas is an unmistakable sign that the heat of midsummer has arrived for good.

The summer solstice occurs in the fifth month according to the reckoning of the Xia calendar, and the arrival of that liminal event injects a clear note of nervousness into the seasonal ordinances. Yang has reached its maximum, and must not be augmented further in any way; hence fires may not be set, nor may crops (such as indigo) that require drying in the sun be harvested. For the same reason, the sun-drying of bolts of cloth is also prohibited. This is a time of danger; "life and death reach a dividing-point," and nobles and officials retire from their duties to fast and practice austerities. The music masters prepare ritual implements for great ceremonials, particularly sacrifices to water gods and prayers for rain, not only to welcome the onset of waxing yin, but in an effort to avert the threat of midsummer drought. People are permitted to ascend to high places to watch symbolically for the turning of the year, and the season of yin is anticipated as the regalia of war dances are inspected and refurbished.

But while yang, having attained its apogee, may not be augmented, the arrival of yin must not be hurried; serious criminal cases are postponed. The benefactions of summer continue—now, however, not to the young and weak, but to the elderly and the dying, as yang reaches the end of its time of dominance. Meanwhile the work of the country folk goes on, as foals are weaned from their dams.

If in this month the ordinances of winter were carried out, the contradiction between yang and yin would be at its most severe, leading to hail and sleet, roads blocked by mud and ice, and foreign invasions. As in the fourth month, if the ordinances of spring were carried out, lesser yang imposed upon greater yang would prevent crops from ripening and unleash plagues of devouring insects. And if the ordinances of autumn were carried out, lesser yin would block greater yang; plants would die without bearing seed, fruit would rot before ripening, and diseases would similarly cut down people before they had reached their allotted span.

Section VI: Sixth Month

[5:8a:8]

1   In the final month of summer, *zhaoyao* points to *wei*.
2   (The Lunar Lodge) Heart culminates at dusk; (the Lodge) Stride culminates at dawn.
3   (Midsummer) occupies the center. Its days are *wu* and *ji*.
4   The fullness of power is in Earth.
5   Its beasts are (those of the) naked (class).
6   Its (pentatonic) note is *gong*.
7   The pitchpipe (of the sixth month) is Hundred Bell [= Forest Bell].
8   The number (of midsummer) is five.
9   Its flavor is sweet.
10   Its smell is fragrant.
11   Its sacrifices are made to the (god of the) drain-hole.
12   From the body of the sacrificial victim, the heart is offered first.
13   The cool winds begin to arrive; crickets dwell in the snug corners (of the house).
14   (Young) geese begin to practice flying; rotting vegetation turns into glow-worms.
15   The Son of Heaven wears yellow clothing. He mounts (a carriage drawn by) black-maned yellow horses. He wears yellow jade (pendants) and flies a yellow banner.
16   He eats millet with beef. He drinks water gathered from the eight winds, and cooks with fire (kindled from) Cudrania branches.
17   The imperial ladies of the Central Palace wear yellow clothing with yellow trim.
18   The weapon (of midsummer) is the sword.
19   The domestic animal (of midsummer) is the bovine.

20 (The Son of Heaven) holds the dawn session of court in the Central Palace (chamber of the Mingtang).

21 (He) commands the Master of Fisheries to spear scaly dragons, capture alligators, fetch up turtles (from the depths), and capture sea-turtles.

22 (He) commands the Marsh-Masters to present timber and rushes.

23 (He) commands the four Supervisory Lords to order all districts (to present) the customary (amount of) fodder to feed the sacrificial beasts.

24 In service to the Supreme Thearch of August Heaven, the illustrious mountains, the great rivers, and the gods of the four directions, he sacrifices millet in the great sanctuary of the (ancestral) temple, praying for the prosperity of the people.

25 (He) carries out benefactions, commanding that the dead should be mourned, the sick enquired after, and the elderly protected and cared for.

26 He causes bran and gruel to be sent to them, and sees to it that their sleeping-mats are (comfortably) thick. (All this is) to speed the ten thousand things on their return (journey, as the year begins to wane).

27 (He) commands the officials of the women's (quarters) to dye (fabrics) in various hues and multicolored designs, patterned and ornamented, bluegreen, yellow, white, and black. There may be none that are not beautiful and fine.

28 (This is to) provide new vestments for the ancestral temple: There must be a display of (things) that are brightly new.

29 In this month, the trees that were planted are fully flourishing; one must not dare to cut them.

30 It is not permitted to call an assembly of the nobles, to raise earthworks, to recruit corvée labor, nor to call up armies.

31 (If these things were done), there inevitably would be calamities called down by Heaven.

32 The soil is richly wet from the humid heat; the great rains fall in season, beneficially bringing to an end the life-cycle of the grassy plants, fertilizing the fields, and enriching the boundary-strips between the fields.

33 If during the last month of summer the ordinances of spring were carried out, the kernels of grain would scatter and fall, (the people would suffer) many colds and coughs, and people would depart the country.

34 If the ordinances of autumn were carried out, hills and lowlands alike would be flooded, the grain that had been sown would not ripen, and there would be many women's calamaties [= miscarriages].

35 If the ordinances of winter were carried out, then winds and cold would arrive out of season, falcons and hawks would snatch their prey (unseasonably) early, and along the four borders of the country people would withdraw to places of safety.

36 The sixth month governs the Lesser Ingathering.

37 Its tree is the hazel.

[5:9b:6]

Commentary to Section VI

The *Huainanzi's* "Treatise on the Seasonal Rules," unlike other versions of the "Yue-ling," treats the sixth month as a special "midsummer" season. The seasonal correlates therefore shift, for this month only, from those of phase fire to those of phase earth; the duodenary correlates continue to make their normal monthly changes. Accordingly, although the summer solstice has already passed and yin has begun its period of accretion, the sixth month here is treated as a special time of balance and centrality. The ruler sacrifices to the Supreme Thearch, to the great gods of natural landmarks and to the four directions; he pays particular care to the preparation of sacrificial animals, continues his benefactions to the elderly, and orders new vestments, in all of the seasonal colors, for use during the coming year.

The ritual color of midsummer is yellow, corresponding to phase earth and to the center. The thearch's carriage is drawn by a yellow black-maned horse, a symbolic equivalent of the Yellow Dragon of the Central Palace of Heaven.

Crops are in their final phase of ripening before the harvest. The seasonal rains arrive, making the ripening grain become full in the ear and making vegetables plump for gathering; the boundary strips between fields provide fodder for domestic animals. Public works are prohibited, so as not to interfere with agricultural pursuits; young trees may not be cut down, lest the crops, by sympathetic magic, fail in the final stage before the harvest. But mature plants may be cut; the Marsh-Masters are told to present timber and rushes to the royal storehouses. A harvest of water creatures signals the onset of the season of yin.

Tentative signs of summer's end appear in the natural world. Occasional cool breezes temper the seasonal heat, and crickets move from the field to the hearth. Young geese begin to be able to fly. Rotting vegetation, we are told, turns into glowworms—a natural conflation of two instances of bioluminescence.

The device of treating the sixth month as a special midsummer season is abandoned in the final lines of this section. Midsummer is subsumed into summer as the customary warnings are given of the dangers of employing the ordinances of the wrong season. Although in the sixth month yang has passed its maximum, summer is still treated as the season of greater yang. Thus again, the employment of the spring ordinances would result in the failure of crops before they ripened, in minor diseases, and—a new element—in the departure of refugees. Employment of the ordinances of autumn would result in an excess of yin, bringing the destruction of crops by floods and, by sympathetic magic, miscarriages (another instance of premature death before ripeness has been attained). Employment of the ordinances of winter would bring wind and cold, an influx of birds of prey (an omen, as the following section makes clear, of criminality and punishments), and general danger.

Section VII: Seventh Month

[5:9b:6]

1 In the first month of autumn, *zhaoyao* points to *shen*.
2 (The Lunar Lodge) Dipper culminates at dusk; (the Lodge) Net culminates at dawn.
3 (Autumn) occupies the west. Its days are *geng* and *xin*.
4 The fullness of power is in Metal.
5 Its beasts are (those of the) hairy (class).
6 Its (pentatonic) note is *shang*.
7 The pitchpipe (of the seventh month) is Tranquil Pattern.
8 The number (of autumn) is nine.
9 Its flavor is pungent.
10 Its smell is rank.
11 Its sacrifices are made to the door-god.
12 From the body of the sacrificial victim, the liver is offered first.
13 Cool winds arrive; the hoar-frost descends. Cold-weather cicadas sing.
14 Hawks sacrifice birds. (This is) used (as a signal to) begin executing criminals.
15 The Son of Heaven wears white clothing. He mounts (a carriage drawn by) black-maned white horses. He wears white jade (pendants) and flies a white banner.
16 He eats hempseed with dog-meat. He drinks water gathered from the eight winds, and cooks with fire (kindled from) Cudrania branches.
17 The imperial ladies of the Western Palace wear white clothing with white trim. They play music on silver bells.
18 The weapon (of autumn) is the halberd.
19 The domestic animal (of autumn) is the dog.
20 (The Son of Heaven) holds the dawn session of court in the corner (chamber of the Mingtang) to the left of the Comprehensive Template (chamber).
21 He promulgates the autumn ordinances.
22 (He commands his officials to) search out the unfilial and unfraternal and those who are oppressive, cruel, tyrannical and ruthless, in order to punish them; thus encouraging the waxing of baleful qi.
23 On the first day of autumn, the Son of Heaven personally leads the Three Sires, the Nine Lords, and the great nobles to welcome the autumn at (the altar of) the western suburbs.
24 Returning (from this ceremony), at court he bestows rewards on the leaders of his armies and on his soldiers.
25 (He) orders the generals and commanders to select soldiers and sharpen weapons, seeking out and selecting men who are heroic and valiant, placing trust in those of proven accomplishments.
26 (This is done) so that he might chastise the unrighteous and indict and punish the overbearing and those who are derelict in their duties.
27 (The execution of these orders) must extend to the furthest reaches of the realm.

28   (He) orders those in authority to set in order the laws and regulations and to repair the prisons, to prohibit licentiousness and bring an end to depravity, to judge criminal cases and adjudicate disputes at law.

29   Heaven and Earth now begin to be severe; it therefore is not permissible to act with mildness.

30   In this month the farmers begin to present their (newly-harvested) grain to the throne. The Son of Heaven (ritually) tastes the new grain and then offers it as the first sacrifical offering in the inner shrine of the (ancestral) temple.

31   (He) orders all of the officials to begin to gather (the tax grain), to complete (the building of) barriers and embankments, to pay careful attention to dikes and groins in order to prepare for floods, to repair city walls and boundary walls, and to refurbish palaces and mansions.

32   There must be no enfeoffment of nobles, nor raising high officials to office; there must be no bestowals of costly gifts, nor any sending forth of important embassies.

33   If the ordinances for this month are observed, the cool winds will arrive in thirty days.

34   If in the first month of autumn the ordinances of winter were observed, the yin qi would be excessive, land-snails would devour the grain, and fierce warriors would invade.

35   If the ordinances of spring were observed, the country would suffer drought; the yang qi would return out of season, and the five kinds of grain would not yield any harvest.

36   If the ordinances of summer were observed, there would be many disastrous fires; cold and heat would not conform to their seasonal order, and the people would suffer fevers.

37   The seventh month governs the armory.

38   Its tree is the tung tree.
    [5:11a:6]

Commentary to Section VII

The seventh month ushers in the season of autumn; five phase correlates are those of the phase metal. The ritual color of autumn is white; the thearch's carriage is drawn by black-maned white horses, symbolically equivalent to the White Tiger of the Western Palace of Heaven.

Hawks are observed stooping upon birds, a sure sign that, with the ascending power of yin, the season for the application of criminal laws and punishments has arrived. Mildness is set aside, and severity reigns; if licentiousness and depravity might have begun to flourish under the forgiving regime of the yang months, a stop is put to them now. The criminal cases postponed during the yang portion of the year are brought to court, and malefactors can expect neither amnesty nor mercy. The time has passed, too, for rewarding civil officials or undertaking peaceable diplomacy.

On the other hand, the military virtues begin to be glorified with the onset of autumn, and plans are made to undertake wars—in the guise of punitive expeditions against the unrighteous. As the ruler's thoughts turn to warfare, defenses are raised against the destructive powers both of man and of nature; city walls and boundary walls are repaired, as are dikes and groins, barriers and embankments.

The harvest that was foreseen in the sixth month is brought home in the seventh. This is an occasion for rejoicing, as the thearch offers the first fruits in sacrifice at the ancestral temple; for individual farmers, however, the rejoicing must have been tempered by the appearance of tax collectors, discharging their duties with the severity appropriate to autumn.

In discussing the consequences of the application of the wrong seasonal ordinances during this month, the authors of the treatise make explicit the conflicts of seasonal yin and yang. If the winter ordinances were applied, yin would be excessive; land snails (emphatically yin creatures) would devour the crops; and armies would invade. If the ordinances of spring were applied, yang qi would be excessive; crop plants would grow excessively without yielding seed or fruit. An even greater influx of unseasonal yang would result from the wrongful application of the ordinances of summer; fires would rage, there would be heat when there should be coolness, and people would suffer from fevers.

Section VIII: Eighth Month

[5:11a:7]

1   In the second month of autumn, *zhaoyao* points to *you*.
2   (The Lunar Lodge) Ox-Leader culminates at dusk; (the Lodge) Turtle-Beak culminates at dawn.
3   (Autumn) occupies the west.
4   Its days are *geng* and *xin*.
5   Its beasts are (those of the) hairy (class).
6   Its (pentatonic) note is *shang*.
7   The pitchpipe (of the eighth month) is Southern Regulator.
8   The number (of autumn) is nine.
9   Its flavor is pungent.
10 Its smell is rank.
11 Its sacrifices are made to the door-god.
12 From the body of the sacrificial victim, the liver is offered first.
13 The cool winds arrive. Look for the wild geese to arrive.
14 Swallows return (to their wintering-grounds); flocks of birds fly to and fro.
15 The Son of Heaven wears white clothing. He mounts (a carriage drawn by) black-maned white horses. He wears white jade (pendants) and flies a white banner.

16 He eats hempseed with dog-meat. He drinks water gathered from the eight winds, and cooks with fire (kindled from) Cudrania branches.

17 The imperial ladies of the Western Palace wear white clothing with white trim. They play music on silver bells.

18 The weapon (of autumn) is the halberd.

19 The domestic animal (of autumn) is the dog.

20 (The Son of Heaven) holds the dawn session of court in the Comprehensive Template (chamber of the Mingtang).

21 He orders those in authority to increase the strictness of all punishments.

22 Beheadings and other capital punishments must be applied with exact appropriateness, with neither excess nor leniency.

23 If the application of punishments is not exactly appropriate, the penalty will revert upon (those in authority).

24 In this month the elderly must be carefully attended to; they are given stools and walking-sticks, congee and gruel, drink and food.

25 (He) commands those in charge of sacrifices and prayer to go to the sacrificial beasts and see to their fodder and grain, examine their fatness or leanness, and see that they are of uniform color.

26 (The officials) check the sacrificial beasts for suitability and color, examine their quality and type, measure whether they are small or large, and see whether they are immature or fully-grown.

27 When (they are sure that) none fail to meet the required standard, the Son of Heaven (sacrifices them) in an exorcism to lead in the autumn qi.

28 (He) takes a dog and (ritually) tastes (its flesh, along with) hemp-seed, and then offers them as the first sacrifical offerings in the inner chamber of the (ancestral) temple.

29 In this month it is permitted to build city walls and outer fortifications, to establish metropolises and walled towns, to dig underground irrigation channels and storage-pits, and to repair granaries and storehouses.

30 (He) also commands those in authority more urgently to collect the tax-levies (due from) the people, to store vegetables, and to accumulate large stores (of all sorts of things).

31 (The officials) exhort the people to plant the (winter) wheat. If any should miss the time for doing this they will be punished without fail.

32 In this month the thunder begins to recede. Hibernating creatures shut up the doors (of their burrows).

33 The deadly (yin) qi gradually becomes abundant; the yang qi daily declines.

34 Water begins to dry up. Day and night are equally divided.

35 (The Son of Heaven orders the Master of Markets to) calibrate correctly the weights and measures, equalize the balance-beam and its weights, correct the weight of the *jun*, the *shi* and the catty (and the volume) of the peck and the pail.

36 (He orders his officials to) regulate barrier-gates and markets, and to bring in (to the

capital) merchants and travellers (to) import goods and wealth so as to promote the affairs of the people.

37 Coming from the four quarters and assembling from distant places, they arrive with wealth and goods.

38 There is no deficiency in what is offered (in the markets), no exhaustion of what is (made available for) use; thus affairs of all sorts are facilitated.

39 If in the second month of autumn the ordinances of spring were carried out, the autumn rains would not fall; plants and trees would blossom (out of season), and the country would be in fear.

40 If the ordinances of summer were carried out, the country would suffer drought; creatures that hibernate would not retire to their burrows, and the five kinds of grain would all (unseasonably) sprout again.

41 If the ordinances of winter were carried out, calamities caused by wind would arise over and over again, the thunder which had abated would come forth again prematurely, and plants and trees would die too soon.

42 The eighth month governs military officers.

43 Its tree is the Cudrania tree.

[5:12a:9]

Commentary to Section VIII

The ordinances of autumn having been faithfully observed in the seventh month, the cool winds arrive seasonably in the eighth. The seasons remain under the sway of metal, while the monthly correlates shift. Geese and swallows begin their migrations, and other birds gather into flocks and fly to and fro—an accurate observation of the behavior of many types of birds when the nesting season has ended.

The degree to which the monthly ordinances balance each other at half-year intervals is increasingly apparent as the text moves into the yin half of the year. (This correspondence is made explicit in Section XIV below.) In the eighth month, as in the second month, the occurrence of the equinox provides the occasion for an inspection of weights and measures, human "balances" that correspond to the celestial balance between daylight and darkness. Where in the second month the use of living sacrificial victims was prohibited, in the eighth month sacrificial animals are reared, fattened, inspected, and then sacrificed in an exorcistic ritual designed to strengthen the accretion of yin. In the second month public works were prohibited, in the eighth month they are encouraged. In the second month the thearch was solicitous of women in childbirth; in the eight month his concern is for the elderly.

As in the seventh month, in this month the leniency of the yang portion of the year is nowhere to be seen; on the contrary, punishments are carried out punctiliously, with any deviation bringing punishment to the responsible officials themselves. The slaughter of sacrificial animals is echoed in the beheading of criminals. Whereas in the spring the thearch was careful to allow the people to pursue their agricultural duties unimpeded, here they plant under compulsion and the threat of punishment.

The harvest is attended by the collection of taxes with increasing severity. The ample harvest of the fields finds a counterpart in the abundant goods made available in the city markets by merchants brought in from distant regions under close supervision and regulation.

The consequences of applying the wrong seasonal ordinances are predictable. In midautumn, a wrongful use of the yang of spring or summer would prevent the proper waning of the year; the premature application of the greater yin of winter would give rise to storms and unseasonable cold.

Section IX: Ninth Month

[5:12a:10]

1   In the last month of autumn, *zhaoyao* points to *xu.*

2   (The Lunar Lodge) Emptiness culminates at dusk; (the Lodge) Willow culminates at dawn.

3   (Autumn) occupies the west.

4   Its days are *geng* and *xin.*

5   Its beasts are (those of the) hairy (class).

6   Its (pentatonic) note is *shang.*

7   The pitchpipe (of the ninth month) is Tireless.

8   The number (of autumn) is nine.

9   Its flavor is pungent.

10 Its smell is rank.

11 Its sacrifices are made to the door-god.

12 From the body of the sacrificial victim, the liver is offered first.

13 Wild geese arrive as guests. Sparrows enter the ocean and turn into clams.

14 Chrysanthemums bear yellow flowers. Dholes sacrifice (small animals), and wild beasts kill small creatures.

15 The Son of Heaven wears white clothing. He mounts (a carriage drawn by) black-maned white horses. He wears white jade (pendants) and flies a white banner.

16 He eats hempseed with dog-meat. He drinks water gathered from the eight winds, and cooks with fire (kindled from) Cudrania branches.

17 The imperial ladies of the Western Palace wear white clothing with white trim. They play music on silver bells.

18 The weapon (of autumn) is the halberd.

19 The domestic animal (of autumn) is the dog.

20 (The Son of Heaven) holds the dawn session of court in the corner (chamber of the Mingtang) to the right of the Comprehensive Template (chamber).

21 (He) commands those in authority to further increase the severity of their procla-
mations.

22 (He) orders all officials (to see to it that) among nobles and commoners (alike), there
is none who does not fulfill his duty to bring in (the harvest), thereby according with
the going-into-storage [= quiescence] of Heaven and Earth.

23 Nothing must be taken out (of storehouses).

24 (He) also issues orders to the Chief Minister that when all agricultural affairs are
settled and (the grain tax has been) received, (he should) present an accounting of
receipts of the five kinds of grain.

25 The grain harvested from the sacred fields is stored in the spirit-granary.

26 In this month the hoarfrost begins to descend; the various artisans rest from their
work.

27 (He) therefore commands those in authority to make (a public announcement) saying, "The cold qi has definitely set in. The people's strength cannot withstand it. All
should (now) stay inside their dwellings."

28 On the first *ding* day of the month (the musicians) enter the Hall of Study to
practice playing wind-instruments.

29 At a great sacrificial feast, the thearch tastes the beasts offered in sacrifice.

30 (The Son of Heaven) assembles the feudal lords and those who govern all of the
districts so that they may receive (the almanac, which sets the) first days of the
months of the coming year.

31 (He) approves the taxes that they have collected from the people.

32 The lightness or heaviness of the laws, and the annual schedule for presenting
tribute, is set according to the distance (of the fief from the royal domain) and the
quality of the land.

33 (He) also instructs them in hunting, so that they may practice the use of the five
weapons.

34 (He) orders the Grand Charioteer and the seven (grades of) grooms to yoke up the
chariots and set out banners.

35 Chariots are assigned (to the nobles) on the basis of rank, and arrayed in correct
order before the screen-of-state (of the ruler).

36 The overseer of the beaters, with his baton of office stuck into his sash, stands facing
north and gives them their instructions.

37 Then the Son of Heaven, wearing martial garb and wide-spreading ornaments,
grasps his bow and holds his arrows, and (goes forth) to hunt.

38 (At the conclusion of the hunt) he orders the Master of Sacrificial Rites to sacrifice
(some of) the game to the (gods of) the Four Directions.

39 In this month (the leaves of) the plants and trees turn yellow and fall; then their
branches are cut and made into charcoal. Hibernating creatures all go (further) into
concealment.

40 Thereupon (those in authority) hasten (the process of) judgement and punishment,
and do not delay in executing the guilty.

41 (The Son of Heaven) receives (the petitions of) those whose emoluments and rank do not correspond (with what is their due), and those who (have) not (received) care and nurture according to right principles.

42 (He orders the Master of Works) to go along the highways and open up the roads, from the frontiers to the capital.

43 In this month the Son of Heaven takes a dog and (ritually) tastes (its flesh, along with) hemp-seed, and then presents them as the first sacrifical offering in the inner chamber of the (ancestral) temple.

44 If, in the final month of autumn, the ordinances of summer were observed, then the country would suffer floods, and the winter stores would be destroyed. The people would suffer respiratory diseases.

45 If the ordinances of winter were observed, there would be many robbers and bandits in the country; the frontiers would be untranquil and the territory (of the state) would be divided and split up (by others).

46 If the ordinances of spring were observed, warm winds would (unseasonably) arrive; the people's energies [qi] would be dissipated accordingly, and battalions and companies (of troops) would thereupon rise up (in rebellion).

47 The ninth month governs the Archer-Lords.

48 Its tree is the sophora.
   [5:13b:9]

Commentary to Section IX

In the final month of autumn, the phase metal remains in control, while the monthly correlates shift. Wild geese arrive from the north to winter in central China; sparrows disappear (having migrated south, but in Chinese folk belief thought to have turned into clams). The chrysanthemum, the quintessential flower of autumn, blooms. Leaves fall from the trees, and the charcoal burners (who were prohibited from working in the spring) prepare fuel for the winter. Rodents scurry about in a last effort to add layers of fat for their hibernation, and are easy prey for carnivores. (For the small wild dog known as the dhole, see the "Technical and Textual Notes.") The ruler and his nobles also engage in a ritual hunt, exercising the weapons that are appropriate to the season governed by metal and engaging in a shedding of animal blood that echoes the sanguinary punishment of criminals.

The hibernation of animals resonates with the storing away of goods in granaries and storehouses. The thearch admonishes the people to stay indoors as well, lest they suffer harm from the cold. There is no relaxation in the severity of the law, and officials are called to account for their collections of taxes.

Just as the third month, the final month of spring, brought the first hint of concern for the coming onset of the season of waxing yin, so here the ruler shows forethought for the coming new year, when the power of yang will increase once again. In this month the ruler promulgates the almanac for the following year, at the same time adjusting taxes and feudal levies and making alterations in the ranks and emoluments of officals who petition for redress. Thus the culmination of the season of lesser yin is balanced by a small but appropriate amount of yang activity.

If in this month the ordinances of summer were observed, there would be a flowing out when there should be a closing in; floods would occur; and an excess of yang would cause grain to rot in the storehouses. The imbalance of yang and yin would lead to diseases of the lungs. If the ordinances of winter were observed, an excess of yin would lead to lawlessness, disorder, and invasion in a month that should be characterized by a strict adherence to the law. If the ordinances of spring were observed, the contradiction of lesser yang imposed upon lesser yin would bring not only unseasonably warm winds but also exhaustion; troops would mutiny in response to the overturning of seasonable yin by unseasonable yang.

Section X: Tenth Month

[5:13b:9]

1   In the first month of winter, *zhaoyao* points to *hai.*
2   (The Lunar Lodge) Rooftop culminates at dusk; (the Lodge) Seven Stars culminates at dawn.
3   (Winter) occupies the north. Its days are *ren* and *gui.*
4   The fullness of power is in Water.
5   Its beasts are (those of the) armored (class).
6   Its (pentatonic) note is *yu.*
7   The pitchpipe (of the tenth month) is Responsive Bell.
8   The number (of winter) is six.
9   Its flavor is salty.
10 Its smell is putrid.
11 Its sacrifices are made to the well-god.
12 From the body of the sacrificial victim, the kidneys are offered first.
13 Water begins to freeze. The earth begins to harden with cold.
14 Pheasants enter the ocean and turn into large clams. The rainbow(-dragon) remains hidden and is not seen.
15 The Son of Heaven wears black clothing. He mounts (a carriage drawn by) black horses. He wears black jade (pendants) and flies a black banner.
16 He eats millet with suckling pig. He drinks water gathered from the eight winds, and cooks with fire (kindled from) pine branches.
17 The imperial ladies of the Northern Palace wear black clothing with black trim. They play music on stone chimes.
18 The weapon (of winter) is the partisan.

19   The domestic animal (of winter) is the pig.

20   (The Son of Heaven) holds the dawn session of court in the corner (chamber of the
      Mingtang) to the left of the Dark Hall (chamber).

21   He promulgates the winter ordinances.

22   He commands those in authority to re-institute the general prohibitions. It is pro-
      hibited to walk abroad. Gates of cities and outer fortifications are closed; strangers
      are placed under detention.

23   Punishments are speedily carried out; those under sentence of death are killed. Those
      who have corruptly abused their positions to confound the law are punished.

24   On the first day of winter the Son of Heaven personally leads the Three Sires, the Nine
      Lords, and the great nobles to welcome the year at (the altar of) the northern suburbs.

25   Returning (from this ceremony), he bestows rewards on (the descendants of) those
      who were killed (while carrying on the ruler's) affairs, and he puts widows and
      orphans under his protection.

26   In this month he commands the Master of Prayers to pray and sacrifice to the gods
      that they might establish (as true and correct) the oracles of the tortoise and the
      milfoil-stalks, enquiring by means of the trigrams and the bone-crackings to foretell
      good fortune and ill fortune.

27   (In this month) the Son of Heaven begins to wear fur garments.

28   (He) commands all of the officials carefully to cover up and store away (all articles
      for which they are responsible).

29   (He) commands inspectors to travel about, (seeing to the) collecting and gathering.

30   City walls and outer fortifications are repaired, and their doors and gates inspected.
      Door-bolts and fastenings are repaired, keys and locks carefully attended to.

31   Earthen mounds and boundary-walls are strengthened; frontier and border
      fortifications are repaired. (The defenses of) important passes are strengthened, and
      narrow defiles and byways are blocked up.

32   Regulations are issued with regard to terms of mourning, and enquiries are made
      (regarding) the quality of inner and outer coffins, burial-clothes, and shrouds.

33   The design of grave-mounds and tumuli are regulated with regard to size and height,
      so that for nobles and commoners, the humble or the honorable, each has its proper
      gradation.

34   In this month the Master of Artisans verifies the results (of the year's) labors, display-
      ing the ritual vessels and examining their conformity to the (prescribed) patterns;
      those that are of fine quality are offered to the throne.

35   If in the carrying out of the work of the artisans there is (anyone who) through hate-
      ful and dilatory (conduct) produces (things that are) meritricious or shoddy, the
      (appropriate) criminal sentence must be carried out.

36   In this month there is a great feast. The Son of Heaven prays (for blessings) for the
      coming year. A grand rite of prayer and sacrifice is conducted at the shrine of the
      lineage-founder, and a general feast is given for the royal ancestors.

37   (The Son of Heaven) rewards the farmers, so that they may rest from their labors.

38 (He) commands the generals and (other) military officers to give lectures on war-craft (to the troops, and have them) practice archery and chariot-driving (and engage in) trials of strength.

39 (He) also orders the Superintendant of Waters and the Master of Fisheries to collect the tax-revenues (due on the products of) the rivers, springs, ponds, and marshes. There must be no embezzlement or over-collection (of these taxes).

40 If in the first month of winter the ordinances of spring were observed, then the freezing-shut (of the earth) would not be complete. The qi of Earth would issue forth and spread about; the people in large numbers would drift away and be lost (to the kingdom).

41 If the ordinances of summer were observed, there would be many hot windstorms. (Even in) the dead of winter it would not be cold; hibernating creatures would re-emerge.

42 If the ordinances of autumn were observed, then snow and frost would not come in season. Minor warfare would break out from time to time; territory would be usurped and seized (by invaders).

43 The tenth month governs the Master of Horses.

44 Its tree is the sandalwood.
   [5:15a:7]

Commentary to Section X

In the first month of winter, the seasonal phase shifts to water; monthly correlates change as usual. The color of winter is black, corresponding to phase water. The the-arch's carriage is drawn by black horses, equine equivalents of the Dark Warrior of the Northern Palace of Heaven.

The influence of waxing yin is seen in the natural world in the freezing of water and soil; pheasants become scarce (in folk belief, because they change into giant clams), and the lowering sun produces few rainbows.

The rapidly shortening days betoken a closing down of the year, and the ruler responds by repairing gates and fortifications, and prohibiting people from leaving their places of residence. Winter definitively ushers in the season of death. Punishments are carried out with increasing severity. The meritorious dead are also attended to, as their widows and orphans are put under government protection; regulations are issued concerning mourning rituals and the design of graves. Apparently in recognition of winter as a season of cosmological danger, attention is paid to the rites and implements of divination. The tree of the tenth month is the sandalwood, presumably because it was used in making incense used in connection with such rites.

The farmers rest from their labors, and officials turn their attention to the products of artisans, from whom levies of goods are collected and inspected, and to the secondary products of the countryside—the rushes and reeds, fish and tortoises, and other products of hunting and gathering.

With the end of the agricultural season, military levies are called up, and the troops are trained and drilled. The office of the tenth month is the Master of Horses, presumably in recognition of this resumption of military training. The weapon of winter is the *sha*, a pole-mounted thrusting weapon with a sword-like blade fitted with crosspieces (quillons). "Partisan" seems the closest English equivalent.[12] The word *sha* itself is rather uncommon, and might be at least to some extent a regional usage of the lower Yangtse/eastern Chu area.

The use of inappropriate seasonal ordinances would have the familiar consequences: excess yang if those of spring or summer were employed, deficient yin if those of autumn were employed. The ruler's mind is very much on military matters, and he is warned of the danger of refugees, bandits, and invaders.

Section XI: Eleventh Month

[5:15a:8]

1   In the middle month of winter, *zhaoyao* points to *zi*.
2   (The Lunar Lodge) (Eastern) Wall culminates at dusk; (the Lodge) Chariot-Platform culminates at dawn.
3   (Winter) occupies the north.
4   Its days are *ren* and *gui*.
5   Its beasts are (those of the) armored (class).
6   Its (pentatonic) note is *yu*.
7   The pitchpipe (of the eleventh month) is Yellow Bell.
8   The number (of winter) is six.
9   Its flavor is salty.
10 Its smell is putrid.
11 Its sacrifices are made to the well-god.
12 From the body of the sacrificial victim, the kidneys are offered first.
13 The ice becomes stronger. The earth begins to crack.
14 The *gandan* bird does not cry. Tigers begin to mate.
15 The Son of Heaven wears black clothing. He mounts (a carriage drawn by) black horses. He wears black jade (pendants) and flies a black banner.
16 He eats millet with suckling pig. He drinks water gathered from the eight winds, and cooks with fire (kindled from) pine branches.
17 The imperial ladies of the Northern Palace wear black clothing with black trim. They play music on stone chimes.
18 The weapon (of winter) is the partisan.
19 The domestic animal (of winter) is the pig.

20 (The Son of Heaven) holds the dawn session of court in the Dark Hall (chamber of the Mingtang).

21 He commands those in authority, saying, "No works having to do with earth may be undertaken, nor may rooms and dwellings be opened.

22 (He also commands them) to call together the masses and say to them, "If anyone opens up what has been shut away by Heaven and Earth, then all hibernating creatures will die; the people will surely suffer illness and pestilence, and in the wake of this will come destruction."

23 It is urgent to arrest thieves and robbers, and to punish those who are debauched, licentious, deceitful, or fraudulent. This is called "fully displaying (the cosmological character of) the month."

24 (He) commands the Superintendant of Eunuchs to re-issue the standing orders of the Palace, and to examine the doors and gates and attend to the rooms and apartments; all must be closed up tightly. (There must be) a general diminution of all affairs having to do with women.

25 (He) also issues orders to the Master Brewer, (saying that) the glutinous millet and rice must be uniform (in quality), the yeast-cakes must be ready, the soaking and cooking must be done under conditions of cleanliness, and the water must be fragrant. The earthenware vessels must be of excellent quality, and the fire must be properly regulated. There must be no discrepancy or error (in these things).

26 The Son of Heaven also commands those in authority to pray to the Four Seas, the great rivers, and the illustrious marshes.

27 In this month, if the farmers have any (crops) that they have not harvested and stored away in granaries, or any cattle, horses, or other domestic animals that they have allowed to stray and get lost, then anyone who takes such things will not be subject to prosecution.

28 If in the mountains, forests, marshes and moors there be those who are able to gather wild food to eat, or to capture rats and other small game, the Superintendant of Uncultivated Land should instruct and guide them (in these activities). If there be any who encroach upon or steal from (such folk), they will be punished without mercy.

29 In this month the day reaches its shortest extent. Yin and yang contend.

30 The Superior Man fasts and practices austerities. His dwelling-place must be closed up; his body must be tranquil. He abstains from music and sex, and forbids himself to feel lust or desire. He rests his body and quiets his whole nature.

31 In this month, lichee buds stand out (on their twigs); the rue plant begins to grow. Earthworms wriggle. The palmate deer shed their antlers. Springs of water stir into movement.

32 Accordingly, (this is the time to) fell trees for wood and collect bamboo for arrow-shafts. Unservicable articles in offices, and articles of equipment which are of no use, are gotten rid of.

33 Gate-towers, pavilions, doors and gates are (repaired with) mud plaster, and prison walls repaired, thus assisting in the closing-up of Heaven and Earth.

34   If in the middle month of winter the summer ordinances were observed, the country would suffer drought. Vapors and fog would spread gloom and obscurity, and the sound of thunder would break out.

35   If the ordinances of autumn were observed, the season would have (excessive) rain. Melons and gourds would not ripen. The country would experience major warfare.

36   If the ordinances of spring were observed, insect pests and caterpillars would cause destruction. The rivers and springs would all run dry. The people would suffer greatly from ulcerating diseases.

37   The eleventh month governs the Metropolitan Guards.

38   Its tree is the jujube.

[5:16b:1]

Commentary to Section XI

The seasonal correlates remain those of phase water; the monthly correlates as usual shift. The auspices of the natural world agree with the increasing influence of yin and the dominance of phase water: ice grows thicker, and the frozen earth cracks. The *gan-dan* bird (which, we are told, does not cry during this month) has proved impossible to identify with any certainty. Gao You identifies it as "a mountain bird." Legge[13] translates it as "the night bird." Among the many variant readings for (and glosses on) the name are some that seem to suggest that this is not a bird at all, but rather a bat. My guess is that this may be a nightjar, a bird that is bat-like in appearance and feeding habits, a night-crier, a bird of the mountains, and a bird of secretive habits (likely to provoke a confused identity).[14]

In this month the winter solstice occurs, bringing with it the shortest day of the year; "yin and yang contend." Thereafter, in the last few days of the month, the power of yang begins to wax once again. Interestingly, this gives rise to a new set of natural observations (in line 31), some of which are of doubtful validity. Palmate deer (similar to the European elk or the American moose) do indeed shed their antlers at the end of the autumn, but litchees and rue are likely still to be in a quiescent state. The statement that "earthworms wriggle" seems to contradict the prohibition against disturbing the earth during this month lest hibernating creatures die; the statement that "springs of water stir into movement" similarly contradicts the earlier observation that "the ice becomes stronger." One has the impression that these auspices reflect the consequences of theory (the movement of the year into its yang phase once again) rather than actual observations of the natural world.

In general this section continues the themes established for the first month of winter. Attention is paid to ritual matters, such as the brewing of grain "wines" for the imperial sacrifices and the offering of prayers to deities of the four directions. The theme of shutting away continues, both with the closing up of buildings and with a prohibition of digging into the earth. There is an indirect acknowledgment that imperial orders are not always obeyed; notice is taken of the possibility that some people might leave crops in the fields, or let domestic animals go astray. The answer to this problem is to "let the punishment fit the crime." Anything not locked away is fair game for anyone who takes it, an ingenious extrajudicial punishment for the negligent and perhaps also a way of providing for the indigent.

A new element comes in with the injunctions that debauchery and lewdness are to be singled out for punishment, women should be shunned, and that the ruler must abstain from sex: with yin at its maximum, any activity that would call forth still more yin energy is to be avoided. Clearly the winter solstice is taken to be a liminal moment, requiring the ruler to be particularly tranquil in mind and body lest anything disturb the cosmic balance.

A general housecleaning in government offices and storerooms betokens a look ahead to the coming new year.

The consequence of employing the summer ordinances in this month of winter show an interesting awareness of a meteorological phenomenon: warm air over cold soil will indeed produce fogs and mist. Thunder is, of course, a common phenomenon of summer, but rare (and thus presumably portentious) in winter. If the ordinances of autumn were employed, the full accretion of yin would be retarded; the reference to melons not ripening is mysterious (presumably no growing melons are left in the fields anyway), but more practical is the worry that gourds would not dry properly for use. An imbalance of yin brings with it a danger of warfare. The consequences of employing the spring ordinances in this month are interesting. Spring will soon arrive in any case, but if the spring ordinances were observed, it would come too soon, bringing drought (too much yang), insect pests (stirred up prematurely by unseasonable warmth), and ulcerating (hot, and therefore yang) diseases.

Section XII: Twelfth Month

1   In the last month of winter, *zhaoyao* points to *chou.*
2   (The Lunar Lodge) Bond culminates at dusk; (the Lodge) Root culminates at dawn.
3   (Winter) occupies the north.
4   Its days are *ren* and *gui.*
5   Its beasts are (those of the) armored (class).
6   Its (pentatonic) note is *yu.*
7   The pitchpipe (of the twelfth month) is Great Regulator.
8   The number (of winter) is six.
9   Its flavor is salty.
10 Its smell is putrid.

11   Its sacrifices are made to the well-god.

12   From the body of the sacrificial victim, the kidneys are offered first.

13   Wild geese head north. Magpies add to their nests.

14   The cock-pheasant cries; hens cluck and lay their eggs.

15   The Son of Heaven wears black clothing. He mounts (a carriage drawn by) black horses. He wears black jade (pendants) and flies a black banner.

16   He eats millet with suckling pig. He drinks water gathered from the eight winds, and cooks with fire (kindled from) pine branches.

17   The imperial ladies of the Northern Palace wear black clothing with black trim. They play music on stone chimes.

18   The weapon (of winter) is the partisan.

19   The domestic animal (of winter) is the pig.

20   (The Son of Heaven) holds the dawn session of court in the (chamber of the Mingtang) to the right of the Dark Hall (chamber).

21   He commands those in authority to conduct a Grand Exorcism, in which sacrificial victims are torn apart on all (four) sides (of the city walls). An earthen ox is set out [to lead away the cold qi].

22   (He) orders the Master of Fisheries to commence fishing. The Son of Heaven personally goes (to take part in) the fish-shooting. (The fish that are caught) are presented as first offerings in the inner temple of the (ancestral) temple.

23   Orders are issued to the people to withdraw (from the storehouses) the five kinds of seed-grain, and to the farmers to calculate (the schedules? for) using the teams (of draft animals), to put in order their plowshares, and to equip themselves with the implements of cultivation.

24   (He) commands the Master of Music to give a grand concert of wind instruments, abstaining from the use (of instruments of other kinds).

25   (He) also commands the Superintendants of the Four Directions to collect and set in order firewood for use in the ceremonies of the inner temple of the (ancestral) temple, as well as firewood and kindling for sacrifices of every kind.

26   In this month the sun completes (its circuit) through the stages (of the twelve divisions of the celestial circle). The moon completes its cycle. The stars have made a complete revolution around the heavens. The year is about to begin again.

27   Orders are given that the farmers and commoners must be rested; they are not to be employed (in any public works).

28   The Son of Heaven calls together his Sires, the lords, and the great officers to promulgate the statutes of the realm and to discuss the seasonal ordinances, in order to plan what is suitable for the coming year.

29   He commands the Grand Recorder to make a list of the nobles in order of rank, assigning to them their (appropriate) levies of sacrificial animals (for the coming year) for use in worship of the Sovereign of Heaven Supreme Thearch and at the shrines of the (gods of) the soil and the grain.

30   (He) also commands the countries (ruled by fief-holders) having the same surname

(as that of the ruler) to provide fodder and feed (for the sacrificial animals) used in worship in the inner temple of the (ancestral) temple.

31 (He also commands all, from) the lords, knights, and great officials to the common people to provide (articles for) use in worship at the sacrifices to the mountains, forests, and illustrious rivers.

32 If, in the last month of winter, the ordinances of autumn were observed, then the white dew would descend too early; shell-bearing creatures would suffer deformities; on the four frontiers people would enter places of refuge.

33 If the ordinances of spring were observed, pregnant females and the young would suffer injury; the country would suffer many intractable diseases. If one were to enquire about this fate, it would be called "adverse."

34 If the ordinances of summer were observed, floods would cause ruin in the country; the seasonable snow would not fall; the ice would melt and the cold dissipate.

35 The twelfth month governs the prisons.

36 Its tree is the chestnut.

[5:17b:1]

Commentary to Section XII

The seasonal correlates remain those of phase water; the monthly correlates shift. In what the Xia calendar defines as the final month of winter, the solstice has already passed and yang is in the ascendant. Accordingly, the auspices of the natural world herald the approach of spring; the geese depart for the north; magpies begin to build their nests; and pheasants mate.

The themes of shutting away and of punishment that dominated the first two months of winter are not emphasized here, another sign that yang has begun to wax again; but in an acknowledgment that the power of yin is still strong, the government function of the twelfth month is prisons.

The season, and with it the old year—which now has completed a full cycle—is ritually destroyed in an exorcistic rite in which animals are torn to pieces at the gates of the four directions. An earthen ox is set out to lead away the cold qi—a variant of the much better-known practice of setting out an earthen dragon to produce rain.[15] The thearch and his nobles take part in fish shooting, in what presumably was an example of the large-scale, formal, and ritualized hunting of the early Chinese ruling class; this may be seen as a final ritual obeisance to the power of water in the winter season. The royal musicians give a palace concert using only wind instruments, thereby through *ganying* resonance helping to conduct the seasonal qi into their next cycle.

In more mundane preparations for the coming spring, workers attached to the royal temples top up their supply of firewood for sacrificial fires for the coming year, before (as any countryman knows) the rising sap and softening ground make wood-cutting impractical. Schedules of levies of sacrificial animals and other necessities of the royal temples are drawn up, to ensure that the nobles will provide their proper share according to their feudal rank; similarly, everyone from lords to commoners is assessed for materials needed for use in local temples and shrines. Farmers are told to make ready their seed grain, and to plan for the spring plowing.

The bad consequences of using inappropriate seasonal ordinances are as expected. The excessive yang of summer would cause floods by melting the mountain snow too early, and drought by preventing seasonal snowfall; the insufficient yin of fall would cause shellfish and snails (yin creatures) to become deformed and fail to develop proper-ly, and lead to unrest on the frontiers ("barbarians" apparently respond aggressively to imbalances of yin and yang in the central regions); the excessive yang of spring would cause the season to hasten unduly, bringing, in this instance, harm to the pregnant and the young (both of which are subjects of special concern in the springtime) as well as unspecified chronic diseases.

Section XIII: The Five Positions

[5:17b:2]

1   There are five positions.
2   The extreme limit of the eastern region begins from Stele-Stone Mountain, passing through the Land of Morning Freshness and the Land of Giants.
3   In the east it reaches the place from whence the sun rises, the land of the Fu [-Sang] tree, the wild fields of the Green-Land trees.
4   The places ruled by Tai Hao and Gou Mang (extend for) 12,000 li.
5   The ordinances of the East say:
6   Hold fast to all prohibitions.
7   Open that which is closed or covered.
8   Penetrate to the utmost all blocked-up passes.
9   Extend out to the frontiers and passes.
10   Wander afar.
11   Reject resentment and hatred.
12   Free slaves and the condemned.
13   Avoid mourning and grief.
14   Desist from imposing corporal punishments.
15   Open gates and dams.
16   Proclaim a (general) distribution of wealth (from the public treasury).
17   Harmoniously resolve (any) resentment (that may be) abroad.
18   Pacify the Four Directions.
19   Act with pliancy and kindness.
20   Put a stop to hardness and (overbearing) strength.

21   The extreme limit of the southern region begins from outside [= beyond] (the country of) the people of North-Facing Doors and passes through the country of Zhuan Xu.

22   It extends to the wild fields of Storing-up-Fire's fiery winds.

23   The regions governed by the Vermilion Thearch and Zhu Rong encompass 12,000 li.

24   The ordinances (of the south) say:

25   Ennoble the virtuous, reward the meritorious.

26   Show kindness to the beneficent and excellent.

27   Come to the aid of the hungry and thirsty.

28   Raise up those who display prowess in agriculture.

29   Relieve the poor and destitute.

30   Show kindness to orphans and widows.

31   Grieve with the infirm and ill.

32   Dispense great emoluments, carry out great bestowals of rewards.

33   Raise up ruined lineages.

34   Support those who have no posterity.

35   Enfeoff nobles.

36   Establish (in office) worthy assistants.

37   The extreme limits of the central region extend from Kunlun east through the region of (the two peaks? of) Constancy Mountain.

38   This is where the sun and the moon have their paths.

39   It is the source of the Han and Jiang [= Yangtse] Rivers.

40   (Here are) the open fields of the multitudes of people, (the lands) suitable for the five (kinds of) grain.

41   At Dragon Gate the He [= Yellow] and the Qi Rivers merge.

42   (Here, Yu the Great) took swelling earth to dam the floodwaters, and traced out the (nine) provinces.

43   (These territories) extend eastward to Stele-Stone Mountain.

44   The territories governed by the Yellow Thearch and the Sovereign of the Soil encompass 12,000 li.

45   The ordinances (of the center) say:

46   Be equable without polarity.

47   Be enlightened without petty fault-finding.

48   Embrace, enfold, cover over, enrich as with dew, so that there is none who is not tenderly enwrapped in (the royal) bosom.

49   Be vast and overflowing, without private considerations.

50   Let government be tranquil, to bring about harmony.

51   Succor, nurture, and feed the old and the weak.

52   Send condolences to (the families of) the dead, enquire after the sick.

53   (All of this), so as to escort the myriad creatures on their return.

54   The extreme limits of the regions of the west extend from Kunlun through the Flowing Sands and the Sinking Feathers, westward to the country of Three Dangers.

55   (They extend to) the Walled City of Stone and the Metal Palace, the open fields of the people who drink qi and do not die.

56   The territories governed by Shao Hao and Ru Shou encompass 12,000 li.

57   The ordinances (of the west) say:

58   Scrupulously use the laws.

59   Punishment of the guilty must be carried out.

60   Take precautions against thieves and robbers.

61   Prohibit sexual license and debauchery.

62   Issue instructions regarding the general collection (of harvest taxes).

63   Attentively make a record of all collections (of revenue).

64   Repair city walls and outer fortifications.

65   Repair and clear out drainage-pipes.

66   Close off footpaths and lanes, block up sluices and ditches.

67   Shut off flowing water, swamps, gorges, and valleys.

68   Guard doors and gates.

69   Set out (in readiness) weapons and armor.

70   Select officials.

71   Punish the lawless.

72   The extreme limits of the regions of the north extend from the Nine Marshes and the *terra ultima* of Exhaust-the-Summer Gloom, north to the Valley Where Ordinances Cease.

73   Here are the open fields of freezing cold, piled-up ice, snow, hail, frost, sleet, and of pooling, soaking, massed-up water.

74   The regions governed by Zhuan Xu and Xuan Ming encompass 12,000 li.

75   The ordinances (of the north) say:

76   Extend all prohibitions.

77   Firmly shut up and store away.

78   Repair (the fortifications of) the frontiers and passes.

79   Fix gates and water-barriers.

80   Prohibit walking abroad.

81   Speedily carry out corporal punishments.

82   Kill those who are under sentence of death.

83   Close up the city gates and the gates of the outer fortifications.

84   On a large scale, conduct investigations of strangers.

85   Put a stop to communications and travel.

86   Prohibit the pleasures of the night.

87   Close up (chambers) early and open them late, in order to restrain lewd folk.

88   If lewd persons are already to be found, they must be seized and held under severe restraint.

89   Heaven has already almost completed its cycle:

90   Punishments and executions must (be carried out) without any being pardoned; even in the case of (royal) relatives of surpassing venerableness, the law must be carried out to the full degree.

91   There must be no travel by water.
92   There must be no opening up of that which is stored away.
93   There must be no relaxation of punishments.
     [5:19a:8]

Commentary to Section XIII

This section summarizes, in language that is very stately in tone and stylistically quite beautiful, the rules for conduct associated with the five phases—correlated in this case, however, not with the calendar but with the five directions. The distinction is, of course, purely a formal one, given the exceptionally tight linkage in five phase theory between the seasons and the directions. The rules of conduct here echo closely those given for the twelve months of the year, and need no further comment.

The picture of the five directions presented here reflects the geographical understanding of *Huainanzi* 4, the "Treatise on Topography": a central region is surrounded by four quarters, each of which extends from the boundaries of the civilized world out to the furthest, myth-embued limits of the earthly plane. The picture here lacks the detailed breakdown of the four quarters into distant regions, outlying regions, and *terrae ultimae* found in *Huainanzi* 4.VI, but many of the far-distant places mentioned there—Kunlun, the Fusang tree, North-Facing Doors, etc.—are repeated here. In general the mythographic landscape here reflects, as does that of *Huainanzi* 4, the cosmography of *Shanhaijing*.

The thearchs and assisting gods of the five seasons, given in other versions of "Yueling" but lacking in the first twelve sections of *Huainanzi* 5, the "Treatise on the Seasonal Rules," are supplied here. They are consistent with those of other versions of the "Yueling"; in addition, they are almost identical to those of the five planets given in *Huainanzi* 3.VI. The only differences are that the thearch and assistant of the south are given here as the Vermilion Thearch (Chi Di) and Zhu Rong; in *Huainanzi* 3.VI.9–10 one finds the rather similar Blazing Thearch (Yan Di) and Zhu Ming. Both Yan Di and Zhu Rong were tutelary deities of the state of Chu.[16] Gao You identifies Yan Di with Shen Nong, and says that he was the son of the Vermilion Thearch; he identifies Zhu Rong as the grandson of Zhuan Xu. In the commentary to 3.VI.10, he identifies Zhu Ming as another name for Zhu Rong.

This section not only summarizes the seasonal ordinances, but also emphasizes the link between the seasons and the directions, and between the directions and the planetary deities. This reminds us that the intersections and divergences between the equatorial plane of earth and the ecliptic circle of the orbits of the heavenly bodies are the determinants of both geographical direction and seasonal time.

Section XIV: The Six Coordinates

[5:19a:8]

1   There are six coordinates.

2   The first month of spring and the first month of autumn are a coordinate.

3   The middle month of spring and the middle month of autumn are a coordinate.

4   The last month of spring and the last month of autumn are a coordinate.

5   The first month of summer and the first month of winter are a coordinate.

6   The middle month of summer and the middle month of winter are a coordinate.

7   The last month of summer and the last month of winter are a coordinate.

8   In the first month of spring (crops) begin to grow; in the first month of autumn (crops) begin to wither.

9   In the middle month of spring (crops) begin to emerge; in the middle month of autumn (crops) begin to be brought in.

10   In the last month of spring (crops) are fully grown; in the last month of autumn (crops) are harvested on a large scale.

11   In the first month of summer (things) begin to slow down; in the first month of winter (things) begin to quicken.

12   In the middle month of summer (the day) reaches its greatest length; in the middle month of winter (the day) reaches its shortest length.

13   In the last month of summer, accretion reaches its climax; in the last month of winter, recision reaches its climax.

14   Thus, if in the first month government fails in its duties, in the seventh month the cool winds will not arrive.

15   If in the second month government fails in its duties, in the eighth month the thunder will not go into hiding.

16   If in the third month government fails in its duties, in the ninth month the frost will not descend.

17   If in the fourth month government fails in its duties, in the tenth month it will not be cold.

18   If in the fifth month government fails in its duties, in the eleventh month hibernating creatures will emerge in the winter.

19   If in the sixth month government fails in its duties, in the twelfth month grasses and trees will not be bare of leaves.

20   If in the seventh month government fails in its duties, in the first month the great cold will not disperse.

21   If in the eighth month government fails in its duties, in the second month the thunder will not break out.

22   If in the ninth month government fails in its duties, in the third month the spring winds will not cease.

23   If in the tenth month government fails in its duties, in the fourth month the grasses and trees will not bear seed.

24   If in the eleventh month government fails in its duties, in the fifth month there will be hail and frost.

25   If in the twelfth month government fails in its duties, in the sixth month the five (kinds of) grain will sicken and become weedy.

26   In spring:

27   If the ordinances of summer are carried out there will be inundations.

28   If the ordinances of autumn are carried out there will be (too much) water.

29   If the ordinances of winter are carried out there will be severity.

30   In summer:

31   If the ordinances of spring are carried out there will be (excessive) winds.

32   If the ordinances of autumn are carried out there will be wild growth of vegetation.

33   If the ordinances of winter are carried out there will be decline.

34   In autumn:

35   If the ordinances of summer are carried out there will be (untimely) blooming of flowers.

36   If the ordinances of spring are carried out there will be (untimely) breaking out of new buds.

37   If the ordinances of winter are carried out there will be spoilage of the harvest.

38   In winter:

39   If the ordinances of spring are carried out there will be excessive flows (of water).

40   If the ordinances of summer are carried out there will be drought.

41   If the ordinances of autumn are carried out there will be fog.
     [5:20a:7]

Commentary to Section XIV

The Six Coordinates here are in effect the same as the Six Departments mentioned in *Huainanzi* 3.XIII. Note that the term "six coordinates" (*liu he*) is being used in a special sense (quite different from its usual meaning of up and down, left and right, front and back). The "Six Departments" of the "Treatise on the Patterns of Heaven" denote six diametral chords across the great circle of the heavens, linking twelve points denoted by the Earthly Branches; here the "Six Coordinates" are six pairs of months, at six month intervals, the months also being denoted in the "Treatise on the Seasonal Rules" by the Earthly Branches and indicated in turn by the marker asterism *zhaoyao* (as engraved on the heaven plate of the *shi* cosmograph).

The coordinates here are used in several ways to demonstrate the cyclical unity of the calendar. First, it is shown that every monthly phenomenon is paired with its opposite at an interval of six months: for example, in midspring crops sprout, in midautumn crops are harvested. Next, it is asserted that any failure to observe the duties of government in any given month will have adverse consequences six months later.

Finally, there is a reiteration of the theme that in any season, bad consequences will ensue from employing the ordinances of any other season.

This section of *Huainanzi* 5 thus represents, one might say, a philosophical step forward in making explicit and systematic the *ganying* theory of yin-yang and the five phases that is only implicit in other versions of the "Yueling."

Section XV: The Six Standards

[5:20a:7]

1   Regulating the standards:
2   For the great regulation of yin and yang, there are six standards.
3   Heaven is the marking-cord, Earth is the level. Spring is the compass, summer is the balance-beam, autumn is the square, winter is the weight.
4   The marking-cord is that whereby the myriad things are marked out.
5   The level is that whereby the myriad things are levelled.
6   The compass is that whereby the myriad things are made round.
7   The balance-beam is that whereby the myriad things are equalized.
8   The square is that whereby the myriad things are made square.
9   The weight is that whereby the myriad things are weighed.
10 The marking-cord as a standard:
11 It is straight without swerving,
12 It is long and inexhaustible.
13 It reaches far into the past without becoming worn out,
14 It reaches to far distances without becoming lost.
15 It matches Heaven in innate power,
16 And the gods in perspicacity.
17 (By its means) what one desires may be obtained,
18 And what one loathes may be caused to perish.
19 From ancient times to the present, there can be no variation in its trueness.
20 Its innate power is vast and subtle; it is broad and capacious.
21 For this reason the High Thearch takes it as the basis of all things.
22 The level as a standard:
23 It is flat but not narrow, equal and not tilted,
25 Broad and capacious, spacious and abundant,
26 So as to be harmonious.
27 It is pliant and not hard,
28 Acute but not injurious,
29 Flowing and not stopped-up,
30 Easy and not disordered,
31 Expanding, penetrating, proceeding in an orderly course.
32 It is comprehensive and subtle but not sluggish.

33　The level makes things perfectly flat without error;
34　Thereby the myriad things are levelled.
35　The people are without malice or scheming; resentment and hatred do not arise.
36　Therefore the High Thearch uses it to make all things level.
37　The compass as a standard:
38　It revolves without ceasing,
39　It is round without turning about.
40　Abundant without excess, broad and spacious,
41　Its motions are ordered.
42　It is penetrating and proceeds on an orderly course.
43　Abundant! Simple!
44　The hundred forms of resentment do not arise.
45　The standard of the compass does not err;
46　It gives birth to both qi and pattern.
48　The balance-beam as a standard:
49　It is measured in its pace, but not behindtimes,
50　It is even, without resentment.
51　It bestows, but is not benevolent,
52　It condoles, but does not rebuke.
53　It adjusts to an appropriate level the people's emoluments,
54　It continues, but does not heap up.
55　Majestic! Brilliant!
56　Only those possessing innate power act thus.
57　Nurturing, bringing to full growth, transforming, rearing;
58　The myriad creatures abundantly flourish.
59　It makes the five (kinds of) grain bear seed, and the bounded fields be fruitful.
60　Government (by this standard) does not err;
61　Heaven and Earth are illumined thereby.
62　The square as a standard:
63　It is majestic and not in disarray,
64　It is hard and undisturbed.
65　It seizes, but without resentment,
66　Takes in, but without doing injury.
67　It is stern and severe, but not coercive;
68　Its ordinances are carried out, but without wasteful destruction.
69　In killing and smiting, its ends are attained;
70　The enemy is brought to submission.
71　The square's trueness is without error;
72　All punishments are (thereby) suitably fulfilled.
73　The weight as a standard:
74　It is hasty, but not excessive.
75　It kills, but it does not slaughter.

76   It is filled to completion;

77   It is comprehensive and subtle but without sluggishness.

78   It inflicts destruction upon things but does not single things out;

79   It punishes and kills without pardon.

80   Sincerity and trustworthiness are its essential character;

81   It is firm in strength and diligence.

82   Cleanse away filth! Chastise the evil!

83   Wickedness may not be tolerated.

84   Therefore if correct (policies) for winter are to be carried out,

85   (The ruler) must appear weak in order to be strong, pliant in order to be firm.

86   The weight's trueness is without error;

87   Through it the myriad things are shut away.

88   In the regulation of the Mingtang,

89   Be tranquil, taking the level as a pattern;

90   Be active, taking the marking-cord as a pattern.

91   For the government of spring, adopt the compass;

92   For the government of autumn, adopt the square;

93   For the government of winter, adopt the weight;

94   For the government of summer, adopt the balance-beam.

95   Thus dryness and dampness, cold and heat, will arrive in their proper seasonal nodes;

96   Sweet rain and fertile dew will descend in their proper times.
     [5:21a:9]

Commentary to Section XV

This passage has been studied in detail by Derk Bodde,[17] and has been the focus of a disagreement between Bodde and Joseph Needham on the question of "laws of nature" in early Chinese thought.[18] Needham is very skeptical about the idea of "natural law" in Chinese philosophy. Bodde's conclusion, with which I concur, is that the employment by the High Thearch (or, perhaps, the "high gods") of the measuring implements mentioned in this section implies a kind of divine sanction lying behind the purely organic operations of the cosmos, and thus points in the direction of an of early Chinese conception of some sort of natural law.

Like Section XIII above, this section is written in classical Chinese prose of unusual beauty, in elevated and nearly liturgical tones. It is a paean to the constancy and unity of the cosmos as represented by heaven, earth, and the four seasons (equivalent, in other words, to the "Six coordinates" in their usual sense of up, down, and the four directions). This constancy and unity is envisioned here as divine, or existing with divine sanction.

The implements denoted here as the "six standards" are similar to, but not quite the same as, the five tools of the builder's trade mentioned in *Huainanzi* 3.VI. There

Figure 5.2. The cosmogonic deities Fu Xi and Nü Gua, as depicted in a relief carving from the Wu Liang Shrine. Fu Xi holds a carpenter's square, Nü Gua holds a compass; both implements symbolize the regularity and constancy of heaven and earth as standards for human behavior. (After Chavannes, *Mission archéologique dans la Chine septentrionale*, vol. 2, plate 70, no. 134. Courtesy of Princeton University Libraries.)

the tools were attributes of the five planetary gods in their guise as creators (possibly) and sustainers (certainly) of the universe as it emerged from the cosmogonic process recounted at the beginning of the "Treatise on the Patterns of Heaven." In that section, the balance beam seems to denote primarily the function of establishing the horizontal, while the weight is a plumb bob for establishing the vertical; here the balance beam instead is the arm of a steelyard, and the weight is employed in weighing rather than in setting out vertical lines; the (water-) level denotes the horizontal.

The distinction is subtle but real. The implements of the planetary gods in 3.VI are those of building and maintaining; the implements here are ideal standards to which the phenomenal world is compared and by which it is judged. The level and the marking cord are taken as standards for the Mingtang, the ideal representation of the 3 × 3 grid of the earth through which the seasons and the months are maintained in their ordered round. They are the standards of heaven and earth (personalized as the High Thearch), the active and passive forces of the cosmos itself. Spring, the season of ascending yang, takes the compass, the symbol of the roundness of heaven; autumn, the season of waxing yin, takes the square, symbol of the squareness of earth. Summer, the season of equable harmony, takes the balance beam as its standard; the standard of winter, the season of harshness, punishments, and shutting away, is the inexorably plunging weight.

Here too, the "Treatise on the Seasonal Rules" takes the philosophy of the "Yueling" to lengths not found in other versions of that text; the rules that govern behavior for the months and the seasons are shown to be equivalent to the eternal and unvarying standards of the cosmos itself.

Appendix A

എ

A CHINESE ERATOSTHENES OF THE FLAT EARTH:
A Study of a Fragment of Cosmology in *Huainanzi*

by Christopher Cullen

This paper[1] attempts to deal with a short passage found at the end of the *Huainanzi*.[2] My first efforts to understand the text led me to the conclusion that it was unique in a number of ways and had points of interest that did not fully appear in the version of Maspero.[3] While there are still some obscurities of language in what appears to be a rather corrupt text, I offer the version given here with a fair degree of conviction that it does not substantially misrepresent the intentions of the unknown author.

I shall argue later that this passage is probably not part of the original *Huainanzi* text. We shall certainly never know who the author was, and we can form only vague notions of when he wrote. Whoever he was, I consider this fragment strong evidence for a powerful and original mind. The text consists largely of a probably hypothetical attempt to find the dimensions of the world by large-scale geometry using the gnomon, or simple vertical pole, which was the basic instrument of ancient Chinese astronomy and surveying. This is nothing unusual in the literature of the pre-Tang cosmological debate. The unique feature of this author, however, is that the main method he proposes is based on a geometrical principle that is simple and accurate, needing none of the false but traditional assumptions used elsewhere. Despite his early date, his work is never referred to again by other astronomers, nor do they use any similar method.

This undeserved oblivion does not detract from the originality of his work, which is, I would suggest, not much below the level of the attempt of Eratosthenes (276–296 B.C.E.) to find the size of the earth by observing the noon solsticial altitude of the sun at Alexandria, a known distance north of Syene (modern Aswan) where at the same instant the sun was directly overhead.[4] Whereas, however, Eratosthenes' computation of the diameter of the earth (on some interpretations) was correct to within 1 percent, the method of the Chinese author was doomed to failure in practice, for he was attempting to find the distance of the sun from the observer using a baseline only one li [≈⅓ mile] long. As the sun is some 93,000,000 miles away the accuracy demanded was far beyond his capacity and only meaningless results would have been obtained (see below, p. 282).

This contrast is a good example of the characteristics of success and failure in science. Eratosthenes had two hypotheses of considerable predictive power, despite the fact that he would have found some difficulty in justifying them: (i) the earth is spherical; (ii) the sun is for practical purposes so far away that its rays reach the earth sensibly parallel. As it will appear, the Chinese author believed neither of these things; that condemned his proposal to sterility. His difficulty sprang from a false idea about the shape of the cosmos common in ancient China. From his writing it is possible to reconstruct the general picture of the universe he thought he lived in, and it turns out to be a rather interesting one. Before considering the text itself, it seems relevant to make some points about Chinese cosmology in general.

In Greece the Ionian philosophers of the seventh and sixth centuries B.C.E. taught cosmologies with a flat earth.[5] This apparently self-evident doctrine continued to be held by the Epicurean Lucretius as late as the first century B.C.E.[6] Four centuries earlier, however, Philolaus, a Pythagorean, stated that the earth was spherical and in motion, not round the sun, but round the "central fire" of the universe.[7] Despite this and the heliocentric suggestion of Aristarchus in the third century B.C.E.,[8] the standard Greek view became that expressed with finality by Aristotle (384–322 B.C.E.): the earth is immobile at the center of the universe.[9] There was, however, never any chance of such a powerful and successful hypothesis as the sphericity of the earth being abandoned so long as rational discussion continued.

In contrast, Chinese thought on the form of the earth remained almost unchanged from early times until the first contacts with modern science through the medium of Jesuit missionaries in the seventeenth century. While the heavens were variously described as being like an umbrella covering the earth (the *gaitian* 蓋天 theory), or like a sphere surrounding it (the *huntian* 渾天 theory), or as being without substance while the heavenly bodies float freely (the *xuanye* 宣夜 theory), the earth was at all times flat, although perhaps bulging up slightly.

A convenient summary of ancient and medieval Chinese cosmological theory is given by Needham.[10] Note, however, that Needham quotes an account of the *gaitian* theory taken from Chatley.[11] In what is perhaps an attempt to make the theory correspond rather more closely to reality, Chatley tacitly assumes that it describes the earth as rather more than a hemisphere, radius 225,000 li, with the result that an observer in

China has his horizon at 25° to that of an observer on top of the earth at the North Pole. However, Chatley's source, the *Zhoubi suanjing* 周髀算經, probably completed by the first century C.E.,[12] states explicitly that heaven and earth are both shaped like Chinese rain hats, are 80,000 li apart and bulge upwards only 60,000 li for a diameter of 476,000 li (*Zhoubi suanjing* 2:1a). If Chatley's interpretation was correct, the *gaitian* theory would never have been subject to the criticisms that led to its downfall; see for instance the eight objections of Yang Xiong 揚雄 (53 B.C.E.–18 C.E.) quoted in *Sui shu* 隋書 19:4a.[13] Fresh difficulties suggest themselves under Chatley's theory, such as the problem of defining what is meant by "down," but no early author mentions any such considerations.

In fact the *gaitian* theory is a not unsophisticated attempt to give at least a qualitatively correct picture of astronomical phenomena under the crippling handicap of the flat earth. The sun and other heavenly bodies perform their long-term motions on the underside of the "umbrella" of the sky, which rotates once daily about an imaginary vertical axis passing through the center of the earth. This position corresponds to the North Pole, and the observer of the *Zhoubi suanjing* is 103,000 li away from it (*Zhoubi suanjing* 1:38a). In summer the sun rotates nearer to the pole than in winter, and the six-month day and night at the pole are clearly described (*Zhoubi suanjing* 1:42a and 2:9a). Since, however, the sun never actually falls lower than 20,000 li above the earth's highest point (*Zhoubi suanjing* 2:3a), the only way that sunrise and sunset can be explained is by saying that they are illusions consequent upon all objects becoming invisible when more than a fairly arbitrary 167,000 li away (*Zhoubi suanjing* 1:43ab); compare the first century C.E. exposition of this doctrine by Wang Chong 王充 (*Lun heng* 論衡 11:8b–9a). This and other flaws led to the widespread rejection of the *gaitian* theory in favor of the *huntian* by the second century C.E. To a certain extent this was a regression, although the *huntian* theory predicted appearances exactly for an observer at the center of the celestial sphere, which was also the center of the flat earth. In contrast to the *Zhoubi suanjing* (2:2a), dawn and dusk occurred simultaneously over the entire earth, and polar conditions were not represented in any way. Further, the latitude of observers at the Chinese centers required that the axis of the sphere be given an apparently arbitrary tilt of 55° to the vertical. On the flat earth assumption progress beyond this point was impossible, and this assumption was not discarded by any Chinese cosmologist on his own initiative.[14]

The text of which the translation now follows also naturally assumes a flat earth. I think it will become evident, however, that it cannot be classified under either the *huntian* or the *gaitian* theories, not because it represents what can in any sense be called a rival theory, but because it has primitive characteristics suggesting an origin before either of these two systems. If this is so, there is a possiblity that this is the earliest known Chinese attempt at quantitative empirically based cosmology.

I have divided the originally continuous text into sections for convenience of comment and reference, without, however, making any attempt at rearrangement. I have followed the text as in *Huainanzi* 3:17ab, *Sibu congkan* edition. Superscript numbers in parentheses refer to points of commentary following the translated segments.

(a) 正朝夕先樹一表東方操一表郤去前表十步以參望日始出北廉日直入又樹一表于東方因西方之表以參望日方入北廉則定東方兩表之中與西方之表則東西之正也。

To fix (the directions of) sunrise and sunset,[1] first set up a gnomon[2] in the east. Grasp another gnomon and retreat ten paces from the former gnomon, sighting[3] on the sun as it first leaves the northern edge.[4] Exactly at sunset plant a further gnomon in the east, sighting in conjunction with the western gnomon on the sun as it is about to enter the northern edge. Thus (the positions are) fixed.[5] The midpoint of the two eastern gnomons, and the western gnomon define (a line running) due east-west.[6]

(1) A parallel to this usage occurs in the section of the *Zhou li* 周禮 known as the "Artificer's Record," *Kao gong ji* 考工記. The eighteenth-century Chinese scholar Jiang Yong 江永 suggested that this may be a state document of Qi 齊 and hence may date from the third century B.C.E. Even if this is true, later editors are not likely to have preserved the text unaltered; but for our purposes its relevance is sufficiently assured so long as it dates before the first century B.C.E.

> 晝參諸日中之影夜考之極星以正朝夕 (*Zhou li* 12:15b)
> By day they observe the noon solar shadow and by night they examine the pole star, in order to fix (the directions of) sunrise and sunset.

Again in *Mozi* 墨子 (fourth century B.C.E.):

> 言而毋儀譬猶運鈞之上而立朝夕者也 (*Mozi* 35:1b)
> Speaking without defined principles is like someone setting out (the directions of) sunrise and sunset on top of a potter's wheel which is free to rotate.

In light of these I am inclined to take *zhaoxi* 朝夕 as a rather formal periphrasis for "east and west" which are referred to as usual by *dongxi* 東西 for the rest of the passage. An alternative might be that this passage is concerned with the fixing of the direction of any given sunrise or sunset with reference to the standard east-west line which is defined by the procedure given. This theory has considerable relevance to the ideas expressed in later sections, which pay attention to the geographical significance of the directions of sunrise and sunset.

(2) In ancient Chinese usage, the gnomon was a simple vertical pole. In this case the height is unspecified and is irrelevant, but a later section suggests the use of a pole ten feet (*chi* 尺) high rather than the eight feet usually found.[15]

(3)   Here and in later sections the usage *can wang* 參望 refers to situations where two objects define a line of sight running in the direction of a third. It is interesting therefore that Karlgren notes early uses of *can* as both "a triad" and "straight."[16] Pronounced *shen*, it is, of course, also used for the line of three stars that forms Orion's belt. The fifty-seventh definition of the Mohist Canon has *zhi can ye* 直參也.[17] As the basic meaning of *zhi* is, of course, "straight," the "alignment" sense of *can* is confirmed.

(4)   The function of the term *beilian* 北廉 is highly problematical, and I have not succeeded in finding a helpful parallel. My first impulse was to take *lian* in its sense of "corner, edge," and make it refer to the sun itself, thus translating: "sighting on the northern limb of the sun as it first rises." There is some point in specifying whether the sight is to be taken on the northern or southern limb; if the gnomons are ten paces apart the sun's angular diameter of ½° would cause an uncertainty of some six inches unless a particular point on the sun is named. It seems, however, that this rendering strains the grammar, and hence we are left with a reference to the sun coming out of the northern *lian* of something else. Since the sun goes into this northern *lian* at sunset as well as apparently coming out of it at dawn, *beilian* cannot very well refer to a part of the earth or some particular direction on the horizon (cf. the use of the term *wei* 維 in (b) below). We are left, therefore, with the possibility that *beilian* refers to the gnomons. Qian Tang accepts this, but then loads the text well beyond the breaking point with an interpretation in terms of the shadow of one gnomon just grazing the edge of another, finishing by attributing to this text a precision of knowlege of solar motion not found, by his own admission, until the fifth century C.E. A simpler explanation seems possible in the following terms:

Assume that the observer does his sighting from close behind one gnomon, and that the gnomons have the not unreasonable diameter of one inch. Then, taking one pace as about sixty inches (a Chinese "pace," *bu* 步, was made up of two steps), the gnomon ten paces away will have an angular diameter Θ as seen by the observer, where

$$\Theta = \tan^{-1} \tfrac{1}{600} \text{ (to a very close approximation)}$$
$$\therefore \Theta \approx \tfrac{1}{12}°$$

For comparison, the sun has an angular diameter of about ½° for observers on the earth and the gnomon thus covers about one-sixth of it.

Further, it is reasonable to suppose that the observer will not bring his eye so close to the nearer gnomon that he cannot focus his eye on it; this distance is, of course, subject to individual variations, but is not far from five inches. The angular diameter Φ, at the eye, of the inch-thick gnomon is then given approximately by

$$\Phi = \tan^{-1} \tfrac{1}{5}$$
$$\therefore \Phi \approx 10°$$

273

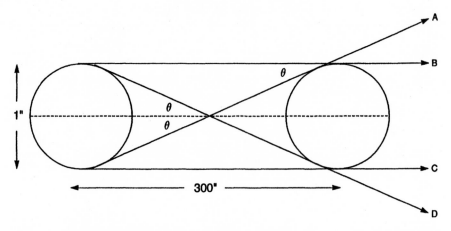

Figure A.1. Main lines of sight obtained with the use of two gnomons (not to scale: diameters of gnomons greatly exaggerated).

Thus, if the nearer gnomon was transparent and provided with some sort of graticule, the sun would cover about 0.05 inches on the scale, while the further gnomon might cover about a sixth of this already very small distance. (This transparency is, of course, introduced only for purposes of illustration.)

Considering the sighting process in more detail, it becomes evident that two gnomons can be used to obtain a number of different lines of sight. In Fig. A.1 (gnomon width much exaggerated) the main ones are shown.

The angle Θ is obviously the quantity calculated earlier as about $\frac{1}{12}°$. Note, of course, that for very distant objects like the sun parallel sightings such as B and C are equivalent. Returning to the text, and noting that the version chosen demands that we find a "northern edge" for the sun to "leave," let us choose the sight line that uses the two northern edges of the gnomons. Then when the center of the sun is just on the horizon in the east we can arrange the gnomons so that the situation in Fig. A.2 will occur.

The line XX' represents the aligned northern edges of both gnomons, arranged so that at rising the sun is just in contact with it. As the sun rises it will take the path shown; the angle of this path to the vertical is equal to the observer's latitude, some 34° for the Han capital Chang'an. It can thus be said to "leave the northern edge" as the text specifies. The situation at sunset will, of course, be a simple reflection of Fig. A.2 in the line XX', the direction of the sun's motion being reversed: at that time the sun "enters" the northern edge.

Notice that if we wish the sun to be just leaving the aligned northern edges of the gnomons at sunrise and just meeting them at sunset, our alignments must be made with the sun's northern limb. It appears, therefore, that the only effect of refer-

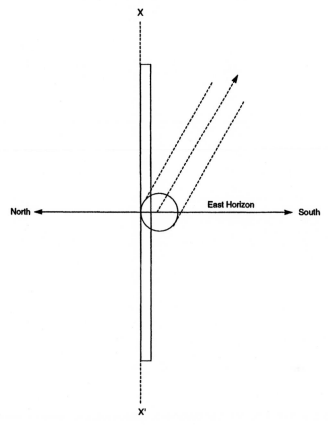

Figure A.2. View toward the eastern horizon, with the northern edge of the rising sun aligned with the northern edges of two gnomons placed in line.

ring *beilian* to the gnomons rather than to the sun is to imply that the observer keeps his eye close enough to a gnomon for its width to be significant; sights must still be taken on the sun's northern limb.

(5) Punctuation is doubtful here. Qian Tang divides after *fang* 方, while Tan Jiefu omits any punctuation.[18] Qian insufficiently emphasizes the fact that we need the midpoint of the two eastern gnomons. By punctuating after *ding* 定, I attempt to indicate a parallel between *ze ding* 則定 for the gnomons and *ze . . . zheng* 則 . . . 正 for the directions. None of these variants makes any practical difference.

(6) A plan view of the final arrangement is shown in Fig. A.3, in which the size of the gnomons is much exaggerated.

275

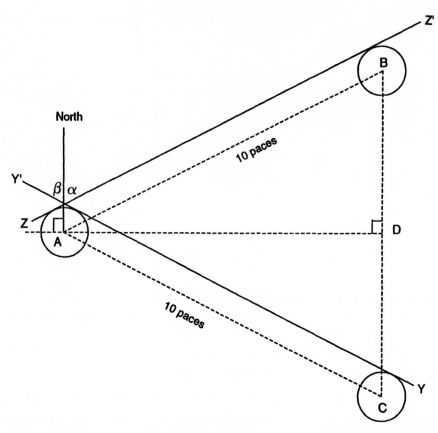

Figure A.3. Diagram showing how three gnomons are used to determine the angles of the rising and setting sun.

I have made the assumption, without which the method will not work, that in planting C the observer retreats ten paces from A, repeating the procedure that he used in planting A. ZZ′ is a line of sight on the rising sun, and YY′ is a line of sight on its setting. The situation shown would occur in the summer; at the solstices the angles α and β would be of the order of 60° for observers near Chang'an. At the equinoxes B and C coincide, and by the winter solstice they have become reversed. To a close approximation the angles α and β are equal, but if we take account of the annual motion of the sun on the celestial sphere, it becomes evident that from the winter solstice to the summer solstice the sun will set a little further north than it rose, making β less than α. From the summer solstice to the winter solstice, β will exceed α. However, this difference is always small, and even at the equinoxes when it reaches its largest value it does not exceed ¼° for a Chang'an observer.

As AB is parallel to ZZ' and CA is parallel to YY', it is evident therefore that if D is the midpoint of the line BC the line DA runs due east-west with an acceptable degree of accuracy; an error of one inch in fixing the position of a gnomon, will as we have seen, cause an error of only ¹⁄₁₂°.

I must confess that I do not feel completely satisfied with the solution of the *beilian* problem in (4) above. In particular I do not think that the terms *chu* 出 and *ru* 入 really apply very well to the supposed motion of the sun relative to the aligned northern edges of the gnomons at rising and setting. Nor does it seem right to ignore the fact that the phrase *ri shi chu* 日始出 occurs elsewhere in contexts where it has no object, and means literally "when the sun first comes out," that is, the moment of dawn itself. (See for instance the story of Confucius and the two small boys in *Liezi* 列子 5:12b, or the example from the *Zhoubi suanjing* on p. 000 below.) On purely practical grounds the observer's closeness to one gnomon involves a very fussy procedure, and speaking personally it seems more natural when checking the alignment of two gnomons to step far enough back from them so that their thickness can be neglected. This would, of course, force us back to referring *beilian* to the sun itself. This may make a clumsy expression of *ri shi chu beilian*, but one might sometimes prefer to yield to the temptation to assume that an author's sense is better than his literary style.

In any case I do not think that any of the several ways of rendering the passage could result in a description of a practical method differing from the others by more than ½° in its definition of an east-west line. Experimental errors would in all likelihood be equal to or greater than this theoretical divergence.

For comparison, here is a short passage from the *Zhoubi suanjing*:

日始出立表而識其晷日入復識其晷晷之兩端相直正東西也中折之指表者正南北也 (*Zhoubi suanjing* 2:8a)

> At dawn set up a gnomon and observe its shadow. At sunset observe its shadow once more. The ends of the shadow align to indicate due east-west. (The line from) their midpoint to the gnomon indicates due north-south.

This method is simpler in that it uses only one gnomon and involves no aligning by the observer. It suffers from the disadvantage that dawn and sunset shadows will naturally have extremely ill-defined ends; this can be overcome, however, by the fairly obvious expedient of marking an equal length along each shadow and thus defining arbitrary shadow ends which will serve the purpose just as well.

(b)   日多至日出東南維入西南維至春秋分日出東中入西中夏至出東北維入西北維。

On the day of the winter solstice the sun rises on the southeast diagonal and sets on the southwest diagonal.[7] On the arrival of the spring and autumn equinoxes the sun rises in the middle of the east and sets in the middle of the west. At the summer solstice it rises on the northeast diagonal and sets on the northwest diagonal.

(7) The term *wei* 維, translated here as diagonal, has a precise meaning in the main body of the chapter:

兩維之閒九十一度 (也) 十六分度之五 (*Huainanzi* 3:6a, SBCK ed.)
Between two *wei* the interval is 91⁵⁄₁₆ *du*. [Cf. 3.XVII.18 above: "Between the two weft-strings is an interval of 91⁵⁄₁₆ᵈ."]

(Comparison with other texts suggests *ye* 也 here is a printing error.) As there are 365¼ᵈ in a complete circle, 91⁵⁄₁₆ᵈ is 90°, a right angle. It will become clearer later on that "diagonal" here refers to a square thought to be formed by the four positions occupied by the sun at the moments of rising and setting at the summer and winter solstices (see Section (i)). In fact it is only for an observer at a latitude of about 57° that these four positions appear to lie along the diagonals of a square centered on the observer; this is far to the north of China. It becomes plain, however, that these statements are not meant approximately, although the author is prepared to concede that some observers may not be at the center of the square and hence will not see the simple situation described here. Despite these modifications the theoretical scheme developed cannot predict the observations of an observer near Chang'an or Luoyang. For such an observer lines running from his position towards sunrise and sunset at the summer solstice include an obtuse angle of about 120°. The same applies to the winter solstice except, of course, that rising and setting are to the south of the observer. The rest of the *Huainanzi* gives us no comparison data about sunrise and sunset.

In the *Zhoubi suanjing*, however, we find:

多至晝極短日出辰而入申 … 夏至晝極長日出寅而入戌 (*Zhoubi suanjing* 2:42b, 43a)
On the winter solstice daylight is shortest. The sun rises in *chen* and sets in *shen*. . . .
On the summer solstice the day is longest. The sun rises in *yin* and sets in *xu.*

Now *chen, shen, yin,* and *xu* are respectively names for the directions 30° south of east, 30° south of west, 30° north of east, and 30° north of west. These data imply the 120° angles between solsticial setting and rising that actually occur.

It is puzzling therefore to find our author putting forward what appear to be obvious inaccuracies; according to him the angle should be 90° for a central observer. Indeed later on he describes a procedure for checking this prediction.

(c)　至則正南

　　At culmination it is due south.[8]

(8)　I am inclined to take this as a misplaced fragment. Normally *zhi* 至 would refer to a solstice, and the sun culminating at noon would be referred to as *zhong* 中. *Zhi* may be used here with reference to the sun having reached its maximum altitude at noon, when it is in fact due south.

(d)　欲知東西南北廣袤之數者立四表以爲方一里距先春分若秋分十餘日從距北表參望日始出及且以侯相應相應則此與日直也輒以南表參望之以入前表數爲法除舉廣除立表表以知從此東西之數也。

　　If you wish to know the figures for breadth and length of east, west, north, and south set up four gnomons to make a right-angled figure one li square. More than ten days before the spring or autumn equinox sight along the northern gnomons of the square on the sun from its first appearance to its rise above the horizon.[9] Wait for (the day when) they coincide. When they coincide they are in line with the sun. Each time[10] take a sight on it [the sun] with the southern gnomons, and take the amount by which it is within the forward gnomons as the divisor. Divide the whole width [and/or?] divide the length (between) the standing gnomons in order to know the measurements east and west from here.[11]

(9)　This is a somewhat provisional rendering of *ri shi chu ji dan* 日始出及且. *Dan* 且 does suggest graphically a situation where the sun's lower limb is only just in contact with the horizon; a different interpretation could scarcely change the practical significance of the passage.

(10)　Presumably on each day of the "more than ten days before" the equinox. The mathematical procedure following only works, however, for the day when the northern gnomons align with the sun.

(11)　This last sentence is very cryptic. There is some help to be gained by adopting the suggestion of D. C. Lau[19] that *ju* 舉 (Karlgren: *kio/kiwo:*) may be a phonetic loan for the earlier *ju* 距 (Karlgren: *g'io/g'iwo:*) itself obviously a loan for *ju* 矩 (Karlgren: *kiwo/kiu:*). If we take this view, then "the whole width" becomes "the square's width" which makes explicit what would otherwise be an obvious inference. One advantage possessed by the translator of scientific texts, however, is that he can often feel fairly sure what the text ought to mean by a simple reference to mathematical or physical facts. Now the geometry of the arrangement described here is obviously as shown in Fig. A.4, which is not, of course, to scale.

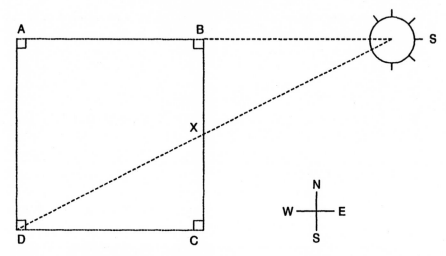

Figure A.4. Diagram showing how four gnomons are used to determine the size of the square earth.

A, B, C, D are gnomons and S is the rising sun. CX is the amount by which it (i.e., the sun) is within the forward gnomons. A, B are the northern gnomons, C, D are the southern gnomons, and B, C are the forward gnomons.

Now the triangles SAD, DCX are similar.

$$\frac{SA}{AD} = \frac{DC}{CX}$$

$$\therefore SA = \frac{(DC \times AD)}{CX} \qquad \text{(Equation 1)}$$

A similar procedure to this one is found in the *Jiuzhang suanshu* 九章算書, perhaps compiled in the first century C.E. Most of this book's techniques were, of course, probably current before its compilation.

有木去人不知遠近立四表相去各一丈令左兩表與所望參相直從後
右表望之入前右表三寸問木去人幾何。
答曰三十三丈三尺三寸少半寸。
術曰令一丈自乘爲實以三寸爲法實如法而一。
(*Suanjing shishu*, edition of Qian Baozong,[20] p. 257.)

There is a tree an unknown distance from a man. He sets up four gnomons ten feet apart [i.e., as a square], so that the left two gnomons align with the object sighted on. Sighting on it from the rear right gnomon it (appears) to be three inches within the forward right gnomon. How far away is the tree?

Answer: 333 feet, 3⅓ inches. [One "foot" *chi* 尺 has ten "inches," *cun* 寸.]

Method: square the ten feet and make that the dividend. Take the three inches as the divisor and divide the dividend by the divisor.

The method here set out in words is, of course, exactly that symbolized by Equation 1 above. Although the *Zhoubi suanjing* does not contain a similar problem, its mathematical language and methods are very similar. What conclusions can be drawn, then, about the strange sentence at the end of (d), which is expressed in terms quite different from the smooth formalism of the *Jiuzhang suanshu?* Note further that in (e) we are given what amounts to an alternative mathematical process for obtaining the results required. I have not succeeded in finding any parallels to the expressions that end (d).

There seem to be three courses open: (i) emend the text until it says clearly what it "ought" to say; (ii) assume that the meaning of a valid but previously unknown expression is now revealed; (iii) treat the text as an abortive and unique attempt to deal with concepts new to the author.

The easiest course is naturally (i); by omitting *chu ju guang* 除舉廣 (or equally *chu li biao mou* 除立表裏), one obtains a prescription for

$$\frac{AD}{CX} \text{ or } \frac{DC}{CX}.$$

As both AD and DC are one li the result will be numerically identical to

$$\frac{(DC \times AD)}{CX},$$

the result for SA in Equation 1 above; it will, however, be a pure number unlike SA which is a length. The spirit of this reading is close to that of the method expressed in (e). Nevertheless it seems rough handling simply to slice three or four characters out of the text, and no more subtle emendation seems possible.

To follow (ii) is a path of despair, especially as it seems very unlikely that a parallel will be found to test the rendering. Even given the "blessed assurance" that we have a very good idea what the text means on mathematical grounds, (ii) demands that we should give up the attempt to understand the author's mental processes. If one is to do this one might as well give up reading the text altogether. Besides, if this method were generally applied it would bring the danger that by ignoring the consistency of the language as a guide, and relying on physical and mathematical precognition instead, one might miss the instances of interesting but incorrect thinking which are a great part of the matter of the history of science.

If we adopt (iii) and bear in mind the subsequent explanations of (e), I am inclined to take *chu ju guang* and *chu li biao mou* as alternatives, translating "Divide the whole width [or] divide the whole length [between] the standing gnomons." This gives us the choice between

$$\frac{AD}{CX} \text{ and } \frac{DC}{CX}$$

as before, these two being equal. If, however, the clauses are in conjunction rather than disjunction, there is the somewhat slender chance that by telling us to divide *both* width and length the author wants us to divide their product as in Equation 1.

However we read this passage it is hard to avoid the conclusion that this author had only relatively primitive mathematical tools at his disposal. The neat expressions of the *Jiuzhang suanshu*, particularly the phrase *shi ru fa* 實如法 for the division process are also found in the *Lüshu* 律書 chapter of the *Shiji* 史記 (25:11a), which may date from before 90 B.C.E. Another parallel is in the *Zhoubi suanjing* (1:70b). Leaving aside the possibility of gross corruption therefore we might conclude that the author of the *Huainanzi* passage wrote either in some isolation or else before such usage became standard.

(e) 假使視日出入前表中一寸是寸得一里也一里積萬八千寸得從此東萬八千里視日方入入前表半寸則半寸得一里半寸而除一里積寸得三萬六千里除則從此西里數也并之東西里數也則極徑也。

Suppose that the rising sun is observed one inch within the forward gnomons. This implies that for an inch one gets one li. One li contains 18,000 inches, so one gets 18,000 eastwards from here to the sun.[12] (Suppose) one observes the sun as it sets, and it sets half an inch within the forward gnomon; then for half an inch one gets one li. Dividing the number of inches in a li by half an inch, one gets 36,000 li.[13] Divide, and then (you have) the number of li westward from here.[14] Add them, (and you have) the number of li east and west, which is the diameter of the extreme limits.[15]

(12) The words *jia shi* 假使, "suppose," make it likely that this passage is based on hypothetical data. It is plain that this must be so for two reasons: (i) An observer at the rear gnomon could not possibly distinguish so small a separation as one inch from a gnomon one li away; this inch would subtend an angle of less than 0.003° at the eye of the observer, less than 1 percent of the sun's angular diameter of 0.5°. (ii) As the sun is in any case some 93,000,000 miles away ($\approx$ 300,000,000 li) the actual distance of the sun within the forward gnomons (given alignment of the northern gnomons) would be given by

$$x = \frac{1 \text{ li} \times 1 \text{ li}}{300,000,000 \text{ li}} \times 18,000 \frac{\text{(inches)}}{\text{(li)}}$$

$\therefore x \approx 0.00006$ inches

Thus any observations made would consist overwhelmingly of experimental error. However, the principle of simple proportion as set down in this section is correct.

(13) This half-inch is, of course, also hypothetical. It is interesting, however, to note that the author conceives the possiblity of being closer to the rising sun than to the setting sun, if, that is, the inch and half-inch are to be taken as measured by the same observer.

(14) If the rather awkward *chu* 除 at the beginning of this sentence could be omitted, this sentence would fit neatly onto the previous one.

(15) As the result of this addition is not stated, the possibility is left open that the pronoun *zhi* 之 is intended to refer to whatever results are obtained when the process pre-

scribed is carried out in practice, rather than to the 18,000 li and 36,000 li already mentioned.

(f) 未春分而直巳秋分而不直此處南也未秋分而直巳春分而不直此處北也分至而直此處南北中也。

If the alignment occurs before the spring equinox and not until after the autumn equinox, this (implies that) you are in the south. If the alignment occurs before the autumn equinox and not until after the spring equinox, this (implies that) you are in the north. If when the equinox arrives the alignment occurs, this (implies that) you are midway between north and south.[16]

(16) "The alignment" referred to is, of course, the dawn alignment of the sun with the northern pair of gnomons. In fact this occurs exactly at the equinoxes for all observers wherever they are on the earth. It is evident from this section, however, that the author has a world conception in which the sun rises over the edge of the earth or out of the earth (which is, of course, flat) at a different position each day. At the summer solstice this position is furthest north, and at the winter solstice it is furthest south; at the equinoxes (probably defined as the days midway between the solstices) the sun rises "midway between north and south" and an observer who is also "midway" will see his gnomons aligned with the sun at dawn. If the observer is further north he will observe alignments at two dates nearer the summer solstice; if he is to the south the dates will be nearer the winter solstice. This lends point to the prescription in (d) above that observations must commence "more than ten days before the spring or autumn equinox": it is thus ensured that a noncentral observer will not miss his alignment. A later section, (j), describes a method of finding how far north or south a particular observer is.

(g) 從中處欲知中南也。

From a central position, to know (the distance) south of the center.

(h) 未秋分而不直此處南北中也。

If the alignment does not occur until the autumn equinox, this (implies that) you are midway between north and south.[17]

(17) Neither of these sections seems properly placed; (g) seems to be a distortion of the beginning of (i), while (h) seems to belong with (f).

(i) 從中處欲知南北極遠近從西南表參望日日夏至始出與北表參則是東與東北表等也正東萬八千里則從中北亦萬八千里也倍之南北之里數也。

From a central position, to know the distance of the limits of north and south, sight on the sun from the southwest gnomon. At the summer solstice, if when the sun rises you (try to) align it with the gnomon to your north [i.e., the northwest gnomon] the result is that it is to the east equally with the northeast gnomon. It

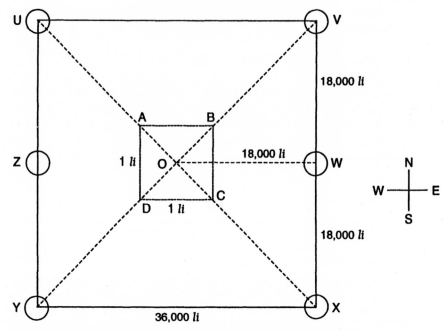

Figure A.5. Diagram of the worldview of the author of the *Huainanzi* 3 section on gnomonics, with a square earth derived from positions of the rising and setting sun.

is 18,000 li due east, so from the center northwards it is also 18,000 li. Double this to obtain the number of li from south to north.[18]

(18) The first two sentences of this section are simply equivalent to the statement of section (h), "At the summer solstice it [the sun] rises on the northeast diagonal." Note that the end of this section now takes for granted the 18,000 li figure that was introduced as the result of the hypothetical one-inch measurement in (e). This figure is also implicit in the statements of section (j). Although the author may have believed that one inch was in fact a correct figure, I am more inclined to believe that he adopted it as a working hypothesis to enable him to work out the implications of his ideas in the absence of a flexible symbolism.

At this stage I feel able to suggest that Fig. A.5 is a likely version of the worldview of this author. The size of the central observer's gnomon-square ABCD is, of course, greatly exaggerated.

The positions V, W, and X represent the rising sun at the summer solstice, equinoxes, and winter solstice respectively, and these positions are fixed explicitly by the text (W by (e) and V, X by (i)). By fixing the setting positions U, Z, Y symmetrically I am relying on the clear statements of (b) and the evidence of any observer's eyes. I have not felt compelled, however, to adopt the half-inch figure for sunset given in (e). As I suggested earlier, it seems to be only an alternative illustration to the one-inch figure, and its adoption here would make VXYU into a trapezoid rather than a square, with UY = 2VX.

As it stands, Fig. A.5 is highly suggestive of the perennial Chinese notion of the square earth. It is, of course, only a diagram of rising and setting solar positions. If, however, the author thought of the sun as rising and setting over the edge of the earth, we have a picture of the shape of the earth in Fig. A.5. It is probable that he also thought of himself as near the center of the earth, in which case his obvious knowledge that the sun is always due south at noon would have forced the conclusion that in its journey from (say) W to Z the sun passed well to the south of O.

Maspero[21] misses the point of the last two sentences. He proposes to read "westwards" for "northwards" and "east to west" for "south to north," which robs section (j) of any rational basis and misses the connection with (b). His object is to avoid contradicting the 20,000 li figure of (k) for the distance south to the subsolar point, but as this is apparently a noon distance it cannot conflict with a sunrise and sunset distance south of 18,000 li. In any case it will soon appear that the 20,000 li figure must refer to the summer solstice, corresponding therefore to the sun rising and setting 18,000 li north of the observer. Further, there is really little point in making drastic emendations in an attempt to avoid clashes between actual data and what are evidently arbitrary hypotheticals.

(j) 其不從中之數也以出入前表之數益損之入一寸寸減日近一里表出一寸寸益
遠一里。

The amount (the observer) is off center is larger or smaller depending on the amount that (the sun) is inside or outside the forward gnomons. If (the sun) is one inch inside the gnomons, that inch brings the sun one li closer. If (the sun) is one inch outside the gnomons, that inch increases the distance by one li.[19]

(19) The geometry of this section is true for observers on a north-south line through the "central position" of section (i).

In Fig. A.6 ABCD represent the gnomon-square of a central observer, while A'B'C'D' are to the north of center. S represents the rising sun at the summer solstice.

As ZD' is parallel to SD

DD' = BB' = ZS = the distance by which the observer is to the north of center.

By similar triangles, $\dfrac{B'X}{D'C'} = \dfrac{ZS}{D'T}$

$\therefore ZS = \dfrac{D'T \times B'X}{D'C'}$

Now D'C' = 1 li, D'T = 18,000 li

$\therefore ZS = 18,000 \ B'X$

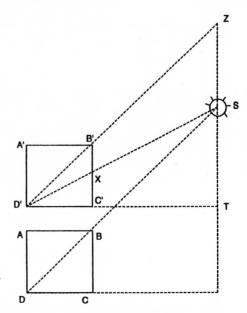

Figure A.6. Method employed to determine the observer's distance from the center of the world.

If B'X is measured in inches, then, as there are 18,000 inches in a li (see section (e)), ZS will measure one li for every inch of B'X, which in this diagram of course is a distance "inside the gnomon."

    An observer near Luoyang would see the sun rising about 60° east of north at the summer solstice, and would thus locate X some 8,000 inches from B' concluding that he was 8,000 li to the north of the center of the earth, which point would lie somewhere near Vietnam. This does not sound like the kind of conclusion that would commend itself to a Chinese audience in ancient times; Latter Han commentators on the *Zhouli* claim that the capital of the Zhou Dynasty was located at the center of the earth, and this capital was of course Luoyang itself.[22] In any case, observation of the winter solstice sunrise would have suggested that, according to the theory given here, the observer was 8,000 li *south* of the center. Once again, we see that the procedure given here is merely hypothetical.

(k) 欲知天之高樹表高一丈正南北相去千里同日度其陰北表二尺南表尺九寸是南千里陰短寸南二萬里則無景是直日下也陰二尺而得高一丈者是南一而高五也則置從此至日下里數因而五之爲十萬里則天高也若使景與表等即高與遠也。

To find the height of heaven, set up [two] gnomons ten feet high and 1,000 li apart due north-south. Measure their shadows (at noon) on the same day. The north gnomon (shadow) is two feet, and the south gnomon (shadow) is one foot nine inches. Thus a thousand li due south shorten the shadow by one inch and twenty thousand li due south there is no shadow at all. This is directly below the sun. A two-foot shadow corresponds to a height of ten feet so for each unit southwards one rises five units. Therefore, if one takes the number of li from this position south to the subpolar point and multiplies by five, making 100,000 li, this is the height of heaven. Supposing the shadow is equal to the gnomon, then the height is equal to the distance.[20]

(20) This section is unrelated to those that precede it, although the style and vocabulary are not sensibly different. The "inch for a thousand li" principle used here is found in all other early Chinese work with gnomons (e.g., *Zhoubi suanjing, passim*). It is a unique feature of this text, however, that it refers to a ten-foot gnomon and not to an eight-foot gnomon which is the size used everywhere else. The shadow principle is not modified in any way, despite this. Thus while here we are given 100,000 li for the "height of heaven," the *Zhoubi suanjing* (1:26b), using the same principle for a smaller gnomon, concludes that the height is 80,000 li.

   Despite this, the two-foot shadow may be the one piece of observed data in the whole text, for it implies a solar altitude of $\tan^{-1} 5 = 78.7°$. (With data of this kind there seems little point in working to greater accuracy.) Using de Sitter's expression for the obliquity of the ecliptic,

$$E = 23° \ 27'8''.29 - 47''.080t - 0''.0059t^2 + 0''.00186t^3$$

where t is measured forward in centuries from 1900 C.E.

   we obtain $E = 23.7°$ for 120 B.C.E.

   If the shadow length given here corresponds to noon at the summer solstice, then the latitude implied for the observer is given by

$$L = 90° + 23.7° - 78.7°$$
$$\therefore L = 35°$$

Several important ancient sites, including the Zhou dynasty capital Luoyang, lie within fifty miles of this line of latitude. There is the further interesting point that the *Zhoubi suanjing* (1:25a) states that the noon summer solsticial shadow of an 8-foot gnomon is 1.6 feet. This corresponds exactly to a 2-foot shadow for a 10-foot gnomon, which is the case given here. We have, of course, no means of deciding whether one figure was obtained from the other, or both drawn from a common literary source, or perhaps both taken from actual observation at the same latitude.

   The 1-foot 9-inch (1.9 feet) shadow would, if it were a summer solstice noon shadow, correspond to a latitude of 34.5° in 120 B.C.E. Taking three li as one mile, this would place the second gnomon only 100 li south of the first rather than 1,000 li. This figure is obviously a fictitious construction.

Let us now take the text as a whole and see what conclusions if any can be drawn about its origin and the thought that lay behind it. This somewhat incomplete and muddled account occurs at the end of a chapter (*Huainanzi* 3) that contains nothing else of a similar nature or style, and is in no way continuous with it. There is an earlier reference to gnomons (3.XVI.41 above}, but to gnomons of 8 feet rather than 10 feet, and with a noon summer solstice shadow of 1.5 feet rather than the 1.6 feet that would correspond to the 2-foot shadow for the 10-foot gnomon given here. A further discrepancy is the use there of *xiu* 修 "length" where one would have expected *biao* 表 "gnomon" as in most other texts of all dates. The main text states (*Huainanzi* 3:2a, SBCK edition) that heaven is 510,000 li away from the earth [see however 3.IV.2 above, where this number has been emended to 150,000 li; see also "Technical and Textual Notes"], and in what is admittedly a different chapter the overall dimensions of the universe are given as 233,500 li and seventy-five paces north-south and east-west, while the inhabited land "within the four seas" is 26,000 li north-south and 28,000 east-west [4.II.1–7 above]. It is hard, therefore, to maintain that our text really belongs in its present position.

It is not, however, inconsistent with what we know of the early history of many Chinese books to suggest that a later editor, attempting to arrange disordered bundles of bamboo strips, came across these isolated notes on the gnomon mixed up with the genuine *Huainanzi* text, and appropriately enough attached them to the end of the astronomy chapter. It may even have been a later author who added his own notes and left them filed in an obvious location in his copy of *Huainanzi*. If he had copied the main text in his own hand, a subsequent copyist would have simply assimilated the notes to the chapter itself without suspecting the interpolation.

If we accept that we are not dealing with a part of the treatise prepared for Prince Liu An, but with what amounts to one man's private notes, it becomes easier to understand the odd way the text veers between fact and hypothesis, with little attention to overall consistency. Sections (i) and (j) for instance take the 18,000 dimension introduced in (e) as obtained from an explicitly hypothetical 1-inch observation, and the figure of 36,000 li, which in conjunction with (b) would imply that the four extreme solar positions form a trapezoid, is not mentioned again. This sort of sequence of thought is, however, familiar to anybody who has tried to work out the implications of a new idea in practice.

Despite the correspondence of the gnomon shadows already mentioned, there is little trace here of the developed *gaitian* cosmology found in the *Zhoubi suanjing*. On the contrary, sections (d) to (j) clearly imply that the sun rises and sets level with the edge of the earth. The primitive notion that the sun's extreme risings and settings mark out a square rules out any possibility that this text is based on the relatively late *huntian* theory, which at least gave an accurate picture of the phenomena for a central observer.

In fact it is easy to draw connections with the archaic descriptions found elsewhere, in which the sun (perhaps a new one each day) rises from some point in the east, *Yanggu* 暘谷, the "Bright Valley" often associated with a magic mulberry tree, *Fusang* 扶桑, in whose branches the suns hang like fruit. It travels over the earth and finally sinks to rest at *Meigu* 昧谷, the "Dark Valley." The earliest reference to this is perhaps in the first chapter of the *Shujing* 書經 (ca. 400 B.C.E.) where the legendary Emperor Yao despatches his astronomers Xi and He to keep watch at those positions (*Shujing* 1:1b). *Huainanzi* itself has a detailed account of the sun's daily journey [see 3.XXV above]. This and similar legends have been discussed by Maspero.[23] Such ideas are obviously prior to the *gaitian* attempt at systematization, which as we have seen suggested that sunrise and sunset were optical illusions. Although therefore we may not be dealing with original *Huainanzi* material, it would still be unwise to set a date very far into the first century B.C.E. for its origin.

In view of the structure of the text and its partly hypothetical nature, the attempt of Maspero followed by Needham[24] to take all of the sections together to form a total cosmological theory seems risky. In Needham's words this leads to "a theory in which the sun at the meridian is five times further away from the earth than at its rising and setting, which would at least involve a very elliptical cover or shell." (This statement should perhaps be revised to refer to distances from a central observer rather than heights above the earth's surface, for as we have seen the rising and setting sun are apparently taken as level with the earth.) Maspero contrasts this with the *gaitian* situation, in which the sun is closest to us when on the meridian, and suggests that we are dealing with an alternative school of cosmology. He goes further, and proposes that we have a reference to the disputes between the rival schools in the *Liezi* (5:12b) where there is a story of Confucius confronted by two small boys quarrelling about the relative distance of the rising, setting, and noonday sun. This argument, however, turns on the apparent contradiction of the sun's larger apparent diameter at dawn with its greater heat at noon, and needs no further explanation than that it is yet another Daoist attempt to present Confucius as a ridiculous figure whose "wisdom" cannot resolve the problem. Although as Needham notes there were actual disputes on this point, the text we have here cannot bear the weight that is placed on it, and for all we know the problem had not occurred to its author who in any case does not seem to have troubled unduly over presenting a clear picture of his views.

Although this early attempt to solve problems of location on the flat earth could not have succeeded I have not so far found any criticism of it by a later writer, nor indeed any reference to it at all. In fact several authors made independent suggestions of their own for finding the center of the earth. An Eastern Han example of the second century C.E. is found in the comments of the two Zhengs on the *Zhouli*. They are

followed in more detail by the Tang editor.[25] Around 490 c.e. we find Zu Gengzhi 祖
暅之 writing at length on the same topic.[26] It may seem odd that the failure of these
proposals was not apparent, especially to Zu Gengzhi who was an expert astronomer as
his other writing shows. It happens, however, that unlike the *Huainanzi* method, all
later procedures automatically lead to the conclusion that the observer is at the center
of the earth. This is exactly the result that would have been expected by an astronomer
working at (probably) the capital city of what was in any case the "Middle Kingdom."

I have repeatedly stressed the hypothetical nature of parts of the text examined
here, and it is this feature that chiefly makes it stand out from its setting in the rest of
the *Huainanzi*. The dimensions found earlier in Chapters 3 and 4 are simply given;
there is no question of any supporting rationale being provided. Here, however, we
have an instance of a hypothesis (the square of sunrises and sunsets) being put forward
and its implications worked out in detail. Now as we have seen this hypothesis predicts
phenomena that are not those actually observed. This does not in any way detract from
the fact that it is a truly scientific hypothesis in that it is vulnerable to testing in a way
that other early Chinese thought schemes were not; the five phase theory predicted
everything and hence predicted nothing. The unknown author of this fragment
deserves great credit for intellectual daring, whatever the long-term results of his
endeavor.

Appendix B

∽

THE HEAVENLY STEMS, THE EARTHLY BRANCHES, AND THE SEXEGENARY CYCLE

THE HEAVENLY STEMS

1. *jia* 甲
2. *yi* 乙
3. *bing* 丙
4. *ding* 丁
5. *wu* 戊
6. *ji* 己
7. *geng* 庚
8. *xin* 辛
9. *ren* 壬
10. *gui* 癸

THE EARTHLY BRANCHES

1. *zi* 子
2. *chou* 丑
3. *yin* 寅
4. *mao* 卯
5. *chen* 辰
6. *si* 巳
7. *wu* 午
8. *wei* 未
9. *shen* 申
10. *you* 酉
11. *xu* 戌
12. *hai* 亥

THE SEXAGENARY CYCLE

1. *jiazi*	13. *bingzi*	25. *wuzi*	37. *gengzi*	49. *renzi*
2. *yichou*	14. *dingchou*	26. *jichou*	38. *xinchou*	50. *guichou*
3. *bingyin*	15. *wuyin*	27. *gengyin*	39. *renyin*	51. *jiayin*
4. *dingmao*	16. *jimao*	28. *xinmao*	40. *guimao*	52. *yimao*
5. *wuchen*	17. *gengchen*	29. *renchen*	41. *jiachen*	53. *bingchen*
6. *jisi*	18. *xinsi*	30. *guisi*	42. *yisi*	54. *dingsi*
7. *gengwu*	19. *renwu*	31. *jiawu*	43. *bingwu*	55. *wuwu*
8. *xinwei*	20. *guiwei*	32. *yiwei*	44. *dingwei*	56. *jiwei*
9. *renshen*	21. *jiaxin*	33. *bingshen*	45. *wushen*	57. *gengshen*
10. *guiyou*	22. *yiyou*	34. *dingyou*	46. *jiyou*	58. *xinyou*
11. *jiaxu*	23. *bingxu*	35. *wuxu*	47. *gengxu*	59. *renxu*
12. *yihai*	24. *dinghai*	36. *jihai*	48. *xinhai*	60. *guihai*

Technical and Textual Notes

In order to avoid a proliferation of superscript numbers in the main body of the text, these notes have been keyed to chapter, section, and line numbers in the translations above; for example, "3.XVIII.4" denotes Chapter 3, Section XVIII, line 4. In these notes, the chapter and section number is listed once, in boldface; individual line numbers follow below. References to the original Chinese text of the *Huainanzi* (HNZ) take the customary form of chapter, page, and line numbers, for example, 4:26a:5. Except as noted, all such references are to the edition edited by Liu Wendian, *Huainan honglie jijie*.

Abbreviations used in these notes include the following:

DDLJ: *Da Dai liji* 大戴禮記.
GY: Gao Yu 高誘 commentary to HNZ.
GSR: Bernhard Karlgren, *Grammata Serica Recensa*.
LJ: *Liji* 禮記.
LSCQ: *Lüshi chunqiu* 呂氏春秋.
LWD: Liu Wendian 劉文典 commentary to HNZ.
SBBY: *Sibu beiyao* 四部備要 edition of HNZ.
SHJ: *Shanhaijing* 山海經.
TPYL: *Taiping yulan* 太平御覽.
WNS: Wang Niansun 王念孫 commentary to HNZ.
WYZ: Wang Yinzhi 王引之 commentary to HNZ.
YY: Yu Yue 俞樾 commentary to HNZ.
ZKJ: Zhuang Kuiji 莊逵吉 commentary to HNZ.

CHAPTER 3

3.I

3 Reading *shi* 始 for *zhao*, following WNZ.
4 WYZ conflates this and the preceding line to read *taishi sheng xukuo* 太始生虛霩, "The Great Inception began in the nebulous void."

5 WNS conflates this and the following line to read *yuqiu shen yuanqi* 宇宙生元氣, as in TPYL.

8 *Yang* 陽 here is taken as an adjective, "bright" (in opposition to *zhuo* 濁, "turbid") in the following line"; yang as a cosmological concept is not mentioned until several lines below.

15 Read *zhuan* 專 as *chuan* 傳, "scattered, distributed."

16 WYZ cites TPYL and other parallel texts to argue that this line should read . . . *jiuzhi sheng huo* 久者生火, "*after a long time* produces fire." Similarly in 3.I.18.

20 Inserting *qi* 氣 before *wei* 爲, as suggested by WYZ.

3.II

6 Reading *yue* 曰 as *ri* 日.

7 "Sucks in" approximates the meaning of *han* 含, lit. "to hold in the mouth."

8 Reading *yue* 曰 as *yue* 月, parallel to 3.II.6.

11 "Unbalanced" approximates *pian* 偏, "partial; inclining to one side."

12 Reading *han* 含 as *he* 合, "harmonious." WNS points out that the similarity of the characters, and the appearance of *han* a few lines earlier, would readily have led to a copyist's error. *He* contrasts with *pian*, while *han* does not.

24 Reading *jiao* 膲 as *shu* 縮, following the commentary of Tao Fangqi.

25 *Tan* 蕈, "nettle," is unexplained here. GY glosses its pronunciation but not its meaning. From the context, it must mean something like "fly up." Perhaps this is an early corruption of some other character.

26 WNS reads *fei* 飛 as *dong* 動, but the emendation seems unnecessary.

33 "Rush" approximates *zhih* 至, "arrive," but also "reach a maximum."

38 GY glosses *ben xing* 賁星 as *ke xing* 客星, "novae," but Tao Fangqi corrects this to *liu xing* 流星, "meteors." Meteors fall, novae do not.

3.III

1 *Xing* 情, "nature, disposition, feeling"; LWD points out that the TPYL version of this passage reads *qing* 精, "spirit, anima."

5 Chatley's draft translation reads "when harvesting is forbidden," apparently reading *ling bushou* 令不收 to mean something like "command to not harvest." This seems an implausible construction of the meaning here.

3.IV

2 Following WNS, who cites parallel passages in *Kaiyuan zhanjing* and TPYL; this must read *yi wuwan li* 億五萬里, not *wuyi wan li*, which makes no sense as a number. *Yi* and *wu* have become transposed in the HNZ text.

Cullen, in Appendix A, reads this figure as 510,000 li.

3.VI

22 *Si* 巳 in the Liu Wendian text is a misprint for *ji* 己.

3.VIII

2 A phrase is missing here; the line must originally have read something like *qi guo shou zhi* 其國受制, as in 3.IX.6 below.

3.IX

1 *Yuan shi* 元始 here means simply "the beginning of the Epoch," and is not the name of a particular calendrical system.
6 The rather odd expression *sui shu* 歲熟 apparently means something like "a year of ripeness"; *shu* could be a copyist's error for *re* 熱, in which case this line would read "the year will be hot."

3.X

1 Following the suggestion of WNS, I emend this line to read *yuan shi yi jiayin, zheng yue yu* . . . 元始以甲寅正月與 instead of *yuan shi yi zheng yue jian yin, yu* . . . 元始以正月建寅與, thus making the text parallel to 3.IX.1.
11 Emending the second *dang chu er buchu* 當出而不出 to read *wei dang chu er chu* 未當出而出, following the suggestion of WNS, and parallel to the analogous text in "Wuxingzhan."

3.XI

2 Tao Fangqi suggests emending *xiao* 効 to *xian* 見; but with reference to celestial bodies, the two terms are synonymous, both meaning "to appear," so the emendation seems pointless. "Wuxingzhan" reads *xiao*.
3 Omitting *yi wu yue xia* 以五月下, which appears to be an erroneous preduplication of the following *yi wu yue xia* 以五月夏.
10 For *buhe* 不和 read *buli* 不利, as in "Wuxingzhan."

3.XII

10 "Wind season" approximates *feng zhi* 風至, "(up until the time the) wind reaches its limit."

3.XIII

5 Read *kong* 空 in the sense of *gong* 工, following GY commentary and also as in the name

of the minor constellation south of the lunar lodge Chariot-Platform (twenty-eighth of the lunar lodges) called *tu si kong* 土司空, "minister of works."

9   Emending *tai yi* 太一 to *tian zi* 天子, following the suggestion in YY's commentary. YY cites the *Tianguan xingzhan* 天官星占 as quoted in TPYL. *Jin shu* 11:9a also reads *tian zi*. The suggestion of WNS that *tai yi* should read *tian yi* is incorrect.

13   Some commentators emend *tian a* 天阿, "Heavenly Slope," to read *tian he* 天河, "Sky River," i.e., the Milky Way, but there does not seem to be any good reason for this.

14   Emending *si gong* 四宮 to read *si shou* 四守, following the suggestion of Tao Fangqi and thus making this list of the "six departments" conform to that given in 3.IV.5 above.

3.XVI

7   *Wei* 維 here is parallel to *sheng* 繩 two lines above. Both words mean "string." *Sheng* has implications of a carpenter's marking string, and here the two diametral chords connect the four cardinal directions, functioning as the "warp-strings" of heaven. The *wei* "weft-strings" thus cross the warp strings to weave the pattern of heaven.

9   Read *yang* 羊 as *yang* 洋.

19   *Cai zang* 閉藏, lit. "shut away in storage"; with reference to animals, this means hibernation. *Shou xue* 首穴, "head for their burrows"; for *shou* as a verb meaning "turn the head towards," see GSR #1102.

23   The significance of *yi qiu* 夷丘 is uncertain; *yi* can mean "level" (GSR #551), and the leveling or terracing of hills seems to be the sense here. Prohibitions on the construction of earthworks are specified for the fourth and sixth months in *Huainanzi* 5, the "Treatise on the Seasonal Rules"; see 5.IV.26 and 5.VI.30 below.

38   GY says that *liuhuang* 流黃, "flowing yellow," means "the essence of soil" (*tu zhi jing ye* 土之精也). My "yellow floods enrich the fields" is an approximation of the meaning of this awkward phrase; *ze* 澤 must have the function of a verb here, parallel to *chu* 出 in the following phrase.

40   *Huang kou* 黃口, "yellow mouths," is a nicely descriptive term meaning newly hatched birds.

3.XVII

18   "Span" translates *sheng* 升, used here in a rather obscure sense to mean "the number of threads in a warp," thus continuing the metaphor seen in 3.XVI.5–7 above of heaven as a woven fabric.

3.XVIII

7   Omit *lei* 雷.

20   WNS reads *lei jie* 雷戒 as *lei zang* 雷藏, to stress the paired opposition to *lei xing* 雷行 in

line 8 above; the emendation does not greatly change the meaning, which must be "thunder ceases" whichever word is used.

3.XIX

12 In this line *tian wei* 天維 "weft-cords of heaven" is perhaps an error for *tian yi* 天儀 (= *taisui*), which would move more smoothly into the following line.

14 WYZ argues that this should read *zhou* 周 rather than *dazhou* 大周. If a distinction between a *dazhou* and a *xiaozhou* 小周 is made at all, then the approximately 12-year Jovian Cycle is a *xiaozhou*, "small circuit." If Jupiter's orbital period is taken to be 11.88 years (as in 3.VII above), then in every 144 years Jupiter would "fall behind" in its orbit by one chronogram, i.e., $\frac{1}{12}$ of the celestial circumference. For Jupiter to come around again to its starting point at *yin* would thus take 1,728 years. This is a *dazhou*, "great circuit." WYZ argues that at the time *Huainanzi* was written this effect of retrograde motion was unknown in China, and so no distinction would have been made between a "small circuit" and a "great circuit"; *da* should be omitted as an interpolation by a later hand.

15 The meaning of "the Grand Monad was in the cyclical year *bingzi*" is uncertain. *Taiyi* 太一 is an important circumpolar star, but it makes no sense to describe it as being "in" a cyclical year. WYZ suggests emending *taiyi* to *tianyi* 天一 (= *tianyi* 天儀 = *taisui*, as in 3.XIX.12 above). This would make this line read "the Jovian Cycle was in the cyclical year *bingzi*," which perhaps accords better with the overall sense of this passage.

16 All commentators point out that this is impossible. *Jiawu* is #31 in the sexagenary cycle; *bingzi* is #13. This would indicate an elapse of forty-three days, but Beginning of Spring starts on the forty-sixth day after the winter solstice.

3.XXII

Much of the material in this section is paralleled in *Chunqiu fanlu* 61.

15 The text reads *gengzi*, but that is impossible; if the year shifts by six days, the sequence must end with *gengwu*.

17 The text reads "seventy years," but that is impossible; the sequence repeats every ten years. A stray "seven" has crept into the text here.

21 Read *shi* 飭 "strengthen" in place of *shi* 飾 "adorn."

3.XXIII

13 Text reads *da gang, yu bu wei* 大岡魚下爲, which makes no sense. WYZ suggests (on the basis of a parallel passage in Dong Zhongshu's *Chunqiu fanlu*) dropping *da* and emending *gang* to read *ze* 則; the line then becomes *ze yu bu wei*, "fish will not grow," with *wei* in the sense of "make, produce, bring forth."

18 Read *xing dui* 星隊 as *xing chui* 星墜, "stars fall."

20 Omit *qi xiang* 其鄉, erroneously duplicated from the previous line.

3.XXIV

3　*Ju* 居 = *juzhe* 居者.

6　*Yi* 夷 means "tranquil," among many other things, so I translate "Woman Yi" as "Tranquil Woman." The graph shows a garlanded arrow (see GSR #551C), not inappropriately for this singing and dancing divinity. GY identifies her as "a goddess of spring and summer, growth and nourishment."

12　The meaning of *gui* 歸, "reverts" (or "returns") with respect to the orbit (or period) of the moon is uncertain.

17　*Yu* 與 here means "stand up against, withstand."

3.XXV

1　LWD suggests emending *yanggu* 暘谷 to *tanggu* 湯谷. I prefer to leave the text unemended; *yanggu* is the form in "Yao dian" 4, which seems to be (in part) the source for this section.

2　The usual meanings of *fu* 拂 do not apply very well here. GY glosses the word as "to reach"; in context, it must mean something like "to rest in" in this case.

6　*Chu* (or *ku*) 朏 refers to the light of the moon a few days after the new moon; more broadly, a faint but growing brilliance.

7　Bent Slope (*qu a* 曲阿) is supposedly the name of a mountain; more likely, an asterism.

9　*Zeng quan* 曾泉; the primary meaning of *zeng* is "a pot for steaming"; secondarily it can mean "multiply, repeat." The image here is of a geyser.

12　*Yan shi* 晏食. For *yan*, see GSR #146; the primary meaning is "late," but it can be used by extension to mean "bright," and also "peaceful, quiet." I take the sense of *yan shi* to be a quiet snack in the brightness of the late morning.

13　I.e., the sun, in approaching its zenith, attains a state of balance as in a balance beam.

14　*Yuzhong* 隅中, "within the angle," i.e., the sun is near its zenith and will soon turn "downwards" in the sky.

17　*Niaoci* 鳥次; *ci* in the sense of "resting-place, lodging." Cf. the familiar Japanese word *torii* 鳥居, "bird roost," for the ceremonial gate of a Shinto shrine.

21　*Nüji* 女紀, "woman's sequence," but possibly also "woman's record" or even "female recorder"; significance unknown.

22　WNS emends *huan* 還 "revolve, return," to *qian* 遷, "remove, shift"; this makes only a slight difference in the meaning however.

23　Emending *yu* 虞 to *yu* 隅, as suggested by WNS.

24　*Gao chong* 高舂. *Chong* means "to pound grain"; here the image is of the sun as a pestle poised to descend. Compare line 26 below.

25　The basic meaning of *lian* 連 is "a kind of carriage" (GSR #213). Here *lianshi* 連石 could also mean "connected-stone (mountain)," reminiscent of the mountain called *jishi* 積石 "Piled-Stone," in 4.IV.1 below.

27 LWD points out that in parallel passages to this one quoted in later sources, this line usually reads " . . . and stops there. Xihe rests her six dragon-steeds [*chi* 螭]."

31 *Menggu* 蒙谷 is equivalent to *meigu* 昧谷 as in "Yao dian" 6.

35 *Qi she* 七舍, "seven resting-places"; the same term is used to describe the seven stages of the sun's annual motion back and forth along the eastern horizon in 3.XVII.1 above, where I translate *qi she* as "seven habitations."

36 WNS suggests emending *Yu* 禹 to *yu* 雕 (= *fen* 分), so that the line would read "[the sun's journey is] divided into dawn, daylight, dusk, and night." But I see no good reason to demythologize the meaning of the text here.

3.XXVI

8–9 Following the suggestion of WYZ, these lines have been transposed to here from 3:20b:10–21a:3 below, where they are clearly out of place.

3.XXVII

This entire section (including the lines that I have transposed to Section XXVI above, for a total of 285 characters) is in a completely different place in the Liu Ji edition of the *Huainanzi* and its descendants; in those editions, the section immediately precedes the chart near the end of the chapter (in Section XLII, in my division of the text). One suspects that this is the result of a disordered bundle of bamboo slips in an early copy of the *Huainanzi*; the last lines of Section XXVI were added to the end of this section, and the entire assembly of 285 characters placed more or less at random at this point in the text. It is impossible to know where the section might originally have been located, but the arrangement in the Liu Ji textual tradition makes sense; this section can serve as an explanatory introduction to the chart itself. (I am grateful to Hal Roth [private communication] for pointing this out to me.)

4 WYZ argues strenuously that this should read, "in the eleventh month it points to *zi*," citing parallel passages quoted in TPYL and other sources. But the effect is the same; if the Dipper points to *zi* in the eleventh (Xia sequence) month, then it points to *yin* in the first month, as the text here says.

6 The pun is between *yin* 寅 and *yinyin* 螾螾, "(wriggle like) earthworms."

7 (1) The pun is between *mao* 卯 and *mao* 茂, "burgeoning."
(2) The pun is between *jiazhong* 夾鐘 "Clasped Bell" and *zhong jia* 種莢, "seeds in a swollen pod."

8 The pun is between *chen* 辰 and *zhen* 振, "to stir up," then linked with *chen* 陳, "withered."

9 (1) There is a visual pun here: *si ze sheng shi ding ye* 巳則生巳定也. *Si* 巳 and *shi* 已 are fundamentally the same graph (see GSR #s 967, 977); here *shi* is used as a loan word for *yi* 以, so the sense of the line is *si, ze sheng yi ding ye*.

(2) The pun is that the center (*zhong* 中) grows (*chong* 充) large, though what is meant by that is unclear.

10   Pun on *wu* 午 and *wu* 忤, "oppose." Perhaps this means that maximum yang "opposes" minimum yin at the summer solstice.

11   (1) Emend *wei* 眛 to *wei* 味, as suggested by WNS on the basis of parallels in *Shiji*, *Shuowen*, *Bohutong*, TPYL, etc., so that the pun is between *wei* 未 and *wei* 味, "flavor."

        (2) The meaning of "extend forth and then stop" (*yin er zhi* 引而止) for Forest Bell perhaps refers to crops reaching maximum growth.

12   Pun on *shen* 申 and *shen* 呻, "chant, drone." The pitchpipe-name Tranquil Pattern has connotations of music and dance; see the name of the goddess Tranquil Woman (or Woman Yi) mentioned in 3.XXIV.6 above.

13   (1) The pun here is based on rhyme: *you* 酉 (*ziôg*) with *bao* 飽, "satiety" (*pôg*); see GSR #s 1096, 1113. There follows a pun between *bao*, "satiety," and *bao* 包, "bundle."

        (2) The phrase *ren bao da ye* 任包大也 makes almost no sense; my "it is recognized that the satiety is great" is a "best-guess" translation.

14   (1) The pun here is visual, between two similar-looking characters: *xu* 戌 and *mie* 滅 ("destruction").

        (2) "Unsatiated" means "bring it in but not be satisfied"; I follow ZKJ's commentary in inserting *zhi* after *ru*, so that the phrase reads *ru zhi wu yan* 入之無厭.

15   This is a rhyme pun, between *hai* 亥 and *ai* 閡, "hindrance."

16   (1) The pun is between *zi* 子 and *zi* 茲, "black"; black is the color of water/north/winter in five phase theory.

        (2) *Chong shi huang* 鐘巳黃; *shi* is used as a loan for *shi* 始, "the bell is beginning to be yellow," but there is also a reference here to yin-yang dualism—Yellow Bell, the pitch pipe note of winter, contains the "germ" (*shi* 巳) of yellow, the color of the opposite season, midsummer.

17   (1) The pun is between *chou* 丑 and *chou* 紐, "to tie."

        (2) There is a pun here between Great Pitchpipe (*dalü* 大呂) and *lülü* 旅旅, "one after another." The meaning here is that with the end of the sequence, the months have passed by one after another.

3.XXVIII

1   For *yue gui* 曰規 read *gu yue* 故曰.

9   *Han* 罕 usually means "net"; here it must be taken in a relatively rare sense to mean "flag." WNS considers that this line makes no sense; he emends *bing chong* 兵重 to read *bing ge* 兵革, so that the whole line reads *bing ge san han* and has a completely different meaning, "armor employs three webbings in its construction."

3.XXIX

38–39   These two lines have been moved to here from 3:24a:7, where they do not belong. In any case these lines were probably originally from a commentary and were transcribed into the text by a copyist's error.

3.XXX

1   The text reads "*zhi* produces *gong, gong* produces *shang*," but that is obviously an error. I have emended the text to give the correct sequence as in 4.XIV.17 below.

3.XXXI

3   WYZ notes that the text seems to require the statement "3 x 3 = 9" at this point.

5–13   The text in these lines is corrupt; my translation follows the reconstructed text of WYZ, for which see HNZ 3:23a:7–11.

      The phrase *xun zi bei* 尋自倍, "if the length of a fathom were doubled," has been omitted; it is a fragment of a sentence that has dropped out of the text.

      WNZ suggests that the sentence *pi zhe, zhong ren zhi du ye* 匹者中人之度也 should be omitted here, but I see no compelling reason for that and so have retained it (as line 13 here).

18   The *Shuowen* reads *fen* 分 in place of *su* 粟.

21   Some phrase such as "if the number of pentatonic notes be doubled" has probably dropped out of this sentence.

23   Reading *zhong* 重 for *liang* 量, as suggested by WNS.

26   The half-ounce (*banliang* 半兩) was the standard weight of a Han coin.

33   A possible translation for *jun* would be "standardweight."

35   The obvious translation for *shi* 石, "stone," doesn't work because of the use of that word in the English system to denote a much smaller weight (fourteen pounds). One could perhaps translate *shi* as "lithon."

3.XXXIII

1   The equation here of the first Jovian Year Shetige with the third chronogram (and first civil month) *yin* confirms HNZ's committment to the Xia sequence calendar. Compare the diagram in Needham, SCC III: 243 and the table in SCC III: 403, (derived from *Lunheng* via de Saussure), in which Shitige is correlated with the chronogram *zi*, and where different lunar lodge correlations for the Jovian Years are given as well. The long commentary of WYZ (HNZ 3:25b–26a) addresses somewhat inconclusively the issue of the chronogram-correlations of the Jovian Years given in 3.XXXIII; it is true that there is something odd about them.

6   單 is usually pronounced *shan* or *dan*; GY specifies the pronunciation *ming* in this instance. Needham, SCC III: 403 gives the pronunciation of this year as *tan-o*, i.e., *dan'e*.

3.XXXIV

2 Another possible reading of *chang zou suo bu sheng* 常徙所不勝 would be, "If it should move constantly, then the place (to which it moves) will not be victorious." The meaning is not very clear, no matter how one translates this line.

7 Read *yue* 曰 in place of *ri* 日.

9 Read *gang* 綱 as *gang* 剛, "unyielding." The meaning here is that the odd-numbered Heavenly Stems (*jia, bing, wu, geng,* and *ren*) are "unyielding" (i.e., yang); the even-numbered Heavenly Stems are "pliant" (i.e., yin). See line 20. The reference to "doubling" here applies only to the first instance: one doubled is two.

10 The line reads *zou suo bu sheng xing*; the first four characters are perhaps transposed from line 2 above, while *xing* 刑 is a fragment of a now-missing phrase; the line as it stands makes little sense.

19 "Follow in accord with this," adopting GY's gloss of *xi* 襲 as meaning *he* 和.

21–26 These lines follow the wording of the chart on p. 3:31a, except that here the word *si* 死, "dies," is used whereas the chart reads *lao* 老, "grows old".

31 Read *qi* 擊 as *ji* 繋, "suspended." But cf. 3.XLI.4.

3.XXXVI

1 Read *liang* 良 in place of *liang* 涼, as suggested by YY and LWD.

9 GY glosses *kang* 康 as *huang* 荒, "wasteland," but all subsequent commentators vehemently disagree. The consensus is that *kang* should read *sheng* 盛, "flourishing," but I see no reason to emend the text here at all. *Kang* in the sense of "repose" seems to fit the context perfectly well.

3.XXXVII

1 WNS argues that the territorial allotment of *gui* should be *Zhao* 趙 rather than *Yue* 越, on the basis of a parallel passage in the *Kaiyuan zhanjing*.

3.XXXVIII

7 WNS suggests that the first *sheng* 勝, "victory," should be emended to read *zhi* 制, "control." This is plausible but not necessary.

3.XL

12 ZKJ notes that the text here reads *Dai* 代 for the territorial allotment of *renzi*, as in the *Daozang* edition of HNZ; other editions read *Zhao* 趙. Dai is correct. All of the places

named here are "outer" states or tribal areas; Zhao must have been one of the "central states" named in the (mutilated) line 13 list that follows, but which cyclical pair it belongs with can no longer be determined.

13   It is possible by inference to restore the two missing stem-branch pairs here (i.e., *wuchen* and *yisi*), but as WNS points out, there is no way of knowing which states were assigned to which pairs in the six cases where the names are missing.

15   It is not clear what the "Lesser Year" (*xiao sui* 小歲) here is. Possibilities include the solar year (in contrast to the twelve-year Jovian Year), the lunar year as opposed to the tropical year, or the 360-day year of the twenty-four seasonal nodes (in contrast to the 365¼ day calendar year). The last seems most likely; cf. 3.XIX.1 above, "The handle of the Dipper makes the Lesser Year."

3.XLI

6   *Xiang zuo* 相錯, "mutual alternation." For *zuo* see GSR #798j.

12   "Heaven has nine layers"; compare the ninefold wall of Kunlun in 4.III.3 below.

16   The text reads "twelve limbs (*zhi* 肢) to regulate the 360 joints (*jie* 節)," but this is obviously an error for "twelve joints" and "360 bones."

17   Read *sheng* 生 as *xing* 性.

3.XLII

This whole section seems mildly textually corrupt; WNS suggests various emendations on the basis of parallel passages in TPYL, but they do not seem to help much. This section may also be a later appendage to HNZ 3 rather than part of the original treatise. Its vaguely Mohist-sounding system of grain rationing does not fit very well with the philosophical stance of HNZ 3 as a whole.

The entry for each of the Jupiter Cycle years ends with a formula, "branch x in stem y is called zz." The appellations are bizarre sounding and can be translated only approximately; they seem to be a kind of fortune teller's mumbo jumbo (perhaps originally in a non-Chinese language), impenetrable to the uninitiated.

3   For *dou* 斗 ("peck"), read *sheng* 升 ("pint") as in TPYL. A *dou* is a dry measure holding ten catties of rice—far too much for a daily household ration, much less a daily reduction thereof. A *sheng* is ⅒ of a *dou*.

16   The text reads "*zi* in *gui*," but this must be an error for "*zi* in *jia*." The sequence of "branches in stems" is 3 in 1; 4 in 2; 5 in 3; . . . 12 in 10; the eleventh in the series should thus be 1 in 1, i.e., *zi* in *jia*.

17   For the same reason given immediately above, the missing appellation at the end of this line must read "*chou* in *yi* is called. . . ."

CHAPTER 4

4.I

1 Omit *xing* 形 in this line; it has been erroneously duplicated from the chapter's title. Compare the opening lines of SHJ 6.

　　This line echoes a similar phrase in *Zhuangzi* 25: *sifang zhi nei, liuhe zhi li* 四方之內六合之裏.

4 WNS argues that *ji* 極 should read *zhu* 柱; the cosmological meaning is the same in either case.

5 The passage beginning with this line and continuing through 4.II.7 is taken directly from LSCQ 13.

8 The name of Shen 神 Province echoes Zou Yan's name for China in his nine-continents scheme, *Chixian shenzhou* 赤縣神州.

9 The appellation *wu* 沃, "fertile," appears again in 4.VI.18, the "fertile wilderness," and in 4.XV.7 and 4.XVI.35, the "Fertile[-land] People."

11 I.e., *bing* 丼 (= 並), usually "parallel" or "united," but here according to GY a synonym for *cheng* 成, "ripe, ready."

15 *Yin* 隱, i.e., the place where yang qi is stored up in anticipation of the next repetition of the annual cycle.

16 GY glosses *shen* 申 as *fu* 復.

22 I find no satisfactory translation for *Juqu* 具區, "utensil place"; this is perhaps a Chinese transcription of a non-Chinese word. The name appears again below in 4.VI.5.

33 On the Black River, Eduard Erkes, in "Das Weltbild des Huai-nan-tze," p. 40, n. 56 remarks, "The Black River in high antiquity was the western boundary of Yungzhou (雍州 or 雝州) [one of the nine provinces of Yu], and thus of the known world. . . . It is mentioned in 'Yu gong,' see *Shujing* III,1,71 and III,2,6. SHJ 11:2a also mentions a Black River Mountain and locates it in the 'Flowing Sands' of the Western Gobi."

　　Richard Wilhelm, in *Frühling und Herbst des Lü Bu we*, p. 492, n. 17, implies an identification of the Black River with the Mekong.

4.II

2 The text reads *shui dao baqian li tong gu qi ming chuan liu bai* 水道八千里通谷其名川六百. Erkes translates ("Weltbild," pp. 40–41), "Die Wasserstrassen [messen zusammen] 8000 meilen. Von ihren bekannten Flusstälern und berühmten Strömen gibt es 600."

　　The HNZ text is obviously garbled here. LSCQ reads *liu* 六 for *qi* 其, which helps a little but not much. My translation is based on the assumption that the text must originally have read something like . . . *tong liu gu. Qi ming chuan you liubai* 通六谷其名川有六百.

8–9 My translation here is an attempt to grapple with a hopelessly garbled sentence. WNS writes, "The *bai* 百 of *sanbai ren* 三百仞, the *li* 里 of *wushi li* 五十里, and the *yuan* 淵 of *jiu yuan* 九淵 are all superfluous characters. This should read *hongshui yuan shu ze*

304

sanren yishangzhe gong you. . . . 鴻水淵藪自三仞以上者共有⋯" This would yield, in translation, "There are 233,559 floods, chasms and marshes that are over three *ren* [in size]." This is a smoother sentence in both Chinese and English, but it still does not seem to make very much sense.

4.III

1   *Xi tu* 息土, "expanding earth," here clearly a magical substance. The same term is used again below in 4.IX.9 in an ordinary sense to mean "fertile soil."

3   YY suggests that this line should be understood to mean "11,000 li long and 114 paces, two feet and six inches thick." He adds, "Of course the numbers are excessive. Perhaps the passage contains omissions or errors."

4   These plants are described as being five *xun* 尋 tall; GY says this means thirty-five feet (*chi* 尺).

7   Crimson Trees, *jiang shu* 絳樹, seem to be otherwise unknown. LSCQ 14 and SHJ 17 mention vermilion trees, *chi shu* 赤樹, which perhaps are the same thing.

10   Omitting the second *li* 里 of *menjian si li, li jian jiu shun* 門間四里里間九純, and reading the second *jian* as *men* 門, as suggested by YY.

     The phrase "one *shun* equals fifteen feet" is undoubtedly from a line of commentary that has crept into the text.

12   Read *peng* 彭 for *heng* 橫, as suggested by GY. LWD cites the TPYL version of this line, which reads *yu heng shou busiyao wei qi xibei zhi yu* 玉橫受不死藥維其西北之隅; my translation is based on this version.

     Hong Xingzu's subcommentary to *Chu ci*, "Tian wen" 43 (SBBY ed., 3:7a) quotes this line as *wu heng* 五橫, but *wu* would seem clearly to be a scribal error for *yu* in that case.

     An entirely different possibility is that *heng* 橫 should be understood to mean *heng* 衡. This would give a completely different complexion to the line, which would then mean, "The northwest corner is the weft-cord of the jade cross-piece." This takes us out of the realm of elixirs of immortality, and into the realm of astronomy. The term "jade cross-piece" has been interpreted to mean the image of the Dipper on the heaven plate of a cosmograph; see Cullen, "Some Further Points on the Shih," p. 39. The term "weft-cord" is used in HNZ 3 to mean one of several diametral lines across the celestial circle. So this line could conceivably refer to the northwest, the direction of Mt. Kunlun and Mt. Buzhou, in connection with the type of astrology associated with the use of the cosmograph. For more on the term *yuheng* 玉衡 and its companion term *xuanji* 璇機, the "rotating device," see Needham et al., *The Hall of Heavenly Records*, pp. 20–21, n. 11.

13   For *beimen* 北門 read *xibeimen* 西北門.

     For *buzhou* 不周 as "non-circumscribing," see 3.XII.16 and the commentary to section 3.XII. *Bohutong* 24 (see Tjan Tjoe Som, *Po Hu T'ung*, vol. 2, pp. 534–35) glosses *buzhou* as *bujiao* 不交, "not connected," a reference to the gap in the northwest caused by the fight between Gong Gong and Zhuan Xu.

14 "Broad Palace," *qinggong* 傾宮; GY says that *qing* means "an area of 100 *mou* 畝." For *fantong* 樊桐 read *fanlin* 樊林 as in SHJ 12.

GY's commentary on the Changhe Gate 閶闔 is of interest: "The Changhe Gate is the gate for beginning an ascent to Heaven. The Gate of Heaven is the gate of the Palace of Purple Tenuity [i.e., the circumpolar stars] where the High Thearch dwells." See also the etymology of Changhe given in *Shiji* 25, the "Treatise on the Pitchpipes": "*Chang* means 'a guide' (*chang* 倡); *he* means 'to shut away' (*zang* 藏). This means that the yang qi lead the myriad creatures to concealment in the Yellow Springs." In other words, the world-pillar that leads upward to the Gate of Heaven also leads downward to the abyss.

15 "Carved-Out Garden," *subu* 疏圃. *Su* means something like "dredged, excavated, scooped-out." This would seem to imply some connection with the engineering works of Yu the Great in the Kunlun region. Erkes takes *su* as equivalent to *su* 疏, "herb," and translates this as "Krautergarten."

18 WNS suggests emending *danshui* 丹 to *baishui* 白水, on the basis of parallels in other texts. His arguments are plausible but not compelling, and I have decided to translate the text in its unemended version.

4.IV

1 This "Yellow River" is not necessarily the same as the actual Yellow River (*he* 河) of North China; see commentary.

3 This sentence is obviously corrupt. WYZ notes that two sentences have become conflated here; they need to be separated and the second moved to its proper place later in the text, as follows:

(1) The phrase *chi shui zhi dong* 赤水之東 is superfluous (from commentary mingled into the text) and should be dropped.

(2) The sentence *ruoshui chu (ze) qiongshi ru yu liusha* 弱水出（自）窮石入流沙 is out of place here. I have moved it to the end of Section XVII below; see 4.XVII.36.

(3) The phrase *ruoshui chu qi xinan chu* 弱水出其西南陬 is restored here, maintaining parallelism with lines 1, 2, and 4.

(4) WYZ argues that the phrase *yupo* 餘波 here is superfluous and should be dropped; there seems no compelling reason to do so, however, and I have left the phrase stand. He also suggests that the phrase *zhi yu Heli* 至于合黎 could be dropped; I have let it stand.

The restored text here thus reads, *Ruoshui chu qi xinan chu, zhi yu Heli, yupo jie liusha nan zhi nan hai.* 弱水出其西南陬至于合黎餘波絕流南至南海.

The "Flowing Sands" are conventionally taken to mean the Gobi; that might be so, but in general it is a mistake to look for too much correspondence between the mythscape of Kunlun and genuine geography.

4 *Yang* 洋 is also sometimes written 養, 漾, or 漾, making it clear that this word is used for phonetic value and is not translatable.

4.V

3　WNS suggests inserting *zhi shan* 之山 after *xianbu* 縣圃.

11　Note the use of the term *gai* 蓋 in this line, with its clear connotations of the *gaitian* cosmological system.

4.VI

1　The word *xun* 純, defined in 4.III.10 above to mean "fifteen feet," here certainly has the meaning "borders."

2　GY glosses *yun* 殞 as *yuan* 遠; LWD cites additional references in favor of defining it as *yan* 埏, "outer boundary." In any case the meaning here is clear.

3　Reversing the order in the text of *wutong* 無通 and *daze* 大澤, to preserve parallelism with the lines that follow, as suggested by YY.

4　Reading *sha* 沙 for *shao* 小, as suggested by LWD. GY's explanation, that "In the east there is a lot of water, therefore it is called Few Seas," does not make sense.

5　GY emends *yuan* 元 to *xue* 穴; ZKJ suggests *wu* 兀. I follow the suggestion of WNS, who reads this as *kang* 亢, the old form of *hang* 沆, "mist."

7　Cinnabar Marsh has already been encountered in 4.IV.2 above; see also the "cinnabar water" of 4.3.18 and the Cinnabar River of 4.XVII.22.

9　I use the conventional translation of Bactria for *Daxia* 大夏, but note Haloun's cautionary remarks (in *Seit wann kannten die Chinesen die Tocharer oder Indogermanen Überhaupt*, esp. p. 136) that Daxia was an old geographical term in China, and its pre-Han location cannot be determined with any accuracy.

12　*Hong* 紘 = *hong* 宏, "outlying region." GY takes it as equivalent to *wei* 維, and says "the *wei* spread across heaven and earth and serve as their measuring-gauge." *Wei* is used throughout HNZ 3 to mean the diametral "weft-cords" of the celestial circle.

13　Harmonious Hill, where phoenixes sing and dance, appears again below in 4.XVI.9, where it is also located in the northeast.

14　"Mulberry Wilderness" in the east suggests a connection with the Fusang tree and the Hollow Mulberry tree.

17　GY says, "*Jiaoyao* 焦僥 is a country of pygmies who do not exceed three feet in height."

　　For "Fiery Earth," compare *Chu ci*, "Da zhao" 10, which says, "Oh soul, do not go to the south. In the south there are blazing fires, and writhing cobras." Erkes, "Weltbild," p. 52, n. 128 adduces Conrady's opinion that "fiery earth" refers to the blazing gas wells of Sichuan. Needham, SCC III: 610, describes these wells and says that knowledge of them predates the Han.

　　Still, this seems superfluous. The important point is that in HNZ's cosmology the south *should be* blazing hot, just as the north is necessarily dark and icebound.

18　GY says that *wu* 沃 here means *bai* 白, "white," but his reasoning is based on five phase theory and has no philological basis. "Fertile" (*wu*) fits perfectly well here.

19　The "Place of Sands" is probably the Gobi. See also 4.IV.3 above.

26 GY comments, "The southeastern gate of every walled city under heaven is called Yang Gate."

29 The location of Changhe in the west here reflects a persistent confusion in Han cosmological texts over whether Changhe was located in the west or in the northwest (with Kunlun).

4.VII

9 Mt. Daiyue 岱嶽 is the same as Mt. Tai 泰, the famous sacred peak in Shandong.

4.VIII

9 WNS argues for reading *zhang* 障, "dikes," as *shui* 水, "water," reasoning that *zhang* represents a transposition and then a miswriting of *ze* 澤 from the previous line. But "dikes" fits the meaning of this passage better than "water"; the idea is one of sympathetic magic: blockage produces blockage. Erkes translates *zhangqi* as "Fieberluft" (feverish winds), a possible reading but unlikely here.

11 For the meaning of *long* 癃 as "paralysis of the legs," see Yu Yunxiu 余雲岫, *Gudai jibing ming hou suyi* 古代疾病名候疏義, p. 148. More commonly *long* means "infirmity," or in the phrase *longbi* 癃閉, "inability to pass urine." Erkes, "Weltbild," p. 57, translates this as "Hühnerbrüstige" (chicken-breasted), apparently as a paired opposite to the following pathological condition, "hunched backs," but otherwise without foundation.

13 Reading *zhong* 腫 as *zhong* 尰, as suggested by WNS.

19 Reading *wang* 尪 in place of *kuang* 狂, "madness," as suggested by WNS.

20 *Ren* 仁 could also be understood in a medical sense here, meaning "(hyper-)sensitivity to touch," but the common meaning of "benevolence" (my "human fellow-feeling") is probably intended here, to contrast with "covetousness" in the following line.

22 *Li* 利 here is used in the sense of "haste"; Erkes, "Weltbild" p. 58 translates it as "heftige," which conveys the meaning nicely.

28 *Busi zhi yao* 不死之藥 here seems more likely to have a botanical than an alchemical meaning: plants that do not die (tropical evergreens), in contrast to the unmelting ice of the north.

30 Another possible reading would be, "The west (is strewn with) mutilated corpses; sleeping, they dwell constantly in dreams. . . ." ZKJ suggests that these may be the same as the headless *xingtian* 形天 people mentioned in SHJ.

4.IX

3 The text beginning with this line and continuing to HNZ 4:10a:1, i.e., most of Section IX and all of Sections X and XI, is also included in DDLJ 81, with minor changes in wording and with the paragraphs in different order; DDLJ also includes three final paragraphs not found in HNZ 4. DDLJ 81 is translated and discussed in Needham, SCC II: 271–72.

6 YY suggests that *fei* 肥, "fat," should be emended to *cui* 脆, "delicate," to preserve the

opposition of meaning with the previous line. The suggestion is plausible but not compelling.

11 I have transposed this line to here, where it fits well, from 4:10a:8 below, where it is obviously out of place.

13 *Hui* 慧 obviously cannot have its usual meaning of "clever, intelligent" here; its less common meaning, "sensitive" (i.e., sensitive to touch; capable of having sensations) must apply. YY suggests emending *er hui* 而慧 to *er buxi* 而不息, "and do not breathe," as in the TPYL version.

16 In the opinion of WNS this line must originally have read *shi sang* 食桑 rather than *shi ye* 食葉.

4.X

19 Erkes, in "Weltbild," p. 62, translates " . . . verwandeln sich die Insekten nach 8 Monaten in Vögel und Fische" (after eight months insects metamorphose into birds and fish). This is quite possibly correct; HNZ gives many instances of such metamorphoses. The problem is that the phrase "birds and fish" also clearly belongs with the first line of the following section (4.XI.1). Possibly *niao yu* 鳥魚 originally appeared twice in succession in the text (see 4:9b:1), but the reduplication was omitted by a later editor.

4.XI

1 Omitting the second *yin* in 4:9b:1, as suggested by WNS. This is mainly to produce a smoother reading; it does not greatly alter the sense of the passage.

7 Cicadas, like sages, were supposed by the ancient Chinese to live on a diet of dew. They were auspicious insects and, because of their conspicuous emergence from the pupal to the adult stage, symbols of the rebirth of the *hun* soul into a state of immortality; thus the custom of placing jade cicadas in the mouths of the dead as part of burial rites in ancient China.

13 Erkes, in "Weltbild," p. 62, n. 191, points out Indian parallels to this belief about dentition.

13–15 These lines are open to different interpretations, particularly in the phrases *er wu qian* 而無前 and *er wu hou* 而無後. The most obvious translation, followed by Erkes, is " . . . are fat, but not in the forequarters," and "are fat, but not in the hindquarters." GY and ZKJ both point to the fact that hornless animals tend to rise from a reclining position front end first, while horned animals (ungulates) stand up hindquarters first. The first interpretation, regarding the distribution of fat, does not correspond to any observable fact of nature; the second one, while correct as to natural fact, requires either a most improbable interpretation of *wu qian* and *wu hou* or, with ZKJ, an equally improbable emendation of the text to *dui qian* 兌前 and *dui hou* 兌後.

My translation here is based on Needham's ingenious translation of these lines as they appear in DDLJ 81; see Needham, SCC II: 271. Needham's successful reconstruction of this passage depends on an implied parallelism in lines 13–15

> (13): *Dai jue zhe . . . wu shang chi* 無角者…無上齒
>
> (14): *Wu jue zhe gao er wu qian [chi]* 無角者膏而無前 [齒]
>
> (15): *You jue zhe zhi er wu hou [chi]* 無角指 [脂] 而無後 [齒]

4.XII

2   My translations "appropriate" here (in lines 2–7) and "suitable" below (in lines 8–14) both translate the same Chinese word, *yi* 宜. The variation is solely for the sake of smoothness in the English version.

3   "Black stone" often means "slate," but the term might be generic here.

4.XIII

4   "Channelled to" translates *tong* 通, a word with more powerful connotations in Chinese than perhaps the English term conveys. Here and in other occurrences of the term below, the implication is that channels of qi run from the bodily orifices to the dominant sensory organ.

11   For *ze* 眦 read *ze* 眦 (= 眥), "eyelids," as in SBBY.

15   Compare 4.VIII.16, "The qi of heat produces many cases of early death."

19   This sentence is unclear and possibly textually corrupt; the commentaries of GY and YY do nothing to clarify it. But the general sense of the passage is clear: the people of the west are misshapen and ugly.

26   For *han shui* 寒水 read *han bing* 寒冰, as in SBBY and as suggested by WNS.

32   An alternative punctuation of this line would yield the meaning "are stupid but longer-lived than birds or beasts." WNS suggests that the phrase "birds and beasts" should be dropped altogether.

    4.VIII.17 also makes a connection between cold and longevity.

4.XV

See the commentary to 4.XV for the identification of the thirty-six countries listed in this section and for variant readings of some of the place names found in SHJ, etc.

22   "Tongue-tied," i.e., *fan she* 反舌; these people supposedly have their tongues backwards in their mouths, so they are mute. Compare the *fan she* "turn-tongue" bird in 5.V.14, which however is not mute, but rather is able to imitate the songs of other birds.

4.XVI

See the commentary to 4.XVI for identification and discussion of these (mostly mythical) persons and places.

3 For "two," read "twenty-eight," as in SHJ 6.

 Erkes, "Weltbild," p. 69, punctuates this line with a full stop after *dihou*. Thus his translation reads "Kaiser und Fürst spielen. Nachts sind sie südwestlich davon"; the second clause is virtually meaningless. In this line *hou* 候 must have the force of a verb, "to watch over."

7 *Qing* 青 (usually "bluegreen") means "grey" when it is applied to the color of horses and cattle, and accordingly I translate *qingma* as Greyhorse. GY takes this as the name of a country. For *qingma* 青馬, SHJ 8 and 9 read *qingniao* 青鳥, "bluegreen bird."

8 The identity of the "sweet *cha* 樝 tree" in line 8 is uncertain; it may be a kind of hawthorn.

14 Chariot pole (*Xuanyuan* 軒轅) is an appellation of Huangdi, the Yellow Thearch; see 3.XVII.11 where that name designates one of the "six departments" (diagonals drawn across the celestial circle).

16 *Tanggu* 暘谷 is an alternate form of *tanggu* 湯谷.

17 *You Song* 有娀 [or *Rong* 戎] is sometimes understood to be a verb-object phrase, "the possessor (= lord) of Song."

25 The reading *xuanshao* 玄燿 is tentative; the same characters, read as *xuanyao*, would mean "Dark Glorious." Also tentative is the parenthetical phrase "(is near)"; the text says only *xuanshao buzhou*, and it may be that this is an alternative name for Mt. Buzhou. In 4.VI.30 "Dark Capital Gate" *youdu zhi men* 幽都之門 is given as another name for Mt. Buzhou, and *xuanshao* in turn may be another version of that one.

4.XVII

3 ZKJ says that *Ju* 雎 is a mistake for *Luo* 洛, which was formerly written *Luo* 雒. But WNS rejects this; both *Luo* 洛 and *Luo* 雒 appear in this list below (lines 10 and 16). Erkes, "Weltbild," p. 74, apparently misreads *Ju* as *Sui* 雎, which appears two lines below (line 5); on the basis of this apparent redundancy he is inclined to follow ZKJ. But *Ju* and *Sui* are clearly meant as the names of two different rivers here.

 Part of this confusion stems from a question about the source of the Ju River. There are two mountains named *Jing* 荆, one in the south, one in the north (*Zhongguo gujin diming dazidian* # 939).

5 *Shuijing* 5 gives Mt. Liang 梁 as the source of the Sui River.

6–7 GY says that these two rivers arise in Shangtang 上黨 (in north-central China), join together, flow through Wei 魏, and merge with the Qing 清 River. See also the commentary of ZKJ on the mountains named here.

8 This Qi 濟 River (also in line 11 below) is said to be the same as the Qi 沛 River in 4.XII.9 above.

9 Neither of the mountains named Mt. Tai (臺, 台) here is the same as the famous sacred Mt. Tai 泰 in Shandong.

11 See the extensive commentaries on this line in HNZ 4:14b:2–8. The problem is that there are two rivers named Wen 汶; the one that flows into the Qi River does not originate at

Mt. Fuqi, but rather east of Mt. Tai in Shandong. The Wen River that originates at Mt. Fuqi is a tributary of the Wei 維 River.

18   Mentioned also in line 35 below. See note to line 11 above.

22   There are several rivers in China named *Danshui* 丹水, Cinnabar River. Which one is meant here is unclear.

23   Reading *Pan* 般 for *Gu* 股, as suggested by WYZ.

24   WYZ and ZKJ both point out that this line is defective, and conflates what should be two lines. Guo Pu's commentary to SHJ 3:14b quotes HNZ 4 as saying, "The Bo 薄 River issues from Mt. Xianyu." Thus this line must originally have been two: *Hao qu [X X]. [Bo qu] Xianyu* 鎬出□□ [薄出] 鮮于.

28–29   Here I follow the reconstruction suggested by WYZ. *Jiejihe* 結給合 (GY: "a name") in the text makes no sense as a place name. WYZ points out that *Jiezhu* 結紐 (read *ji* 給 as *zhu* 紐) is another name for *Longshan* 龍山, "Dragon Mountain." Thus the text here must originally have read, *Jin qu Ziezhu [comm. inserted into text: yiming Longshan]. He qu Fengyang* 晉出結紐 [一名龍山] 合出封羊.

33   *Hutuo* 呼沱 is usually written 滹沱. ZKJ says that *Luping* 魯平 should read *Luhu* 魯乎.

34   The *Nituyuan* 泥塗淵 River is not identifiable, and there is no way to tell whether this name represents one river or three (i.e., the Ni, the Tu, and the Yuan).

35   ZKJ says that *Shi* 濕 is a mistake for *Lei* 灅. Erkes, "Weltbild," p. 76, takes this as the name of a single river, the Weishi.

36   This line has been extracted from the garbled passage in 4:3b:7–8 (4.IV.3 above) and inserted here, where it belongs.

4.XVIII

9   YY argues convincingly that *Ba* 突 should be written *Ba* 胈, meaning "fine body hair" of the sort that Yu the Great is said to have worn from his shanks in the course of his exertions. This fits well with the other lines in this section; "all feathered creatures," "all hairy creatures," etc. invite the parallel, "all creatures with fine body hair."

I find no satisfactory translation for *Ruojun* 若菌, which overtly means "like-a-mushroom." SHJ 15 says "there are small people called the Jun People"; perhaps that line is related to this name. If there is a connection between "small people" and "like-a-mushroom," Ruojun might signify something like "small and phallic."

18   My translation "Scaly One" reflects the ambiguity of this line. YY argues that *jielin* 介鱗 is a mistake; that *jie* is mistakenly duplicated here from line 20 below, and that a character is missing after *lin*.

Kunkeng 鯤鯁 is apparently the same as the giant Kun Fish in *Zhuangzi* 1.

24–27   These lines are garbled beyond recovery. The commentators ignore them, and when that happens one can generally assume that they either regard something as obvious or as tangled beyond their grasp. The second assumption must hold true here. For a somewhat desperate attempt to sort these lines out, see my earlier version of this translation in "Topography and Cosmology in Early Han Thought," p. 170, n. 444.

29 The name Sun-Climber (*riping* 日馮) has connotations of the Fusang tree of 4.V.8. "Brightness-Blocker" similarly recalls the Jian tree of 4.V.11 above, which "forms a canopy over the center of the world."

31 Reading *zhaoyao* 招搖, "quivering leaves," for *genpa* 根拔 (or 芨), "rooted stem," which (as WNS suggests) has probably been transposed to here from the following line.

32 Reading *pa* 拔 as *pa* 芨. *Pa* 拔 means "to weed, to uproot," and "Root-plucker" would translate the unemended version of this line, but the context seems to require something like "Rooted Stem."

33 *Chengruo* 成若; "Established Ruo[-tree]" would be a possible translation; in any case this term has echoes of the Ruo tree of 4.V.12 above.

36 GY says that *jue long* 屈龍 is the same as *you long* 游龍, as in *Shiji*, Mao Ode 84. "Swimming Dragon" fits the context here very well. Another possible reading would be *jian long* 潜龍, "Latent Dragon."

36 *Ronghua* 容 (= 蓉) 華, according to GY, is the same as *furong* 芙蓉. Both *fu* and *rong* usually mean "hibiscus," but the name of an aquatic plant seem to be called for here. Bretschneider, in *Botanicum Sinicum*, vol. 2, no. 99, identifies *furong* as a kind of lotus, *Nelumbium*. So "lotus" seems like a safe, if slightly tentative, translation here.

37–38 This passage is textually corrupt. WNS says that *ping* 萍, "duckweed," is synonymous with *biao* 薸 (= 瀌), and that all three occurrences of the word *ping* should be eliminated here. I prefer to retain the first, as a compound, *pingcao*.

   I prefer to reconstruct here on the basis of parallelism with the previous paragraphs; my translation is based on this reconstruction:

   [Ping]cao sheng [shu] fucao. Fan bugen pazhe sheng yu [shu] fucao [萍] 草生 [庶] 浮草几不根芨者生於 [庶] 浮草.

4.XIX

1 *Jue* 缺, glossed as yellow jade, must mean some kind of translucent yellow stone. The word is sometimes translated as realgar, which is yellow but not translucent. Amber would seem to be a plausible candidate here.

2 Consolidating the text here to read *jue wubai sui sheng huang hong* 缺五百歲生黃澒, to preserve the parallelism with the following four paragraphs.

5 *Jiyang* 激揚, "arising and spreading out"; my translation "rising to a crescendo" attempts to convey the orgasmic implications of this phase.

7 The text reads *qing* 清, "clear"; this is an obvious error for *qing* 青, "bluegreen."

12 *Zhuang* 壯, "vigorous," in contrast to *pin* 牝 in line 25 below. WNS emends *zhuang* to *mu* 牡, in which case the contrast between lines 12 and 25 would be not "vigorous-passive" but "male-female." Either way, the contrast is between maximum yang/south/vermilion and maximum yin/north/black.

CHAPTER 5

5.I

7   The text reads *luzhong taicou* 律中太蔟; the *zhong* signifies that the note is within the primary octave.

15   LSCQ reads "he mounts a *luan* 鸞 ("phoenix") carriage drawn by azure dragon(-horses)."

17   This formulaic line is standard for each of the twelve months in HNZ 5; it is absent in the LSCQ version of the "Yueling."

5.II

2   *Hu* 弧, "Bow," is a constellation south of the lunar lodge Spirit-Bearer. *Jianxing* 建星, "Establishing-Stars," is a six-star constellation north of the lunar lodge Southern Dipper.

22   Read *ju* 句 as *gou* 苟, "young sprout."

23   *Yuan* 元, glossed by GY as *shan zhi chang* 善之長, "auspicious."

27   A *jun* 鈞 equals thirty catties (*jin* 觔); a *shi* 石 equals 120 catties. See 3.XXXI.31–35. A *dou* 斗 ("peck") is a dry measure holding ten catties of rice; see 3.XLII.2. For *cheng* 稱, read *tong* 桶, "pail," a dry measure holding six catties of rice. This correction of weights and measures is carried out twice a year at the solstices; see also 5.VIII.35 below.

30   The "barbarians" here are the *Rong* 戎.

5.III

21   For *wu* 烏, read *yan* 焉 (= *yu* 於), as in LSCQ.

24   Read *ju* as *gou*, as in II.22 above.

26   *Ming shi* 名士; by the late Warring States and early Han *shi* was more likely to mean "scholar" than "knight," though in either case there is an implication of aristocratic virtue.

30   *Yu* 虞, "forester."

32   For *pu* 撲, read *po* 樸 ("simple, unadorned"), as suggested by WNS. For *qu* 曲 read *qu* 笛 ("cocoon frame"); for *qin* 親 read *jiu* 就 ("go to"); for *sheng* 省 read *zhe* 者 (particle); for *quan* 勸 read *guan* 觀 ("oversee"); all as in TPYL and as suggested by LWD.

5.IV

2   *Wunü* 婺女, "Widow," is an asterism north of the tenth lunar lodge, Serving-Maid.

20   The term Mingtang is used to mean both the entire structure and (as here) its south-central chamber.

28   *Chang mai* 嘗麥, "sacrificial wheat." LSCQ 4 includes a line (missing in the HNZ text) previous to this one that says "the farmers present their (newly-harvested) wheat." This is

what the ruler eats for his sacrifical meal. The word *chang* is associated with sacrifices for good harvests.

33   *Xiu cao* 秀草, "flourishing plants": the implication is that plants would spring up too quickly but then wither before bearing fruit or grain.

5.V

13   "Lesser Heat": fourteenth of the twenty-four solar nodes, in the order as given in 3.XVIII above.

14   *Fanshe* 反舌, "turn-tongue," a kind of bird. See commentary to 5.V.

17   *Guan* 管, "reed-pipe," a straight bamboo flute (like the Japanese *shakuhachi*).

20   Mingtang Great Chamber = the Mingtang south-central hall of the Mingtang building.

24   GY glosses *zhi* 雉 as "a young chicken" (it usually means "pheasant"); WNS says that *zhi* is simply a mistake for *ji* 雞.

28   Read *zheng* 正 for *zheng* 政, as in LSCQ.

33   GY identifies the *banxia* 半夏 only as "a medicinal plant." Of the *mujin* 木堇, he says that "it is a shrub whose flowers bloom in the morning and fall in the evening. It reaches a height of five or six feet. Its leaves are similar to the pomegranate; it blooms in this month. It can be used for kindling. . . . (other names) are 'morning-born' and *shun* 蕣 (hibiscus)." Legge, *Li Chi*, vol. 2, p. 275, calls it the *Hibiscus syriacus*.

5.VI

The HNZ differs from LSCQ and LJ in treating the section for the fifth month as a separate and artificial "midsummer" season; those two versions of the "Yueling" text have a "supplementary" midsummer section at the end of this section. The older scheme of following the natural order of the four seasons is reflected in *Guanzi* 40, "Si shi 四時" (The Four Seasons), which says, "The center is called (phase) earth. The power of earth circulates among (all) four seasons." Thus in the pre-Han development of five phase theory there was no perceived need for a separate season assigned to phase earth.

5   Naked = hairless, i.e., human beings. The HNZ text has *luo* 蠃 ("a small wasp"; "a mollusk"), which is homophonous with *luo* 倮 ("naked"). Five phase theory calls for the "hairless" group of animals here, correlated with midsummer, center, etc.

11   *Liu* 霤 means "drain-hole" or "rain-spout"; see GSR #1114y. Another possible meaning is "smoke-hole" or "chimney."

17   The expected information about the musical instruments that they play is missing here.

22   *Pangren* 滂人, "heavy-rain men," which GY glosses as "officials in charge of springs and marshes." YY says this should read *bengren* 榜人, "oarsmen," but this fits the context less well. *Ru* 入 here can mean "gather in," but also "present at court."

23   *Sijian daifu* 四監大夫, "four inspecting great officials," which I translate as Four Supervisory Lords. GY says that they were in charge of commanderies; the "hundred districts" were subordinate to them.

26 This sentence (not in LSCQ) is somewhat obscure, and my translation is really more of a paraphrase.

27 *Fufu* 黼黻; this would seem to indicate figured embroideries, but GY takes this phrase to mean specific color combinations—black and white and green and red, respectively. Similarly *wenzhang* 文章 would seem to mean "patterned and ornamented"; GY says that this phrase indicates color combinations of black and red and red and white.

31 *Tianyang* 天殃, "heaven(-sent) catastrophes."

32 *Sha* 殺, "killing" the grasses, but here the implication is not a negative one. "Boundary-strips": These benefited from being enriched, because they were used to grow fodder.

34 *Qiang* 牆 ("wall") in this phrase seems out of place. The commentators ignore it.

36 I.e., the first phase of the harvest.

37 *Xin* 梓 is a variant of *zhen* 榛, "hazel.

5.VII

13 The "cold-weather" cicada is perhaps the green cicada of late summer.

14 Migrating birds make easy prey for hawks; this natural phenomenon is used as a sympathetic magic signal to begin the season of criminal punishments.

17 WNS argues that the "white" of "white bells" in this passage is an error of reduplication from the previous line. This is perhaps so, but metals did have color correlates in five phase theory, and silver (= white metal) bells is not implausible here.

18 WNS argues that *ge* 戈 is a mistake for *yue* 戉, "battle-axe," on the grounds that the weapons of the five seasons should all be of different types, and that the halberd is too similar to the weapon of summer, the glaive (both being pole weapons).

22 *Sunqi* 損氣, "baleful qi," emphasizing again the onset of the half-year of increasing severity and injuriousness.

27 LSCQ and LJ begin this line with the phrase "thus making clear (his) love (of virtue) and his hatred (of vice), extending outward. . . .

34 *Jiechong* 介蟲, shelled creatures in general, but here clearly land snails. *Rongbing* 戎兵 could also be translated as "Rong 'barbarian' warriors."

36 Omitting *dong* 冬 ("in winter") in this line; it makes little sense and does not appear in the LSCQ/LJ version.

38 I have not been able to identify the *dong* 棟 ("ridge-pole") as the name of a tree. GSR #1175f identifies it only as "a kind of tree." GY says that phoenixes eat its fruit.

5.VIII

13 The arrival of the cool winds was forecast in 5.VIII.33 above.

14 Cf. 4.IX.2 above, "swallows and geese fly in succession." For the second clause here, LSCQ and LJ have "flocks of birds store up provisions," which with rare exceptions (e.g., the shrike), birds in fact do not do.

25 Piebald oxen cannot be used for sacrifices. Cf. *Zhuangzi* 4, "oxen with white foreheads . . . cannot be offered to the river god."

30 "To store vegetables"; reading *chu* 畜 as *xu* 蓄 and *cai* 采 as *cai* 菜, as in LSCQ.

31 "Plant winter wheat"; omitting *su* 宿, which is superfluous here.

34 This is an observation from nature, not based on cosmological theory. With the force of yin increasing, one would expect more, not less, water.

35 This was also done at the spring equinox; cf. 5.II.27 above.

36 *Li* 理, "regulate"; GY glosses this as *tong* 通, "open up" or "facilitate." LSCQ and LJ have *yi* 易, "make easy"; Legge, *Li Chi*, vol. 2, p. 289 takes this to mean "reduce tariffs" at the barrier gates.

41 Read *zao* 蚤 as *zao* 早.

42 *Wei* 尉, "military officers (of junior grade)."

5.IX

13 Cf. 4.XI.4 above: "At the beginning of winter swallows and sparrows enter the sea and turn into clams."

14 The *chai* 豺, often translated as "wolf" (e.g. GSR #943t), has been conclusively identified by Schafer as the dhole, a small Asian wild dog known for its ferocity and for its habit of hunting in packs. GY says, "It kills small creatures and lays them out facing in the four directions; people say that it 'sacrifices' them." See Edward H. Schafer, "The Chinese Dhole," *Asia Major* 4.1 (new ser., 1991), pp. 1–6. My thanks to David Goodrich for bringing Schafer's article to my attention while this book was in press.

22 *Wu bu wu ru* 無不務入, "none who does not fulfill his duty to bring in (the harvest)"; see line 23.

23 *Wu you xuan chu* 無有宣出 must be parallel to the phrase in line 22; hence, "nothing must be taken out of the storehouse." Legge, *Li Chi*, vol. 2, p. 293 ignores the parallelism and translates "They must not allow anything to remain out in the field"; Wilhelm, in *Frühling und Herbst*, p. 104 retains the parallelism and translates "Es darf nichts den Scheunen entnommen werden."

24 *Zhong zai* 冢宰, "Chief Minister," but possibly this should be understood as a generic title, "great stewards."

25 The *diji* 帝籍 "sacred fields" were fields ritually plowed in person by the ruler; the *shen-cang* 神倉 "spirit-granary" stored the harvest from those fields for use in state sacrifices.

28 The Heavenly Stem *ding* is correlated with phase fire, south, summer, and wind instruments. This musical performance may be a way of encouraging the retention, in autumn, of a small amount of yang influence, lest the yin qi grow too strong too quickly.

31 I take *yu* 與 in the sense of "to approve"; it could also mean "to receive." The general import of the line is the same in either case.

33 "Five weapons": GY says these are the knife, the sword, the spear, the halberd, and the bow, but compare the weapons of the five seasons given in this treatise, i.e., spear, glaive, sword, halberd, and partisan.

317

34 Reading *jing* 旌 ("banners") for *ren* 茬.

39 LSCQ and LJ texts read " . . . all hunker down in (*fu* 俯) their burrows and block up their doors."

42 I follow WNS in reading *hou* 后 as *zhi* 止, as in 5.III.28 above.

46 GY says that a *shi* 師 is a military unit of 2,500 men, while a *zu* 旅 is a unit of 500 men.

47 I have usually followed the old convention of translating *hou* 侯 as "marquis"; here the literal emphasis on archery in the etymology of that term seems worth preserving. Schafer translates this title as "Marksman." It is also possible that in this passage the word is to be taken as a generic term for the feudal aristocracy in general.

5.X

17 Stone chimes were made of dark grey or black stone, and had strong yin connotations. See Edward H. Schafer, "The Yin-Transmitting Lithophones," Part One of his "Two Taoist Bagatelles," p. 1–9 (1981).

18 *Sha* 鍛, "partisan"; see commentary to this section.

19 *Zhi* 彘, used in line 5.X.16 above in its more exact sense of suckling pig, but here as a term for swine in general.

23 "Those who have corruptly abused their positions (*a shang* 阿上). . . ." In the LSCQ and LJ texts this line is at the end of the passage about divination (line 26 below). Legge, in *Li Chi*, vol. 2, p. 298 translates it in that context as "(In this way) all flattery and partizanship in the interpretation of [the oracles] (will become clear) and the crime of the operators be brought home."

29 I.e., making sure that the farmers are harvesting and storing away their crops properly.

31 Reading *jiang* 疆 ("boundary fortifications") in place of *xi* 壐, as in LSCQ and as suggested by WNS. *Wan* 完 means "strengthened" in this context.

32 Terms of mourning, i.e., the number of months of mourning according to the gradations of kinship propinquity.

    Bohou 薄厚, "paltriness and substantiality," i.e., the "quality" of coffins.

33 Read *bei* 痺 as *bei* 卑; *gaobei* 高卑 = "height."

34 *Xiao gong* 効功; Legge, *Li Chi*, vol. 2, p. 299 translates this "prepare a memorial on the work of the artificers." Wilhelm, *Frühling und Herbst*, p. 118 has "die Liste der ausgeführten Arbeiten einzureichen"; he apparently takes *xiao* 効 as *xiao* 效 in its sense of "to announce," thus "announce (which of the workers were) of extraordinary merit."

36 *Da yin zheng* 大飲蒸, "great drinking and steam-cooking," i.e., a great feast. GY glosses *zheng* as "winter feast."

    Gong 公 here should be understood in the sense of "lineage-founder." Legge, *Li Chi*, vol. 2, p. 300 takes *gongshe* in a general sense, "the public altar of the spirits of the land," which weakens the impact of the phrase.

37 *Lao* 勞: GSR 1135a, "(acknowledge somebody's toil:) to recompense."

40 *Wang* 亾 (= 亡) could mean "perish" or "be lost to the state" (through emigration), or both.

42   *Xiao bing* 小兵, "minor warfare" in contrast with the "major warfare" of line 5.XI.35 below; another possible meaning here is "small bands of armed men."

5.XI

14   For the *gandan* 鴉鶪 bird, see the commentary to this section.

26   *Ming* 名, "illustrious," can also mean "named" (cf. 4.II.2 above). Here and below (5.XII.31), the implication is that these are features of the natural landscape having an indwelling god (cf. the Japanese *kami*) that is referred to and worshiped by name.

28   *Ye yu* 野虞, "Superintendant of Uncultivated Lands," but perhaps here a generic term, "wardens and foresters."

31   *Yun* 芸, a flowering plant of some kind, perhaps the rue (*Ruta* sp.).

32   Legge, *Li Chi*, vol. 2, p. 305, translates "offices in which there is no business may be closed."

35   The "ripening" (*cheng* 成) here refers to the drying out of bottle gourds that had been harvested previously. If the season were too damp, they would rot instead of drying.

     "Major warfare" (*dabing* 大兵) contrasts with "minor warfare" in 5.X.42 above.

5.XII

13   Corvids do sometimes reuse old nests augmented with new material. WNS points out that HNZ 3 (3.XVI.36 above) says that this happens in the eleventh month.

21   A similar exorcism takes place in the third month; see 5.III.36 above. GY says that the winter exorcism was to defend against pestilence.

     LSCQ and LJ add that the earthen ox was set out "to lead away the cold qi." GY notes that in the Latter Han this practice was still current among peasants (though he says it took place at the beginning of spring), who placed an earthen ox outside the boundaries of their tilled fields.

22   *Wang shi yu* 往射漁; evidently this refers to shooting fish with bows and barbed arrows. After the line "The Son of Heaven personally goes (to take part)", LSCQ and LJ add the usual formula, missing in the HNZ text, "He then (ritually) tastes the fish, first offering some. . . ."

23   *Ji* 計, "calculate," here probably meaning to plan a schedule for the use of draft animals; but possibly meaning to reckon up how many teams of animals are available for plowing.

     Leisi 耒耜, traditionally the two-pronged digging stick used by Yu the Great, but here clearly meaning the plowshare of an ox-drawn plow.

24   "Abstaining from the use of (instruments of other kinds)"; Legge, *Li Chi*, vol. 2, p. 308, takes *er ba* 而罷 to mean "and with this (the music of the year) is closed." Wind instruments are correlated with summer; perhaps the intent here is to conjure up a bit of yang in the yin last month of winter.

26   *Qiong* 窮, "exhausts," here = "completes."

27   On the basis of the slightly different wording in LSCQ and LJ, Legge (*Li Chi*, vol. 2, p.

308) and Wilhelm (*Frühling und Herbst*, p. 144) take this to mean that the people must engage in agriculture and do nothing else. But the HNZ version clearly implies a cessation of all activity.

28 For *shi* 飾 read *chi* 飭 ("promulgate"), as in LSCQ.

29 Omitting *chu* 剹, transposed by mistake from the following sentence.

31 See 5.XI.26 above.

32 Reading *yao* 祅 as *yao* 妖, as in LSCQ.

33 This refers to pregnant animals as well as to women.

5.XIII

2 "Stele-Stone Mountain" reappears in line 43 below as the eastern limit of the central region.

   "Land of Morning Freshness" is *chaoxian* 朝鮮, later a name for Korea.

3 WNS argues that *qingtu* 青土 should read *qingqiu* 青丘, "Green Hill."

15 *liang* 梁, a wooden sluice-gate on a small waterway.

17 An alternative translation would be "Deal harmoniously with the resentment of those outside the realm [i.e., the 'barbarians']."

21 *Beihu sun* 北戶孫, "north(-facing) doors progeny," i.e., the people of the land of north-facing doors. The land of "reversed" (i.e., north-facing) doors also appears in 4.VI.16; it is so far to the south that doors must face north to catch the sunlight during the day.

   Zhuan Xu is commonly associated with southern lands in Chinese mythology; Zhu Rong in line 23 below is said by GY to be a grandson of Zhuan Xu. Interestingly, Zhuan Xu is also the ruling god of the north (see line 74 below); this is sometimes explained on the grounds that he was exiled to the far north after his battle with Gong Gong.

35 *Hou* 侯, "marquis," "marksman," "archer-lord," etc., but here probably a generic term for the feudal nobility.

36 *Fu* 輔, usually "chariot-pole," but here, by extension, a non-aristocratic aide to an official.

37 The character *liang* 兩 ("two" or "paired") is probably superfluous here. GY says, "the use of *liang* with Heng Shan ["Constancy Mountain"] is unknown"; ZKJ notes that *liang* does not appear in this text as quoted in TPYL.

41 *Xiangguan* 相貫, "thread into each other," = "merge."

43 Stele-Stone Mountain, see 5.XIII.2 above.

52 *Tiao si* 弔死, "send condolences to (the families of) the dead."

53 A similar phrase is found in 5.VI.26 above; the idea is that the "myriad creatures" are being speeded on their journey in the waning half of the year. The year is "returning" to yin; the myriad creatures are symbolically returning as well, to the Yellow Springs—the ultimate yin place that lies at the base of the *axis mundi*.

54 "Sinking Feathers" (*jianyu* 沈羽) is a reference to the Weakwater (see 4.IV.3), on the water of which not even a feather will float.

   Three Dangers Mountain is associated with the Weakwater and with Kunlun; see 4.XVI.21 above.

62 Read *chi* 飭 in place of *shi* 飾, as in line 5.XII.28 above.

72 "Valley Where Ordinances Cease," reading *zhi* 止 in place of *zheng* 正, as suggested by ZKJ. The implication is that the thearch's writ does not run in the furthest reaches of the icebound north.

82 *Sha dang zui* 殺當罪, "kill those who deserve to die."

83 WNS suggests that *guan* 關 should be read as *men* 門 here.

86 Another reading would be *jin ye yue* 禁夜樂, "prohibit music at night," but that is less plausible and fits the context less well than "prohibit the pleasures of the night (*jin ye le*)" i.e., sexual intercourse.

87–88 Here I follow the emendations suggested by WNS: for *sai* 塞 read *su* 索; repeat the phrase *jianren* 姦人; read *de* 德 as *de* 得.

89 The word *zhong* 終 is implied in the phrase *tian jie yi [zhong] ji* 天節已 [終] 幾, "the heavenly nodes have already [completed] their revolution."

5.XIV

27 Reading *yan* 奄 (= 淹) for *xie* 池, on the basis of parallels with *Guanzi, Fangyan,* and *Guangya* pointed out by YY. *Xie* has been transposed to here from line 39 below.

29 *Su* 肅, "severity"; the implication is that there would be excessive sternness in the policies of government.

33 Reading *ke* 格 as *luo* 落, "scattering, dropping of leaves, decline," as suggested by WNS.

5.XV

11 Reading *zheng* 爭 as *zheng* 繪, as suggested by YY.

30 *Wei* 穢, "weed-like, disordered."

46 *Qi* 氣 and *li* 理, echoing the proto-Neo-Confucian cosmology also found in 3.I.

54 For *zu* 足 as "heap up," see GSR #1219a.

60 Or, reading *zheng* 正 for *zheng* 政, "its rules are unerring."

75 "Does not slaughter (*ge* 割)," i.e., the killing is judicious, not wanton or excessive.

77 This duplicates line 32 above, and perhaps should be omitted here.

Reference Notes

NOTES TO CHAPTER 1

1 For the translation of *di* as "thearch," and other questions of terminology, see the section entitled "Conventions Employed in This Book" at the end of this chapter.

2 See my "Two Cultural Styles in Early China: A Speculative Essay," in the companion volume to this work, *Essays on the Huainanzi and Other Topics in Early Chinese Intellectual History.*

3 See for example the opinion of Fung Yu-lan (which most scholars now would reject), that the *Huainanzi*, "like the *Lü-shih Ch'un Ch'iu*, is a miscellaneous compilation of all schools of thought, and lacks unity." *A History of Chinese Philosophy*, trans. Derk Bodde. 2 vols. (Princeton: Princeton University Press, 1952–53), vol. 1, p. 395.

4 Roger Ames, *The Art of Rulership: A Study in Ancient Chinese Political Thought* (Honolulu: University of Hawaii Press, 1983); includes a translation of *Huainanzi* Chapter 9.

5 Charles Le Blanc, *Huai-Nan Tzu: Philosophical Synthesis in Early Han Thought* (Hong Kong: Hong Kong University Press, 1985); includes a translation of *Huainanzi* Chapter 6.

6 Harold D. Roth, *The Textual History of the Huai-nan Tzu*, Association for Asian Studies Monograph 46 (Ann Arbor: Association for Asian Studies, 1992).

7 These issues are explored in Roth, *The Textual History of the Huai-nan Tzu*, pp 16–26.

8 For more on the circumstances under which the *Huainanzi* was written, see Roth, *The Textual History of the Huai-nan Tzu*, chap. 1.

9 Benjamin Wallacker, "Liu An, Second King of Huai-nan," *Journal of the American Oriental Society* 92 (1972): 36–49.

10 Le Blanc, *Huai-Nan Tzu*, p. 83.

11 For a brief account of the composition and compilation of the *Shanhaijing*, see Michael Loewe, *Ways to Paradise: The Chinese Quest for Immortality* (London: George Allen and Unwin, 1979), p. 148. Briefly, it is generally (but not universally) agreed that *Shanhaijing* 1–5, often known as the *Wuzang shanjing*, dates in some form from the Warring States period, possibly incorporating earlier material; that *Shanhaijing* 6–13 date from the Former Han, and were edited by Liu Xiang and published by his son Liu Xin in 6 B.C.E.; and that *Shanhaijing* 14–18 were added to the text only in the fourth century C.E. by Guo Pu, who also wrote the principal commentary to the entire text. Nevertheless, it appears that both

Huainanzi 4 and *Shanhaijing* 14–18 drew on some common body of material, so that even the latest chapters of *Shanhaijing* have their roots in Han or pre-Han times. See also Riccardo M. Fracasso, "Teratoscopy or Divination by Monsters: Being a Study on the *Wu-tsang Shan-ching*," *Hanxue yanjiu/Chinese Studies* [Taipei] I.2 (1983): 657–700.

12 W. Allyn Rickett, *Guanzi: Political, Economic and Philosophical Essays from Early China*, vol. 1 (Princeton: Princeton University Press, 1985), p. 23.

13 Fung Yu-lan, *A History of Chinese Philosophy*, trans. Derk Bodde, vol. 1 (Princeton: Princeton University Press, 1952), p. 383.

14 Wei-ming Tu, "The 'Thought of Huang-Lao': A Reflection on the Lao Tzu and Huang Ti Texts in the Silk Manuscripts of Ma-wang-tui." *Journal of Asian Studies* 39.1 (1979): 95–110. See also K. C. Hsiao, *A History of Chinese Political Thought*, trans. F. W. Mote, vol. 1 (Princeton: Princeton University Press, 1979), pp. 552–56.

15 Guo Moruo, *Shi pipan shu* (Ten critical essays) (Beijing, Science Press, 1962).

16 See also Uchiyama Toshihiko, "Maōtai bosho *Keihō, Judaikyō, Shō, Dōgen* shō kō" (A brief study of the Mawangdui silk texts "Jingfa," "Shidajing," "Cheng," and "Daoyuan"), *Tohogaku* 56 (1978): 1–16.

17 Harold D. Roth, "Who Compiled the *Chuang Tzu?*" In Henry Rosemont, Jr., ed., *Chinese Texts and Philosophical Contexts: Essays in Honor of Angus Graham* (La Salle, Ill.: Open Court Publishing Co., 1991), pp. 79–128.

18 Angus Graham, "Reflections and Replies: Roth," in Rosemont, *Chinese Texts and Philosophical Contexts*, p. 281.

19 These issues were raised by Roth in "Who Compiled the *Chuang Tzu?*" and further explored by Roth, Kidder Smith, and Sarah Queen in a very fruitful panel session on Huang-Lao at the April 1991 meeting of the Association for Asian Studies in New Orleans. See especially Queen's paper for that session, "A Confucian with a Taoist Face: Huang-Lao Influence on Tung Chung-shu."

20 For example, in my doctoral dissertation, "Topography and Cosmology in Early Han Thought," Harvard University, 1973.

21 See Michael Loewe's eloquent paraphrase of *Huainanzi* 8 in *Chinese Ideas of Life and Death: Faith, Myth and Reason in the Han Period (202 B.C.–A.D.)* (London: George Allen and Unwin., 1982), pp. 44–45.

22 See for example Peerenboom's articles "Natural Law in *Huang-Lao Boshu*," *Philosophy East and West* 40 (1990): 309–29 and "*Heguanzi* and Huang-Lao Thought," *Early China* 16 (1991): 169–86, and his book-length study of the *Heguanzi* forthcoming from SUNY Press.

23 The following summary draws heavily on the articles by Tu and Peerenboom cited above.

24 Tu, "The 'Thought of Huang-Lao,'" p. 103.

25 Peerenboom, "*Heguanzi* and Huang-Lao Thought," p. 170.

26 Tu, "The 'Thought of Huang-Lao,'" p. 104.

27 See Ames, *The Art of Rulership*, pp. 14–15.

28 Ibid., pp. 167–68.

29 Ibid., p. 178.

30 Among readily available editions of *Huainanzi*, Roth strongly prefers the version in the

Sibu congkan (SBCK) collection; he regards the (rare) edition of Liu Ji as the best version overall. For his critique of the Liu Wendian edition and his arguments in favor of Liu Ji, see *The Textual History of the Huainanzi*, pp. 170–187, 298–302.

31   See Wang Kuo-wei, "Chinese Foot-Measures of the Past Nineteen Centuries," *Journal of the North China Branch of the Royal Asiatic Society* 59 (1928): 111–23.

32   See Xi Zezong, "Chinese Studies in the History of Astronomy, 1949–1979," *Isis* 72 (1981): 466; Yi Shitong, "Liangtian chi kao" (A study of the "sky-measure" foot), *Wenwu* 1978.2: 10–17; also Institute of Archaeology, Chinese Academy of Sciences, eds., *Zhongguo gudai tianwen wenwu tuji* (Illustrations of ancient Chinese astronomical artifacts) (Beijing: Wenwu Press, 1978), plates 42–43, text on p. 118.

33   This convention was, as far as I know, first employed in the book that I wrote jointly with Joseph Needham, Lu Gwei-djen, and John Combridge, *The Hall of Heavenly Records: Korean Astronomical Instruments and Clocks, 1380–1780* (Cambridge: Cambridge University Press, 1986). Because of its convenience, accuracy, and lack of ambiguity, I hope that it will come to be accepted as a standard practice.

34   Sarah Allan, "Water in Early Chinese Philosophical Thought," paper presented at the annual meeting of the Association for Asian Studies, Washington, D.C., 4 April, 1992.

35   John S. Major, "A Note on Two Technical Terms in Chinese Science: *wu-hsing* and *hsiu*," *Early China* 2 (1976): 1–3; also "Reply to Richard Kunst's Comments on *Hsiu* and *Wu-hsing*," in *Early China* 3 (1977): 69–70.

36   Richard A. Kunst, "More on *Hsiu* 宿 and *Wu-hsing* 五行, with an Addendum on the Use of Archaic Reconstructions," in *Early China* 3 (1977): 67–69; A. C. Graham, *Disputers of the Tao* (La Salle, Ill.: Open Court Publishing Co., 1989), pp. 325–26; Bodde, *Chinese Thought, Society, and Science*, pp. 100–101; Chauncey S. Goodrich in his review of Twitchett and Loewe, eds., *The Cambridge History of China, Volume One* in *Journal of the American Oriental Society* 108 (1988): 461.

37   Major, "A Note on Two Technical Terms in Chinese Science"; Richard A. Kunst, "More on *Hsiu* and *Wu-hsing*"; Major, "Reply to Richard Kunst."

38   Willard Peterson, in "Making Connections: 'Commentary on the Attached Verbalizations' of *The Book of Change*," *Harvard Journal of Asiatic Studies* 42 (1982): 67–122, suggests "numen" as a translation for *shen*; that translation, appropriate in many instances, does not seem right for these chapters of *Huainanzi*, where the use of the term almost always refers to divinities or their attributes. See also Harold D. Roth, "The Early Taoist Concept of *Shen*: A Ghost in the Machine?" in Kidder Smith, ed., *Sagehood and Systematizing Thought in Warring States and Han China* (Brunswick, Maine: Bowdoin College Asian Studies Program, 1990), pp. 11–32.

39   Schafer, however, cautions that this word can also mean a dusty or dark blue or green, as for example the color of lichens or of the sea beneath a cloudy sky; he prefers the old English word "watchet" in such instances. Edward H. Schafer, "Fusang and Beyond: The Haunted Seas to Japan," *Journal of the American Oriental Society* 109 (1989): 389.

40   Edward Schafer, *Pacing the Void: T'ang Approaches to the Stars* (Berkeley: University of California Press, 1977), p. 5.

41   See below, Chapter 2, pp. 39–43.

42 Stephen Field, "Cosmos, Cosmograph, and the Inquiring Poet: A New Answer to the 'Heavenly Questions,'" *Early China* 17 (forthcoming, 1992).

43 See Ho Peng Yoke, *Li, Qi and Shu: An Introduction to Science and Civilization in China* (Hong Kong: Hong Kong University Press, 1985), pp. 155–56.

NOTES TO CHAPTER 2

1 For translations of *Huainanzi* 1 and 2, see Evan Morgan, *Tao, The Great Luminant: Essays from Huai Nan Tzu* (Shanghai: Kelly and Walsh, 1933; reprint, New York: Paragon Book Reprint Corp., 1969), pp. 2–56; and, more reliably, Eva Kraft, "Zum Huai-nan-tzu. Einführung, Übersetzung (Kapitel I und II) und Interpretation," *Monumenta Serica* 16 (1957): 191–286, 17 (1958): 128–207.

   The cosmogony of the *Huainanzi* has been analyzed brilliantly by N. J. Girardot, *Myth and Meaning in Early Taoism* (Berkeley and Los Angeles: University of California Press, 1983), pp. 134–56 (part of the chapter entitled "Cosmogony and Conception in the *Huai Nan Tzu* and *Lieh Tzu*"; see also the rigorous study of parallels between *Zhuangzi* 2 and *Huainanzi* 2 by Charles Le Blanc, "From Ontology to Cosmogony: Notes on *Chuang Tzu* and *Huai-Nan Tzu*," in Charles Le Blanc and Susan Blader, eds., *Chinese Ideas About Nature and Society: Studies in Honour of Derk Bodde* (Hong Kong: Hong Kong University Press, 1987), pp. 117–29.

2 Girardot, *Myth and Meaning*, p. 137.

   A private communication from Hal Roth, received just as this book was about to go to press, makes me realize that this point needs further clarification. Roth writes, "I have never been persuaded by the arguments of Girardot that Chinese cosmogony exemplifies the theme of 'creation and paradise lost' because I cannot see how the Void before the generation (not the creation) of the cosmos is any kind of 'paradise.' Isn't the 'paradise' in the *Huainanzi* the simple, unself-conscious community of the Taoist Primativist that has little to do with a pre-cosmic Void or state?"

   This is a key point, and the question has a definite answer: The "paradise lost" in this cosmology is not the cosmic void, but rather the primative state of being that exists after the spontaneous self-organization of the cosmos from the void but *before* the cosmic disasters (symbolized in the *Huainanzi* 3 cosmogony by the fight between Gong Gong and Zhuan Xu) that led to the universal flood, calendrical time, and human government.

3 Compare Le Blanc, "From Ontology to Cosmogony," p. 118.

   Hal Roth (private communication) criticizes my use of the term "Lao-Zhuang" here. He writes: "I don't think there was a Lao-Zhuang before the Dark Learning thinkers. For the *Huainanzi* authors, *Laozi* is a major and acknowledged influence; *Zhuangzi* is a major and unacknowledged influence. But there is no Lao-Zhuang influence on *Huainanzi* because at the time there was no Lao-Zhuang school or lineage."

   Moreover, he continues, "It seems to me that the *Zhuangzi* 2 passage that *Huainanzi* 2 restates and comments on is, if anything, 'anti-metaphysics.' I read it as an attempt to point out the futility of the kind of reasoning that seeks to work out a cosmogony, as we find in the *Laozi*."

These points are well taken; accordingly, my references here to "Lao-Zhuang" should be read simply as shorthand for *Laozi* and *Zhuangzi* as (separate) influences on the *Huainanzi* (and especially on the cosmogonic opening passages of *Huainanzi* 1 and 2 respectively) and not as implying the existence or influence of a "Lao-Zhuang" school in the early Han.

4   Le Blanc, "From Ontology to Cosmogony," pp. 127–28.

5   Girardot, *Myth and Meaning*, pp. 150–52.

6   The commentaries to *Huainanzi* 3 Sections I and II below deal with some specific issues arising from the text. I have commented on some of the broader themes of this cosmogony in "Substance, Process, Phase: *Wuxing* in the *Huainanzi*," in Henry Rosemont, Jr., ed., *Chinese Texts and Philosophical Contexts: Essays in Honor of A. C. Graham* (La Salle, Ill.: Open Court Publishing Co., 1991), pp. 67–78; and "Celestial Circles" in the forthcoming companion volume to this book, *Essays on the Huainanzi and Other Topics in Early Chinese Intellectual History*.

7   A. C. Graham, "Reflections and Replies: Major," in Rosemont, ed., *Chinese Texts and Philosophical Contexts*, p. 279.

8   Bernhard Karlgren, "The Book of Documents," *Bulletin of the Museum of Far Eastern Antiquities* 22 (1950): 74.

9   Randall Peerenboom, "*Heguanzi* and Huang-Lao Thought," *Early China* 16 (1992): 169–86. See also Peerenboom's article, "Natural Law in *Huang-Lao* Boshu," *Philosophy East and West* 40 (1990): 309–29.

10   See Joseph Needham's famous essay on natural law in *Science and Civilisation in China*, vol. 2 (Cambridge: Cambridge University Press, 1956), pp. 518–83 and Bodde's rather different conclusions "Organicism and Laws of Nature," in *Chinese Thought, Society, and Science* (Honolulu: University of Hawaii Press, 1991), pp. 332–55.

11   A. C. Graham, *Yin-Yang and the Nature of Correlative Thinking*. IEAP Occasional Paper and Monograph Series, 6 (Singapore: Institute of East Asian Philosophies, 1986).

12   See Charles Le Blanc, "The Idea of *Kan-ying* in *Huai-nan Tzu*," chap, 6 in *Huai-Nan Tzu: Philosophical Synthesis in Early Han Thought* (Hong Kong: Hong Kong University Press, 1985), pp. 191–206.

13   Michael Loewe, "The Religious and Intellectual Background," chap. 12 of Denis Twitchett and Michael Loewe, eds., *The Cambridge History of China. Volume One: The Ch'in and Han Empires, 221 B.C.–A.D. 220* (Cambridge: Cambridge University Press, 1986); Ho Peng Yoke, *Li, Qi and Shu: An Introduction to Science and Civilization in China* (Hong Kong: Hong Kong University Press, 1985); Nathan Sivin, in his long introductory essay in *Traditional Medicine in Contemporary China* (Science, Medicine, and Technology in East Asia, 2. Ann Arbor: University of Michigan Center for Chinese Studies, 1987); Derk Bodde, *Chinese Thought, Society, and Science*; A. C. Graham, *Yin-Yang and the Nature of Correlative Thinking*; and the chapter "The Cosmologists" in Graham, *Disputers of the Tao* (La Salle, Ill.: Open Court Publishing Co., 1989), which reproduces some of the same material in modified form.

See also the relevant works (listed in the bibliography below) of Wolfram Eberhard, Alfred Forke, Fung Yu-lan, Gu Jiegang, John Henderson, Iijima Tadaō, Joseph Needham, Manfred Porkert, and Benjamin Schwartz.

14 Sarah Allan, "The Shape of the Cosmos," in *The Shape of the Turtle: Myth, Art, and Cosmos in Early China* (Albany: SUNY Press, 1991), pp. 74–111, esp. pp. 75–79.

15 Graham, *Yin-Yang and the Nature of Correlative Thinking*, p. 70.

16 In Allan, *The Shape of the Turtle,*"pp. 74–111.

17 Edward H. Schafer, *Pacing the Void: Tang Approaches to the Stars* (Berkeley: University of California Press, 1977), pp. 34–35.

18 See also the example in Thomas Lawton, *Chinese Art of the Warring States Period* (Washington: Freer Gallery of Art, 1982), p. 86, and in Bernhard Karlgren, "Han and Huai," *Bulletin of the Museum of Far Eastern Antiquities* 13 (1941): 1–125, plate 18.

19 See also Wu Hung, *The Wu Liang Shrine: The Ideology of Early Chinese Pictorial Art* (Stanford: Stanford University Press, 1989), p. 279. Scale-model bronze chariots of similar type from the tomb of Qin Shihuangdi are on display at the National Historical Museum, Beijing.

20 For more on the 3 × 3 grid, see my article, "The Five Phases, Magic Squares, and Schematic Cosmography," in Henry Rosemont, Jr., ed., *Explorations in Early Chinese Cosmology* (JAAR Thematic Studies 50/2, Chico, Calif.: Scholar's Press, 1984), pp. 133–66, reprinted in *Essays on the Huainanzi* (forthcoming).

21 I have attempted to sort out these images in my essay "The Cosmic Pillar," in *Essays on the Huainanzi* (forthcoming).

22 See the brilliant discussion of these issues in the section entitled "Symmetry and Centrality" in Bodde, *Chinese Thought, Society, and Science*, pp. 103–22; also Allan, "The Shape of the Cosmos," pp. 106–7; and John Henderson, *The Development and Decline of Chinese Cosmology* (New York: Columbia University Press, 1984), pp. 59–87.

23 Henderson, *Development and Decline*, pp. 68–70.

24 Nakayama Shigeru, *A History of Japanese Astronomy: Chinese Background and Western Impact* (Cambridge: Harvard University Press, 1969), pp. 24–35; see also, less reliably, Needham in *Science and Civilisation in China*, vol. 3 (Cambridge: Cambridge University Press, 1959), pp. 210–16, which relies on Herbert Chatley, "'The Heavenly Cover': A Study in Ancient Chinese Astronomy," *Observatory* 61 (1938): 10–21.

25 David Hawkes, *Ch'u Tz'u: The Songs of the South* London: Oxford University Press, 1959), p. 211. I am grateful to David Pankenier for drawing to my attention this passage, which is the clearest explanation I've seen of a very confusing subject.

26 Schuyler Cammann, "The 'TLV' Pattern on the Cosmic Mirrors of the Han Dynasty," *Journal of the American Oriental Society* 68 (1948): 159–67.

27 On TLV mirrors, see Cammann, "The 'TLV' Pattern on Cosmic Mirrors of the Han Dynasty"; Michael Loewe, *Ways to Paradise: The Chinese Quest for Immortality* (London: George Allen and Unwin, 1979), pp. 60–85; and Major, "The Five Phases, Magic Squares, and Schematic Cosmography," in *Essays on the Huainanzi*. For references to the cosmograph, see Chapter 3, note 16, below.

28 See Nakayama, *A History of Japanese Astronomy*, pp. 35–39 for a useful brief summary of the *huntian* system. Nakayama correctly points out that the egg analogy does not imply that the Han Chinese had the concept of a spherical earth; the earth was still flat, and "'the yolk of the egg' suggested not the shape but the position of the earth" (p. 39).

29 See Stephen Field, "Cosmos, Cosmograph, and the Inquiring Poet: A New Answer to the 'Heaven Questions,'" in *Early China* 17 (1992): 83–110.

30 Some of these issues are explored further in Stephen Field, "Cosmos, Cosmograph, and the Inquiring Poet."

31 See Loewe, *Ways to Paradise*, pp. 1–2.

32 One such candidate for a hitherto-unidentified astronomical instrument (or part thereof) is a collapsible, and therefore readily portable, bronze tripod in the Freer Collection; see Lawton, *Chinese Art of the Warring States Period*, pp. 68–70. Tentatively identified as a "mirror stand," this tripod seems to me much more likely to have been a mount for an equatorial-plane sundial (which, like all gnomonic instruments, was useful for many astronomical measurements in addition to telling time), or possibly even for an instrument akin to the *shi* cosmograph. The mounting slot at the tripod's apex is set at a polar elevation of slightly less than 40°, just about right—possibly a degree or two too high—to hold an equatorial-plane instrument for use at the approximate latitude of the North China Plain.

33 David W. Pankenier, "Astronomical Dates in Shang and Western Zhou," *Early China* 7 (1981–82): 2–37; David S. Nivison and Kevin D. Pang, "Astronomical Evidence for the *Bamboo Annals'* Chronicle of Early Xia," *Early China* 15 (1990): 87–95; see also the "Forum" comments of Pankenier, Major, et al., and the responses of Nivison and Pang, in same issue of *Early China*, pp. 97–196. Nivison and Pankenier do not always agree, and sometimes disagree sharply; yet from the point of view of an outsider to their disagreements, they both have contributed to an understanding that Chinese astronomy and astrology go back at least to the beginning of the dynastic period, i.e., the early second millennium B.C.E.

34 Allan, "Sons of Suns," in *The Shape of the Turtle*, pp. 19–56.

35 Li Xueqin, "A Neolithic Jade Tablet and Early Chinese Cosmology," paper presented at the annual meeting of the Association for Asian Studies, Washington, D.C., 4 April, 1992.

36 For the Changsha square *ding*, see *The Exhibition of Archaeological Finds of The People's Republic of China* (Washington: National Gallery of Art, 1975), p. 52, and Hayashi Minao, "The Twelve Gods of the Chan-kuo Period Silk Manuscript Excavated at Ch'ang-sha," in Noel Barnard, ed., *Early Chinese Art and Its Possible Influence in the Pacific Basin*, 3 vols. (New York: Intercultural Arts Press, 1972), vol. 1, 168–69. See also the remarkable *taotie*-like masks excavated at Matianping, Xupu County, Hunan and reported in *Hunan kaogu jikan* 2 (1984; see illus. on p. 57); these quite plausibly may be interpreted as representations of gods of the months or directions.

    The idea of the *taotie* as an axial image is briefly alluded to in Schuyler Cammann, "Symbolic Expressions of Yin-Yang Philosophy," in Le Blanc and Blader, eds., *Chinese Ideas about Nature and Society*, pp. 109–16, on pp. 115–16; Cammann elaborated on it in an unpublished manuscript on the *taotie* motif itself (Cammann, private communication).

See also Hayashi Minao, "Iwayuru 'taotie' mon wa nani o arawashita mono ka?" (A Consideration of the meaning of the so-called *taotie* motif), *Tōhō gakuhō* (Kyoto) 56 (1984): 1–97.

37 See Major, "The Five Phases, Magic Squares, and Schematic Cosmography."

38 Giorgio de Santillana and Hertha von Dechend, *Hamlet's Mill* (Boston: Gambit, 1969), *passim.*

39 For more on the theme of the Grand Origin Myth in China, see my article "Myth, Cosmology, and the Origins of Chinese Science," *Journal of Chinese Philosophy* 5 (1978): 1–20, reprinted with revisions in *Essays on the Huainanzi*, forthcoming.

40 Cesare Emiliani et al., "Paleoclimatological Analysis of Late Quaternary Cores from the Northeastern Gulf of Mexico," *Science* 189 (1975): 1083–88.

41 See Sarah A. Queen, "A Confucian with a Taoist Face: Huang-Lao Influence on Tung Chung-shu," paper presented at the annual meeting of the Association for Asian Studies, New Orleans, 13 April, 1991.

42 See Loewe, *Ways to Paradise*; also Ying-shih Yü, "Life and Immortality in the Mind of Han China," *Harvard Journal of Asiatic Studies* 25 (1965): 80–122.

NOTES TO CHAPTER 3

1 For more on calendrical cycles in the Former Han, see Nathan Sivin, *Cosmos and Computation in Early Chinese Mathematical Astronomy*, *T'oung Pao* LV.1–3 (1969); reprinted, Leiden: E. J. Brill, 1969, pp. 12–19.

2 For a detailed analysis of lines 1–22 of this section, see my article, "Substance, Process, Phase: *Wuxing* in the *Huainanzi*," in Henry Rosemont, Jr., ed., *Chinese Texts and Philosophical Contexts: Essays Dedicated to A. C. Graham* (La Salle, Ill.: Open Court Publishing Co, 1991), pp. 67–78, as well as my essay "Celestial Circles," which will appear in the companion volume to this work, *Essays on the Huainanzi and Other Topics in Early Chinese Intellectual History* (forthcoming). For lines 23–29, see "The Cosmic Pillar" in the same volume.

3 Compare also translations of the opening sections of *Huainanzi* 3 by Derk Bodde in his translation of Fung Yu-lan, *A History of Chinese Philosophy* vol 1 (Princeton: Princeton University Press, 1952), pp. 396–98, and by A. C. Graham in *Disputers of the Tao* (La Salle, Ill.: Open Court Publishing Co., 1991), p. 132. See also the discussion of this passage in N. J. Girardot, *Myth and Meaning in Early Taoism* (Berkeley and Los Angeles: University of California Press, 1983), pp. 143–50.

4 I am grateful to Stephen Field for sharing a draft of this "bifurcated" translation with me in advance of its publication. The first eight lines of this translation appear in his article "Cosmos, Cosmograph, and the Inquiring Poet: A New Answer to the 'Heaven Questions,'" in *Early China* 17 (1992): 83–110. Translations of the remaining lines are based on Field's work in progress on the narrative sequence of the "Tian wen," though in some instances I have substituted my own reading of the text for his.

5   These terms have been discussed illuminatingly by Girardot in *Myth and Meaning in Early Taoism*, pp. 146–47. See also Field, "Cosmos, Cosmograph, and the Inquiring Poet."

6   See the discussion of this term in Derk Bodde, *Chinese Thought, Society, and Science* (Honolulu: University of Hawaii Press, 1991), pp. 105–7, and Graham, "Reflections and Replies: Major," in Rosemont, ed., *Chinese Texts and Philosophical Contexts*, p. 279.

7   See Chapter 2 above. The concept of resonance is necessarily discussed in every scholarly work dealing with Chinese cosmological thinking; one of the best treatments is found in Charles Le Blanc, *Huai-Nan Tzu: Philosophical Synthesis in Early Han Thought* (Hong Kong: Hong Kong University Press, 1985), pp. 191–206. Compare also the translation and analysis of this passage in Graham, *Disputers of the Tao*, pp. 332–33.

8   Jean-Pierre Diény, *Le Symbolisme du dragon dans la Chine antique*. Bibliothèque des Hautes Études Chinoises, vol. 27. (Paris: Collège de France, Institut des Hautes Études Chinoises, 1987).

    Studies of dragons, simurghs (Schafer's term for the *luan* "phoenix"), and other mythical beasts are found throughout the works of Edward Schafer; see in particular *The Vermilion Bird* (Berkeley: University of California Press, 1967) and *The Divine Woman: Dragon Ladies and Rain Maidens in T'ang Literature* (Berkeley: University of California Press, 1973).

    See also Paul W. Kroll's review of Diény's book in *Journal of the American Oriental Society* 102.9 (1989): 325–30, where he offers the splendid suggestions of "wyverne" for the *chi* 螭 dragon and "spirax" for the *qiu* 虯 dragon; he also disputes Schafer's choice of "krakon" for the *jiao* 蛟 dragon, offering instead the possibly no better "lamia."

    These mythical beasts and many others are catalogued and analyzed in Käte Finsterbusch, *Verzeichnis und Motifindex der Han-darstellungen* (Weisbaden: Otto Harrassowitz, 1966).

9   I first encountered the phrase, and the accompanying figure, in Sivin's graduate seminar on Chinese science at MIT in 1965. See Sivin, "Cosmos and Computation," p. 7.

10 Sarah Allan, "The Shape of the Cosmos," in *The Shape of the Turtle: Myth, Art and Cosmos in Early China* (Albany: SUNY Press, 1991), pp. 74–111, on p. 105; also John S. Major, "New Light on the Dark Warrior," in N. J. Girardot and John S. Major, eds., *Myth and Symbol in Chinese Tradition* (Symposium Issue, vols. 13 and 14 of the *Journal of Chinese Religions* (Boulder: Society for the Study of Chinese Religions, 1986), pp. 65–86, reprinted in *Essays on the Huainanzi* (forthcoming).

11 See my article "The Five Phases, Magic Squares, and Schematic Cosmography, in Henry Rosemont, Jr., ed., *Explorations in Early Chinese Cosmology* (JAAR Thematic Studies 50/2, Chico, Calif.: Scholar's Press, 1984), pp. 133–66. The published version of that article contains numerous significant typographical errors that will be corrected in the reprinted version in *Essays on the Huainanzi* (forthcoming). On the nine palaces, see also my "New Light on the Dark Warrior."

12 Joseph Needham, Lu Gwei-djen, John Combridge, and John S. Major, *The Hall of Heavenly Records: Korean Astronomical Instruments and Clocks, 1380–1780* (Cambridge: Cambridge University Press, 1986), pp. 4–6.

13 See Xi Zezong, "Zhongguo tianwenxue shi di yige zhongyao faxian—Mawangdui Hanmu boshu zhong di 'Wuxingzhan,'" (An important discovery for the history of Chinese astronomy: The Mawangdui silk manuscript "Prognostications of the Five Planets"), in *Zhongguo tianwenxue shi wenji* (Collected essays in the history of Chinse astronomy) (Beijing: Science Press, 1978), pp. 14–33.

14 See also my discussions of this section of *Huainanzi* 3 in "Substance, Process, Phase: *Wuxing* in the *Huainanzi*," and in "New Light on the Dark Warrior."

I am grateful to Hal Roth for pointing out (private communication) that the marking cord is already found in a similar symbolically important usage in the first line of the "Dao fa" section of the Mawangdui silk text "Jingfa." This emphasizes the point made in Chapter 1 above: the Mawangdui Huang-Lao corpus and the *Huainanzi* have many points in common, both in textual details and in philosophical outlook.

15 Edward H. Schafer, *Pacing the Void: Tang Approaches to the Stars* (Berkeley: University of California Press, 1977) pp. 211–19.

16 See Donald Harper, "The Han Cosmic Board (*Shih* 式)," *Early China* 4 (1978–79): 1–10; Christopher Cullen, "Some Further Points on the *Shih*," *Early China* 6 (1980–81): 31–46, and Harper, "The Han Cosmic Board: A Response to Christopher Cullen," *Early China* 6 (1980–81): 47–56. See also Michael Loewe, *Ways to Paradise: The Chinese Quest for Immortality* (London: George Allen and Unwin, 1979), pp. 75–80, 204–8; Marc Kalinowski, "Les Instruments astro-calendriques des Han et la méthode *liu ren*," *Bulletin de l'École Française d'Extrême-Orient* 72 (1983): 309–419; Field, "Cosmos, Cosmograph, and the Inquiring Poet"; and Li Ling, "'Shitu' yu Zhongguo gudai de yuzhou moshi (shang, xia)" (The cosmograph diagram and the ancient Chinese model of the cosmos (Parts 1 and 2)), *Jiuzhou xuekan* 1991.4: 5–52; 1991.7 49–79.

17 Ho Peng Yoke, *The Astronomical Chapters of the Chin Shu* (Paris and The Hague: Mouton and Co., 1966), p. 123.

18 David S. Nivison, "Evolution of the Chinese Lunar *hsiu* System," *duduan 03* (Stanford, Calif.: privately circulated, 1984); for the lunar lodges in the fifth century B.C.E., see Hubei Provincial Museum, *Suixian Zeng Houyi mu* (The tomb of Marquis Yi of Zeng at Suixian) (Beijing: Wenwu Press, 1980), color plate 89, showing a lacquered wooden casket the lid of which is decorated with a depiction of the twenty-eight lunar lodges, the Northern Dipper, and the White Tiger and Bluegreen Dragon.

19 See Xi Zezong, "Zhongguo tianwenxue shi de yige zhongyao faxian," appendix, p. 33.

20 For a detailed study of these and other wind names in the *Huainanzi*, see my article "Notes on the Nomenclatures of Winds and Directions in the Early Han," *T'oung Pao* 65 (1979): 66–80, to be reprinted with substantial revisions in *Essays on the Huainanzi* (forthcoming).

21 See "The Cosmic Pillar" in *Essays on the Huainanzi* (forthcoming).

22 See "The Cosmic Pillar" in *Essays on the Huainanzi* (forthcoming).

23 See Ho, *The Astronomical Chapters of the Chin Shu*, for the names and identifications of these asterisms.

24 Ho, *Chin Shu*, pp. 67ff., modified.

25 Ho, *Chin Shu*, pp. 76ff., modified.

26   Ho, *Chin Shu,* p. 93, modified.

27   Ho, *Chin Shu,* p. 91, modified.

28   Ho, *Chin Shu,* p. 74, modified.

29   For a more detailed analysis of this passage, see my article, "The Meaning of *Hsing-te,*" in Charles Le Blanc and Susan Blader, eds., *Chinese Ideas about Nature and Society: Essays in Honour of Derk Bodde* (Hong Kong: Hong Kong University Press, 1987), pp. 281–91, to be reprinted in *Essays on the Huainanzi* (forthcoming).

30   See for example Joseph Needham, *Science and Civilisation in China,* vol. 3 (Cambridge: Cambridge University Press, 1959), pp. 404–6 [hereafter Needham, SCC III]; Ho Peng Yoke, "Calendrical Science" in *Li, Qi and Shu: An Introduction to Science and Civilization in China* (Hong Kong: Hong Kong University Press, 1985), pp. 153–58, esp. pp. 154–55; Bodde, *Chinese Thought, Society, and Science,* pp. 120–21.

31   E.g. that found in Needham, SCC III: 405.

32   See his commentary in Liu Wendian, *Huainan honglie jijie* 3:14ab.

33   Xi Zezong, "'Huainanzi tianwenxun' shulue," (Outline of the "Treatise on the Patterns of Heaven" of *Huainanzi*), *Kexue tongbao* 1962.6: 35–36.

34   Derk Bodde, "The Chinese Cosmic Magic Known as Watching for the Ethers," in Else Glahn and Søren Egerod, eds., *Studia Serica Bernhard Karlgren Dedicata* (Copenhagen: Munksgaard, 1959), pp. 14–35; reprinted in Bodde, *Essays on Chinese Civilization,* ed. and intro. by Charles Le Blanc and Dorothy Borei (Princeton: Princeton University Press, 1981), pp. 351–72.

35   I am grateful to Christopher Cullen and David Pankenier for their helpful comments on this section (private communications).

36   David Pankenier has pointed out to me (private communication) that there are a number of instances in Zhou texts which indicate that "facing" Jupiter brings disaster, whereas "turning away from" Jupiter brings good fortune.

37   See Sivin, "Cosmos and Computation in Early Chinese Mathematical Astronomy," pp. 3–15; Ho, "Calendrical Science," in *Li, Qi and Shu,* pp. 153–58, esp. p. 156; and Nakayama Shigeru, *A History of Japanese Astronomy: Chinese Background and Western Impact* (Cambridge: Harvard University Press, 1969), pp. 67–69.

38   See Bernhard Karlgren, "The Book of Documents," *Bulletin of the Museum of Far Eastern Antiquities* 22 (1950): 3, para. 8.

39   See W. Allyn Rickett, *Guanzi: Political, Economic, and Philosophical Essays from Early China,* vol. 1 (Princeton: Princeton University Press, 1985), pp. 160–61.

40   See Edward Schafer, *The Divine Woman: Dragon Ladies and Rain Maidens in T'ang Literature* (Berkeley: University of California Press, 1973).

41   In Sarah Allan, *The Shape of the Turtle: Myth, Art and Cosmos in Early China* (Albany: SUNY Press, 1991), pp. 19–56.

42   Needham, SCC III: 188, modified.

43   See Robert G. Henricks, "On the Whereabouts and Identity of the Place Called 'K'ung-sang' (Hollow Mulberry) in Early Chinese Mythology" (Paper presented at the annual meeting of the Association for Asian Studies, Washington, D.C., 4 April, 1992).

44 Allan, "Sons of Suns," in *The Shape of the Turtle*, p. 29.

45 Wolfgang Bauer, *China and the Search for Happiness: Recurring Themes in Four Thousand Years of Chinese Cultural History* (New York: Seabury Press, 1976), pp. 191–92. See also Norman Girardot's comments on Bauer's observations in *Myth and Meaning in Early Taoism*, pp. 147–48.

46 Ho, *Chin Shu*, p. 67. See also Schafer, *Pacing the Void*, p. 46; Cullen, "Some Further Points on the *Shih*," p. 41.

47 For an analysis of the complex symbolism associated with one, two, and three in *Laozi* 42, see Girardot, *Myth and Meaning in Early Taoism*, pp. 56–63.

48 See Cheng-Yih Chen, "The Generation of Chromatic Scales in the Chinese Bronze Set-Bells of the -5th Century," in Cheng-Yih Chen, ed., *Science and Technology in Chinese Civilization* (Singapore: World Scientific Publishing Co., 1987), pp. 155–97, esp. pp. 165–83; also Edouard Chavannes, *Les Mémoires historiques de Se-Ma Ts'ien*, vol. 3 (Paris: E. Leroux, 1898), pp. 313–16.

49 Needham (with Kenneth Robinson), SCC IV.1: 126–228, especially pp. 160-83. See also the following studies:

Jean Joseph-Marie Amiot, "Mémoire sur la musique des chinois tant anciens que moderns," in Amiot et al., *Mémoires concernant l'histoire . . . des Chinois . . .* (Paris, 1780).

John H. Levis, *Foundations of Chinese Musical Art* (Peiping: Henri Vetch, 1936).

Willy Hartner, "Some Notes on Chinese Musical Art," *Isis*, July, 1938; reprinted in Nathan Sivin, ed., *Science and Technology in East Asia* (New York: Science History Publications, 1977), pp. 32–54.

Laurence Pickin, "The Music of Far Eastern Asia, I: China," in *The New Oxford History of Music* (Oxford: Oxford University Press, 1957), pp. 83–134.

E. Chavannes, translation of *Shiji* 25, the "Treatise on Mathematical Harmonics," *Les Mémoires historiques de Se-Ma Ts'ien*, vol. 3 (Paris: Leroux, 1898), pp. 293–19.

E. Chavannes, "Des Rapports de la musique Grecque avec la musique Chinoise," in Chavannes, *Mémoires historiques* III, Appendix 2, pp. 630–45.

Cheng-Yih Chen, "The Generation of Chromatic Scales in the Chinese Set-Bells of the -5th Century," in Chen, ed., *Science and Technology in Chinese Civilization*, pp. 155–97.

Lothar A. von Faulkenhausen, "Ritual Music in Bronze Age China: An Archaeological Perspective," (Ph.D. diss., Harvard University, 1988).

50 Chen, "The Generation of Chromatic Scales in the Chinese Set-Bells of the -5th Century." Qian Tang's "Supplementary Commentary to the *Huainanzi* 'Treatise on the Patterns of Heaven'" (in the Liu Wendian edition of the *Huainanzi*) is also particularly helpful on these sections dealing with mathematical harmonics.

51 See Chen, "The Generation of Chromatic Scales in the Chinese Set-Bells of the -5th Century," pp. 181–83. See also the table of shifting fundamentals on p. 124 of Qian Tang's "Supplementary Commentary" in Liu Wendian's edition of the *Huainanzi*.

52 See Dubs's translation of this passage and his lengthy commentary on it, in Homer H. Dubs, *The History of the Former Han Dynasty*, vol. 3 (Baltimore: The Waverly Press,

1955), vol. 3, pp. 255–57. As Dubs points out, "the particular branch used to denote a day . . . is given an astrological significance which depends on which branch denotes the month. [The passage] says, 'If *yin* is *chien*, [which clause means both of two things in accordance with two meanings of the word *chien*: "If the day having the branch *yin* occurs in the month having the branch *yin*" and "The day *yin* is (in that case) the day for establishing"].'" Dubs feels that this passage establishes a paradigm for use with the branch designation of all of the months, so that as the months succeed each other the astrological rules simply shift by one place each time.

53 See Needham, SCC III: 251, 404.

54 See Needham, SCC III: 402–3; and Schafer, *Pacing the Void*, pp. 76–78.

55 Qian Tang, "Supplementary Commentary," pp. 88ab points out that the system of "accretion and recision" here is unrelated to, and operates on very different principles from, the solar calendar accretion-and-recision system described in 3.XVII above, despite the apparent similarity of the terms used.

56 Qian Tang, "Supplementary Commentary," p. 92a.

57 See the illustration in Cullen, "Some Further Points on the *Shih*," p. 35.

58 See Christopher Cullen, "The Han Cosmic Model: A Rejoinder to Donald Harper," *Early China* 7 (1981–82): 130–33, on p. 131; and Xi Zezong, "Chinese Studies in the History of Astronomy, 1949–1979," ed. John S. Major, *Isis* 72 (1981): 456–470, p. 464. See also the table of lodge extensions in Needham, SCC III: 234–37, table 24, and the notes on variant systems on p. 234.

59 See for example the table in Schafer, *Pacing the Void*, pp. 76–77.

60 *Jinizi* 1:3a, in Ma Guohan, *Yuhan shanfang jiyishu* (1853). See the translation of the longer *Jinizi* passage of which this is an excerpt in Needham, SCC III: 402. Needham ascribes the *Jinizi* to a "southern naturalistic tradition" of the fourth century B.C.E.

61 In *Chinese Thought, Society, and Science*, p. 260.

62 Roger Ames, *The Art of Rulership: A Study in Ancient Chinese Political Thought* (Honolulu: University of Hawaii Press, 1983), p. 186.

63 Qian Tang, "Supplementary Commentary," pp. 98a, 98b.

64 Qian Tang, "Supplementary Commentary," pp. 98b–99b.

65 Harper, "The Han Cosmic Board (*Shih* 式)," p. 4.

66 Hal Roth points out that in the Liu Ji edition of the *Huainanzi* (and other editions in that lineage) this diagram is printed as a circle instead of as a rectangle. The data are essentially the same, but the arrangment is different. The two Heavenly Stems correlated with earth (*wu* and *ji*) are placed in the center, surrounded by the remaining eight Stems arrayed in the eight directions. The next ring (reading outwards) has the twelve Earthly Branches; next gives the "birth-maturity-old age" sequence; the outermost ring has the twenty-eight lunar lodges. This is perhaps a more elegant arrangement; it is impossible to tell which version (the rectangle or the circle) is the original one, or whether either goes back to the original compilation of the *Huainanzi*. See Harold D. Roth, *The Textual History of the Huai-nan Tzu*, Association for Asian Studies Monograph 46 (Ann Arbor: Association for Asian Studies, 1992), Plates 7–8 and 20–21.

NOTES TO CHAPTER 4

1   Fragments of Zou Yan's works that survive as quotations in later works are collected and analyzed in Wang Meng'ou, *Zou Yan yishuo kao* (Taipei: Commercial Press, 1966).

2   In the interest of saving space in what is already a very long book, I will not here attempt to provide identifications of all of the actual (as opposed to legendary or mythical) place names in *Huainanzi* 4. The identification of such place names generally is only worth undertaking for particular reasons in individual cases. The commentary of Gao You gives Han locations for all of the place names that he could identify, and in Liu Wendian's edition of the *Huainanzi*, supplementary commentaries often provide additional information.

   The notes to Eduard Erkes's translation ("Das Weltbid des Huai-nan-tze," *Ostasiatische Zeitschrift* 5 [1916–17]: 27–80) locate identifiable place names in terms of *xian* and province, the political divisions that he uses being, of course, those of the early twentieth century. In addition, he gives, when available, a reference number to G. M. H. Playfair, *The Cities and Towns of China: A Geographical Dictionary*, 2d ed. (Shanghai: Kelly and Walsh, 1910) or, when appropriate, to Playfair, Appendix 7, "The Principal Rivers and Lakes of China."

   The notes to the earlier version of this translation incorporated in my doctoral dissertation ("Topography and Cosmology in Early Han Thought," Harvard University, 1973), contain many place name identifications drawing on these and other sources (such as the *Zhongguo gujin diming dazidian* and Qian Mu's *Shiji diming kao*); the dissertation is on file at the Harvard-Yenching Library for anyone who might care to consult it. Note, however, that both the translation and the commentary in that dissertation are superseded by the version presented here.

   The province names in this section are discussed further in my article "The Five Phases, Magic Squares, and Schematic Cosmography," in Henry Rosemont, Jr., ed., *Explorations in Early Chinese Cosmology* (JAAR Thematic Studies 50/2, Chico, Calif.: Scholar's Press, 1984), pp. 133–66; the wind names are discussed further in my article "Notes on the Nomenclature of Winds and Directions in the Early Han," *T'oung Pao* 65 (1979): 66–80. Both of these articles will be reprinted in revised form in the companion volume to this book, *Essays on the Huainanzi and Other Topics in Early Chinese Intellectual History* (forthcoming).

3   See "The Five Phases, Magic Squares, and Schematic Cosmography," in *Essays on the Huainanzi*.

4   See "The Five Phases, Magic Squares, and Schematic Cosmography," in *Essays on the Huainanzi*.

5   I am grateful to Stephen Field for sharing with me his "bifurcated translation" of "Tian wen" from a work in progress on the narrative sequence of the Heavenly Questions. My translations are based on his, though his final versions are likely to differ from mine.

6   In "Handai yiqian Zhongguoren de shijie guannian yu yuwai jiaotong de gushi" (The worldview and foreign relations of the pre-Han Chinese), *Yugong banyue kan* 5:3 and 4 (1936): 106–7.

7 For a comparison of various measurements of the earth in pre-Han and Han works, see Riccardo M. Fracasso, "Teratoscopy or Divination by Monsters: Being a Study on the *Wu-tsang Shan-ching*," *Hanxue yanjiu/Chinese Studies* [Taipei] 1.2 (1983): 691–94.

8 Nakayama Shigeru, *A History of Japanese Astronomy: Chinese Background and Western Impact* (Cambridge: Harvard University Press, 1969), p. 29.

9 Nathan Sivin, "The Limits of Empirical Knowledge in the Traditional Chinese Sciences," in J. T. Fraser et al., eds., *Time, Science, and Society in China and the West. The Study of Time, V* (Amherst: University of Massachusetts Press, 1986), pp. 151–69; see pp. 156–63.

10 For more on this wall, see Paul Wheatley, *The Pivot of the Four Quarters* (Chicago: Aldine Publishing Co., 1971), pp. 442–44.

11 Confusingly, there are also circumpolar constellations in Chinese astronomical nomenclature called Eastern Wall and Western Wall; see the star map in Ho Peng Yoke, *Li, Qi and Shu: An Introduction to Science and Civilization in China* (Hong Kong: Hong Kong University Press, 1985), p. 136. These names may also echo the concept of Kunlun as an axial magical place, but they are not connected with the lunar lodge system under discussion here.

12 Léopold de Saussure, *Les Origines de l'astronomie chinoise* (Paris: Maisonneuve, 1930), p. 134.

13 David Hawkes, *Ch'u Tz'u: The Songs of the South* (London: Oxford University Press, 1959), p. 63.

14 Hawkes, *Ch'u Tz'u*, p. 136.

15 See Ying-shih Yü, "Life and Immortality in the Mind of Han China," *Harvard Journal of Asiatic Studies* 25 (1965): 91.

16 See Giorgio de Santillana and Hertha von Dechend, *Hamlet's Mill* (Boston: Gambit Press, 1969), pp. 238–39; and Chapter 2 above.

17 In the Indian tradition the link between architecture and cosmology is explicit. In Balinese Hinduism, for example, multitiered (often nine-tiered) temple towers are called *meru*, imitative in name as well as in structure of the classical Indian nine-tiered *axis mundi* or cosmic mountain.

18 Edward H. Schafer, "The Transcendent Vitamin: Efflorescence of Lang-kan," *Chinese Science* 3 (1978): 27–38.

19 On the latter, see Suzanne Cahill, "Reflections of a Metal Mother: Tu Kuang-t'ing's Biography of Hsi Wang Mu," in N. J. Girardot and John S. Major, eds., *Myth and Symbol in Chinese Tradition* (Symposium Issue, vols. 13 and 14 of *Journal of Chinese Religion*, Boulder: Society for the Study of Chinese Religions, 1986), pp. 127–42.

20 See Deborah Porter, "Myth and History in the *Mu T'ien-tzu chuan*" (Paper presented at the annual meeting of the Association for Asian Studies, Washington, D.C., 3 April, 1992).

21 Edward H. Schafer, "Fusang and Beyond: The Haunted Seas to Japan," *Journal of the American Oriental Society* 109 (1989): 394.

22 A. F. P. Hulsewé, "Texts in Tombs," *Asiatische Studien/Études Asiatiques* 18/19 (1965): 89.

23 Joseph Needham, *Science and Civilisation in China*, vol. 3 (Cambridge: Cambridge University Press, 1959), pp. 607–8 [hereafter, SCC III].

24   Hawkes, *Ch'u Tz'u*, p. 83. See also Yü, "Life and Immortality, p. 100, n 122.

25   See for example Wei Tingsheng, *Mu Tianzi zhuan jinkao* (A modern scientific study of King Mu's travels), 3 vols. (Taibei: Zhonghua xueshu yuan, 1970).

26   In "The Cosmic Pillar" in *Essays on the Huainanzi* (forthcoming). Meanwhile see Riccardo M. Fracasso, "Manifestazioni del simbolismo assiale nelle tradidizioni cinese antiche, *Numen* 28 (1981): 194–215.

27   In her essay "Sons of Suns," in Sarah Allan, *The Shape of the Turtle: Myth, Art, and Cosmos in Early China* (Albany: State University of New York Press, 1991), pp. 19–56; see especially pp. 27–36.

28   See Allan, "Sons of Suns," pp. 28–29.

29   Though at first glance this section of text seems fairly straightforward, on closer examination it contains numerous difficulties. For an attempt to disentangle them, see my article "The Five Phases, Magic Squares, and Schematic Cosmography" in *Essays on the Huainanzi* (forthcoming).

30   See Timoteus Pokora, "The Notion of Coldness in Huai-nan-tzu," *Nachrichten der Gesellschaft für Natur- und Völkerkunde Ostasiens, Hamburg: Zeitschrift für Kulture und Geschichte Ost- und Südostasiens* 125 (1979): 69–74.

31   Edward Schafer, "The Transcendent Vitamin: Efflorescence of Lang-kan."

32   Berthold Laufer, *Jade: A Study in Chinese Archaeology and Religion* (Chicago: Field Museum, 1912); Zhang Hongzhao, *Shi ya* (Added title in English: *Lapidarium Sinicum: A Study of the Rocks, Fossils, and Minerals as Known in Chinese Literature*) (Beijing: Chinese Geological Survey, 1927).

33   Francis Adams, *The Genuine Works of Hippocrates*, vol. 1 (London, 1849), pp. 180–222.

34   R. Bruce Gillie, "Endemic Goiter," *Scientific American* (June 1971): 92–7.

35   Erkes, "Das Weltbild des Huai-nan-tze," p. 58; Yü, "Life and Immortality in the Mind of Han China," pp. 90–91.

36   See the illustration of the *xingtian* from the *Shanhaijing* in Needham, SCC III: 506.

37   See Michael Loewe, "The Cult of the Dragon and the Invocation for Rain," in Charles Le Blanc and Susan Blader, eds., *Chinese Ideas about Nature and Society: Essays in Honour of Derk Bodde* (Hong Kong: Hong Kong University Press, 1987), pp. 195–213.

38   Translated and discussed by Needham, SCC II:271–72.

39   See Needham, SCC I:150, and SCC II:269.

40   See Helmut Wilhelm, *Change: Eight Lectures on the I Ching*, trans. Cary F. Baynes. (New York: Pantheon Books, Bollingen Series 62, 1960), pp. 27–28.

41   Erkes, "Das Weltbild des Huai-nan-tze," p. 62, n. 191.

42   For more extensive comments on this section of *Huainanzi* 4, see my articles, "The Five Phases, Magic Squares, and Schematic Cosmography" in *Essays on the Huainanzi*, and "Substance, Process, Phase: *Wuxing* in the *Huainanzi*," in Henry Rosemont, Jr., ed., *Chinese Texts and Philosophical Contexts: Essays Dedicated to A. C. Graham* (La Salle, Ill.: Open Court Publishing Co, 1991), pp. 67–78.

43   The five phase correspondences (Zou Yan used the term *wude*, "five powers") for successive dynasties are specified in one of the authentic fragments of Zou Yan's writings, translated

in Needham, SCC II: 238. For a dispute in the Han about how to apply that sequence to current affairs, see Schuyler Cammann, "The Magic Square of Three in Old Chinese Philosophy and Religion," *History of Religions* 1 (1961): 48–49, and Gu Jiegang, "Wude zhongshi shuoxia de zhengzhi he lishi" (Politics and history in light of the five-powers cyclical theory), *Gushi bian* 5: 430–35.

44 Wei Tingsheng, *Mu Tianzi zhuan jinkao*, vol. 2, pp. 317–46.

45 Hulsewé, "Texts in Tombs," pp. 88–89.
For some notable early attempts to identify the strange lands beyond China's frontiers, see Albert Herrmann, *Die Alten Seidenstrassen zwischen China und Syria* (Wittenburg: Herrose & Ziemsen, 1910), and *Lou-lan: China, Indien, und Rom im Lichte der Ausgrabungen am Lobnor* (Leipzig, 1931); and Gustave Schlegel, in a series of articles entitled "Problèmes géographiques: Les peuples étrangers chez les historiens Chinois," *T'oung Pao*, vols. 3–6, (1892–95). See also Roy Andrew Miller, trans., *Accounts of Western Nations in the History of the Northern Chou Dynasty* (Berkeley and Los Angeles: University of California Press, 1959).
Place names are extensively discussed in Hsu Cho-yun and Katheryn M. Linduff's *Western Chou Civilization* (New Haven: Yale University Press, 1989). Constance A. Cook, in her review of that book in the *Journal of the American Oriental Society* 111 (1991): 615–17, criticizes the authors for trying to identify the Zhurong People mentioned in Han sources with aboriginal peoples in Henan, Shandong, and Anhui, and with the ancestors of Chu. One might expand this critique to draw out a larger lesson: Some Han texts are better sources for ethnography than others, but all must be used with extreme care.

46 Eduard Erkes has diligently listed other early texts in which these thirty-six countries are also named; see "Das Weltbild des Huai-nan-tze," pp. 65–68.

47 Ying-shih Yü, *Trade and Expansion in Han China* (Berkeley and Los Angeles: University of California Press, 1967), p. 133.

48 The "hairy people" appear also in *Shanhaijing* 9. The commentary of Guo Pu to that passage says that they live on islands and dwell in pits; this fits the Ainu (or Ainu-like people) who were the original inhabitants of Japan, with their notable hairiness and semisubterranean dwellings. Guo also mentions that in 310 C.E. a salt merchant on the China coast found and cared for a boatload of shipwrecked "hairy people." See also Komai Kazuchika, "The Ainu in Age of T'ang Dynasty," *Acta Asiatica* 6:1–10 (1964), and Erkes, "Das Weltbild des Huai-nan-tze," p. 67, n. 230.

49 David Hawkes, *Ch'u Tz'u: Songs of the South*, p. 104.

50 Schlegel, "Problèmes geographiques," *T'oung Pao* 4 (1893): 410.

51 Edouard Chavannes, *Les Mémoires historiques de Se-Ma Ts'ien*, vol. 1 (Paris: E. Leroux, 1895), p. 37, n. b; Schlegel, "Problèmes geographiques, *T'oung Pao* 4 (1893): 355; August Conrady, "Indischer Einflüß in China im 4. Jahrhundert v. Chr." *Zeitschrift der Deutschen Morgenländischen Gesellschaft* 60 (1906): 335–51.

52 Needham, SCC III: 505–7.

53 See Hayashi Minao, "The Twelve Gods of the Chan-kuo Period Silk Manuscript Excavated at Ch'ang-sha," in Noel Barnard, ed., *Early Chinese Art and Its Possible Influence in*

the Pacific Basin, vol. 1 (New York: Intercultural Arts Press, 1972), pp. 123–86.

54 N. J. Girardot, *Myth and Meaning in Early Taoism* (Berkeley and Los Angeles: University of California Press, 1983), pp. 165, 206, 235–39, 326–28.

55 See Allan, "Sons of Suns," pp. 38–40.

56 See also *Shanhaijing* 6 and 15 and *Lüshi chunqiu* 22. For a discussion of the term "no death" see Ying-shih Yü, "Life and Immortality," pp. 90–91.

57 In Allan, *The Shape of the Turtle*, pp. 19–56, esp. pp. 27–46.

58 See Qian Mu, *Shiji diming kao* (Hong Kong: Longmen shudian, 1968), p. 166.

59 On the Jian Di myth, see Allan, "Sons of Suns," pp. 38–41.

60 See Girardot, *Myth and Meaning*, pp. 232–33.

61 See my article "The Cosmic Pillar" in *Essays on the Huainanzi*.

62 See for example Ying-shih Yü, "Life and Immortality," pp. 96ff.; Homer H. Dubs, "Han Hill Censers," in Else Glahn and Søren Egerod, eds., *Studia Serica Bernhard Karlgren Dedicata* (Copenhagen: Munksgaard, 1959), pp. 259–64; Dubs, "An Ancient Chinese Mystery Cult," *Harvard Theological Review* 35 (1942): 221–40; J. R. Hightower, *The Poetry of T'ao Ch'ien* (Oxford: Oxford University Press, 1970), pp. 229–48; Suzanne Cahill, "Reflections of a Metal Mother," pp. 127–42; Loewe, *Ways to Paradise*, pp. 86–126; and Wu Hung, *The Wu Liang Shrine: The Ideology of Early Chinese Pictorial Art* (Stanford: Stanford University Press, 1989), pp. 108–41. See also Riccardo Fracasso, "Holy Mothers of Ancient China: A New Approach to the Hsi-Wang-Mu Problem," (Taipei, 1985, mimeographed), and a forthcoming book-length study by Suzanne Cahill (Stanford University Press, in press, 1992).

63 It is interesting, given Xiwangmu's location in the northwest, that whistling is a distinctive feature of the vocal music of the nomadic peoples of China's Inner Asian frontier.

64 Fracasso, "Holy Mothers of Ancient China," pp. 8–9.

65 In Balinese Hinduism, which incorporates aspects of ancient (pre-Hindu) folk belief that in many respects show parallels with the ancient coastal-riverine cultures of China, the figure of Jero Gede (depicted as a gigantic puppet mask or *barong landung*) is both feared as a bringer of epidemics and revered as a protector of villages from epidemics—in the latter case, especially when the intercession of his lascivious wife Jero Luh is invoked.

66 Loewe, *Ways to Paradise*, pp. 98–100.

67 In addition to those noted below, see *Shujing*, "Yugong" I,78 and II,6; also *Lüshi chunqiu* 14:3b and 22:4a. See also Qian Mu, *Shiji diming kao*, p. 41.

68 See Allan, "Sons of Suns," pp. 44–45.

69 For the question of whether the sky covers up the "corners" of the earth, see Chapter 2, pp. 41–43 above, and my article "The Cosmic Pillar" in *Essays on the Huainanzi* (forthcoming).

70 See also Allan, "Sons of Suns," pp. 28–29.

71 The suggestion that the serpent-tailed figure at the apex of the Mawangdui 1 banner represents the *hun* soul of the tomb's occupant, the Lady Dai, was made somewhat hesitantly by Michael Loewe in *Ways to Paradise*, p. 59. To me this point has always seemed so obvious as hardly to need further demonstration. The painted banner is a cosmic map of both space

and time: space, because (read from the bottom up) it depicts the underworld, the plane of the earth, the Changhe Gate of Heaven, and the realm of the heavenly bodies; time, because it depicts the separation at death of the *po* and *hun* souls, the first descending into the tomb, the second ascending to the heavens.

This interpretation contradicts the opinions of virtually all Chinese authorities, who have tended to identify the serpent-bodied figure as either Fu Xi or the Torch Dragon (see Loewe's discussion of this point, with references appended). It should be noted, however, that those opinions were mostly expressed during the Cultural Revolution, a time when (as I was assured in private conversations with historians at both Beijing University and Sichuan University in 1978) it would have been far too dangerous politically for anyone to suggest that the painting depicted the afterlife of an immortal soul or any other such religious theme.

72 For an analysis of the associations cosmic egg/Pan Gu/dog ancestors of human beings, see Girardot, *Myth and Meaning in Early Taoism*, pp. 192–93.

73 Marcel Granet, *Danses et légendes de la Chine ancienne* (Paris: Alcan, 1926), p. 326, n. 3.

74 Girardot, *Myth and Meaning in Early Taoism*, p. 153.

75 See Giorgio de Santillana and Hertha von Dechend, *Hamlet's Mill* (Boston: Gambit Press, 1969), pp. 125–28; also Granet, *Danses et légendes*, pp. 507–9.

76 De Santilana, *Hamlet's Mill*, illustrations facing p. 273; see also An Zhimin, "Changsha xin faxiande Xi Han bohua shitan" (A tentative interpretation of the Western Han silk painting recently discovered at Changsha), *Kaogu* 1973.1: 47, 52.

77 See note 2 above.

78 Needham, SCC IV.3:548–50.

79 See Needham, SCC III: 523.

80 See Allan, "Sons of Suns," pp. 29–30.

81 For the names of these winds, see the commentary to 3.XII above, and also my article "Notes on the Nomenclature of Winds and Directions in the Early Han," in *Essays on the Huainanzi*.

82 For dragons and allied creatures, see Jean-Pierre Diény, *Le Symbolisme du dragon dans la Chine antique* (Paris: Collège de France, Institut dese Hautes Études Chinoises, 1987), and Jean-Pierre Diény, "Le *Fenghuang* et le phénix," *Cahiers d'Extrême-Asie* 5 (Special Issue: Taoist Studies II, 1989–90), pp. 1–15.

83 Diény, *Le Symbolisme du dragon dans la Chine antique*, p. 140.

84 Diény, *Le Symbolisme du dragon dans la Chine antique*, pp. 211–13.

85 See the admirably cautious translation of Hu Shih in *The Development of the Logical Method in Ancient China* (Shanghai: Oriental Book Co., 1922), pp. 135–36, quoted in modified form in Needham, SCC II: 78–79, and Needham's analysis of it, SCC II: 79–80.

86 Homer H. Dubs, "The Beginnings of Alchemy," *Isis* 38 (1947): 62–86; Needham, SCC III: 641–42; Nathan Sivin, "The Theoretical Background of Elixer Alchemy," in Needham, SCC V.4 (1980); Nathan Sivin, "Reflections on Theory and Practice in Chinese Alchemy" (Paper presented at the Conference on Taoism, Bellagio, 7–14 September 1968). Summarized in Holmes Welch, "The Bellagio Conference on Taoist Studies," *History of Religions*

9.2 and 3: 114–17 (but see also Sivin's comments in *History of Religions*, May 1973); Ho, *Li, Qi and Shu*, pp. 26–27.

87   Sarah Allan, "Sons of Suns," p. 29; see also Girardot, *Myth and Meaning in Early Taoism*, pp. 147–48.

88   Sivin, "Reflections on Theory and Practice in Chinese Alchemy," p. 7.

89   Sivin, "Reflections on Theory and Practice in Chinese Alchemy," p. 12.

90   Joseph Needham, *Time and Eastern Man: The Henry Myers Lecture 1964* (London: Royal Anthropological Institute of Great Britain and Ireland, Occasional Paper 21, 1965), p. 21.

NOTES TO CHAPTER 5

1   Translated in Richard Wilhelm, *Frühling und Herbst des Lü Bu We* (Jena: E. Diedrichs, 1928). See also the partial translation in Wm. Theodore De Bary *et al.*, *Sources of Chinese Tradition* (New York and London: Columbia University Press, 1960), pp. 208–10.

2   See the translation by James Legge, *Li Chi: Book of Rites*, vol. 1 (Sacred Books of the East, 27–28. Oxford: Oxford University Press, 1885; reprinted, New Hyde Park, N.Y.: University Books, 1967), pp. 249–310.

3   "You guan" is translated in W. Allyn Rickett, *Guanzi: Political, Economic and Philosophical Essays from Early China* (Princeton: Princeton University Press, 1985), pp. 169–92. The other chapters mentioned are described briefly in the same work, on pp. 160–161.

4   Translated as an appendix to William Soothill, *The Hall of Light: A Study of Early Chinese Kingship* (London: Lutterworth Press, 1951).

5   See Noel Barnard, ed., *Early Chinese Art and Its Possible Influence in the Pacific Basin*, vol. 1, *Ch'u and the Silk Manuscript* (New York: Intercultural Arts Press, 1972), especially the contributions to that volume by Jao Tsung-yi and Hayashi Minao.

6   Excellent discussions of the "Yueling" texts, with reviews of the appropriate scholarly literature, are found in John B. Henderson, *The Development and Decline of Chinese Cosmology* (New York: Columbia University Press, 1984), pp. 20–24ff., and in Rickett, *Guanzi*, pp. 148–69. See also Fung Yu-lan, *A History of Chinese Philosophy*, trans. Derk Bodde, vol. 1 (Princeton: Princton University Press, 1952), pp. 164–65; Needham, *Science and Civilisation in China*, vol. 3, pp. 194–5, 245–8 (hereafter Needham, SCC III); Derk Bodde, *Festivals in Classical China: New Year and Other Annual Observances during the Han Dynasty, 206 B.C.–A.D. 220* (Princeton: Princeton University Press; Hong Kong: Chinese University of Hong Kong Press, 1975); Hsü Dau-lin, "Crime and Cosmic Order," *Harvard Journal of Asiatic Studies* 30 (1970): 111–25; and William G. Boltz, "Philological Footnotes to the Han New Year Rites," *Journal of the American Oriental Society* 99 (1979): 423–39. On *ganying* resonance, see Henderson, *The Development and Decline of Chinese Cosmology*, pp. 22–28, and Charles Le Blanc, "The Idea of *Kan-Ying* in *Huai-nan Tzu*," Chapter 6 of his *Huai-nan Tzu: Philosophical Synthesis in Early Han Thought* (Hong Kong: Hong Kong University Press, 1985), pp. 191–206.

7   See Donald Harper, "The Han Cosmic Board (*Shih* 式)," *Early China* 4 (1978–79): 1–10,

p. 2; Christopher Cullen, "Some Further Points on the *Shih*," *Early China* 6 (1980–81): 37, fig. 6.

8 See Soothill, *The Hall of Light*. For a very interesting account of Qing scholars' criticisms of the Mingtang as portrayed in the *Yueling*, see Henderson, *The Development and Decline of Chinese Cosmology*, pp. 217–18.

9 See the illustration in Zeng Zhaoyue et al., *Yinan gu huaxiang shimu fajue baogao* (Report on the excavation of an ancient carved stone tomb at Yinan) (Shanghai: Cultural Relics Bureau, 1956), plate 98.

10 I am grateful to Elling Eide for helping me to identify this tree (private communication).

11 See The Diagram Group, *Weapons: An International Encyclopedia from 5000 B.C. to 2000 A.D.* (London: Macmillan, 1990), p. 56.

12 Ibid.

13 Legge, "Yüeh Ling," *Li Chi*, vol. 1, p. 302.

14 I am grateful to Elling Eide (private communication) for helping me think through the identification of this bird.

15 See Michael Loewe, "The Cult of the Dragon and the Invocation for Rain," in Charles Le Blanc and Susan Blader, eds., *Chinese Ideas about Nature and Society: Studies in Honour of Derk Bodde* (Hong Kong: Hong Kong University Press, 1987), pp. 195–213. In this article Loewe cites several examples of rain–dragon sympathetic magic recounted in the *Huainanzi*.

16 Constance A. Cook, "Auspicious Metals and Southern Spirits: An Analysis of the Chu Bronze Inscriptions" (Ph.D. diss., University of California at Berkeley, 1990), p. 270.

    See also Jeffrey K. Riegel, "Kou-mang and Ju-shou," *Cahiers d'Extrême-Asie* 5 (Special Issue on Taoist Studies, II 1989–90.): 55–83. Riegel identifies Gou Mang (cf. 5.XIII.4) and Ru Shou as tutelary gods of the east and west, respectively, and he equates them (pp. 80–83) with Dongwanggong and Xiwangmu.

17 "Organicism and the Laws of Nature," in Bodde, *Chinese Thought, Society, and Science* (Honolulu: University of Hawaii Press, 1991), pp. 332–45, and esp. pp. 338–41; this section of Bodde's book is closely similar to his "Chinese 'Laws of Nature': A Reconsideration," *Harvard Journal of Asiatic Studies* 39 (1979): 139–55, reprinted in Bodde, *Essays in Chinese Civilization*, ed. by Charles Le Blanc and Dorothy Borei (Princeton: Princeton University Press, 1981), pp. 299–315; which in turn was a revision of "Evidence for 'Laws of Nature' in Chinese Thought," *Harvard Journal of Asiatic Studies* 20 (1957): 709–27.

18 See Needham's long essay on human law and natural law in China and the West in SCC III: 518–83, and his translation of this passage—which differs markedly from Bodde's and from my own—in SCC IV.1: 15–17.

NOTES TO APPENDIX A

1 Reprinted, with minor revisions, from the *Bulletin of the School of Oriental and African Studies* (BSOAS) (February 1976), by permission of BSOAS and Christopher Cullen.

2 I first became interested in this passage after reading the tantalizing reference in Joseph

Needham, *Science and Civilisation in China*, vol. 3 (Cambridge: Cambridge University Press, 1959) p. 224 (hereafter Needham, SCC III). (It occurs to me that the preceding sentence or some variant of it is likely to occur in learned journals with a high frequency for the next fifty years at least.) Professors A. C. Graham and D. C. Lau both gave very generously of their time in discussions of my first draft. Professor Graham brought to my notice a commentary by the Qing scholar Qian Tang, "Huainanzi tianwenxun buzhu." Preface dated 1788. (Shanghai: Datong shuju, 1935.) Also in Liu Wendian, *Huainan honglie jijie* (reprint ed., Shanghai: Commercial Press, 1933). I did not feel able to follow Qian in all that he wrote, but was relieved to find that we reached the same general conclusions about what the text was saying, although Qian seems to miss much that is important. Since the original publication of this article Professor Graham has discussed this passage in his *Later Mohist Logic, Ethics, and Science* (Hong Kong: Chinese University of Hong Kong Press, 1978), pp. 369–371.

    Unless otherwise noted, all citations of Chinese works in the body of this appendix refer to the *Sibu congkan* editions of those texts.

3 Henri Maspero, "L'Astronomie chinoise avant les Han," *T'oung Pao* 26 (1929): 348ff.

4 J. L. E. Dreyer. *History of the Planetary Systems from Thales to Kepler* (Cambridge: Cambridge University Press, 1906); reprinted as *A History of Astronomy from Thales to Kepler* (New York: Dover Publications, 1953), p. 174. For a recent review of the debate on Eratosthenes, see G. E. R. Lloyd, *The Revolutions of Wisdom* (Berkeley: University of California Press, 1987), p. 231ff.

5 Dreyer, *History of the Planetary Systems*, pp. 11ff.

6 Lucretius [ca. 40 B.C.E.]. *De rerum natura*, ed. and trans. by C. Bailey, 3 vols. (Oxford: Clarendon Press, 1947), trans. by R. E. Latham as *The Nature of the Universe* (Penguin Classics) (Harmondsworth: Penguin Books, 1951). See I, 1050; V, 546.

7 Dreyer, *History of the Planetary Systems*, pp. 40ff.

8 Dreyer, Ibid., p. 137.

9 Dreyer, Ibid., pp. 108ff.

10 Joseph Needham, SCC III: 210–29.

11 Herbert Chatley, "'The Heavenly Cover', A Study in Ancient Chinese Astronomy," *Observatory* 61 (1938): 10–21; see Needham, SCC III: 212.

12 Qian Baozong, *A History of Chinese Mathematics* (Peiping: Academia Sinica, 1932), pp. 23ff. See also Qian Baozong, *Suanjing shishu* (Ten classics of calculation [collated and punctuated]) (Beijing: Zhonghua shuju, 1963). For a detailed study and full translation of the *Zhoubi*, see C. Cullen *Astronomy and Mathematics in Ancient China: The Zhou bi suan jing* (Cambridge: Cambridge University Press, forthcoming).

    Citations from the *Zhoubi suanjing* in the text of this appendix are from the *Sibu congkan* (SBCK) edition.

13 *Sui shu* (History of the Sui Dynasty), compiled by Wei Cheng and others, 636–656 C.E. Punctuated and collated edition. Beijing: Zhonghua shuju, 1973.

    Quotations in this appendix are from the SBCK edition.

14 The version of this article previously published in the *Bulletin of the School of Oriental and*

African Studies (1976) includes at this point a critique (omitted here to maintain the focus more closely on the *Huainanzi* materials) of Needham's contention (in SCC III: 498) that some Chinese cosmologists dissented from the idea of the flat earth. It is shown that the flat-earth assumption was consistently maintained in Chinese cosmology until recent times, and that no convincing examples of a spherical-earth assumption in traditional Chinese cosmology can be adduced. Some ancient Chinese cosmologists objected to the idea that the earth was *square*, but all assumed that it was flat.

15 As for example in the main body of *Huainanzi* 3. For the translation of *chi* as "foot" (early Han length ≈ 9 English inches), see "Conventions Employed in this Book" in Chapter 1 above, p. 16.

16 Bernhard Karlgren, "Grammata Serica Recensa" (hereafter GSR), *Bulletin of the Museum of Far Eastern Antiquities* 29 (1957): 1–332, #647a.

17 Tan Jiefu, *Mojing yijie* (Shanghai: Commercial Press, 1935), p. 50. See also Graham, *Later Mohist Logic, Ethics, and Science,* pp. 306–307.

18 Tan Jiefu, *Mojing yijie,* p. 50.

19 Private communication.

20 Qian Baozong, *Suanjing shishu.*

21 Henri Maspero, "L'Astronomie chinoise avant les Han," *T'oung Pao* 26 (1929): 350.

22 *Zhouli* 10:13a ff., in *Shisanjing zhusu* (Thirteen classics with collected commentaries and subcommentaries) (Jinchang shuye tang edition, 1778).

23 Henri Maspero, "Légendes mythologiques dans le *Chou king,*" *Journal Asiatique* 204 (1924): 1–100.

24 Maspero, "L'Astronomie chinois avant les Han," pp. 350 ff.; Needham, SCC III: 224.

25 Two Zhengs, Tang editor; both in *Zhouli* 10:13a, *Shisanjing zhusu* edition.

26 *Sui shu* 19:21a.

Bibliography

This bibliography lists all works cited in the reference notes, plus a much larger number of works consulted in the course of preparing this book.

ABBREVIATIONS

AM	*Asia Major*
BMFEA	*Bulletin of the Museum of Far Eastern Antiquities*
EC	*Early China*
HJAS	*Harvard Journal of Asiatic Studies*
HR	*History of Religions*
JAS	*Journal of Asian Studies*
JAOS	*Journal of the American Oriental Society*
JNCB/RAS	*Journal of the North China Branch of the Royal Asiatic Society*
KG	*Kaogu* 考古
KGXB	*Kaogu xuebao* 考古學報
SBBY	*Sibu beiyao* 四部備要
SBCK	*Sibu congkan* 四部叢刊
TP	*T'oung Pao*
TSS	*Tōyō shisō no shōmondai* 東洋思想の諸問題 (Various problems of eastern thought), Vol. 13 of *Tōyō shichō* 東洋思潮 (Currents of eastern thought). Tokyo: Iwanami shoten, 1934.
WW	*Wenwu* 文物
YG	*Yugong banyue kan* 禹貢半月刊

Abe Takeo 安部健夫. *Chūgokujin no tenka gannen* 中國人の天下觀念 (added title page in English: *T'ien-hsia Idea of the Chinese*). Kyoto: Harvard-Yenching Institute Doshisha University Lectures on Eastern Culture, 1956.

Adams, Francis. *The Genuine Works of Hippocrates.* (London, 1849)

Akatsuka Kiyoshi 赤塚忠. *Chūgoku kodai no shūkyō to bunka—In ōchō no saishi* 中國古代の

宗教と文化: 殷王朝の祭祀 (Ancient Chinese religion and culture—sacrificial rituals of the Yin kings). Tokyo, 1977.

Allan, Sarah. *The Heir and the Sage: Dynastic Legend in Early China.* Taipei: Chinese Materials Center, 1981.

Allan, Sarah. *The Shape of the Turtle: Myth, Art, and Cosmos in Early China.* Albany: State University of New York Press, 1991.

Sarah Allan, "Water in Early Chinese Philosophical Thought." Paper presented at the annual meeting of the Association for Asian Studies, Washington, D.C., 4 April, 1992.

Ames, Roger T. *The Art of Rulership: A Study in Ancient Chinese Political Thought.* Honolulu: University of Hawaii Press, 1983.

Amiot, Jean Joseph-Marie. "Mémoire sur la musique des chinois tant anciens que moderns," in Amiot et al., *Mémoires concernant l'histoire . . . des chinois. . . .* Paris, 1780.

An Zhimin 安志敏. "Changsha xin faxiande Xi Han bohua shitan 長沙新發現的西漢帛畫試探" (A tentative interpretation of the Western Han silk painting recently discovered at Changsha). KG 1973.1: 43–53.

Aoki Seiji 青木正兒. "Shina no shizenkan 支那の自然觀" (The Chinese view of nature). TSS 6. See esp. pp. 8–20, "Kisetsu no jinji 季節と人事" (Man and the seasons).

Balfour, Frederic Henry. "The Principle of Nature: A Chapter from the 'History of Great Light' by Huai-nan-tsze, Prince of Kiang-ling." *The China Review* 9 (1880–81): 281–97.

Balfour, Frederic Henry. *Taoist Texts, Ethical, Political, and Speculative.* London: Trubner and Co.; Shanghai: Kelly and Walsh, 1884.

Barnard, Noel. "The Ch'u Silk Manuscript and Other Archaeological Documents of Ancient China." In Noel Barnard, ed., *Early Chinese Art,* vol. 1, pp. 77–101.

Barnard, Noel. *The Ch'u Silk Manuscript—Translation and Commentary* (Studies on the Ch'u Silk Manuscript, Part 2). Canberra: Australian National University Monographs on Far Eastern History 5, 1973.

Barnard, Noel, ed. *Early Chinese Art and Its Possible Influence in the Pacific Basin.* 3 vols. New York: Intercultural Arts Press, 1972.

Barnard, Noel. *The Origin and Nature of the Art of Ancient Ch'u* (Studies on the Ch'u Silk Manuscript, Part 3). Canberra: Australian National University Monographs on Far Eastern History 6, 1974.

Barnard, Noel. *Scientific Examination of an Ancient Chinese Document as a Prelude to Decipherment, Translation, and Historical Assessment—The Ch'u Silk Manuscript* (Studies on the Ch'u Silk Manuscript, Part 1). Rev. and enlarged ed. Canberra: Australian National University Monographs on Far Eastern History 4, 1972.

Bauer, Wolfgang. *China and the Search for Happiness: Recurring Themes in Four Thousand Years of Chinese Cultural History.* New York: Seabury Press, 1976.

Bennett, Stephen J. "Patterns of the Sky and Earth: A Chinese Science of Applied Cosmology." *Chinese Science* 3 (1978): 1–26.

Bielenstein, Hans. "An Interpretation of the Portents in the Ts'ien Han Shu." BMFEA 22 (1950): 127–43.

Bibliography

Biot, Edouard. *Le Tcheou-li ou rites des Tcheou.* Paris: Imprimerie nationale, 1851.

Blacker, Carmen, and Michael Loewe, eds. *Ancient Cosmologies.* London: George Allen and Unwin, 1975.

Bo Shuren. "Astrometry and Astrometric Instruments." In Institute of the History of Natural Sciences, Chinese Academy of Sciences, *Ancient China's Technology and Science,* pp. 15–32. Beijing: Foreign Languages Press, 1983.

Bodde, Derk. "The Chinese Cosmic Magic Known as Watching for the Ethers." In Glahn and Egerod, eds., *Studia serica Bernhard Karlgren dedicata,* pp. 14–35. Copenhagen: Munksgaard, 1959. Also in Bodde, *Essays,* pp. 351–72.

Bodde, Derk. "'Chinese Laws of Nature,' A Reconsideration." HJAS 39 (1979): 139–55. Also in Bodde, *Essays,* pp. 299–315. See also "Organicism and Laws of Nature" in Bodde, *Chinese Thought, Society, and Science,* pp. 332–355.

Bodde, Derk. *Chinese Thought, Society, and Science.* Honolulu: University of Hawaii Press, 1991.

Bodde, Derk. *Essays on Chinese Civilization,* ed. and intro. by Charles Le Blanc and Dorothy Borei. Princeton: Princeton University Press, 1981.

Bodde, Derk. "Evidence for 'Laws of Nature' in Chinese Thought." HJAS 20 (1957): 709–27.

Bodde, Derk. *Festivals in Classical China: New Year and Other Annual Observances during the Han Dynasty, 206 B.C.–A.D. 220.* Princeton: Princeton University Press; Hong Kong: Chinese University of Hong Kong Press, 1975.

Bodde, Derk. "Harmony and Conflict in Chinese Philosophy." In Arthur F. Wright, ed., *Studies in Chinese Thought,* pp. 19–80. Chicago: University of Chicago Press, 1953. Also in Bodde, *Essays,* pp. 237–98.

Bodde, Derk. "Myths of Ancient China." In Samuel N. Kramer, ed., *Mythologies of the Ancient World,* pp. 369–406. New York: Doubleday and Co., 1961. Also in Bodde, *Essays,* pp. 45–84.

Bodde, Derk. "Types of Chinese Categorical Thinking." JAOS 59.2 (1939): 293–99. Also in Bodde, *Essays,* pp. 141–60.

Bodde, Derk. "Sexual Sympathetic Magic in Ancient China." HR 3 (1963): 293–99. Also in Bodde, *Essays,* pp. 373–80.

Bohutong 白虎通. SBCK edition.

Boltz, William G. "Kung-kung and the Flood: Reverse Euhemerization in the *Yao tien.*" TP 67 (1981): 141–53.

Boltz, William G. "Philological Footnotes to the Han New Year Rites." JAOS 99 (1979): 423–39.

Bretschneider, E. *Botanicum Sinicum: Notes on Chinese Botany from Native and Western Sources.* 3 vols. London, 1882.

Bulling, Annaliese. *The Decoration of Mirrors of the Han Period.* Ascona, 1960.

Bulling, Annaliese. "The Decoration of Some Mirrors of the Chou and Han Periods." *Artibus Asiae* 18 (1955): 20–43.

Bulling, Annaliese. "The Guide of the Souls Picture in the Western Han Tomb in Ma-Wang-Tui near Ch'ang-sha." *Oriental Art* 20 (1974): 158–73.

Cahill, Suzanne. "Reflections of a Metal Mother: Tu Kuang-t'ing's Biography of Hsi Wang Mu." In Girardot and Major, eds., *Myth and Symbol in Chinese Tradition*, pp. 127–42.

Cammann, Schuyler. "The Evolution of Magic Squares in China." JAOS 80 (1960): 116–24.

Cammann, Schuyler. "The Magic Square of Three in Old Chinese Philosophy and Religion." HR 1 (1961): 37–80.

Cammann, Schuyler. "Old Chinese Magic Squares." *Sinologica* 7 (1963): 14–53.

Cammann, Schuyler. "Symbolic Expressions of *Yin-yang* Philosophy." In Le Blanc and Blader, eds., *Chinese Ideas about Nature and Society*, pp. 101–16.

Cammann, Schuyler. "The 'TLV' Pattern on the Cosmic Mirrors of the Han Dynasty." JAOS 68 (1948): 159–67.

Cammann, Schuyler. "Types of Symbols in Chinese Art." In Arthur F. Wright, ed., *Studies in Chinese Thought*, pp. 195–231. Chicago: University of Chicago Press, 1953.

Cao Wanru 曹婉如. "Wuzang shanjing he Yugong de dili zhishi 五藏山經和禹頁的地理知識" (Geographical knowledge in the *Wuzang shanjing* and in "Yugong"). *Kexueshi jikan* 科學史集刊 1 (1958):77–85.

Chan, Ping-leung. "*Ch'u Tz'u* and Shamanism in Ancient China." Ph.D. diss., Ohio State University, 1962.

Chang, Kwang-chih. *The Archaeology of Ancient China.* Rev. ed. New Haven: Yale University Press, 1986.

Chang, Kwang-chih. *Art, Myth, and Ritual: The Path to Political Authority in Ancient China.* Cambridge: Harvard University Press, 1983.

Chang, Kwang-chih. "A Classification of Shang and Chou Myths." In Chang, *Early Chinese Civilization*, pp. 155–73.

Chang, Kwang-chih. *Early Chinese Civilization: Anthropological Perspectives.* Cambridge: Harvard University Press, 1976.

Chang, Kwang-chih. "Major Aspects of Ch'u Archaeology." In Noel Barnard, ed., *Early Chinese Art*, vol. 1, pp. 5–52.

Chang, Leo S. "The Metamorphosis of Han Fei's Thought in the Han." In Rosemont and Schwartz, eds., *Studies in Classical Chinese Thought*, pp. 503–47.

Changsha Chumu bohua 長沙楚墓帛畫 (The silk painting from a Han tomb at Changsha). Beijing: Wenwu Press, 1973.

Chao Wei-pang. "The Chinese Science of Fate-Calculation." *Folklore Studies* 5 (1946): 279–315.

Chatley, Herbert. "'The Heavenly Cover,' A Study in Ancient Chinese Astronomy." *Observatory* 61 (1938): 10–21.

Chatley, Herbert. "*Huai-nan-tsu* Chapter Three." Unpublished draft translation, n.d.

Chatley, Herbert. "The Lunar Mansions in Egypt." *Isis* 3 (1940): 394–97.

Chavannes, Edouard. *Les Mémoires historiques de Se-Ma Ts'ien.* 5 vols. Paris: E. Leroux, 1895–1905.

Chavannes, Edouard. *Mission archéologique dans la Chine septentrionale.* 2 vols. + portfolio of plates. Paris: E. Leroux, 1913.

Chavannes, Edouard. *Le Tai chan: Essai de monographie d'un culte Chinois.* Paris: E. Leroux, 1910.

Chen, Cheng-yih. "The Generation of Chromatic Scales in the Chinese Bronze Set-Bells of the -5th Century." In Chen et al., eds., *Science and Technology in Chinese Civilization*, pp. 155–97.

Chen, Cheng-yih et al., eds. *Science and Technology in Chinese Civilization*. Singapore: World Scientific Publishing Co., 1978.

Chen Jiujin. "Chinese Calendars." In Institute of the History of Natural Sciences, Chinese Academy of Sciences, *Ancient China's Technology and Science*, pp. 33–49. Beijing: Foreign Languages Press, 1983.

Chen Jiujin 陳久金. "Cong Mawangdui boshu 'Wuxing zhan' de chutu shishen woguo gudai de suixing jinian wenti 從馬王堆帛書 '五星占' 的出土試探我國古代的歲星紀年問題" (An essay on the question of year-reckoning by the Jupiter cycle, based on the excavation of the Mawangdui silk manuscript "Prognostications of the five planets"). In *Zhongguo tianwenxue shi wenji*, pp. 48–65.

Chen Mengjia 陳夢家. "Wuxing zhi qiyuan 五行的起源" (On the origin of the five-phase system). *Yanjing xuebao* 燕京學報 24 (1938): 35–53.

Chen Xinxiong 陳新雄 and Yu Dacheng 于大成, eds. *Huainanzi lunwen ji* 淮南子論文集 (Collected essays on the *Huainanzi*). Taipei: Muduo chupanshe, 1976.

Chen Zhun'gui 陳遵媯. *Zongguo tianwenxue shi* 中國天文學史 (A history of Chinese astronomy). 3 vols. Shanghai: People's Press, 1980–84.

Cheng Faren 陳發靱. "Chunqiu diming tu kao 春秋地名圖考" (Illustrated study of geographical names in the Chunqiu Period). *Shida xuebao* 師大學報 6 (1961): 1–158.

Cheng Faren. "Yugong dili buyi 禹貢地理補義" (Geographical annotations on "Yugong"), *Shida xuebao* 師大學報 2 (1957): 121–35.

Cheng, Hsiao-Chieh et al., trans. *Shan Hai Ching: Legendary Geography and Wonders of Ancient China*. Taipei: National Institute for Compilation and Translation, 1985.

Cheng Te-k'un. "The Travels of the Emperor Mu." JNCB/RAS 64 (1933): 124–42; 65 (1934): 128–49.

Cheng Te-k'un, see also Zheng Dekun.

Christie, Anthony. *Chinese Mythology*. 2d ed. London: Newnes, 1983.

Chu ci 楚辭. Hanfenlou photo reprint of a Song edition. Shanghai: Commercial Press, n.d.

Chu ci buzhu 楚辭補注. SBBY edition.

Chu wenhua yanjiu lunji 楚文化研究論集 (Collected studies in Chu culture). Wuhan: Xing Chu Publishing Co., 1987.

Chunqiu fanlu 春秋繁露. By Dong Zhongshu 董仲舒 (ca. 100 B.C.E.). Edition of Su Yu 蘇輿, *Chunqiu fanlu yicheng* 義證, 1910.

Combridge, John H. "Chinese Sexagenary Calendar-Cycles." *Antiquarian Horology* 5.4 (1966): 134.

Conrady, August. "Indischer Einflüß in China im 4. Jahrhundert v. Chr." *Zeitschrift der Deutschen Morgenlandischen Gesellschaft* 60 (1906): 335–51.

Cook, Constance Anne. "Auspicious Metals and Southern Spirits: An Analysis of the Chu Bronze Inscriptions." Ph.D. diss., University of California at Berkeley, 1990.

Cook, Constance Anne. Review of *Western Chou Civilization* by Hsu Cho-yun and Katheryn M. Linduff. JAOS 111 (1991): 615–17.

Couvreur, Seraphin. [*Yili*] *Ceremonial: Texte chinois et traduction.* Xianxian: Imprimerie de la mission catholique, 1928.

Couvreur, Seraphin. [*Liji*] *Mémoires sur les bienseances et les ceremonies.* 2 vols. Paris: Cathasia, 1950.

Creel, H. G. *Shen Pu-hai: A Political Philosopher of the Fourth Century B.C.* Chicago: University of Chicago Press, 1974.

Creel, H. G. "What is Taoism?" JAOS 76 (1956): 139–152. Reprinted in Creel, *What is Taoism?.*

Creel, H. G. *What is Taoism? And Other Studies in Chinese Cultural History.* Chicago: University of Chicago Press, 1970.

Cullen, Christopher. *Astronomy and Mathematics in Ancient China: The Zhou bi suan jing.* Cambridge: Cambridge University Press, forthcoming.

Cullen, Christopher. "The Han Cosmic Model: A Rejoinder to Donald Harper." EC 7 (1981–82): 130–33.

Cullen, Christopher. "Some Further Points on the *Shih.*" EC 6 (1980–81): 31–46.

Da Dai liji 大戴禮記. 1888 edition. Reprint. Taipei: World Book Co., 1966.

Davis, Tenny L. "The Dualistic Cosmogony of Huai-nan-tzu and Its Relation to the Background of Chinese and European Alchemy." *Isis* 25 (1936): 327–40.

De Bary, Wm. Theodore, et al. *Sources of Chinese Tradition* (New York and London: Columbia University Press, 1960).

Deishi Masahiko 出石誠彦. "Jodai Shina ni okeru shinwa oyobi setsuwa 上代支那における神話及び説話" (Myths and legends in ancient China). TSS 3. See esp. pp. 46–54, "Shirei—ryu ki rin ho—no setsuwateki homen 四靈一龍龜麟鳳一の説話方面" (Mythological aspects of the four numena—dragon, tortoise, *qilin*, phoenix).

DeRosny, L., trans. *Chan-Hai-King: Antique géographie Chinoise.* Paris: Maisonneuve, 1891.

De Woskin, Kenneth. *Doctors, Diviners, and Magicians of Ancient China: Biographies of Fang-shih.* New York: Columbia University Press, 1983.

Diagram Group, The. *Weapons: An International Encyclopedia from 5000 B.C. to 2000 A.D.* London: Macmillan, 1990.

Diény, Jean-Pierre. "Le *Fenghuang* et le phénix." *Cahiers d'Extrême-Asie* 5 (Special Issue: Taoist Studies II) (1989–90): 1–15.

Diény, Jean-Pierre. *Le Symbolisme du dragon dans la Chine antique.* Paris: Collège de France, Institut des Hautes Études Chinoises, 1987.

Dreyer, J. L. E. *History of the Planetary Systems from Thales to Kepler.* Cambridge: Cambridge University Press, 1906. Reprinted as *A History of Astronomy from Thales to Kepler.* New York: Dover Publications, 1953.

Du Erwei 杜而未. *Feng lin gui long kaoshi* 鳳麟龜龍考譯 (Research on the phoenix, qilin, tortoise, and dragon). Taipei: Commercial Press, 1966. Includes summary and bibliography in English.

Bibliography

Du Erwei. *Kunlun wenhua yu busi guannian* 崑崙文化與不死觀念 (Added title in English: The Kunlun Culture and the Concept of Immortality). Taipei: Huaming shuju, 1962.

Dubs, Homer H. "An Ancient Chinese Mystery Cult." *Harvard Theological Review* 35 (1942): 221–40.

Dubs, Homer H. "The Beginnings of Alchemy." *Isis* 38 (1947): 62–86.

Dubs, Homer H. "The Beginnings of Chinese Astronomy." JAOS 78 (1958): 295–300.

Dubs, Homer H. "Han Hill Censers." In Glahn and Egerod, *Studia serica Bernhard Karlgren dedicata*, pp. 259–64.

Dubs, Homer H. *The History of the Former Han Dynasty*. 3 vols. Baltimore: Waverly Press, 1938–55.

Dubs, Homer H. "Standard Weights and Measures in Han Times." In Dubs, trans., *The History of the Former Han Dynasty*, vol. 1, chap. 4, appendix 1, pp. 276–80.

Eberhard, Wolfram. "Beiträge zur Kosmologischen Spekulation Chinas in der Han Zeit." *Baessler Archiv* 16 (Berlin: Museum für Völkerkunde, 1933): 1–100.

Eberhard, Wolfram. "Index zu den Arbeiten über Astronomie, Astrologie, und Elementlehre." *Monumenta Serica* 7 (1942): 242–66.

Eberhard, Wolfram. *The Local Cultures of South and East China*. Leiden: E. J. Brill, 1968.

Eberhard, Wolfram. *Lokalkulturen im alten China*. 2 vols. Leiden: E. J. Brill, 1942.

Eberhard, Wolfram. Review of Karlgren, "Legends and Cults in Ancient China." *Artibus Asiae* 6 (1946): 1–10.

Eberhard, Wolfram. "The Political Function of Astronomers and Astronomy in Han China." In John K. Fairbank, ed., *Chinese Thought and Institutions*, pp. 33–70. Chicago: University of Chicago Press, 1957.

Eisman, Harriet Lentz. "Shan Hai Ching (The Classic of Mountains and Seas)." M.A. diss., Cornell University, 1975.

Eliade, Mircea. "Centre du monde, temple, maison." In *Le Symbolisme cosmique des monuments religieux*. Serie Orientale Roma, 14. Roma: Istituto Italiano per il Medio ed Estremo Oriente, 1957.

Eliade, Mircea. *The Forge and the Crucible*. New York: Harper and Bros., 1962.

Eliade, Mircea. *The Myth of the Eternal Return, or, Cosmos and History*. Princeton: Princeton University Press, Bolingen Series 40, 1954.

Eliade, Mircea. *Shamanism*. Princeton: Princeton University Press, Bolingen Series 76, 1964.

Emiliani, Cesare, et al. "Paleoclimatological Analysis of Late Quaternary Cores from the Northeastern Gulf of Mexico." *Science* 189 (1975): 1083–88.

Eno, Robert. "Creating Nature: Juist and Taoist Approaches." In Smith, ed., *Chuang Tzu:: Rationality::Interpretation*, pp. 3–28.

Eno, Robert. "Was There a High God *Ti* in Shang Religion?" EC 15 (1990): 1–26.

Erkes, Eduard. "Der Chinese un das Tier." *Sinologica* 1 (1948): 273–91.

Erkes, Eduard. "Chinesisch-amerikanische mythenparallelen." TP 24 (1926): 32–54.

Erkes, Eduard. "Spuren einer kosmogonischen Mythe bei Lao-tze." *Artibus Asiae* 8 (1940): 16–35.

Erkes, Eduard. "Das Weltbild des Huai-nan-tze." *Ostasiatische Zeitschrift* 5 (1916–17): 27–80.

The Exhibition of Archaeological Finds of The People's Republic of China. Washington: National Gallery of Art, 1975.

von Falkenhausen, Lothar A. "Ritual Music in Bronze Age China: An Archaeological Perspective." Ph.D. diss., Harvard University, 1988.

Fehl, N. E. *Li: Rites and Propriety in Literature and Life.* Hong Kong: Chinese University of Hong Kong Press, 1971.

Field, Stephen. "Cosmos, Cosmograph, and the Inquiring Poet: A New Answer to the 'Heaven Questions.'" EC 17 (1992): 83–110.

Field, Stephen. *T'ien Wen: A Chinese Book of Origins.* New York: New Directions, 1986.

Finsterbusch, Käte. "Shan-hai-ching Buch 13: Das Buch vom Osten innerhalb des Meeres." In *Asiatica: Festschrift Friedrich Weller*, pp. 103–18. Leipzig: Otto Harrassowitz, 1954.

Finsterbusch, Käte. *Verzeichnis und Motivindex der Han-darstellungen.* Weisbaden: Otto Harrassowitz, 1966.

Forke, Alfred. *Lun-Heng: Philosophical Essays of Wang Ch'ung.* 2 vols. Leipzig: Otto Harrassowitz, 1907.

Forke, Alfred. *The World-Conception of the Chinese: Their Astronomical, Cosmological, and Physico-philosophical Speculations.* London: Probsthain, 1925.

Forte, Antonino. *Mingtang and Buddhist Utopias in the History of the Astronomical Clock.* Serie Orientale Roma, 59. Rome: Istituto Italiano per il Medio ed Estremo Oriente, 1988.

Fracasso, Riccardo. "Holy Mothers of Ancient China: A New Approach to the Hsi-Wang-Mu Problem." Taipei: mimeographed, 1985.

Fracasso, Riccardo. "Manifestazioni del simbolismo assiale nelle tradizioni cinesi antiche." *Numen* 28 (1981): 194–215.

Fracasso, Riccardo. "Teratoscopy or Divination by Monsters: Being a study on the *Wu-tsang Shan-ching.*" *Hanxue yanjiu/Chinese Studies* [Taipei] 1.2 (1983): 657–700.

Fukui Kojun 福井康順 et al., eds. *Dōkyō* 道教 (Daoism). 3 vols. Tokyo: Hirakawa, 1983.

Fung Yu-lan. *A History of Chinese Philosophy*, trans. Derk Bodde. 2 vols. Princeton: Princeton University Press, 1952–53.

Giles, Lionel. *A Gallery of Chinese Immortals.* London: J. Murray, 1912.

Gillie, R. Bruce, "Endemic Goiter." *Scientific American* (June 1971): 92–97.

Girardot, N. J. "Chaotic 'Order' (*hun-tun*) and Benevolent 'Disorder' (*luan*) in the *Chuangtzu.*" *Philosophy East and West* 28.3 (1978): 300–21.

Girardot, N. J. *Myth and Meaning in Early Taoism.* Berkeley and Los Angeles: University of California Press, 1983.

Girardot, N. J., and John S. Major, eds. *Myth and Symbol in Chinese Tradition* (Symposium Issue, vols. 13 and 14 of *Journal of Chinese Religions*). Boulder: Society for the Study of Chinese Religions, 1986.

Glahn, Else, and Søren Egerod, eds. *Studia serica Bernhard Karlgren dedicata.* Copenhagen: Munksgaard, 1959.

Gong nong kaogu jichu zhishi 工農考古基礎知識 (Basic archaeology for workers and peasants). Beijing: Wenwu Press, 1978.

Goodrich, Chauncey S. "A New History of Early Imperial China" [review of Twitchett and Loewe, eds., *The Cambridge History of China, Volume One: The Ch'in and Han Dynasties, 221 B.C.–A.D. 220*], JAOS 108 (1988): 457–63.

Graham, A. C. *The Book of Lieh-tzu*. London: J. Murray, 1960.

Graham, A. C. *Chuang-tzu: The Seven Inner Chapters and Other Writings from the Book of Chuang-tzu*. London: Allen and Unwin, 1981.

Graham, A. C. *Disputers of the Tao*. LaSalle, Ill.: Open Court Publishing Co., 1989.

Graham, A. C. "How Much of *Chuang Tzu* did Chuang Tzu Write?" In Rosemont and Schwartz, eds., *Studies in Classical Chinese Thought*, pp. 459–501.

Graham, A. C. *Later Mohist Logic, Ethics, and Science*. Hong Kong: Chinese University of Hong Kong Press; London: School of Oriental and African Studies, 1978.

A. C. Graham, "Reflections and Replies." In Rosemont, ed., *Chinese Texts and Philosophical Contexts*, pp. 267–322.

Graham, A. C. *Yin-Yang and the Nature of Correlative Thinking*. IEAP Occasional Paper and Monograph Series, 6. Singapore: Institute of East Asian Philosophies, 1986.

Granet, Marcel. *Danses et légendes de la Chine ancienne*. 2 vols. Paris: Alcan, 1926.

Granet, Marcel. *Fêtes et chansons anciennes de la Chine*. Paris: Leroux, 1929.

Granet, Marcel. *La pensée chinoise*. Paris: La Renaissance du Livre, 1934.

Gu Jiegang. 顧頡剛. "Handai yiqian Zhongguoren de shijie guannian yu yuwai jiaotong de gushi 漢代以前中國人的世界觀念與域外交通的故事" (The world-view and foreign relations of the Han Chinese). YG 5.3 and 4 (1936): 97–120.

Gu Jiegang. *Qin Han de fangshi yu rusheng* 秦漢的方士與儒生 (Masters of techniques and Confucians in the Qin and Han). Shanghai, 1955. Originally published in 1934 as *Handai xueshu shilue* 漢代學術史略.

Gu Jiegang. "Wude zhongshi shuoxia de zhengzhi he lishi 五德終始說下的政治和歷史" (Politics and history in light of the five-powers cyclical theory). *Qinghua xuebao* 6 (1930): 71–268; also in *Gushi bian* 5: 404–617. German abstract by Wolfram Eberhard in *Sinica* 6 (1931): 136–37.

Gu Jiegang and Yang Xianggui 楊向奎. *Sanhuang kao* 三皇考 (added title page in English: *The History of the "Three Emperors" in Ancient China*). *Yenching Journal of Chinese Studies*. Monograph Series No. 8. Peiping: Harvard-Yenching Institute, 1936.

Gu Jiegang et al., eds. *Gushi bian* 古史辨 (Symposium on ancient history). 7 vols. Vols. 1–5, Peiping, 1926–35; vols. 6–7, Shanghai, 1938–41.

Gu Tiefu 顧鐵符. "Mawangdui boshu 'Tianwen qixiang zazhan' neirong jianshi 馬王堆帛書 '天文氣象雜占' 內容簡述" (added title in English: "Notes on the Silk Manuscript of Astrology Found in Tomb No. 3 at Mawangdui, Changsha"). WW 1978.2: 1–4.

Guan Donggui 管東貴. "Zongguo gudai shi ri shenhua zhi yanjiu 中國古代十日神話之研究" (Studies of the ten-suns myths of ancient China). *Bulletin of the Institute of History and Philology, Academia Sinica* 33 (1962): 287–330.

Guanzi 管子. SBBY edition.

Guo Moruo 郭沫若. *Shi pipan shu* 十批判書 (Ten critical essays). Beijing: Science Press, 1962.

Guoyu 國語. SBBY edition.

Haloun, Gustav. *Seit wann kannten die Chinesen die Tocharer oder Indogermannen überhaupt.* Leipzig: Otto Harrassowitz, 1926.

Han shu 漢書. *Bonaben* and SBCK editions.

Hansen, Chad. "Reason in the Translation and Interpretation of Chinese Philosophy." In Smith, ed., *Chuang Tzu::Rationality::Interpretation*, pp. 53–70.

de Harlez, Charles Joseph. "Textes taoistes." *Annales du Musée Guimet* 20 (1891).

Harper, Donald J. "A Chinese Demonography of the Third Century B.C.." HJAS 45: 459–98 (1985).

Harper, Donald J. "The Han Cosmic Board (*Shih* 式)." EC 4 (1978–79): 1–10.

Harper, Donald J. "The Han Cosmic Board: A Response to Christopher Cullen." EC 6 (1980–81): 47–56.

Harper, Donald J. "A Summary of the Contents of the Ma-wang-tui Silk-Scroll Book 'Assorted Astronomical and Meteorological Prognostications.'" *Chinese Studies in Archaeology* 1 (1979): 56–74.

Harper, Donald J. "Tekhnê in Han Natural Philosophy: Evidence from Ma-wang-tui Medical Manuscripts." In Smith, ed., *Sagehood and Systematizing Thought*, pp. 33–45.

Harper, Donald J. "Warring States, Qin, and Han Manuscripts Related to Natural Philosophy and the Occult." In Edward L. Shaughnessy, ed., *Paleographic Sources of Early China* (Hong Kong: Chinese University of Hong Kong Press, forthcoming).

Hart, James A. "The Speech of Prince Chin: A Study of Early Chinese Cosmology." In Rosemont, ed., *Explorations in Early Chinese Cosmology*, pp. 35–66.

Hartner, Willy. "Some Notes on Chinese Musical Art," *Isis*, July, 1938; reprinted in Nathan Sivin, ed., *Science and Technology in East Asia* (New York: Science History Publications, 1977), pp. 32–54.

Hawkes, David. *Ch'u Tz'u: The Songs of the South.* London: Oxford University Press, 1959; 2d ed., London and New York: Penguin Books, 1985.

Hayashi, Minao 林巳奈夫, "Chugoku kodai no shinpu 中國古代の神巫" (Shamanism in ancient China). *Tōhō gakuhō* (Kyoto) 38 (1967): 199–224.

Hayashi, Minao. "Iwayuru 'taotie' mon wa nani o arawashita mono ka? 所謂饕餮紋は何を表はしたものか" (added title in English: A consideration of the meaning of the so-called tao-tie motif). *Tōhō gakuhō* (Kyoto) 56 (1984): 1–97.

Hayashi, Minao. "Kan kyō no zuhyō ni, san ni tsuite 漢鏡の図柄二三について (A few remarks on Han TLV mirrors). *Tōhō gakuhō* (Kyoto) 44 (1973): 1–65.

Hayashi, Minao. "The Twelve Gods of the Chan-kuo Period Silk Manuscript Excavated at Ch'ang-sha." In Noel Barnard, ed., *Early Chinese Art*, vol. 1, pp. 123–86.

He Cejun 賀次君. "Shuijingzhu jingliu qiliu mu 水經注經流枝流目" (Index of rivers in the *Shuijingzhu*). YG 2.8 (1934): 27–34; 2.10 (1935): 39–43.

He Guanzhou 何觀州. "Shanhaijing zai kexueshang de piping ji zuozhe zhi shidai kao 山海經在科學上的批刊及作者之時代考" (The *Shanhaijing*: The date of its authorship and its scientific value), *Yanjing xuebao* 燕京學報 (*Yenching Journal of Chinese Studies*) 7

(June 1930): 1347–75. English abstract in *Yenching Journal of Chinese Studies Supplement* 1 (1932): 62–64.

Henderson, John B. *The Development and Decline of Chinese Cosmology.* New York: Columbia University Press, 1984.

Henricks, Robert G. *Lao-Tzu Te-Tao Ching: A New Translation Based on the Recently Discovered Ma-wang-tui Texts.* New York: Ballantine Books, 1989.

Henricks, Robert G. "On the Whereabouts and Identity of the Place Called 'K'ung-sang' (Hollow Mulberry) in Early Chinese Mythology." Paper presented at the annual meeting of the Association for Asian Studies, Washington, D.C., 4 April, 1992.

Hentze, Carl. "Mythologische Bildsymbole im alten China." *Studium Generale* 6 (1953): 264–77.

Hentze, Carl. *Tod, Auferstehung, Weltordnung.* 2 vols. Zürich: Origo Verlag, 1955.

Herrmann, Albert. *Die Alten Seidenstrassen zwischen China und Syria.* Wittenburg: Herrose and Ziemsen, 1910.

Herrmann, Albert. *Lou-Lan: China, Indien, und Rom im Lichte der Ausgrabungen am Lobnor.* Leipzig, 1931.

Herrmann, Albert. "Die Westlander in d. chinesischen Kartographie." In Sven Heyden, *Southern Tibet: Discoveries in Former Times Compared with My Own Researches in 1906–1908,* vol. 3, pp. 91–406. Stockholm: Swedish Army General Staff Lithographic Institute, 1922.

Hightower, James R. "Ch'ü Yüan Studies." In *The Silver Jubilee Volume of the Zimbun-Kagaku-Kenkyuso* 1 (Kyoto, 1954): 92–233.

Hightower, James R. *The Poetry of T'ao Ch'ien.* Oxford: Oxford University Press, 1970.

Hirth, F. *China and the Roman Orient.* Shanghai: Kelly and Walsh, 1885.

Ho Peng Yoke. *The Astronomical Chapters of the Chin Shu.* Paris and The Hague: Mouton and Co., 1966.

Ho Peng Yoke. *Li, Qi and Shu: An Introduction to Science and Civilization in China.* Hong Kong: Hong Kong University Press, 1985.

Howard, Jeffrey A. "Concepts of Comprehensiveness and Historical Change in the *Huai-nan-tzu.*" In Rosemont, ed., *Explorations in Early Chinese Cosmology,* pp. 119–32.

Hsiao, K. C. *A History of Chinese Political Thought,* trans. by F. W. Mote. Princeton: Princeton University Press, 1979.

Hsu Cho-yun and Katheryn M. Linduff. *Western Chou Civilization.* New Haven: Yale University Press, 1989.

Hsü Dau-lin, "Crime and Cosmic Order." HJAS 30 (1970): 111–25.

Hu Shih. *The Development of the Logical Method in Ancient China.* Shanghai: Oriental Book Co., 1922.

Huainanzi 淮南子. SBBY and SBCK editions; see also Liu Wendian, *Huainan honglie jijie.*

Huainanzi tongjian 淮南子通檢 (*Index du Hoai Nan Tseu*). Beijing: Centre Franco-Chinois d'études Sinologiques, 1944.

Hubei Provincial Museum. *Suixian Zeng Houyi mu* 隨縣曾侯乙墓 (The tomb of Marquis Yi of Zeng at Suixian). Beijing: Wenwu Press, 1980.

Hughes, E. R. "Chinese Religion in the Third Century B.C.." *Asiatic Review* 31 (1935): 721–33.

Hulsewé, A. F. P. "Texts in Tombs." *Asiatische Studien/Études Asiatiques* 18/19 (1965): 78–89.

Hunan Provincial Museum. "Hunan Changde Deshan Chumu fajue baogao 湖南常德德山楚墓發掘報告" (Report on the excavation of the Chu tombs at Deshan, Changde County, Hunan). KG 1963.9: 461–73.

Hunan Provincial Museum. *Mawangdui Hanmu yanjiu* 馬王堆漢墓研究 (Research on the Mawangdui Han tombs). Changsha: Hunan Provincial Museum, 1981.

Hunan Provincial Museum, Huaihua 怀化 Area Cultural Relics Work Team. "Hunan Xupu Matianping Zhanguo Xi Han mu fajue baogao 湖南淑浦馬田坪戰國西漢墓發掘報告" (Report on excavations of Warring States and Western Han tombs at Matianping, Xupu County, Hunan). *Hunan kaogu jikan* 湖南考古輯刊 2 (1984) 38–69.

Hunan Provincial Museum and Institute of Archaeology, Chinese Academy of Sciences. *Changsha Mawangdui yihao Hanmu* 長沙馬王堆一號漢墓 (The Han tomb no. 1 at Mawangdui, Changsha). 2 vols. Beijing: Wenwu Press, 1973.

Iijima Tadaō 飯島忠夫. "In'yō gogyō no setsu 陰陽五行の說" (The yin-yang/five phase theory). *Tōyō shichō* vol. 4 no. 4. Tokyo: Iwanami Shoten, 1935.

Iijima Tadaō. *Tenmon rekihō to in'yō gogyō setsu* 天文歷法と陰陽五行說 (Astronomy, calendrical science, and yin-yang/five phase theory). Tokyo, 1939.

Institute for the History of the Natural Sciences, Chinese Academy of Science. *Zhongguo gudai keji chengjiu* 中國古代科技成就 (Accomplishments of ancient Chinese science and technology). Beijing: China Youth Press, 1978.

Institute of Archaeology, Chinese Academy of Sciences, eds. *Zhongguo gudai tianwen wenwu tuji* 中國古代天文文物圖集 (Illustrations of ancient Chinese astronomical artifacts). Beijing: Wenwu Press, 1980.

Jao, Tsung-yi. "Some Aspects of the Calendar, Astrology, and Religious Concepts of the Ch'u People as Revealed in the Ch'u Silk Manuscript." In Noel Barnard, ed., *Early Chinese Art*, vol. 1, pp. 113–22.

Jinizi 計倪子. Assembled fragments in Ma Guohan 馬國翰, *Yuhan shanfang ji yishu* 玉函山房輯佚書 (Jade Box Mountain Studio collection of reconstituted lost books). 1853. Chap. 69.

Kalinowski, Marc. *Cosmologie et divination dans la Chine ancienne: Le Compendium des cinq agents (Wuxing dayi, VIe siècle)*. Paris: École Française d'Extrême-Orient, 1991.

Kalinowski, Marc. "Les Instruments astro-calendriques des Han et la méthode *liu jen*." *Bulletin de l'École Française d'Extrême-Orient* 72 (1983): 309–416.

Kaltenmark, Max. *Le Lie Sien Tchouan*. Beijing: Centre Franco-Chinois d'études Sinologiques, 1953.

Kaltenmark, Max. "La Naissance du monde en Chine." In *La Naissance du monde*, pp. 453–67. Paris: Éditions du Seuil, 1959.

Kaltenmark, Max. *Lao Tzu and Taoism*. Stanford: Stanford University Press, 1969.

Kanaya Osamu 金谷治. *Rō-Sō teki sekai, Enanji no shisō* 老莊的世界淮南子の思想 (The thought of *Huainanzi* in the world of Lao-Zhuang Daoism). Kyoto, 1959.

Kandel, Barbara. "Der Versuch einer politischen Restauration—Liu An von Huai-nan." *Nachrichten der Gesellschaft für Natur- und Völkerkunde Ostasiens, Hamburg* 113 (1973): 33–96.

Kaplan, Sidney M. "On the Origin of the TLV Mirror." *Revue des arts asiatiques* 11 (1937): 21–24.

Karlgren, Bernhard. "The Book of Documents." BMFEA 22 (1950): 1–81.

Karlgren, Bernhard. "Glosses on the Book of Documents." BMFEA 20 (1948) and 21 (1949). Reprinted, Stockholm: Museum of Far Eastern Antiquities, 1950.

Karlgren, Bernhard. "Grammatica Serica Recensa." BMFEA 29 (1957): 1–332.

Karlgren, Bernhard. "Han and Huai." BMFEA 13 (1941): 1–125.

Karlgren, Bernhard. "Legends and Cults in Ancient China." BMFEA 18 (1946): 199–365.

Keightley, David N. "Akatsuka Kiyoshi and the Culture of Early China: A Study in Historical Method." HJAS 42 (1982): 267–320.

Keightley, David N. "Late Shang Divination: The Magico-Religious Legacy." In Rosemont, ed., *Explorations in Early Chinese Cosmology*, pp. 11–34.

Keightley, David N., ed. *The Origins of Chinese Civilization*. Berkeley: University of California Press, 1983.

Keightley, David N. "The Religious Commitment: Shang Theology and the Genesis of Chinese Political Culture." HR 17.3 and 4 (1978): 211–25.

Kimura Eichi 木村英一. *Rōshi no shinkenkyū* 老子の新研究 (New studies of *Laozi*). Tokyo: Sobunsha, 1959.

Knoblock, John. *Xunzi: A Translation and Study of the Complete Works*. 3 vols. Stanford: Stanford University Press, 1988.

Kobayashi Shimmei 小林信月. *Chugoku jōdai in'yō gogyō shisō no kenkyū* 中国上代陰陽五行思想の研究 (Research on yin-yang/five phase thought in ancient China). Tokyo, 1956.

Komai Kazuchika, "The Ainu in Age of T'ang Dynasty," *Acta Asiatica* 6 (1964):1–10.

Kongzi jiayu 孔子家語. SBBY edition.

Kraft, Eva. "Zum Huai-nan-tzu. Einfürung, Übersetzung (Kapitel I und II) und Interpretation." *Monumenta Serica* 16 (1957): 191–286; 17 (1958): 128–207.

Kroll, Paul W. Review of Jean-Pierre Diény, *Le Symbolisme du dragon dans la Chine antique*. JAOS 109 (1989): 325–30.

Kume Kunitake 久米邦武. "Konron saiōbō ko 崑崙西王母考" (Studies of Kunlun and the Queen Mother of the West). *Shigaku zasshi* 史學雜誌 4 (1893): 197–214, 288–302.

Richard A. Kunst, "More on *Hsiu* 宿 and *Wu-hsing* 五行, with an Addendum on the Use of Archaic Reconstructions." EC 3 (1977): 67–79.

Kuraishi Takeshiro 倉石四郎. "Enanji no rekishi 淮南子の歴史" (History of the *Huainanzi*). *Shinagaku* 支那学 3 (1923): 334–68.

Lanciotti, L. "The Shan Hai Ching." *East and West* 4 (1953): 52–54.

Lao Ge 勞格. *Dushu zazhi* 讀書雜識, 1878.

Larre, Claude. *Le Traite VIIᵉ du Houai Nan Tseu: "Les Ésprits légers et subtils animateurs de l'essence*. Paris: Institut Ricci, 1982.

Lau, D. C., trans. *Lao Tzu Tao Te Ching*. Harmondsworth, Middlesex: Penguin Books, 1963.

Laufer, Berthold. *Chinese Clay Figures*. Part 1: "Prolegomena on the History of Defensive Armor." Chicago: Field Museum, 1914. See esp. pp. 73–173, "The History of the Rhinoceros."

Laufer, Berthold, "Ethnographische Sagen der Chinesen." In *Aufsätze z. Kultur u. Sprach-geschichte vornehmlich des Orients Ernst Kuhn gewidmet (Kuhn Festschrift).* Breslau: Mara-cus, 1916.

Laufer, Berthold. *Jade. A Study in Chinese Archaeology and Religion.* Chicago: Field Museum, 1912.

Lawton, Thomas. *Chinese Art of the Warring States Period: Change and Continuity.* Washington: Freer Gallery of Art, 1982.

Lawton, Thomas, ed. *New Perspectives on Chu Culture During the Eastern Zhou Period.* Wash-ington: Smithsonian Institution, Sackler Gallery of Art, 1991.

Le Blanc, Charles. "From Ontology to Cosmogony: Notes on *Chuang Tzu* and *Huai-nan Tzu.*" In Le Blanc and Blader, eds., *Chinese Ideas about Nature and Society,* pp. 117–29.

Le Blanc, Charles. *Huai-Nan Tzu: Philosophical Synthesis in Early Han Thought.* Hong Kong: Hong Kong University Press, 1985.

Le Blanc, Charles. "A Re-Examination of the Myth of Huang-ti." In Girardot and Major, eds., *Myth and Symbol in Chinese Tradition,* pp. 45–63.

Le Blanc, Charles. "The Taoist Cosmology of the *Huai-nan-tzu.*" Ph.D. diss., University of Pennsylvania, 1976.

Le Blanc, Charles, and Susan Blader, eds. *Chinese Ideas about Nature and Society: Studies in Honour of Derk Bodde.* Hong Kong: Hong Kong University Press, 1987.

Le Blanc, Charles, and Rémi Mathieu, eds. *Mythe et philosophie à l'aube de la Chine impériale; Études sur le Huainan zi.* Montréal: Les Presses de l'Université de Montréal, 1992.

Legge, James. *The Chinese Classics.* 5 vols. Hong Kong and London, 1861–72.

Legge, James, trans. *Li Chi: Book of Rites.* 2 vols. Sacred Books of the East, 27–28. Oxford: Ox-ford University Press, 1885. Reprinted, New Hyde Park, N.Y.: University Books, 1967.

Levis, John H. *Foundations of Chinese Musical Art.* Peiping: Henri Vetch, 1936.

Li Guohao, Zhang Mengwen, and Cao Tianqin, eds. *Explorations in the History of Science and Technology in China.* Shanghai: Chinese Classics Publishing House, 1982.

Li Ling 李零. "'Shitu' yu Zhongguo gudai de yuzhou moshi (shang, xia) '式圖' 與中國古代的宇宙模式 (上, 下)" (The cosmograph diagram and the ancient Chinese model of the cosmos (Parts 1 and 2)). *Jiuzhou xuekan* 九州學刊 1991.4: 5–52; 1991.7 49–79.

Li Shizhen 李時珍. *Bencao gangmu* 本草綱目. *Wanya wenku* edition.

Li Xueqin. *Eastern Zhou and Qin Civilizations.* New Haven: Yale University Press, 1985.

Li Xueqin 李學勤. "Lun Chu boshu zhong de tianxiang 論楚帛書中的天象" (A discussion of astronomical materials in Chu silk manuscripts). *Hunan kaogu jikan* 1 (1981–82): 68–72.

Li Xueqin. "A Neolithic Jade Tablet and Early Chinese Cosmology." Paper presented at the annual meeting of the Association for Asian Studies, Washington, D.C., 4 April, 1992.

Li Xueqin. *The Wonder of Chinese Bronzes.* Beijing: Foreign Languages Press, 1980.

Liezi 列子 SBBY ed. See also the edition of Yang Bojun 楊伯峻. *Liezi jishi* 列子集釋. Shanghai, 1958.

Lim, Lucy, et al. *Stories from China's Past: Han Dynasty Pictorial Tomb Reliefs and Archaeological Objects from Sichuan Province, People's Republic of China.* San Francisco: Chinese Cultural Foundation, 1987.

Lin Tung-chi. "The Chinese Mind: Its Taoist Substratum." *Journal of the History of Ideas* 8 (1947): 259–72.

Liu Dunyuan 劉敦愿. "Shilun Zhanguo yishupin zhong de niao she xiangdou ticai 試論戰國 藝術品中的鳥蛇相斗題材" (Preliminary discussion of paired bird-snake motifs in Warring States art). *Hunan kaogu jikan* 1 (1981–82): 73–81.

Liu Wendian 劉文典 (Liu Shuya 劉叔雅), ed. *Huainan honglie jijie* 淮南鴻烈集解. Shanghai: Commercial Press, 1926. Reprinted, Taipei, 1969.

Lloyd, G. E. R. *The Revolutions of Wisdom.* Berkeley: University of California Press, 1987.

Loewe, Michael. *Chinese Ideas of Life and Death: Faith, Myth and Reason in the Han Period (202 B.C.–A.D. 220).* London: George Allen and Unwin, 1982.

Loewe, Michael. *Crisis and Conflict in Han China.* London: George Allen and Unwin, 1974.

Loewe, Michael. "The Cult of the Dragon and the Invocation for Rain." In Le Blanc and Blader, eds., *Chinese Ideas about Nature and Society,* pp. 195–213.

Loewe, Michael. *Everyday Life in Early Imperial China: During the Han Period, 202 B.C.–A.D. 220.* London: Batsford, 1968.

Loewe, Michael. "K'uang Heng and the Reform of Religious Practices (31 B.C.)." AM 17.1 (1971): 1–27.

Loewe, Michael. "Man and Beast: The Hybrid in Early Chinese Art and Literature." *Numen* 25.2 (1978): 97–117.

Loewe, Michael. "Manuscripts Recently Found in China: A Preliminary Survey." TP 93.2/3 (1977): 99–136.

Loewe, Michael. *The Pride That Was China.* Sidgwick and Jackson Great Civilisations Series. London: Sidgwick and Jackson; New York: St. Martin's Press, 1990.

Loewe, Michael. *Records of Han Administration.* 2 vols. Cambridge: Cambridge University Press, 1967–68.

Loewe, Michael. *Ways to Paradise: The Chinese Quest for Immortality.* London: George Allen and Unwin, 1979.

Louton, John. "Concepts of Comprehensiveness and Historical Change in the *Lü-Shih Ch'un-ch'iu.*" In Rosemont, ed., *Explorations in Early Chinese Cosmology,* pp. 105–18.

Lucretius (ca. 40 B.C.E.). *De rerum natura.* Ed. and trans. by C. Bailey. 3 vols. Oxford: Clarendon Press, 1947. Trans. by R. E. Latham as *The Nature of the Universe* (Penguin Classics). Harmondsworth: Penguin Books, 1951.

Lunheng 論衡 by Wang Chong 王充 (ca. 83 C.E.). SBCK ed. See also the edition of Lin Pansui 劉盼遂, ed. *Lunheng jijie* 論衡集解. Beijing, 1957.

Lüshi chunqiu 呂氏春秋. SBBY edition.

Ma Peitang 馬培堂, "Huainan jiuzhou qianshen houying 淮南九州前身後影" (The origin and later influence of the nine provinces as given in *Huainanzi*). YG 3.5 (1935): 1–6.

Ma Peitang. "Jizhou kaoyuan 冀州考原" (A study of Ji Province). YG 1.5 (1934): 2–6.

Ma Peitang. "Yugong yu Yudu 禹貢與禹都" (The Tribute of Yu and Yu's capital). YG 2.8 (1934): 21–24.

Maenchen-Helfen, Otto. "The Later Books of the Shan-Hai-Ching." AM 1 (1924): 550–86.

Maeyama, Yasukatsu. "The Oldest Star Catalogue in China, Shih Shen's *Hsing Ching.*" In

Maeyama Yasukatsu and W. G. Salzer, eds., *Prismata: Naturalwissenschaftgeschichtliche Studien—Festschrift für Willy Hartner* (Wiesbaden: Franz Steiner Verlag, 1977), pp. 211–45.

Major, John S. "Astrology in the *Huai-nan-tzu* and Some Related Texts." *Society for the Study of Chinese Religions Bulletin* 8 (1980): 20–31.

Major, John S. "The Efficacy of Uselessness: A Chuang-tzu Motif." *Philosophy East and West*, 25 (1975): 265–79.

Major, John S. "The Five Phases, Magic Squares, and Schematic Cosmography." In Rosemont, ed., *Explorations in Early Chinese Cosmology*, pp. 133–66.

Major, John S. "The Meaning of *Hsing-te*." In Le Blanc and Blader, eds., *Chinese Ideas about Nature and Society*, pp. 281–91.

Major, John S. "Myth, Cosmology, and the Origins of Chinese Science." *Journal of Chinese Philosophy* 5 (1978): 1–20.

Major, John S. "New Light on the Dark Warrior." In Girardot and Major, eds., *Myth and Symbol in Chinese Tradition*, pp. 65–86.

Major, John S. "A Note on Two Technical Terms in Chinese Science: *wu-hsing* 五行 and *hsiu* 宿." EC 2 (1976): 1–3.

Major, John S. "Notes on the Nomenclature of Winds and Directions in the Early Han." TP 65 (1979): 66–80.

Major, John S. "Numerology in the *Huai-Nan-Tzu*." In Smith, ed., *Sagehood and Systematizing Thought*, pp. 3–10.

Major, John S. "Reply to Richard Kunst's Comments on *Hsiu* and *Wu-hsing*." EC 3 (1977): 69–70.

Major, John S. "Research Priorities in the Study of Ch'u Religion, HR 17.3 and 4 (1978): 226–43.

Major, John S. "Substance, Process, Phase: *Wuxing* 五行 in the *Huainanzi*." In Rosemont, ed., *Chinese Texts and Philosophical Contexts*, pp. 67–78.

Major, John S. "Topography and Cosmology in Early Han Thought: Chapter 4 of the *Huai-nan-tzu*." Ph.D. diss., Harvard University, 1973.

March, Andrew L. "An Appreciation of Chinese Geomancy." JAS 27 (1968): 253–67.

Maspero, Henri. "L'Astronomie chinoise avant les Han." TP 26 (1929): 267–356.

Maspero, Henri. "L'Astronomie dans la Chine ancienne, histoire des instruments et des découvertes." In Maspero, *Mélanges posthumes sur les religions et l'histoire de la Chine*. Vol. 3, *Études historiques*, pp. 13–34. Paris: Publications du Musée Guimet, 1950.

Maspero, Henri. *La Chine antique*. Paris: DeBoccard, 1927. Trans. by Frank A. Kierman, *China In Antiquity*. Amherst: University of Massachusetts Press, 1978.

Maspero, Henri. "Légendes mythologiques dans le *Chou king*." *Journal Asiatique* 204 (1924): 1–100.

Maspero, Henri. "Le Ming-T'ang et la crise religieuse chinoise avant les Han." *Mélanges Chinois et Bouddhiques* 9 (1948–51): 1–71.

Maspero, Henri. "Les Procédés de 'nourrir le principe vital' dans la religion taoïste ancienne." *Journal Asiatique* 229 (1937): 177–252, 353–430.

Maspero, Henri. *Le Taoisme.* Vol. 2 of Maspero, *Mélanges posthumes sur les religions et l'histoire de la Chine.* Paris: Publications du Musée Guimet, 1950.

Maspero, Henri. *Le Taoïsme et les religions chinoises.* Paris: Gallimard, 1971. Trans. by Frank A. Kierman, *Taoism and Chinese Religion.* Amherst: University of Massachusetts Press, 1978.

Mathieu, Rémi. *Le Mu tianzi zhuan, traduction annotée, étude critique.* Paris: Collège de France, Insitut des Hautes Études Chinoises, 1978.

Mawangdui Silk Manuscripts Study Group, "Mawangdui Hanmu boshu 'Wuxing zhan' cewen 馬王堆漢墓帛書《五星占》釋文" (Transcription of the Manwangdui silk manuscript "Prognostications of the five planets"), in *Zhongguo tianwenxue shi wenji,* pp. 1–13.

McClain, Ernest G. "The Bronze Chime Bells of the Marquis of Zeng: Babylonian Biophysics in Ancient China." *Journal of Social and Biological Structures* 8 (1985): 147–73.

Miller, Roy Andrew. *Accounts of Western Nations in the History of the Northern Chou Dynasty.* Chinese Dynastic History Translations, 6. Berkeley and Los Angeles: University of California Press, 1959.

Morgan, Evan. "The Operations and Manifestations of the Tao Exemplified in History [Translation of *Huainanzi* 12]." JNCB/RAS 52 (1921): 1–39.

Morgan, Evan. "The Taoist Superman." JNCB/RAS 54 (1923): 229–45.

Morgan, Evan. *Tao, the Great Luminant: Essays from Huai Nan Tzu.* Shanghai: Kelly and Walsh, 1933; reprint, New York: Paragon Book Reprint Corp., 1969.

Morohashi Tetsuji 諸橋轍次. *Dai Kanwa jiten* 大漢和辭典. 13 vols. Tokyo: Taishukan shoten, 1955–60.

Mu Tianzi zhuan 穆天子傳. *Han Wei congshu* edition.

Münke, Wolfgang. *Die klassische chinesische Mythologie.* Stuttgart: Ernst Klett Verlag, 1976.

Munro, Donald J. "Afterword." In *Zhuangzi Speaks: The Music of Nature,* adapted and illus. by Tsai Chih Chung, trans. Brian Bruya. Princeton: Princeton University Press, 1992.

Munro, Donald J. *The Concept of Man in Early China.* Stanford: Stanford University Press, 1969.

Nakayama Heijiro 中山平次郎. "Shina kō shōmei no saiōbō ni tsuite 支那古鐘銘の西王母について" (Xiwangmu in ancient Chinese bell-inscriptions). *Kōkogaku zasshi* 11 (1921): 324–32.

Nakayama, Shigeru. "Characteristics of Chinese Astrology." *Isis* 57 (1966): 442–54. Also in Sivin, *Science and Technology in East Asia,* pp. 94–106.

Nakayama, Shigeru. *A History of Japanese Astronomy: Chinese Background and Western Impact.* Cambridge: Harvard University Press, 1969.

Nakayama, Shigeru, and Nathan Sivin, eds. *Chinese Science: Explorations of an Ancient Tradition.* MIT East Asian Science Series No. 2. Cambridge: MIT Press, 1973.

Nasr, Seyyid Hossein. *Science and Civilization in Islam.* Cambridge: Harvard University Press, 1968.

Needham, Joseph. "The Cosmology of Early China." In Blacker and Loewe, eds., *Ancient Cosmologies,* pp. 87–109.

Needham, Joseph, with various collaborators. *Science and Civilisation in China.* 7 vols., projected. Cambridge: Cambridge University Press, 1954– . See esp. vol. 3, "Mathematics and the Sciences of the Heavens and the Earth." 1959.

Needham, Joseph. *Time and Eastern Man: The Henry Myers Lecture 1964.* London: Royal Anthropological Institute of Great Britain and Ireland, Occasional Paper 21, 1965.

Needham, Joseph, Lu Gwei-djen, John Combridge, and John S. Major. *The Hall of Heavenly Records: Korean Astronomical Instruments and Clocks, 1380–1780.* Cambridge: Cambridge University Press, 1986.

Ngo Van Xuyet. *Divination, magie et politique dans la Chine ancienne.* Paris: Presses Universitaires de France, 1976.

Nivison, David S. "Evolution of the Chinese Lunar *hsiu* System." *duduan 03.* Stanford, Calif.: Privately circulated, 1984.

Nivison, David S. "Stems and Branches: Toward a Unified Theory of the Calendar." *duduan 02.* Stanford, Calif.: Privately circulated, 1984.

Nivison, David S. and Kevin D. Pang. "Astronomical Evidence for the *Bamboo Annals'* Chronicle of Early Xia." EC 15 (1990): 87–95.

Nomura Gakuyō 野村岳陽. "Bunkenjō yori mitaru konron shisō no hattatsu 文獻上より見たる崑崙思想の發達" (The development of the idea of Kunlun as seen in the *Wenxian*). *Shigaku zasshi* 史學雜誌 29 (1918): 458–94, 583–601.

Nylan, Michael, and Nathan Sivin. "The First Neo-Confucianism: An Introduction to Yang Hsiung's 'Canon of Supreme Mystery' (*Tai hsuan ching,* ca. 4 B.C.)." In Le Blanc and Blader, eds., *Chinese Ideas about Nature and Society,* pp. 41–99.

Pankenier, David W. "Astronomical Dates in Shang and Western Zhou." EC 7 (1981–82): 2–37.

Pankenier, David W. "Early Antecedents of Five Phases Correlative Thought: Sandai Celestial Revelations and Religious Time." paper for the annual meeting of the Association for Asian Studies, San Francisco, 26 March, 1988.

Pankenier, David W. "Early Chinese Astronomy and Cosmology: The 'Mandate of Heaven' as Epiphany." Ph.D. Diss., Stanford University, 1983.

Pankenier, David W. "Early Chinese Positional Astronomy: The *Guoyu* Astronomical Record." *Archaeoastronomy* 5 (1982): 10–20.

Parker, E. H. "Hwai-nan-tsz, Philosopher and Prince." *The New China Review* 1 (1919): 505–21.

Parker, E. H. "Some More of Hwai-nan-tsz's Ideas." *The New China Review* 2 (1920): 551–62.

Peerenboom, Randall. "Natural Law in *Huang-Lao* Boshu." *Philosophy East and West* 40 (1990): 309–29.

Peerenboom, R. P. "*Heguanzi* and Huang-Lao Thought." EC 16 (1991): 169–86.

Peterson, Willard. "Making Connections: 'Commentary on the Attached Verbalizations' of *The Book of Change.*" HJAS 42 (1982): 67–122.

Pelliot, Paul. "L'Étude du *Mou t'ien tseu tchouan.*" TP 21 (1922): 98–102.

Pfizmaier, August. "Die Könige von Hoai-Nan aus dem Hause Han." *Sitzungsberichte der Akademie der Wissenschaften Wien, Philosophisch-Historische Klasse* 39 (1862): 575–618.

Picken, Laurence. "The Music of Far Eastern Asia, I: China." In *The New Oxford History of Music,* pp. 83–134. Oxford: Oxford University Press, 1957.

Pirazzoli t'Serstevens, Michèle. *The Han Dynasty,* trans. Janet Seligman. New York: Rizzoli International, 1982.

Playfair, George M. H. *The Cities and Towns of China: A Geographical Dictionary.* 2d ed. Shanghai: Kelly and Walsh, 1910.

Pokora, Timoteus. "The Notion of Coldness in Huai-nan-tzu." *Nachrichten der Gesellschaft für Natur- und Völkerkunde Ostasiens, Hamburg: Zeitschrift für Kultur und Geschichte Ost- und Südostasiens* 125 (1979): 69–74.

Porkert, Manfred. *The Theoretical Foundations of Chinese Medicine: Systems of Correspondence.* MIT East Asian Science Series, 3. Cambridge: MIT Press, 1974.

Porter, Deborah. "Myth and History in the *Mu T'ien-tzu chuan.*" Paper presented at the annual meeting of the Association for Asian Studies, Washington, D.C., 3 April, 1992.

Porter, L. C. "Climate, Calendar, and Philosophy in Ancient China, Suggested Relationships." *Yenching Journal of Social Studies* 5 (1950): 143–56.

Powers, Martin J. *Art and Political Expression in Early China.* New Haven: Yale University Press, 1991.

Pregadio, Fabrizio. "The Medical Texts of Ma-wang-tui: The Taoist 'Cultivation of Life,'" *Cahiers d'Extrême-Asie* 5 (Special Issue: Taoist Studies II) (1989–90): 381–86.

Prusek, Jaroslav. *Chinese Statelets and the Northern Barbarians in the Period 1400–300 B.C.* New York: Humanities Press, 1971.

Przyluski, J. "Les Unipeds." *Mélanges Chinois et Bouddhiques* 2 (1933): 307–32.

Pulleyblank, E. G. "The Chinese and Their Neighbors in Prehistoric and Early Historic Times." In Keightley, ed., *The Origins of Chinese Civilization,* pp. 411–66.

Qian Baozong. *A History of Chinese Mathematics.* Peiping: Academia Sinica, 1932.

Qian Baozong 錢寶琮, *Suanjing shishu* 算經十書 (Ten classics of calculation [collated and punctuated]). Beijing: Zhonghua shuju, 1963.

Qian Mu 錢穆. *Qin Han shi* 秦漢史. Taipei: San Min Book Co., 1957.

Qian Mu. *Shiji diming kao* 史記地名考 (A Study of place-names in the *Shiji*). Hong Kong: Longmen shudian, 1968.

Qian Mu. *Zhongguo sixiang shi* 中國思想史 (A history of Chinese thought). Taipei: Zhonghua wenhua chupan she, 1952.

Qian Mu. *Zhuangzi cuanjian* 莊子纂箋. 3d. ed. Hong Kong, 1957.

Qian Tang 錢塘. "*Huainanzi* tianwenxun buzhu 淮南子天文訓補注" (Supplementary commentary to the *Huainanzi* Treatise on the Patterns of Heaven)." Preface dated 1788. Shanghai: Datong shuju, 1935. Also in Liu Wendian, *Huainan honglie jijie.*

Queen, Sarah A. "A Confucian with a Taoist Face: Huang-Lao Influence on Tung Chung-shu." Paper presented at the annual meeting of the Association for Asian Studies, New Orleans, 13 April, 1991.

Rawson, Jessica. *Ancient China: Art and Archaeology.* London: British Museum, 1980.

Rawson, Jessica. *Chinese Bronzes: Art and Ritual.* London: British Museum, 1987.

Rickett, W. Allyn. "An Early Chinese Calendar Chart." TP 48 (1960): 195–251.

Rickett, W. Allyn. *Guanzi: Political, Economic, and Philosophical Essays from Early China.* vol. 1. Princeton: Princeton University Press, 1985.

Rickett, W. Allyn. "*Kuan-tzu* and the Newly Discovered Texts on Bamboo and Silk." In Le Blanc and Blader, eds., *Chinese Ideas About Nature and Society*, pp. 237–48.

Riegel, Jeffrey K. "Kou-mang and Ju-shou." *Cahiers d'Extrême-Asie* 5 (Special Issue on Taoist Studies, II) (1989–90): 55–83.

Riegel, Jeffrey K. "Mawangdui Tomb Three: Documents." EC 2 (1976): 68–72.

Riegel, Jeffrey K. "A Summary of Some Recent *Wenwu* and *Kaogu* Articles on Mawangdui Tombs Two and Three." EC 1 (1975): 10–15.

Robinet, Isabelle. *Meditation taoïste*. Paris: Dervy-Livres, 1979.

Robinet, Isabelle. "Les Radonnées extatiques des taoïstes dans les astres." *Monumenta Serica* 32 (1976): 159–73.

Rosemont Jr., Henry, ed. *Chinese Texts and Philosophical Contexts: Essays in Honor of A. C. Graham*. La Salle, Ill.: Open Court Publishing Co., 1991.

Rosemont, Jr., Henry, ed. *Explorations in Early Chinese Cosmology*. JAAR Thematic Studies 50/2. Chico, Calif.: Scholar's Press, 1984.

Rosemont Jr., Henry, and Benjamin I Schwartz, eds. *Studies in Classical Chinese Thought*. JAAR Thematic Studies 48. American Academy of Religion, 1979.

Roth, Harold D. "The Early Taoist Concept of *Shen*: A Ghost in the Machine?" In Smith, ed., *Sagehood and Systematizing Thought*, pp. 11–32.

Roth, Harold D. "Psychology and Self-Cultivation in Early Taoistic Thought." HJAS 51 (1991): 599–650.

Roth, Harold D. *The Textual History of the Huai-nan Tzu*. Association for Asian Studies Monograph No. 46. Ann Arbor: Association for Asian Studies, 1992.

Roth, Harold D. "Who Compiled the *Chuang-tzu*?" In Rosemont, ed., *Chinese Texts and Philosophical Contexts*, pp. 79–128.

Rubin, Vitaly A. "Ancient Chinese Cosmology and *Fa-chia* Theory." In Rosemont, ed., *Explorations in Early Chinese Cosmology*, pp. 95–104.

Rudolph, Richard C., and Yu Wen. *Han Tomb Art of West China*. Berkeley and Los Angleles: University of California Press, 1951.

Sailey, Jay. "A. C. Graham's *Disputers of the Tao* and Some Recent Works in English on Chinese Thought." JAOS 112 (1992): 42–54.

Sailey, Jay. "An Annotated Translation of *Huai Nan Tzu* Chapter XVI." Mimeographed, 1971.

Sailey, Jay. *The Master Who Embraces Simplicity: A Study of the Philosopher Ko Hung, A.D. 283–343*. San Francisco: Chinese Materials Center, 1978.

Sakai Tadaō 酒井忠夫. "Hō-jutsu to dō-jutsu 方術と道術" (added title in English: Fang-shu and tao-shu, religious and political art in Taoism). *Tōyō shigaku ronshu* 東洋史學論集 1 (1953): 19–59.

Sakai Tadaō and Yamazaki Hiroshi 山崎宏. "Dōkyō to wa nani ka? 道教とは何か (What is Daoism?). In Fukui et al., eds., *Dōkyō*, vol. 1, pp. 10–17.

Salmony, Alfred. *Antler and Tongue: An Essay on Ancient Chinese Symbolism*. Ascona, 1954.

de Santillana, Giorgio, and Hertha von Dechend. *Hamlet's Mill*. Boston: Gambit Press, 1969.

Sargent, C. B. "Index to the Monograph on Geography in the History of the Former Han Dynasty." *Journal of the West China Border Research Society*, Series A, 12 (1940): 173–216.

de Saussure, Léopold. "The Calendar of Mu T'ien-tsz Chuan." *North China Review* 2 (1920): 513–16.

de Saussure, Léopold. "L'Étymologie du nom des Monts K'ouen louen." TP 20 (1921): 370–71.

de Saussure, Léopold. *Les Origines de l'astronomie chinoise.* Paris: Maisonneuve, 1930.

de Saussure, Léopold. "La relation des voyages du Roi Mou." *Journal Asiatique*, 11th ser., nos. 197, 198 (1921).

de Saussure, Léopold. "Le Système cosmologique des Chinoise." *Revue générale des Sciences* 32 (1921): 729–36.

de Saussure, Léopold. "Le voyage de Mou Wang de l'hypothese d'Ed. Chavannes." TP 20 (1921): 19–31.

Schafer, Edward H. "The Chinese Dhole," *Asia Major* 4.1 (New ser.; 1991): 1–6.

Schafer, Edward H. *The Divine Woman: Dragon Ladies and Rain Maidens in T'ang Literature.* Berkeley: University of California Press, 1973.

Schafer, Edward H. "Fusang and Beyond: The Haunted Seas to Japan." JAOS 109 (1989): 379–99.

Schafer, Edward H. *The Golden Peaches of Samarkand.* Berkeley: University of California Press, 1963.

Schafer, Edward H. "Mineral Imagery in the Paradise Poems of Kuan-hsiu." AM 10 (1963): 73–102.

Schafer, Edward H. *Pacing the Void: T'ang Approaches to the Stars.* Berkeley: University of California Press, 1977.

Schafer, Edward H. "The Sky River." JAOS 94 (1974): 401–7.

Schafer, Edward H. "The Transcendent Vitamin: Efflorescence of Lang-kan." *Chinese Science* 3 (1978): 27–38.

Schafer, Edward H. "Two Taoist Bagatelles." *Bulletin of the Society for the Study of Chinese Religions* 9 (1981): 1–16.

Schafer, Edward H. *The Vermilion Bird.* Berkeley: University of California Press, 1967.

Schatzman-Steinhardt, Nancy. "The Han Ritual Hall." In Nancy Schatzman-Steinhardt et al., eds., *Chinese Traditional Architecture*, pp. 69–78. New York: China Institute in America, 1984.

Schatzman-Steinhardt, Nancy. "The Mingtang of Wang Mang." *Orientations* (November 1984): 109–19.

Schipper, Kristopher M. *L'Empéreur Wou des Han dans la légende taoiste: Han Wou-ti nei-tchouan.* Paris: Publications de l'École Française d'Extrême-Orient, 1965.

Schlegel, Gustav, "Probléms géographiques: Les Peuples étrangers chez les historiens Chinois." TP 3 (1892): 101–68, 490–510; 4 (1893): 323–62, 402–14; 5 (1894): 179–233; 6 (1895): 1–64, 165–215, 247–57.

Schlegel, Gustav. *Uranographie chinoise.* 2 vols. Leiden: E. J. Brill, 1875.

Schwartz, Benjamin I. *The World of Thought in Ancient China.* Cambridge: Belknap Press, 1985.

Seidel, Anna. "The Image of the Perfect Ruler in Early Taoist Messianism." HR 9.2 and 3 (1969–70): 216–47.

Seidel, Anna. "Tokens of Immortality in Han Graves." *Numen* 29 (1982): 79–122.

Shanhaijing jiansu 山海經箋疏. SBBY edition.

Shaughnessy, Edward L. "Historical Geography and the Extent of the Earliest Chinese King-doms." AM 2 (New ser.; 1989): 1–22.

Shaughnessy, Edward L. *Sources of Western Zhou History.* Berkeley: University of California Press, 1991.

She Shiran 社石然 et al., eds. *Zhongguo kexue jishu shigao* 中國科技術史稿 (Outline of Chinese science and technology), vol. 1. Beijing: Science Press, 1982.

Shiji 史記: *Shiki kaichū kōshō* 史記會註考證 edition. 10 vols. Tokyo, 1932–34.

Shimada Kan 島田翰. *Kōbun kyushō ko* 古文舊書考 (Studies of ancient literature). Tokyo: Minyusha, 1905.

Shinjō Shinzō 新城新藏. *Tōyō tenmongakushi kenkyū* 東洋天文學史研究 (Researches on the history of East Asian astronomy). Kyoto: Kobun-do, 1930.

Shisanjing zhusu 十三經注疏 (Thirteen classics with collected commentaries and subcommen-taries). Jinchang shuye tang 金閶書業堂 edition, 1778.

Sivin, Nathan. "Chinese Alchemy and the Manipulation of Time." *Isis* 67 (1976): 513–26. Also in Sivin, *Science and Technology in East Asia,* pp. 108–22.

Sivin, Nathan. "Chinese Alchemy as a Science." *Transactions of the International Conference of Orientalists in Japan* 13 (1968): 117–29.

Sivin, Nathan. *Chinese Alchemy: Preliminary Studies.* Harvard Monographs in the History of Science. Cambridge: Harvard University Press, 1968.

Sivin, Nathan. "Chinese Conceptions of Time." *The Earlham Review* 1 (1966): 82–92.

Sivin, Nathan. "Cosmos and Computation in Early Chinese Mathematical Astronomy." TP 55 (1969): 1–73; reprinted, Leiden: E. J. Brill, 1969.

Sivin, Nathan. "The Limits of Empirical Knowledge in the Traditional Chinese Sciences." In J. T. Fraser et al., eds., *Time, Science, and Society in China and the West. The Study of Time, V,* 151–69. Amherst: University of Massachusetts Press, 1986.

Sivin, Nathan. "On the Word 'Taoist' as a Source of Perplexity: With Special Reference to the Relations of Science and Religion in Traditional China." HR 17 (1978): 303–30.

Sivin, Nathan. "Reflections on Theory and Practice in Chinese Alchemy." Paper presented at the Conference on Taoism, Bellagio, 7–14 September, 1968. For a summary and discus-sion of this paper, see Holmes H. Welch, "The Bellagio Conference on Taoist Studies." HR 9.2 and 3 (1970): 114–17; but see also Sivin's response in HR, May 1973.

Sivin, Nathan. "Science and Medicine in Imperial China—The State of the Field." JAS 47: 41–90 (1988).

Sivin, Nathan, ed. *Science and Technology in East Asia.* New York: Science History Publications, 1977.

Sivin, Nathan. "The Theoretical Background of Elixer Alchemy." In Needham, *Science and Civilisation in China,* vol. 5, Part 4 (1980), pp. 210–323.

Sivin, Nathan. *Traditional Medicine in Contemporary China.* Science, Medicine, and Technol-ogy in East Asia, 2. Ann Arbor: University of Michigan Center for Chinese Studies, 1987.

Smith, Kidder, ed. *Chuang Tzu::Rationality::Interpretation.* Brunswick, Maine: Bowdoin College Asian Studies Program, 1991.

Smith, Kidder, ed. *Sagehood and Systematizing Thought in Warring States and Han China.* Brunswick: Bowdoin College Asian Studies Program, 1990.

Soothill, William E. *The Hall of Light: A Study of Early Chinese Kingship.* London: Lutterworth Press, 1951.

Soymié, Michel. "La Lune dans les religions chinoises." In *La Lune: Mythes et Rites* (Sources Orientales, V), pp. 291–321. Paris: Éditions du Seuil, 1962.

Spencer, J. E., and William L. Thomas. *Asia, East by South: A Cultural Geography.* 2d ed. New York: John Wiley and Sons, 1971.

Stein, Rolf A. "Architecture et pensée religieuse en extrême-orient." *Arts Asiatiques* 4 (1957): 163–86.

Stein, Rolf A. "Review of *Tao, the Great Luminant.*" *Journal asiatique* 227 (1935): 314–20.

Stein, Rolf A. *The World in Miniature: Container Gardens and Dwellings in Far Eastern Religious Thought,* trans. Phyllis Brooks. Stanford: Stanford University Press, 1990.

Su Xuelin 蘇雪林. *Kunlun zhi mi* 崑崙之謎 (The riddle of Kunlun). Taipei, 1956.

Sui shu 隋書. Compiled by Wei Cheng 魏徵 and others, 636–56. Punctuated and collated edition, Beijing: Zhonghua shuju, 1973. Also SBCK and *Bonaben* editions.

Sun Zuoyun 孫作云. "Changsha Mawangdui yihao Hanmu chutu huafan kaoshi 長沙馬王堆一號漢墓出土畫幡考釋" (Studies on the silk painting unearthed from Han tomb no. 1 at Mawangdui, Changsha), KG 1973.1: 54–61.

Swanson, Gerald. "The Concept of Change in the *Great Treatise.*" In Rosemont, ed., *Explorations in Early Chinese Cosmology,* pp. 67–94.

Tan Jiefu 譚介甫. *Mojing yijie* 墨經易解. Shanghai: Commercial Press, 1935.

Tao Fangqi 陶方琦. *Huainan xuju yitong gu* 淮南許注異同詁 (Explanations of variations in the Xu Shen commentary to *Huainanzi*). 1882.

Teboul, Michel. *Les Premières théories planétaires chinoises.* Paris: Collège de France, 1983.

Teiser, S. F. "Engulfing the Bounds of Order: The Myth of the Great Flood in *Mencius.*" In Girardot and Major, eds., *Myth and Symbol in Chinese Tradition,* pp. 15–43.

Tianwenxue shi zhuanji 天文學史傳集 (Essays in the history of astronomy). Vol. 1. *Kejishi wenji* 科技史文集 (Essays in the history of science and technology), 1. Shanghai: Science Press, 1978.

Tianwenxue shi zhuanji 天文學史傳集 (Essays in the history of astronomy). Vol. 2. *Kejishi wenji* 科技史文集 (Essays in the history of science and technology), 6. Shanghai: Science Press, 1980.

Tjan Tjoe Som. *Po Hu T'ung--The Comprehensive Discussions in the White Tiger Hall.* 2 vols. Leiden: E. J. Brill, 1949–52.

Toda Toyosaburō 戶田豐三郎. "Gogyō setsu seiritsu ni kansuru ichikosatsu 五行說成立に觀する一考察" (A Study of the formation of the five phase system). *Shinagaku kenkyū* 那支学研究 12 (1955): 38–45.

Treistman, Judith. *The Prehistory of China.* New York: American Museum of Natural History/ Doubleday and Co., 1972.

Tsuda Sōkichi 津田左右吉. *Dōka no shisō to sono tenkai* 道家の思想と其の展開 (Taoist thought and its development). Tokyo: Iwanami shoten, 1939. See esp. pp. 82–88, "Ryoshi shunju oyobi Enanji 呂氏春秋及び淮南子" (*Lüshi chunqiu* and *Huainanzi*).

Tsuda Sōkichi. *Jukyō no kenkyū* 儒教の研究 (Researches in Confucianism). 2 vols. Tokyo: Iwanami shoten, 1950–51. See esp. vol. 2, pp. 109–304, "Zen Kan no jukyō to inyo-setsu 前漢の儒教と陰陽說" (Confucianism and yin-yang theory in the Former Han).

Tu, Wei-ming. "The 'Thought of Huang-Lao': A Reflection on the Lao Tzu and Huang Ti Texts in the Silk Manuscripts of Ma-wang-tui." JAS 39 (1979): 95–110.

Twitchett, Denis, and Michael Loewe, eds. *The Cambridge History of China, Volume One: The Ch'in and Han Dynasties, 221 B.C.–A.D. 220*. Cambridge: Cambridge University Press, 1986.

Uchiyama Toshihiko 內山俊彥. "Maōtai bosho *Keihō*, *Judaikyō*, *Shō*, *Dōgen* shō kō 馬王堆帛書經法十大經稱道原小考" (A brief study of the Mawangdui silk texts "Jingfa." "Shidajing." "Cheng." and "Daoyuan"). *Tohogaku* 56 (1978): 1–16.

van Aalst, J. A. *Chinese Music.* (Shanghai, 1884).

van Gulik, Robert H. *Sexual Life in Ancient China.* Leiden: E. J. Brill, 1961.

Veith, Ilza. *The Yellow Emperor's Classic of Internal Medicine.* 1949. New ed., Berkeley: University of California Press, 1966.

Waley, Arthur. *The Analects of Confucius.* London: George Allen and Unwin, 1938.

Waley, Arthur. *The Book of Songs.* London: George Allen and Unwin, 1937.

Waley, Arthur. *Chiu Ko--The Nine Songs. A Study of Shamanism in Ancient China.* London: George Allen and Unwin, 1955.

Waley, Arthur. *Three Ways of Thought in Ancient China.* Garden City, N.Y.: Doubleday and Co., 1956.

Waley, Arthur. *The Way and Its Power.* London: George Allen and Unwin, 1934.

Wallacker, Benjamin. *Huai-nan-tzu, Book Eleven: Behavior, Culture, and the Cosmos.* New Haven: The American Oriental Society, 1962.

Wallacker, Benjamin. "Liu An, Second King of Huai-nan (180?–122 B.C.)." JAOS 92 (1972): 36–51.

Wang, C. H. *The Bell and the Drum: Shih Ching as Formulaic Poetry in an Oral Tradition.* Berkeley: University of California Press, 1974.

Wang, Kuo-wei. "Chinese Foot-Measures of the Past Nineteen Centuries." JNCB/RAS 59 (1928): 111–23.

Wang Meng'ou 王夢鷗. "Gu mingtang tu kao 古明堂圖考 (Illustrated study of the ancient mingtang). *Kong Meng xuebao* 孔孟學報 11 (1966): 221–29.

Wang Meng'ou. *Zou Yan yishuo kao* 鄒衍遺說考 (Study of the surviving sayings of Zou Yan). Taipei: Commercial Press, 1966.

Wang Niansun 王念孫 and Wang Yinzhi 王引之. "Du *Huananzi* zazhi 讀淮南子雜誌" (Miscellaneous reading notes on *Huainanzi*). In Wang Niansun, *Dushu zazhi* 讀書雜誌 (1832), chap. 9. Reprinted, Shanghai: Commercial Press, 1934.

Wang Shumin 王叔岷. "Huainanzi jiaozheng 淮南子斠證 (Textual annotations on *Huainanzi*). *Wenshi zhexue bao* 文史哲學報 5 (1953): 15–90; 6 (1954): 1–73; 7 (1956): 9–22.

Wang Shumin. "Huainanzi yu Zhuangzi 淮南子與莊子." *Tsing Hua Journal of Chinese Studies* 2 (1960): 69–82.

Bibliography

Wang Zhong 汪中. *Shu xue* 述學. 1816; reprinted, Taipei, Kuang-wen Bookstore, 1970.

Waters, Geoffrey. *Three Elegies of Ch'u: An Introduction to the Traditional Interpretation of the Ch'u Tz'u.* Madison: University of Wisconsin Press, 1986.

Watson, Burton. *Chuang-tzu: Complete Works.* New York: Columbia University Press, 1968.

Watson, Burton. *Records of the Grand Historian of China.* New York: Columbia University Press, 1961.

Watson, William. *Cultural Frontiers in Ancient East Asia.* Edinburgh, 1971.

Watson, William. *Inner Asia and China in the Pre-Han Period.* Inaugural Lecture, 2 December 1968. London: University of London, School of Oriental and African Studies, 1969.

Watson, William. "Traditions of Material Culture in the Territory of Ch'u." In Noel Barnard, ed., *Early Chinese Art,* vol. 1, pp. 53–75.

Wei Tingsheng 衛挺生. *Mu Tianzi zhuan jinkao* 穆天子傳今考 (Added title in English: A modern scientific study of King Mu's travels). 3 vols. Taipei: Zhonghua xueshu yuan, 1970.

Welch, Holmes H. "The Bellagio Conference on Taoist Studies." HR 9.2 and 3 (1968) 107–36.

Welch, Holmes H. *The Parting of the Way.* Boston: Beacon Press, 1957.

Welch, Holmes H. "Syncretism in the Early Taoist Movement." *Papers on China from the Regional Studies Seminar, X.* Cambridge: Harvard University Committee on International and Regional Studies, 1956.

Welch, Holmes H. and Anna Seidel. *Facets of Taoism: Essays in Chinese Religion.* New Haven: Yale University Press, 1979.

Wen Yiduo 聞一多. "Shenxian kao 神仙考" (Studies of immortals). In *Wen Yiduo quanji xuankan zhi yi: Shenhua yu shi* 聞一多全集選刊之一: 神話與詩 (Selected works of Wen Yiduo, vol. 1: Mythology and poetry). Beijing: Guji chupan shi, 1956.

Wheatley, Paul. *The Pivot of the Four Quarters.* Chicago: Aldine Publishing Co., 1971.

Wieger, Léon. *Textes philosophiques.* Xianxian: Imprimerie de la mission catholique, 1930.

Wilhelm, Helmut. *Change: Eight Lectures on the I Ching,* trans. Cary F. Baynes. New York: Pantheon Books, Bollingen Series 62, 1960.

Wilhelm, Helmut. *Heaven, Earth and Man in the Book of Changes: Seven Eranos Lectures.* Seattle: University of Washington Press, 1977.

Wilhelm, Richard. *Dschuang Dsi. Das wahre Buch vom südlichen Blutenland, Nan hua dschen ging.* Jena: E. Diederichs, 1920.

Wilhelm, Richard. *Frühling und Herbst des Lü Bu We.* Jena: E. Diederichs, 1928.

Wilhelm, Richard. *The I Ching or Book of Changes,* trans. Cary F. Baynes. New York: Pantheon Books, Bollingen Series 19, 1950.

Wu Hung. *The Wu Liang Shrine: The Ideology of Early Chinese Pictorial Art.* Stanford: Stanford University Press, 1989.

Wu Kuang-tsing. "Libraries and Book-collecting in China Before the Invention of Printing." *T'ien-hsia Monthly* 5 (1937): 237–60.

Wu Lu-ch'iang and Tenney L. Davis. "An Ancient Chinese Treatise on Alchemy Entitled *Ts'an T'ung Ch'i.*" *Isis* 18 (1932): 210–89. See pp. 227–30, on the life of Liu An.

Wylie, Alexander. *Chinese Researches.* Shanghai: Kelly and Walsh, 1897.

Xi Zezong. "Chinese Studies in the History of Astronomy, 1949–1979." ed. by John S. Major. *Isis* 72 (1981): 456–70.

Xi Zezong 席澤宗 "'Huainanzi tianwenxun' shulue 淮南子文訓述略." (Outline of the "Treatise on the Patterns of Heaven" of *Huainanzi*). *Kexue tongbao* 科學通報 1962.6: 35–39.

Xi Zezong. "Mawangdui boshu zhong de huixing tu 馬王堆帛書中的彗星圖" (The comet chart found among the Mawangdui silk manuscripts). WW 1978.2: 5–9.

Xi Zezong. "Zhongguo tianwenxue shi de yige zhongyao faxian—Mawangdui Hanmu boshu zhong de 'Wuxing zhan' 中國天文學史的一個重要發現——馬王堆帛書中的五星占" (An important discovery for the history of Chinese astronomy: The Mawangdui silk manuscript "Prognostications of the five planets"). In *Zhongguo tianwenxue shi wenji*, pp. 14–33.

Xia Nai 夏鼐 *Kaoguxue he kejishi* 考古學和科技史 (added title in English: Essays on Archaeology of Science and Technology in China). Beijing: Science Press, 1979.

Xiong Zhuanxin 熊傳新. "Tan Mawangdui sanhao Xi Han mu chutu de liubo 談馬王堆三號西漢墓出土的陸博" (On the *liubo* set excavated from tomb 3 at Mawangdui). WW 1979.4: 35–39.

Xu Dishan 許地山. *Daojiao shi, shangpian* 道教史上編 (A history of Daoism, vol. 1). Shanghai: Commercial Press, 1934.

Xu Xusheng 徐旭生 (Xu Bingchang 徐炳昶). *Zhongguo gushi de zhuanshuo shidai* 中國古史的傳說時代 (The mythic era in ancient Chinese history). Beijing: Science Press, 1962.

Xu Zhentao 徐振韜. "Cong boshu 'Wuxing zhan' kan 'xian Qin hunyi' de chuangzhi 從帛書五星占看先秦渾儀的創制" (The invention of the "pre-Qin armillary sphere" as seen from the silk manuscript "Prognostications of the five planets), in *Zhongguo tianwenxue shi wenji*, pp. 34–47.

Yabuuti, Kiyosi. "Chinese Astronomy: Development and Limiting Factors." In Nakayama and Sivin, eds., *Chinese Science: Explorations of an Ancient Tradition*, pp. 91–103. Cambridge: MIT Press, 1973.

Yabuuti, Kiyosi. "Indian and Arabian Astronomy in China." In *Silver Jubliee Volume of the Zinbun-Kagaku-Kenkyusyo*, pp. 585–603. Kyoto, 1954.

Yabuuti, Kiyosi. "The Observational Date of the *Shih-shih Hsing-ching*" (in Japanese with English summary). In Li, Zhang, and Cao, eds., *Explorations in the History of Science and Technology in China*, pp. 133–42.

Yamada Keiji. "The Formation of the *Huang-ti nei-ching*." *Acta Asiatica* 36 (1979): 67–89.

Yamada Toshiaki 山田利明 "Shisendō 神仙道" (The Dao of the immortals). In Fukui et al., eds., *Dōkyō*, vol. 1, pp. 347–61.

Yan Dunjie 嚴敦杰. "Guanyu Xi Han chuqi de shipan he zhanpan 關于西漢初期的式盤和占盤" (added title in English: Notes on the Diviner's Boards of Early Western Han). KG 1978.5: 334–37.

Yan Kejun 嚴可均. *Quan shanggu sandai Qin Han sanguo liuchao wen* 全上古三代秦漢三國六朝文 (Complete collection of pre-Tang fragments). 1836. Reprinted, Beijing, Zhonghua shuju, 1958, 1965.

Yang Chao 楊超. "Xian Qin yinyang wuxing shuo 先秦陰陽五行說" (The yin-yang/five phase theory in the pre-Qin period). In *Zhongguo gudai zhexue luncong* 中國古代哲學論叢 (Collected essays on ancient Chinese philosophy), pp. 32–55. Beijing, 1957.

Yang Kuan 楊寬. "Zhongguo shanggu shi daolun 中國上古史導論" (Introduction to ancient Chinese history). In Gu Jiegang et al., eds., *Gushi bian* vol. 7, part 1, pp. 65–421.

Yang, Lien-sheng. "An Additional Note on the Ancient Game Liu-po." HJAS 15 (1952): 124–39.

Yang, Lien-sheng. "A Note on the So-Called TLV Mirrors and the Game Liu-po." HJAS 9 (1947): 202–6.

Yang, Lien-sheng. "Numbers and Units in Chinese Economic History." HJAS 12 (1949): 216–25.

Yang Shuda 楊樹達. *Huainanzi zhengwen* 淮南子證聞 (1953). Reprint, Shanghai: Guji chupanshe, 1985.

Yang Xiangkui 楊向奎. "Wuxing shuo de qiyuan ji qi yanbian 五行說的起原及其演變 (The origin and transformation of the five-phase theory), in *Zhongguo gudai zhexue luncong* 中國古代哲學論叢 (Collected studies in ancient Chinese philosophy), pp. 13–31. Beijing: Zhonghua shuju, 1957.

Yao San-yu. "The Cosmological and Anthropological Philosophy of Tung Chung-shu." JNCB/RAS 73 (1948): 40–68.

Yates, Robin R. E. "The Mohists on Warfare: Technology, Technique, and Strategys." In Rosemont Jr. and Schwartz, eds., *Studies in Classical Chinese Thought*, pp. 549–603.

Yearley, Lee H. "Hsün-tzu on the Mind: His Attempted Synthesis of Confucianism and Taoism." JAS 39 (1980): 465–80.

Yetts, W. Percival. *The Cull Chinese Bronzes*. London: The Courtauld Institute, 1939.

Yi Shitong 伊世同. "Liangtian chi kao 量天尺考" (A study of the "sky-measure" foot). WW 1978.2: 10–17.

Yin Difei 殷滌非 "Xi Han Ruyin hou mu de zhanpan he tianwen yiqi 西漢汝陰侯墓的占盤和天文儀器" (The chronograph from the Western Han tomb of the Marquis of Ruyin and other astronomical instruments). KG 1978.5: 338–43.

Yosida, Mitukuni. "The Chinese Concept of Nature." In Nakayama and Sivin, eds. *Chinese Science*, pp. 70–91. Cambridge: MIT Press, 1973.

Yu Dacheng 于大成. *Huainanzi jiaoshi* 淮南子校釋 (Collation and explanation of *Huainanzi*). 2 vols. Taipei: National Normal University, 1969.

Yu Shinan 虞世南. *Beitang shuchao* 北堂書鈔. Printed from a traced and recut Song blockprint edition, 1888.

Yu Xingwu 于省吾. *Shuangjianchi zhuzi xinzheng* 雙劍誃諸子新證 (New studies of various philosophers). 1940; Reprinted, Beijing: Zonghua shuju, 1962.

Yu Xun 余遜. "Zaoqi daojiao zhi zhengzhi xinnian 早期道教之政治信念" (Early Daoist political beliefs). *Furen xuezhi* 輔仁學誌 11 (1942): 1–136. See esp. pp. 6–12 on yin-yang and the Huang-Lao School.

Yü, Ying-shih. "Interactions between Formal and Popular Thoughts in Han China." Cambridge: mimeographed, n.d.

Yü, Ying-shih. "Life and Immortality in the Mind of Han China." HJAS 25 (1965): 80–122.

Yü, Ying-shih. *Trade and Expansion in Han China*. Berkeley and Los Angeles: University of California Press, 1967.

Yu Yue 俞樾. *Zhuzi pingyi* 諸子平議 (Explanation of various philosophers). In *Chunzaitang chuanshu* 春在堂全書, 1889.

Yu Yunxiu 余雲岫. *Gudai jibing ming hou suyi* 古代疾病名候疏義 (Glosses on ancient pathological terminology). Beijing, 1953.

Yuan Ke 袁珂. *Zhongguo shenhua ziliao huibian* 中國神話資料會編 (Collected materials on Chinese mythology). Chengdu: Sichuan Social Science Press, 1985.

Zeng Zhaoyue 曾昭燏 et al. *Yinan gu huaxiang shimu fajue baogao* 沂南古畫象石墓發掘報告 (Report on the excavation of an ancient carved stone tomb at Yinan). Shanghai: Cultural Relics Bureau, 1956.

Zhang Anzhi 張安志. "Xi Han bohua de yishu chengjiu 西漢帛畫的藝術成就. WW 1973.9: 66–70.

Zhang Hongzhao 章鴻釗. *Shi ya* 石雅 (added title in English: *Lapidarium Sinicum: A Study of the Rocks, Fossils and Minerals as Known in Chinese Literature*). Beijing: Chinese Geological Survey, 1927.

Zhang Mengwen 張孟聞. "Siling kao 四靈考" (added title and summary in English: "The Four Sacred Animals"). In Li, Zhang, and Cao, eds., *Explorations in the History of Science and Technology in China*, pp. 525–52.

Zheng Dekun 鄭德坤. "[He Guanzhou xiansheng de 'Shanhaijing zai kexueshang de pipan ji zuozhe zhi shidai kao'] shu hou 何觀洲先生的山海經在科學上的批判及其作者時代考書後" (Postscript [to He Guanzhou's 'The *Shanhaijing*: The date of its authorship and its scientific value']). *Yanjing xuebao* 燕京學報 (*Yenching Journal of Chinese Studies*) 7 (June 1930): 1376–80. English abstract in *Yenching Journal of Chinese Studies Supplement* 1 (1932): 65.

Zheng Liangshu 鄭良樹. "*Huainanzi* zhuanben zhijian ji 淮南子傳本知見記" (The editions of *Huainanzi*). *Guoli zhongyang tushuguan guankan* 國立中央圖書館館刊 (Bulletin of the National Central Library [Taipei]), new ser., 1.1 (October 1967): 27–39.

Zheng Wenguang 鄭文光. *Zhongguo tianwenxue yuanliu* 中國天文學源流 (Evolution of Chinese astronomy). Beijing: Science Press, 1979.

Zheng Wenguang and Xi Zezong. *Zhongguo lishishang de yuzhou lilun* 中國歷史上的宇宙理論 (Cosmological theories in Chinese history). Beijing: People's Publishing Co., 1975.

Zhongguo gujin diming dazidian 中國古今地名大字典 (Dictionary of ancient and modern Chinese geography). Shanghai: Commercial Press, 1931.

Zhongguo tianwenxue shi wenji 中國天文學史文集 (Collected essays in the history of Chinese astronomy). Beijing: Science Press, 1978.

Zhou Junfu 周駿富. "*Huainanzi* yu *Zhuangzi* zhi guanxi 淮南子與莊子的關係" (The relationship between *Huainanzi* and *Zhuangzi*). *Dalu zazhi* 大陸雜誌 14.2 (1957): 14–17.

Zhou Shaoxian 周紹賢. *Daojia yu shenxian* 道家與神仙 (Daoists and immortals). Taipei: Zhonghua shuju, 1974.

Zhu Kezhen 竺可槙. *Zhu Kezhen wenji* 竺可槙文集 (Collected works of Zhu Kezhen). Beijing: Science Press, 1979.

Zou Shuwen 鄒樹文, rev. by Zhang Mengwen 長孟聞. "Zhongguo gudai de dongwu fenlei xue 中國古代的動物分類學 (added title and summary in English: "On Ancient Chinese Zootaxonomy"). In Li, Zhang, and Cao, eds., *Explorations in the History of Science and Technology in China*, pp. 511–24.

Index

This index serves also as a glossary; characters as well as page references are given for Chinese names and terms mentioned in the main body of the text. Characters are not given in the index, however, for works and authors listed in the Bibliography, nor for the Heavenly Stems and Earthly Branches listed in Appendix B, nor for commonplace names and terms (e.g. Yangtse River).

This is designed as analytical index of terms and ideas in context. References to terms in the chapter synopses for Chapters 3-5 are omitted, as are terms mentioned only in passing. Names of items that constitute parts of lists (e.g. the twenty-eight lunar lodges, the twenty-four solar nodes, the twelve pitch pipes) are not indexed separately. Thus references to the lunar lodge Ox-Leader, for example, would be found by consulting relevant page numbers under "Lunar lodges." Finally, stereotypical features of the *Huainanzi* 5 "Seasonal Rules" that can readily be located in each of the twelve monthly sections of that chapter (pitch pipes, lunar lodges, etc.) are not indexed separately.

9 - 9:19
1 - 6
10:02 - 11:42
6 - 32
2:12 - 2:41
32 - 43
3:34 - 3:49
43 - 49
8:35 - 9:15
49 - 80
7:49 - 8:06
80 - 98
12:50 - 1:10
98 - 112
2:00 - 2:37
112 - 132
8:19 - 8:47
132 - 150
8:36 - 8:51
217 - 230

19
40
39
98
15
113
40
153
17
20
190
27
217
28
245

60
6
34 53 7
20
360
-190
170

360
-120
240

gaitten
sky
Earth
rotate around
North pole staw
humtian
Earth in spheical
neaven
?

Printed in the United States
55713LVS00003B/124

9 780791 415863